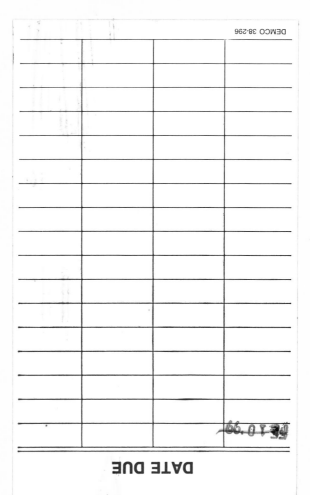

DEMCO 38-296

DATE DUE

RECONSTRUCTING A WOMEN'S PRISON

CLARENDON STUDIES IN CRIMINOLOGY

Published under the auspices of the Institute of Criminology, University
of Cambridge, the Mannheim Centre, London School of Economics,
and the Centre for Criminological Research, University of Oxford

GENERAL EDITOR: ROGER HOOD (University of Oxford)

EDITORS: ANTHONY BOTTOMS and TREVOR BENNETT
(University of Cambridge)

DAVID DOWNES and PAUL ROCK
(London School of Economics)

LUCIA ZEDNER and ANDREW SANDERS
(University of Oxford)

Other titles in this series:

*Prison Systems: A Comparative Study of Accountability in England,
France, Germany, and The Netherlands*
JON VAGG

Reporting Crime: The Media Politics of Criminal Justice
PHILIP SCHLESINGER & HOWARD TUMBER

Grendon: A Study of a Therapeutic Prison
ELAINE GENDERS and ELAINE PLAYER

The State of Our Prisons
ROY D. KING AND KATHLEEN MCDERMOTT

Community Policing
NIGEL FIELDING

RECONSTRUCTING A WOMEN'S PRISON

The Holloway Redevelopment Project
1968–88

Paul Rock

CLARENDON PRESS · OXFORD
1996

n Street, Oxford OX2 6DP
York
gkok Bombay
r es Salaam Delhi
Florence Hong Kong Istanbul Karachi
Kuala Lumpur Madras Madrid Melbourne
Mexico City Nairobi Paris Singapore
Taipei Tokyo Toronto

and associated companies in
Berlin Ibadan

Oxford is a trade mark of Oxford University Press

Published in the United States
by Oxford University Press Inc., New York

British Library Cataloguing in Publication Data
Data available

Library of Congress Cataloguing in Publication Data
Rock, Paul Elliott.
Reconstructing a women's prison: the Holloway redevelopment project,
1968–88/Paul Rock.
p.   cm.— (Clarendon studies in criminology)
Includes bibliographical references and index.
1. HM Prison Holloway.   2. Reformatories for women—Great Britain—
London—Case studies.   3. Prisons—Great Britain—London—Design and
construction—Case studies.   4. Female offenders—Rehabilitation—
Great Britain—London—Case studies.   5. Women prisoners—Rehabilitation—
Great Britain—London—Case studies.   I. Title.   II. Series.
HV9650.L4H57   1996
365'.43'0942143–dc20   95–46255

ISBN 0–19–826095–4

1 3 5 7 9 10 8 6 4 2

Typeset by J&L Composition Ltd, Filey, North Yorkshire.
Printed in Great Britain
on acid-free paper by
Bookcraft Ltd., Midsomer Norton, Avon

'I do believe that Holloway will eventually show that constructive forms of treatment of people and help with their attitudes and relationships that they can carry away with them will prevail and that it will be seen that repression breeds violence and is destructive.' (Joanna Kelley)

General Editor's Introduction

Clarendon Studies in Criminology, the successor to *Cambridge Studies in Criminology*, which was founded by Leon Radzinowicz and J.W.C. Turner more than fifty years ago, aims to provide a forum for outstanding work in criminology, criminal justice, penology and the wider field of deviant behaviour. It is edited under the auspices of three criminological centres: the Cambridge Institute of Criminology, the Mannheim Centre for Criminology and Criminal Justice at the London School of Economics, and the Oxford Centre for Criminological Research.

Professor Paul Rock's book, *Reconstructing A Women's Prison*, like so much of his work, breaks new ground. In approach and method it builds upon the *genre* of contemporary criminological history which he has developed in his recent publications on the Victim's Movement in this country and in Canada. Drawing on a range of sources, but particularly on official documents and interviews with those involved, he analyses how policies germinate and how, through the influences exercised by key individuals, ideas are translated into working practices. In this engrossing saga of the redevelopment of Holloway Prison between 1968 and 1988, Professor Rock shows that post-war conceptions of female criminality, together with the influence of the rehabilitative 'medical model', led to the proposal for an entirely new type of penal institution for women: the prison as hospital. It is a fascinating account of the ways in which this hoped-for transformation of Holloway from grim Victorian fortress to therapeutic community was thwarted by many interacting forces – economy, architecture, changing conceptions and experiences of women prisoners, shifting penal priorities, changing leadership and staff conflicts. This blow-by-blow account, set as it is in the broader social, political and penal contexts, provides a remarkable insight into the pressures which so often transform penal ideals into penal disasters. Yet, despite the recent severe indictment of conditions at Holloway, Paul Rock shows that it had been possible, at least for a period, to devise a regime for women which was both humane and responsive to their needs. It is a tale which in turn is depressing and uplifting. The story needed to be told and Professor Rock has done us a great service by telling it so well.

The editors welcome this, the eighth volume, of the *Series*.

Roger Hood
Oxford, December 1995

Foreword

Jailcraft is a matter of balance. 'Her Majesty's Prison Service', says the concise statement of purpose hung up in every prison, 'serves the public by keeping in custody those committed by the courts. Our duty is to look after them with humanity and help them lead law abiding and useful lives in custody and after release'. The balance is between security, humanity and help. Nowhere has it proved more difficult to maintain than at Holloway over the twenty years covered in this book.

The original prison was modelled on Jebb's Pentonville and Warwick Castle, with a fine jagged skyline but a somewhat eerie atmosphere. It became in 1902 solely a prison for women. Under the inspiration of Joanna Kelley, Governor in the late 1950s and early 1960s, and the guidance of David Faulkner, that most valuable of civil servants involved with crime and justice, the move came to make Holloway a therapeutic centre for disturbed women. It was the age when most prisoners were felt to need treatment, when an Assistant Governor rather trendily declared, 'all women that commit offences must have some sort of personality or psychiatric disorder'. It took so long to demolish and re-build Holloway that penal theory meanwhile changed. In came Sir John May's 'positive custody'. 'The rhetoric', he wrote, 'of treatment and training has had its day and should be replaced.'

But there was plenty more rhetoric to come. Professor Rock steers the reader through the uncertain reign of Megan Bull, the increased standing of the Prison Officers Association that came in with Joy Kinsley, the new architecture unsuitable for new purposes, and the growth of the horrid cavern of C1. Everybody seemed to have plenty to say.

The pendulum swung. In 1986 and again in 1988, a new and younger Governor, Colin Allen, attempted to restore the balance. He could not restore the concept of Holloway as a secure hospital, or even as a wholly therapeutic prison such as Grendon, but he took on (without much support from his superiors in the Prison Service, who are not named in this book) the might of local union forces and hostile pressure groups, and established a relatively civilised institution where hospital and prison existed alongside each other.

I wrote in 1992 that 'it is difficult to appreciate the extent of all the changes that have occurred at Holloway in the past five years'. Self-mutilations had declined from around 1,000 a year to 150; there were fewer assaults, suicides and attempted suicides; the level of offending by prisoners at Holloway was very much reduced. Without the battle waged by Colin Allen and those who did support him there in 1988 this could not have happened. The balance, to which I referred at the start, would, I believe, have been altogether lost. It is a story worth reading.

His Honour Judge Stephen Tumim
HM Chief Inspector of Prisons

February 1995

Acknowledgements

Empirical research depends on the kindness of friends and strangers, and the writing of recent history makes that dependancy especially evident. After all, sociology is not much more than a re-working of others' interpretations of action, a series of 'constructs of the constructs made by actors on the social scene',[1] and if a key person or institution refuses to co-operate, the whole project may founder for want of a vital piece. This book was written because no significant refusal occured and I owe a great debt to all those who helped me.

John Donat first inspired the venture, and he and Lucia Zedner were generous in allowing me to branch out on my own. I am particularly grateful to John Donat for allowing me to reproduce four of his original photographs of the first Holloway and for shooting four new photographs of the second Holloway expressly for this book. Chris Nuttall again acted as the gatekeeper of first instance, and I am grateful to him for guiding me to people and papers. David Faulkner once more gave me patient help and advice. I would like to thank Phillippa Drew of the Prison Department for supporting the project, and her colleagues, Michael Loughlin and Jacquie Jee for their unfailing courtesy in supplying me with files, space and coffee. I consulted the Home Office and Prison Department libraries (and am particularly grateful to Nick Barnes, the Prison Department librarian); the libraries of the *Guardian* (thanks to Malcolm Dean) and *The Sunday Times* (thanks to Alistair Brett); recent minutes of the Holloway Board of Visitors (thanks to Freda Evans) and older minutes (thanks to Jeffrey Bayes and Jane Blom-Cooper); and records of the Prison Officers Association (thanks to Peter Rudkin) and the Victorian Society (thanks to Richard Holder). I owe much to people who spoke to me, many showing me their papers: Colin Allen, Charmian Bollinger (earlier Blackler), Nick Davies, Frances Heidensohn, Joanna Kelley, Alison Liebling, Mike Maguire, Elaine Player and Dorothy Speed. I am grateful to Mary Eaton for introducing me to WIP, Women in Prison, and to Chris Tchaikovsky

---

[1] A. Schutz, 'Common-Sense and Scientific Interpretation of Human Action', in *Collected Papers* Vol. 1 (The Hague: Martinus Nijhoff, 1964), 6.

and her colleagues in and around WIP for their help in discussing Holloway with me. And I would like to thank all those whom I interviewed and whose voices will appear in the course of this book. Those voices would have been silent had it not been for Seeta Persaud who transcribed hours of sometimes dimly audible tapes with consistent patience and cheerfulness.

A book about architecture needs its plans and illustrations, and Jane Pugh of the Graphics Department of the London School of Economics was more than helpful in the preparation of much of the visual material. Towards the centre of the book are eight plates, showing four photographs of the old Holloway and four of the new: each of these was taken by John Donat and is reproduced by his kind permission.

Money and time are essential for research, and I must finally express my gratitude to the Social Research Division of the London School of Economics for funding a considerable portion of this research and, above all, to the Nuffield Foundation which awarded me a Social Science Research Fellowship in the Summer Term of the year 1993–4. The Foundation has been a constant source of support for my work over the years, and I am ever mindful of the straightforward, sensible and helpful way in which it goes about promoting research.

A number of people read this book in draft, and I am particularly grateful to Collin Allen, David Downes, David Faulkner, Frances Heidensohn, Norman Hindson, Roger Hood, Glennys Howarth, Joanna Kelley, Joy Kinsley, Susan McCormick, Ken Neale, Elaine Player, Chris Tchaikovsky and Lucia Zedner for their helpful comments.

Paul Rock

Contents

Dramatis Personae*

Colin Allen	1971–77, Deputy Governor of Feltham; 1977–81, Governor of Huntercombe; 1981–85, Governor of Maidstone Prison; 1985–88, Governor of Holloway Prison; 1988– , Deputy Chief Inspector of Prisons.
Francis Baden-Powell	Architect, member of Robert Matthew, Johnson-Marshall and Partners, principally responsible for the new Holloway, 1967–77.
Jeffrey Bayes	Member and sometime Chairman of the Board of Visitors at Holloway in the 1980s.
Megan Bull	1967–73, Medical Officer at Holloway; 1973–82, Governor of Holloway Prison.
Nick Davies	Home affairs correspondent of the *Guardian* newspaper.
Malcolm Dean	Journalist on the *Guardian* newspaper and member of the Holloway Board of Visitors, 1978–81.
David Faulkner	Assistant Secretary in charge of P4, 1970–74.
Gordon Fowler	Assistant Secretary in charge of P7 and the Holloway project, February–October 1974.
Trevor Gibbens	Professor of Forensic Psychiatry, Maudsley Hospital; 1964–66, Member of the Royal Commission on Penal Reform; member of the Home Office Advisory Council on the Penal System.
Ann Hair	1985, Secretary of the Holloway Project Review Committee; 1985–89, Deputy Governor of Holloway Prison.
Norman Hindson	1986–92, Senior Medical Officer, Holloway Prison.
Joanna Kelley	1947–52, Assistant Governor, Holloway Prison; 1952–59, Governor of Askham Grange; 1959–66, Governor III of Holloway Prison; 1966–74, Assistant Director (Women).
Joy Kinsley	1972–77, Governor of Bullwood Hall;

	1977–79, Governor of Pucklechurch; 1979–82, working in South East Region to become Deputy Regional Director for women's establishments; 1982–84, Governor of Holloway.
Kenneth Neale	1967–70, Assistant Secretary in charge of P4; 1970–75, Director of Industries and Supply; 1976–80, Controller, Planning and Development.
Sydney Norris	1974–79, appointed Assistant Secretary in charge of P7; 1979–81, seconded to HM Treasury; 1982, Assistant Under-Secretary of State, Home Office; 1982–5, seconded to Northern Ireland Office; 1985–88, Director of Operational Policy, Prison Department; 1988–90, Police Department.
William Pile	1962–66, Assistant Under-Secretary of State, Department of Education and Science; 1966–68, Ministry of Health; 1967–70, Deputy Under-Secretary of State at the Home Office; 1968–70, Director General of the Prison Service; Permanent Under-Secretary, Department of Education and Science.
Dorothy Speed	1986–90, Principal Medical Officer, Holloway Prison.
Victor (Lord) Stonham	1964–67, Joint Parliamentary Under-Secretary of State, Home Office; 1967–69, Minister of State, Home Office.
Charity Taylor	1947–59, Governor of Holloway Prison.
Chris Tchaikovsky	Former inmate of Holloway and founder of WIP, Women in Prison.
Terence Weiler	1962–66, 1971–80, Member of the Prisons Board; 1967–80, Assistant Under-Secretary of State, Home Office.
Austin Wilson	1974–77, Assistant Secretary in charge of P4.
Dorothy Wing	1967–73, Governor of Holloway Prison.

*   Only biographical information pertinent to principal figures and themes in this book is given.

Glossary

Banging-up	Locking in cells
BBC	British Broadcasting Corporation
Category A	Category defined by the Mountbatten Report of 1964 as prisoners whose escape would be highly dangerous to the public or the police or to the security of the State
Category B	Prisoners defined as those for whom the very highest conditions of security are not necessary but for whom escape must be made very difficult
Category C	Prisoners defined as those who cannot be trusted in 'open' conditions but who do not have the ability or resources to make a determined escape attempt
Category D	Prisoners defined as those who can reasonably be trusted to serve their sentence in 'open' conditions
C1	The unit for 'disturbed prisoners' in C block, level 1, of the new Holloway Prison
CNA	Certified Normal Accommodation
COHSE	Confederation of Health Service Employees
DATA	Dalmeny Avenue Tenants Association
DHSS	Department of Health and Social Security
Fresh Start	Review and structural reform of the prison service inaugurated in 1986
GBH	Grievous Bodily Harm
GDP	Gross Domestic Product
GLC	Greater London Council
HMG	Her Majesty's Government
HMP	Her Majesty's Prison

IRA	Irish Republican Army
ITN	Independent Television News
MO	Medical Officer
MP	Member of Parliament
NCCL	National Council for Civil Liberties
NEC	National Executive Committee
NEPO	New Entrant Prison Officer
P1	Prison Department division responsible, *inter alia*, for strategic planning of buildings
P3	Prison Department division responsible for adult male offenders
P4	Prison Department division established in 1967 and responsible, *inter alia*, for women
P5	Prison Department division responsible for security matters
P7	Prison Department division responsible for the development of existing sites and buildings
PMO	Principal Medical Officer
POA	Prison Officers Association
POUT	Prison Officer Under Training
PSA	Property Services Agency
RAP	Radical Alternatives to Prison
RMJM	Robert Matthew, Johnson-Marshall and Partners, the architects responsible for the new Holloway
SER	South East Region (of the Prison Service)
SMO	Senior Medical Officer
WIP	Women in Prison, a charity formed in 1983

Introduction

The Inception of the Book

I seem to have been interested in Holloway prison for a long while. Its high Gothic tower was part of the landscape to be seen out of my bedroom window as a boy. Some time before the publication of the work of Ward and Kassebaum[1] and of Giallombardo,[2] I floated the idea of studying Holloway for a doctorate, but my supervisor advised me that a women's prison would never let me in. Much later, I wondered a little about the history of ideas that might unite the work of Cesare Lombroso in the 1890s and that of Grace Pailthorpe[3] in the 1930s with the rebuilding of the prison in the 1970s.[4]

But it was only a chance conversation with John Donat, a friend and architectural photographer, that inflamed that interest strongly enough to lead to research. Donat had been commissioned in 1970 to make a visual record of the old Victorian Holloway Prison before it was demolished and replaced by a new 'medically-orientated establishment'. His cache of photographs was outstanding, it had never been published, and, together with Lucia Zedner, we discussed working on what would have been a largely pictorial book centred on the social life of women in a radial prison (four of those original photographs and four new photographs are displayed in this book). It would have been my job to describe and analyse the decision to build anew, and I approached the Home Office Prison Department about studying policy papers on the matter. Philippa Drew of the

[1] D. Ward and G. Kassebaum, *Women's Prison: Sex and Social Structure*, (London: Weidenfeld and Nicolson, 1965).
[2] R. Giallombardo, *Society of Women: A Study of a Women's Prison,* (New York: John Wiley, 1966).
[3] C. Lombroso and W. Ferrero, *The Female Offender*, (London: T. Fisher Unwin, 1895) and G. Pailthorpe, *Studies in the Psychology of Delinquency*, (London: HMSO, 1932). It was Terry Morris who first pointed me to the importance of Grace Pailthorpe.
[4] See D. Downes and P. Rock, *Understanding Deviance*, (Oxford: Oxford University Press, 1988), 293.

Department was more than helpful, she supported the project, and, in time, I was shown into a room housing a small mountain of files on the Holloway Redevelopment Project. The sheer bulk of the files was unexpected and daunting (they even surprised members of the Prison Department who could not recollect another project being so lavishly documented) but it would have been foolish to forego such a chance. Thereafter, one thing led to another, and it became clear that the scale and interest of the materials justified preparing not only the original photographic book but also a full-blown academic monograph.

The files of the Holloway Redevelopment Project became the foundation and core of a practical programme of research. They mapped out a future calendar of interviews with critical people (interviews that would lead, in their turn, to further interviews),[5] a list of books and papers to be read (and yet more books and papers in their wake), and the project mushroomed in characteristic fashion.[6] Little by little, questions crystallized, a history was revealed, and the research acquired shape.

Reconstructing A Women's Prison is the outcome and its title is intended to convey a triple meaning and purpose. It refers to a chain of reforming efforts to reconstruct a penal regime and a social world for inmate women, efforts that were focussed initially on the loftily idealistic work of transforming a Victorian radial prison into a 'secure hospital' that would be, as a eulogistic article put it, 'a tremendous breakthrough in penal institutions';[7] next, on the struggle to impose order on the disorganization that ensued, a struggle that seemed at times only to exacerbate disorder; and, finally, on a dramatic confrontation and a culminating catharsis that led to a revelatory glimpse of new possibilities of policy and practice. The book refers, secondly, to the companion, seventeen-year long, Herculean task of physically re-building an occupied prison *in situ*, a task

---

[5] In the event, I interviewed more than fifty people, including four journalists; one former MP; six former staff of governor grade who had served in Holloway; three former prison officers; two former nurses; one psychologist; two psychiatrists; one probation officer; four former inmates; one former education officer; eight former officials of the Prison Department; three members of the Board of Visitors; two medical officers; and one of the principal architects of the new prison. A number of those people were interviewed more than once.

[6] I have described this method of working before in 'A Natural History of Research on Policy-Making' in N. Fielding (ed.), *Actions and Structures: Research Methods and Social Theory*, (London: Sage, 1988), 99–116.

[7] K. FitzHerbert, 'New Holloway?', *New Society*, 25 Feb. 1971, 301.

never before attempted by its author, the Home Office, and described in an official press notice as 'the first urban prison site to be redeveloped while remaining operational'[8] and by David Faulkner, the official administering the work for a while, as 'as large and as important as any penological project which has been undertaken in this country in the past'.[9] And, thirdly, it refers to the intellectual project of writing this history itself: *Reconstructing A Women's Prison* is spun out of a skein of different narratives about an institution, narratives that were found in letters, briefing notes and minutes, in newspaper reports and in interviews with those whose lives centred for a while on the rebuilt prison.

Methods and Materials

It was inevitable that evidence about the history of Holloway should have been uneven in its completeness and accessibility. Working papers in the prison and Prison Department were never really produced or kept for scholarly purposes (although books about Holloway have been written,[10] and others were planned)[11]; what remains is patchwork. Some matters were covered in exquisite detail. I have already observed that the main bureaucratic work of planning and executing the designs for the new prison between July 1968 and 1985 was documented meticulously. Joanna Kelley, a former Governor of Holloway Prison, Assistant Director of the Prison Department and prime mover of those plans, recalled:

We needn't have kept anything like this . . . we had a very nice man . . . in the clerical staff and he made this his job and his desk and he did nothing else— he thought this was going to be the best project ever documented.[12]

---

[8] 'Holloway Prison to be Rebuilt: New Approach to Women Offenders', Press Notice, Home Office, 30 Sept. 1970.

[9] D. Faulkner, 'The Redevelopment of Holloway Prison', *The Howard Journal of Penology and Crime Prevention*, 1971, Vol. XIII, No. 2, 126.

[10] See, for instance, J. Camp, *Holloway Prison*, (Newton Abbot: David and Charles, 1974); S. Casale, *Women Inside: The experience of women remand prisoners in Holloway*, (London: The Civil Liberties Trust, 1989); J. Kelley, *When the Gates Shut*, (London: Longmans, 1967); and M. Size, *Prisons I Have Known*, (London: George Allen and Unwin, 1957).

[11] In 1971, there was talk in the Prison Department about commissioning Tom Clayton to commemorate the new prison, but he was obliged to withdraw from the project. Joanna Kelley began collecting papers for a history of Holloway, a history she did not begin to write. I was fortunate enough to be given those papers to study.

[12] Interview. From henceforth, it should be assumed that all unattributed quotations stem from interviews.

All the 280 files of the Holloway Redevelopment Project have survived intact. Other collections of papers have not. Decisions to retain official papers at the main Home Office repository at Hayes appear to have been a little arbitrary on occasion. Whilst much survives, papers touching on the original proposal to rebuild the prison have been destroyed or lost and it was impossible to find any unpublished documents covering pertinent events between the 1930s and the early 1960s. The Home Office's own paper memory is evidently deficient, and officials themselves could not always unravel their own past (on one occasion in May 1975, for example, it was reported to the Prison Department's Steering Committee to Oversee Redevelopment Schemes that 'it has not yet been possible to trace the specific decision of the Prisons Board on the Redevelopment' of Holloway Prison).

Holloway's own record-keeping was in a worse state. The prison was obliged to retain records of 'occurrences', discharges, punishments and the like for five years. They seemed to have been stored chiefly for purposes of form, being piled haphazardly in a muniments room that was 'cleared out every two or three years', and I was not allowed to sift through them. Other prison papers were no better preserved. There had been a bonfire of the old prison's books and records when the Victorian building was evacuated in 1977. Governors tend to destroy or keep their personal papers and letters when they leave. The Board of Visitors held none of its own papers and minutes from before November 1987. Members of staff have written booklets about the prison's history, and I shall draw on what they have said, but there is an overriding impression that Holloway Prison, like any other prison, is a busy place with a transient population of staff[13] and inmates overwhelmingly preoccupied with the problems of the here-and-now, and lacking much of an organized, collective memory. The past was practically immaterial to many of those who lived in the prison. The officers in post whom I met in the 1990s certainly professed to know little about the events of the 1970s and 1980s. They had not been working in Holloway then.

[13] In late 1983, at a time critical to this history, an internal report prepared by the prison's senior psychologist showed that the average time served by officers at Holloway was two and a half years, that a quarter of the officers had been in post for less than 2 years and a half less than 3 years. I. Posen, 'Sickness and Resignation Rate of Staff at Holloway', Dec. 1983.

To be sure, some missing papers could be found elsewhere in the private possession of people who had been involved in the history of Holloway,[14] but their survival over the years was a matter of chance, and this book cannot but mirror their fragmentary character. I learned more about management and the Board of Visitors than about the Prison Officers Association, and my narrative cannot but mirror that imbalance.

So too with the portions of this book that are based on interview. It was impossible to trace all the individuals who were at the centre of events some twenty or thirty years ago. A number have died and others were too ill to be approached, and analytic gaps have arisen in consequence. Yet only a few of those individuals who were still alert refused to speak to me, and most were surprisingly candid and helpful. The generosity of strangers is a constant astonishment to the fieldworker. Some were undoubtedly no more than courteous. Others were evidently pleased to reminisce. And others still retained strong memories of a momentous local history which had left its stamp and made Holloway into a small obsession. A former deputy governor observed 'I actually think you might get hooked because . . . it is one of the things about Holloway that there is this huge fascination . . . [and there is] the very strong sense of the place that I have from my period there'. Some people, indeed, talked as if to exorcize themselves of a difficult past.

The result was a great mass of interviews, reports and papers touching patchily on the development of a substantial institution between 1968 and 1988. They embodied stocks of knowledge, motive and expectation that had shifted over the twenty one years of that history, sometimes smoothly but more often erratically. They recorded realities that may have been sensed initially as open and uncertain but quickly enough became fixed and established, for all practical purposes parts of a more or less opaque pre-history (one official who took over the management of the redevelopment project reflected that 'I got involved at the point where the main decisions had already been taken'). They recorded realities that were shaped, re-shaped, forgotten, re-discovered, disowned and destroyed over the years: thus, what had originally been conceived as a rational and

---

[14] For instance, Jane Blom-Cooper was generous in giving me a complete set of papers relating to her membership of the Board of Visitors between Aug. 1972 and Mar. 1984.

progressive penal policy, described in 1969 as 'a new and modern approach . . . [whose] scale and sophistication . . . [are] bound to impose new methods and standards on the female penal system as a whole',[15] could reverse its meaning so radically that it was later to be dismissed summarily by a very senior Home Office official as 'deranged, a new Piranesi world . . . when I saw the place, I thought it was a mad-house'. They reflected the exigencies of time and place: the recollections of a prison officer, governor, a probation officer or former inmate could never have been quite the same. They were recursive: pragmatically so, as decision built on decision in the official papers; dialectically, when events generated conditions to which people were obliged to respond; and heuristically, as my own questions invited people to review their own and others' past actions.

In short, the mass of reports engendered a kaleidoscopic vision in which the prison was, as the American sociologist, Peter Manning, might have said, 'polysemic', phenomenologically unstable, not one thing but many.[16] A former assistant governor reflected that 'there are lots of stories to be told about Holloway and they exist on all sorts of different levels and, if it's possible to tap into them all (it probably isn't), it'd be a life-time's work to do it'. One task of this book will be to simplify, condense and elide, cutting through all that complexity to supply a framework that can contain and explain some of those stories and the diverse levels on which they existed.

Some Presuppositions

As I write, I have been mindful of all that has had to be neglected and obscured in the interests of finding a coherent analytic path. I have been mindful of the fact that, unusually and unavoidably, this is not a detailed ethnographic study but a work based solely on second-hand accounts of events now closed. I could not supplement others' narratives with my own observations, and many gaps have had to remain obstinately unfilled. I have also been aware that the regime at Holloway has changed more than once since 1988, the date at which I

[15] 'Holloway Redevelopment Project: Note by Chairman of the Project Group', March 1969.

[16] MacFarlane has reminded us that, if it is difficult enough to study social relations in the present, their scale and complexity are multiplied dizzily as one moves back in time. A. MacFarlane, *Reconstructing Historical Communities*, (Cambridge: Cambridge University Press 1977), 8.

chose to finish. I cannot pretend that the Holloway which was left in Chapter 10 remains intact and unaltered, but a narrative conclusion had to be found somewhere, and 1988 did mark a clear end to the process of settling in to a new building.

The main argument of this book will be informed by a set of sensitizing concepts or expectancies that developed and were expounded at some length in earlier books and articles on policy-making in the criminal justice system.[17] Put briefly, I shall assume, first, that the division of labour in policy circles is so refined that very few problems in their early stages can be entrusted to more than three or four officials, and that the experiences, relations and reputations of those officials will inevitably affect what can and will be done. A new initiative will be associated with specific people, it will define them as a group or policy circle, and it will become a symbolic part of the identities they can assume in the work setting. Attitudes and actions directed towards the policy will necessarily refract the social relations of the circle in which they are embedded.

Pari passu, my second assumption is that attitudes and actions towards members of the circle will affect the course of the policy. To be sure, what can be done must always rest on general bureaucratic mandates, rules and procedures, but individuals count in the micro-environments of the policy process, and especially in the beginning when so much is fluid and uncertain. Description must therefore focus on how named individuals mediated action.

Policy circles are never stable. Their members change, particularly in the government service where officials are transferred from post to post with managed regularity. The circles themselves change, it being a part of the policy-making process that initiatives commonly pass through a series of hands as tasks alter and grow in scale. The members of each circle will tend inevitably to assess the motives, meanings and intentions of their predecessors and successors at each stage, and their judgements will affect how they treat the policies that come before them. An understanding of the social relations of the policy process must therefore embrace not only transactions conducted between individuals within circles but between the individuals of different circles as they succeed one another over time. In

---

[17] I have laid out those assumptions at greater length in *A View from the Shadows* (Oxford: Oxford University Press, 1986), and *Helping Victims of Crime*, (Oxford: Oxford University Press, 1990) and, most recently, in 'The Opening Stages of Criminal Justice Policy Making', *British Journal of Criminology*, Winter 1995, 1–16.

the case of the Holloway Redevelopment Project, matters were to become more complicated still because two principal sites of activity, one at the prison and the other at the Prison Department, developed in parallel to influence one another at a distance.

I assume, third, that officials and others generally experience policy-making *in situ* as a blend of the closed and determinate, on the one hand, and the open and emergent, on the other. Policy-makers must observe routines: there are planning timetables to follow, conferences and meetings to attend, ministers to brief, and officials prepare for all that activity in orderly fashion. A predictability of structure and development are the consequence, and a competent official should be reasonably confident about the broad forms of almost any emerging issue. But there can be less confidence about the content and ultimate success of particular pieces of policy-making. Only retrospectively will an official be able to construct a clear story about the steps that appeared, after all, to lead one by one and inexorably to what was to become the only conceivable outcome of planning. In prospect, before that outcome has been established, there seem always to have been too many uncertainties, too little firm knowledge about what one was doing and what others may have been doing around one, to be sanguine about what was about to happen. Officials can know only that most sequences of policy-making will be affected at different points by unforeseeable crises, contingencies and catalysts, and their skill is to combine a competence in handling the ordinary with a capacity to manage the extraordinary when it does arise.

The process I shall describe was situated, emergent and dialectical. It engendered at each stage new definitions, problems, judgements, facts, structures of action, histories, commitments, interests and physical structures. In short, it continually engendered new realities to which officials and others were obliged to respond. My fourth assumption will then be that policy-making must be understood as an interpretive process. A book about policy-making has to be a study of the practices and fruits of bureaucratic reasoning; my job, in part, must be to reanimate that reasoning phase by phase so that key decisions and actions can become intelligible again. Accordingly, *Reconstructing a Women's Prison* will reproduce the growth and transformation of the logic-in-use deployed in the rebirth of Holloway. In doing so, it will attempt to trace how that logic unfolded, baring its broad composition and ruling presuppositions at each stage, not anticipating over-much and prematurely how well those presuppositions would eventually be fulfilled, but waiting until the appropriate place in the narrative to show what actually did transpire. If I seem to refrain from criticism or correction at points it is because I wish to give an appreciative, thick description of what drove the actors on the social scene at material times, not what I, they or others could say with the condescension of hindsight.

The logic-in-use of the Holloway Redevelopment Project defined fields of action and relevance. It was real to officials and real enough in its consequences, and my own analysis has followed in its path. I have, in effect, tried to be at once inside and outside the phenomenal reality of those who worked on the Project, not accepting it wholly as my own, giving it adequate context, perspective and history, but nevertheless heeding the importance of things heeded by officials themselves, tracking the official mind as it illuminated problems, and, by extension, awarding lesser importance to the things that that mind itself neglected. As I present that reasoning, I shall make heavy use of what officials themselves have had to say. I shall do so not only because their words have an evidential authority but because it is their social reality that I wish to recapture. And pertinent quotation from interviews and letters is the most direct and honest route to such an end.

The Plot

Reconstructing A Women's Prison is quite centrally a history of ideas. More precisely, it will begin with a description of the old radial prison that was to be regarded more and more as a 'grim Victorian fortress' quite inappropriate to the administration of an enlightened regime for women. It will then move quickly on to follow the grain of the records by describing how criminal women were defined by officials in prisons and the Home Office in the 1960s and how it was decided in 1967 to build a new establishment to house them, an establishment whose physical design would bear the impress of a new penology. Internally, the establishment ('prison' was a word in declining currency at the time) was to be arrayed as a therapeutic continuum, a string of small, linked, flexible spaces that would plot a moral career for the inmate. Externally, the new institution was to be a prison that would not look like a prison. It was instead to be a 'secure hospital' that might eventually be surrendered to the Health

Service when the supply of delinquent women dwindled altogether. The new Holloway was to be slipped unobtrusively into its urban setting, a place to which the local community might come, an out-patients' clinic to which former prisoners and women on bail might be referred. Its boundaries with the outer world were correspondingly designed to be as slight and reassuring as security would allow.

The book will then proceed to describe the extraordinary delays that prolonged the project, delays which propelled it through a series of intellectual and penological regimes and under the control of a succession of groups of officials, delays when almost everything seemed to go wrong,[18] frustrating officers and officials (one recalled that there was 'a little joke in the prison system at the time that there was a right way to do things, the wrong way and the Holloway').[19] Tardiness brought it about that the world in which the new building came to be completed in 1985 was very different from the world of the 1960s that had conceived it. Holloway was a collection of special therapeutic spaces used instead for conventional purposes of control, containment and discipline, and discontents flowing from the parti-cular character of the institution and from a wider, national tide of industrial conflict swept over the prison and flooded it for a while.

In the mid-1980s, Holloway was known publicly as an unhappy place, said in an article in the *Solicitors Journal* to have 'achieved notoriety with tales of violence, ill treatment of inmates and no association between the women',[20] and riddled with complaints about staffing levels, oppressive conduct, threats and mistrust between management, inmates, staff and the Board of Visitors. Prisoners were locked-up ('banged-up' as they put it) for long periods. There were publicly-debated cases of attempted and success-ful suicide, self-mutilation and arson, particularly in C1, the unit for 'severely disturbed' women. The work of the education, industrial and other departments was severely curtailed. Prisoners were 'locked-out' in police cells as discipline staff refused to admit new receptions at certain times and above certain numbers. There were reports of

---

[18] One senior and experienced official wrote in 1975: 'I think it is no exaggeration on my part to say that I have never been involved with a scheme which has run into so many problems'.

[19] However, it must be said that Joanna Kelley, the Governor of Holloway in the 1960s, remembered that that had been an old joke when she had joined the prison service in 1947.

[20] J. Morton, 'Inside Holloway', *Solicitors Journal*, 10 Apr. 1987, Vol. 131, No. 15, 457.

abnormal rates of staff sickness, resignation and stress. And all this was followed avidly by the mass media, pressure groups and both Houses of Parliament.

Matters came to a theatrical climax in August and September 1988 when Colin Allen, a reforming Governor who had been in post for some three years, confronted what management called a discipline officers' strike and the POA, the Prison Officers Association, called a 'lock-out'. With a skeleton staff of 'strike-breakers' and a few assistant governors drafted in from other establishments, the prison continued to function, and it did so peacefully and relatively amicably. Allen succeeded because he had managed to win the tacit co-operation of inmates who were allowed a greater freedom than they had known since the 1960s. The events of 1988 were to be, in effect, a vivid enactment of the anarchists' dream, a vision of what people can be when authoritarian constraints are removed, not unlike the film *King of Hearts* which the sociologist Robert Scott once showed to his students at Princeton University, the film in which the lunatics quit the madhouse to take over a town evacuated by its inhabitants in time of war, behaving perfectly 'normally', not identifiably different from those whom they had replaced.

The crisis of 1988 marked a turning-point, and Holloway has yet to make a full and recognizable return to the oppressive conditions that preceded it. Just as early Roman history was measured by its consulships, so prison history can be measured by its Governors. It seemed dramatically appropriate to conclude the narrative with the Governorship of Colin Allen. What was done in his time effectively renders problematic conclusions that might otherwise have been reached about the character of penal regimes, the links between architecture and behaviour, and much else. It was an unambiguous cæsura in time and analysis.

That is the substance and plot of the book, and it stirs up a crowd of attendant questions about the formation and transformation of official typifications of deviant women; the manner in which those typifications could be inscribed in the architecture of a place designed to change lives; the relations between space, control and action, and, perhaps more interestingly still, the way in which those relations could become caught up in a rhetoric of dissatisfaction and conflict; the character and importance of boundaries between places where 'dirty work'[21] is

---

[21] See E. Hughes, 'Good People and Dirty Work', in *The Sociological Eye,* (Chicago: Aldine-Atherton, 1971).

done and the surrounding social terrain; the internal boundaries and spaces of prisons, and the fears they can excite; in short, questions about the interplay between symbolic and physical representations of the bad, the mad and the sad (a cluster of attributes often listed by those working in Holloway) and between that cluster and other representations of normality and goodness. And in all this, *Reconstructing A Women's Prison* may be read as a practical iconography of an ideology and a penology.

1

The Noble Castle: Holloway as a Victorian Radial Prison

'I suppose to many people it doesn't mean anything but to most of us in my era, we appreciated it, it spoke with our expectations of things, and we were very, very fond of the building, and we thought it was a sin before God that it was destroyed' (former discipline officer).

Introduction

I shall begin by describing something of the architecture and social organization of the first Holloway Prison whose demolition and replacement are to be the substantive theme of this book. The old prison had a strong identity which must be appreciated before other matters can be understood, and I shall distil, simplify and exaggerate its characteristics for purposes of effect. Holloway was a paradigmatic radial prison, 'said when built to represent the last word in modern prison design',[1] which nevertheless came to be condemned by the Home Office as unfit for the exercise of a progressive penology. What had enabled the practice of one style of control was held in time to thwart another. The benign became malign, and it was to be the almost dialectical clash between the two, between what were held to be the faults of the old and the promise of the new, that fired administrators and architects in the 1960s and 1970s.

The second Holloway Prison was to be an inversion of the first. It would turn its predecessor upside down and inside out. Instead of a centre, there would be a green space. Instead of the long wings and straight sight-lines, there would be an undulating band of small units laid out as a chain. And it was to be that contrast between the strong disciplinary prison with its centre and the therapeutic building with none, which lay vividly before officers, prisoners and others to feed

[1] M. Size, *Prisons I Have Known,* (London: George Allen and Unwin, 1957), 91.

their discontents when the new prison opened phase by phase between 1977 and 1985.

The New City Prison

In 1832, the Privy Council bought 19.5 acres of what was then gently-sloping country in Holloway, north of London, to serve as a burial ground for cholera victims. But the cholera abated and no cemetery was created. Plate 1 shows how it was to be another House of the Dead that came to be established there when 10 of those acres were sold in 1845 to the City of London as a site for a modern house of correction. Seven years later, in October 1852, the New City Prison opened with 120 men and 27 women prisoners transferred from the now outmoded City prisons: from Newgate (whose great bell may still be seen in the works office), from Bridewell and the Poultry, Borough and Giltspur Street Compters, and, in 1870, from the Whitecross Street Compter.

Holloway continued to be the responsibility of the City of London until 1878 when, under the Prison Act of 1877, all local prisons came under the control of the Secretary of State. In February 1902, it became a prison solely for women, its male inmates having been removed to Wormwood Scrubs, and it remained a women's prison thereafter. By the 1930s, it was regarded by the Home Office as the principal establishment of the English female penal system.

The Architecture of the Radial Prison

The first Holloway Prison was confident in its architecture and appearance. It was one of the 54 radial prisons launched with 'astonishing rapidity' and 'immense enthusiasm'[2] in the six years after the opening of the great English prototype, the new model prison constructed by Sir Joshua Jebb nearby at Pentonville in 1842 (Pentonville itself having been fashioned after Haviland's Eastern Penitentiary at Philadelphia).[3] Holloway was modelled on Pentonville,[4] coming in

---

[2] L. Fairweather, 'Prison Architecture in England', *The British Journal of Criminology*, Apr. 1961, Vol. 1, No. 4, 339.

[3] See *Report of the Surveyor-General of Prisons on the Construction, Ventilation and Details of Pentonville Prison*, (London: HMSO, 1844), 5. To be sure, Haviland's penitentiary was not the first radial prison. Precursors could be found in Blackburn's design of 1786 for a prison at Ipswich and Steuart and Cockburn's design of 1782 for Edinburgh Bridewell (see N. Teeters and J. Shearer, *The Prison at Philadelphia*, (New York: Columbia University Press, 1957), 161–2).

[4] Its architect, James Bunning, inscribed the plans for Holloway as 'designed on the principles of Pentonville' ('Holloway Prison Islington', unpublished, undated briefing document in the possession of the Victorian Society, 1).

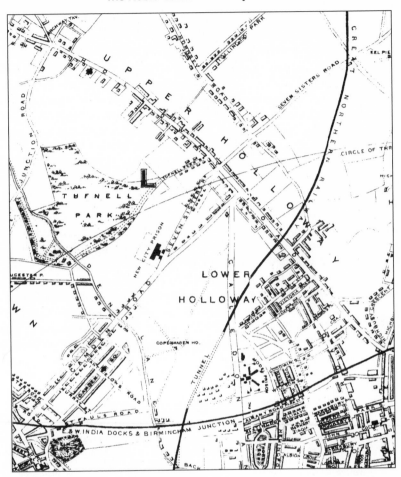

Plate 1.1: The New City Prison Under Construction in 1851 (detail from *Tallis Illustrated Plan of London and Environs*, 1851, reproduced courtesy of the Royal Geographical Society)

time to be recognized as its sister penitentiary,[5] and, fathered by Jebb[6] and descended from the Eastern Penitentiary, its pedigree showed.

Like the Eastern Penitentiary, it was a fantastic recapitulation of a medieval fortress, castellated, decked with towers and heraldic beasts, 'rising like a giant's castle from the means [sic] streets of North London'.[7] There is a story, so often told that it has become threadbare, that its facade mimicked Warwick Castle to mollify suburban neighbours unhappy about the construction of a prison in the midst of their new-built homes.[8]

The first Holloway Prison was intended to reform inmates, to make them penitent, submissive and good, the agents of their own redemption. It would work by making solitary prisoners[9]—immured in their cells, left alone with the Bible and simple, hard work, quarantined against every influence but that of God, officers and the chaplain— reflect on their sins and acquire habits of discipline. Holloway's physical grandeur echoed its elevated aspiration. Mayhew and Binney described how 'the battlements and the lofty tower of the prison rose conspicuously before us, reminding us of some noble castle of the olden feudal times'.[10] But it was also designed to frighten and deter, to inspire awe and dread, to 'strike chill into the heart'.[11] It was a forbidding variation on a Gothic theme and it had about it much of the donjon and the *oubliette*. On its foundation stone was inscribed the malediction 'may God preserve the City of London and make this

[5] See X. Field, *Under Lock and Key*, (London: Max Parrish, 1963), 84.

[6] See J. Carlebach, 'Major-General Sir Joshua Jebb, K.C.B. 1793–1863', *The Prison Service Journal*, April 1965, Vol. IV, No. 15, 26. Jebb inspired the design and influenced its execution although its principal author was James Bunning, the City architect. Bunning was elected Clerk of the City's Works in 1843, the title being changed to City Architect and Suveyor in 1847. His major buildings, almost all subsequently demolished, included the City of London School, 1837; the Coal Exchange, 1849; Billingsgate Market, 1853: the Metropolitan Cattle Market, 1855; and The Roger's Almshouses, 1856. In the judgement of the Victorian Society, he was not a distinguished architect of the time, and that judgement diluted their will to campaign against the demolition of Holloway Prison itself in 1968.

[7] 'The babies of Holloway', *Birmingham Evening Mail*, 17 Mar. 1971.

[8] That is certainly the story that new staff and visitors were told in an anonymous, undated booklet, *An Introduction to H.M.P. Holloway*, distributed within the prison.

[9] Holloway was actually a slight modification of the separate system, allowing some measure of limited association for special groups of prisoners, but the principle of isolation was at its core.

[10] H. Mayhew and J. Binney, *The Criminal Prisons of London*, (London: Griffin, Bohn, and Company, 1862), p. 539.

[11] S. Hobhouse and A. Brockway, *English Prisons Today*, (London: Longmans, Green and Co., 1922), p. 86.

place a terror to evil doers',[12] and it was a photographic plate of Holloways main gateway that was used by Tomlinson to underscore her contention that 'the use of castellated facades in the design of the Victorian prison was a conscious attempt to make prisons appear repulsive, symbolising on the outside the terrors to be expected within'.[13]

Like its fellow penitentiaries (Pentonville, Wormwood Scrubs and Brixton, for instance) Holloway was a strong building. It gave an impression of great *physical* strength, a Tiryns of the penitentiary system, and mythœpic stories would later dwell on the resilience of its walls when it fell. One former prisoner recalled:

I was actually there in the exercise yard when workmen were attempting to take down the wall of, I think, it was F Wing, and they swung this great big concrete ball on a chain back. All these workmen were standing around with crash caps on, and we were obviously really enjoying this, and the ball swung back, hit the wall, and a tiny bit of like talcum powder came off the wall. . . . They said, and I'm sure this was entirely untrue, they said that they were 15 foot thick, the walls, and that allowed for much embroidery and exaggeration, but they had to dynamite it in the end because they couldn't get it down in a normal way.

Holloway was strong *symbolically*, as much expressive as practical, an extravagant, ornate, imposing, melodramatic (perhaps even absurd)[14] place designed to fever the imagination. Plate 2 makes it clear how it summoned up a fairytale imagery of castles and dungeons, of barons, kings and giants. The building was a 'stronghold designed not only to keep the enemy out but also the prisoner in'.[15] Inmates would say that they felt as if they were in a 'B'-movie when they went there: 'I just thought, "wow!, look at this place, this is fantastic!" . . . it was imposing and forbidding, all those things, but it was very beautiful'. A deputy governor said of his first view of the prison, 'I saw it for what it was—a replica of Warwick Castle and an impression of all the dungeons that go with it'.[16] And a former assistant governor said of her first view:

---

[12] 'History of the Prison', Directorate of Works, Home Office, 1982, 1. Perhaps the malediction was more myth than real. Joanna Kelley reflected that 'this was said to be so but I understood when the foundation stone was uncovered it was not inscribed'.

[13] H. Tomlinson, 'Design and reform: the 'separate system' in the nineteenth-century English prison', in A. King (ed.), *Buildings and Society*, (London: Routledge and Kegan Paul, 1980), 111.

[14] I have spoken to a number of people who had visited it in the 1960's and called it absurd.   [15] 'Holloway Prison Islington', 3.

[16] 'Holloway, as I see it—by the first *man* to be deputy governor', *Daily Mail*, 10 Aug. 1976.

PRISON FOR THE CITY OF LONDON, AT HOLLOWAY.

Mr. BUNNING, F.S.A. Architect.

Plate 1.2: The new City Prison at Holloway in 1851 (from *The Builder*, 14 June 1851)

I had just never experienced anything like the Victorian radial prison. So coming on to the centre with wings opening off, the feeling of space, although . . . in retrospect [it] was very good, at the time it felt a little overwhelming. I can only imagine that prisoners coming through these huge wooden doors into an imposing pile like Warwick Castle, feeling that sense of enormous space and people tucked away behind doors. That must have been quite an experience. For me it was certainly an alarming experience. It took a while to adjust.

Even more elegiac was Jean Scarlett who worked in a therapeutic unit with young women:

In the morning, as I pass under the impressive Victorian baronial battlements through the door crowned with great heraldic dragons,[17] I sometimes expect to meet not women, however frail, but some of the captives of the Inquisition or of feudal monarchs, the heretics, pirates or political assassins who, with cannon balls chained to their feet, mouldered in dungeons in the middle ages.[18]

Holloway had *functional* strength as a huge instrument of social engineering. If architectural 'power is to be found in hierarchical structures, control, surveillance',[19] Holloway was powerful indeed. Jebb observed in 1844 that his new prisons rested on a 'uniform principle of construction'[20] and, he persisted ten years later, 'no alteration of any importance has suggested itself for [their] construction.[21] That principle of construction, pragmatically-founded, clearly laid down, not permitting of deviation, was the radial design. Pentonville and its progeny, Holloway, supplanted the seeming disorganization of the old gaols and compters with a strict and rational regulation that accomplished the greatest effect with the least labour. The result was palpable. Hepworth Dixon wrote of Pentonville in 1850:

There is perfect order, perfect silence. The stillness of the grave reigns in every part. To a person accustomed to see only such gaols as Giltspur-street and Horsemonger-lane—with all their noise, filth, and disorder—the change is

---

[17] Actually griffins, the City of London's heraldic beasts.
[18] J. Scarlett, 'A Therapeutic Community for Borstal Girls in Holloway Prison', in P. de Berker (ed.), *Interaction: Human Groups in Community and Institution*, (Oxford: Cassirer, 1969), 95.
[19] T. Markus, *Buildings and Power*, (London: Routledge, 1993), 23.
[20] *Report of the Surveyor-General*, 3.
[21] *Seventh Report on the Discipline and Management of Convict Prisons*, (London, 1853), 88.

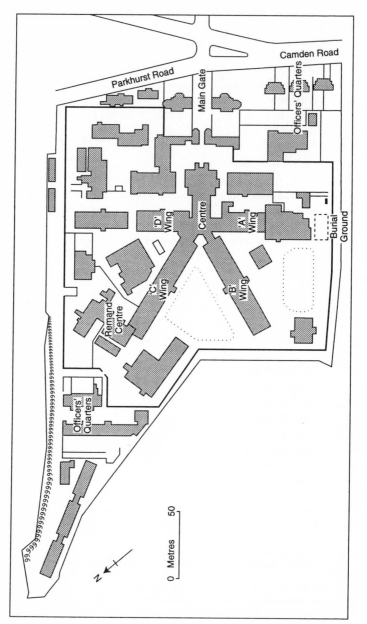

Figure 1.1 HM Prison Holloway in 1967 (simplified chart based on Prison Department Plan)

striking in the extreme. The observer feels as if he had come upon a new and different world.[22]

Figure 1.1 shows how, enclosed within a high, 20′ wall that offered protection against escapes, rescue, weather and observation, the new penitentiary was laid out like a great cartwheel. Each spoke of that wheel was a wing that allowed inmates to be classified, separated and segregated; each housed tiers of 'spacious corridors'; and each stretched out from the inspection hall at the hub, 'the point of observation commanding a view, and from which access is afforded in all directions'.[23] Almost everything of note could be seen from that central point, the Governor and his staff being able to subject prisoners to 'unobserved inspection' as they gazed down the straight, unencumbered lines of the galleries around them. One officer who had worked in the first Holloway Prison recalled that 'you could see if anyone stuck their nose out the door'. And Joanna Kelley, the Governor between 1959 and 1966, wrote that 'a single person [could] survey the whole prison from one spot'.[24] That was the very point of the Panopticon.[25]

Holloway's six wings were paired, two being some 280′ in length, two 140′ and two 110′.[26] They were four-storeys high, surmounted by arched ceilings, penetrated by 16′ wide corridors, and finished by great windows. They enclosed cavernous spaces suffused by a dim light, and some called the prison a 'black cathedral'. Individual wings and their adjoining exercise yards could be sealed off; they could be used to isolate different groupings (Jebb wrote that 'it is an object to keep all the departments quite distinct from each other');[27] and they could be reached rapidly in crisis by staff moving from wing to wing through the centre. They conferred a capacity to govern: a former education officer said 'geographically and architecturally [the officers] loved it because it's easy to control from the centre'.

[22] H. Dixon, *The London Prisons* (London: Jackson and Walford, 1850), 157–8.

[23] J. Jebb, *Modern Prisons: Their Construction and Ventilation*, (London: John Weale, 1844), 3.

[24] J. Kelley, *When the Gates Shut*, (London: Longmans, 1967), 11.

[25] See M. Foucault, *Discipline and Punish*, (London: Allen Lane, 1977).

[26] For a technical description of the newly-built prison, see 'The New City Prison, Holloway', *The Builder*, 14 June 1851.

[27] *Report of the Surveyor-General of Prisons*, 1844, 4.

The Population of the Radial Prison

I shall dwell on the Holloway of the 1960s and early 1970s,[28] the time when the central events of this book began to unfold. Women have always formed a small fraction of the prison population in England and Wales. By the 1960s, they were especially sparse, they had few previous convictions, and their sentences were often short.[29] Their numbers declined absolutely and relatively for a while, falling from an average daily population of 971 (3.2 per cent of the total prison population) to 882 (3.0 per cent) between 1963 and 1964,[30] and to 805 (2.5 per cent) in 1968. Holloway had been designed for 800, it had a capacity to house 450 in the late 1960s, but its actual occupancy was only about 300 throughout the 1960s. It seemed on occasion to be near-empty. Indeed, its prisoners were said in 1963 to have 'rattled about the place like dried peas in a pod'.[31] And, being the principal establishment and thinly occupied, set in the capital and centre of population, it was required to play an omnibus role in the criminal justice system of the south of England, serving a vast catchment area from Lyme Bay to the Wash. It became Sir Lionel Fox's *omnium gatherum,* at once a central, regional and local prison and a prison hospital. There was little scope for a proliferation of specialist institutions within the women's system.

The prison was a closed, all-purpose, category B establishment that housed just over a third of the entire female inmate population of England and Wales (276 out of 805 in 1968) and its inner social world was correspondingly complex, a penal system in microcosm. It held remands, convicted and unconvicted (in a ratio of 8 to 10): almost half the women received in 1969 were referred for medical reports

---

[28] I have explained that many papers touching on the history of Holloway were not retained by the Home Office, the prison or any other body, and documentation is consequently patchy. This section necessarily reflects some of those problems of piecemeal survival. It makes use of the varying data I have been able to unearth, reporting different items recorded at different dates. My chief source was the collection of data put together for the two Steyning Conferences of 1968 (I shall describe those conferences in Ch. 4). In effect, the first efforts to plan the new prison were based on materials assembled by Prison Department officials who relied on the best and most recent information they could find at the time. A set of those materials remained intact in the personal possession of Joanna Kelley but not, it seems, anywhere else, and I am indebted to her for bequeathing them to me.

[29] See A. Smith, 'The Treatment of Women Offenders', *The British Journal of Criminology,* October 1969, Vol. 9, No. 4, 396–8.

[30] *Report on the Work of the Prison Department 1964,* (London: HMSO, 1965), Cmnd. 2708, 1.   [31] X. Field, *Under Lock and Key,* 83.

(1,900 of 4,000 admissions) and most, 80 per cent, were subsequently given non-custodial disposals.[32] In 1967, the average daily population of remand prisoners was 105. Holloway held short and long term recidivists; 'stars' (women serving their first custodial sentence) and stars awaiting transfer; 'borstal recalls' (there were some 25–30 at a time in the mid-1960s);[33] maximum security prisoners (there were two life prisoners in 1965); civil prisoners; women serving sentences of less than six months; all prostitutes sentenced by the criminal courts; and what were called 'highly disturbed women and girls from all over the country'.[34]

Of the offences for which women were sentenced to Holloway in January 1965, the two largest categories in the daily average population were simple larceny (some 25 per cent) and fraud and false pretences. Sentences served in Holloway were comparatively brief, as they were for women in the country at large: in early 1965, a third of the inmates were committed for terms of three months or less and about two thirds for terms of over three months to four years.[35] In short, the Holloway of the 1960s contained a small, heterogeneous, rapidly changing population composed in almost equal parts of women sent by the courts for medical and psychiatric observation and prisoners sentenced to short periods principally for property offences.

The administrative structure of Holloway mirrored the complexity and diversity of its tasks. Joanna Kelley, its former Governor, recorded in 1968 that its functions were to:

accept on *remand* such prisoners as may be sent by the Courts . . . When required, to make reports to the Courts on these prisoners. . . . To keep in safe custody all those prisoners received from and *sentenced* by the Courts and to try to enable them to rehabilitate themselves . . . To afford such medical and psychiatric treatment to all prisoners in custody as may be necessary. Good order and discipline must be maintained throughout the establishment.[36]

---

[32] S. Dell, 'The Remanding of Women to Prison for Medical Examination', *Women Offenders Research Bulletin*, (London: Home Office Research Unit, 1971), No. 11, 4.

[33] See T. Sturges, 'Experiment in Holloway', *Prison Service Journal*, January 1965, Vol. IV, No. 14, 24.

[34] *Prison Policy: Women and Girls*, P.D. 4 Study No 1, (London: Prison Department, 1968), 2.

[35] See N. Goodman and J. Price, *Studies of Female Offenders*, (London: HMSO, 1967), 65.

[36] J. Kelley, *The Functions of Holoway*, unpublished typescript, 1968.

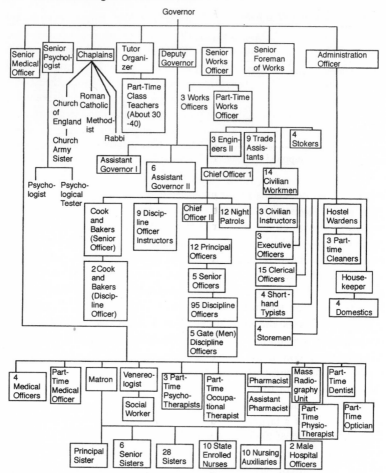

Figure 1.2 *The Administration of Holloway Prison in 1968 (based on chart prepared for Steyning Conference, 1968)*

It may be seen from Figure 1.2 how substantial and elaborate was the organization required to fulfil those functions and provide comprehensive services for what was, in effect, an autonomous world. Social life inside the prison was a reflection of life without: women had to be taught, fed, clothed and sheltered as they would have been anywhere else. But it is also apparent that the two largest groups of the staff were devoted to the maintenance of order and discipline, on the one

Table 1.1. *Analysis of Patients in Holloway, early 1969*

	Actual Number of Patients in Early 1969	Maximum Number in 1969
'Mental observation'	150	160
Medical Cases	22	32
Surgical	8	15
Epileptics	10	20
V.D.	10	16
Drug addicts	10	15

Source: Figures supplied by Medical Officer to Second Steyning Conference.

hand, and to medical and diagnostic work, on the other. Holloway was heavily invested in the activity of guarding, testing, classifying and treating women often regarded as problematic, ill, disordered or psychiatrically disturbed (four successive Governors between 1909 and 1947 had been medically trained). In early 1969, according to the Senior Medical Officer of the time, there would have been 210 patients in the prison hospital and between 20 and 60 not in hospital but who were 'on treatment'.

The prison was the very epitome of a rational bureaucracy, an organization, not unlike the army, with its serried ranks, titles and clear lines of command and communication. At its apex sat the Governor and, beneath her, were Assistant Governors charged with the management of the different wings, the NCOs and the rank and file of the discipline officers. Also formally answering to the Governor, in charge of a large, semi-detached unit, was the Senior Medical Officer, a person of consequence not only because of the number of people that worked under him or her, or the distinct regime which he or she represented, but because of the centrality of medicine to the rehabilitative project of Holloway. Somewhat dramatically, Sim wrote of the women's prison being founded on 'a regulation, discipline and process of normalization quite different and distinct from the experience of male prisoners. And at the centre of this iron therapy stood the figure of the medical man [*sic*]'.[37]

The Senior Medical Officers and their staff could not always be neatly assimilated within a simple hierarchy built on instruction, discipline and quasi-legal rules. Medical expertise has its own

[37] J. Sim, *Medical Power in Prisons*, (Milton Keynes: Open University Press, 1990), 129.

professional mandate that stands outside the rational–legal authority of the prison service and acts as a competing source of legitimacy. It may indeed have been the dominant source in Holloway. It does not always speak the language of will, accountability and blame.[38] Relations between discipline and medicine, the discipline officer and the medical officer, could become entangled, and nowhere could they be more fraught than in deliberations about a woman's fitness for punishment, particularly when that woman had been defined as 'disturbed' or 'disordered'. It is about such relations that some of the plot of this book will turn.

The Social Organization of the Radial Prison

Conceived originally to enforce a system of strict separation between inmates, modified in the construction of Holloway to allow limited association, and passing through a succession of penal regimes, Jebb's radial design continued to mould the life of prisoners and staff. It was intended to do so. Evans remarked: 'These buildings with their proliferating components and patterned plans, were to map the location of staff and inmates, guide their movements and mediate the transactions between them . . . it was always architecture that fixed the shape of experience'.[39] The impact of physical design on the social organization of Holloway was to be perfectly plain.

First, the high walls stamped the prison as a total institution, as a place set apart, in which 'a large number of like-situated individuals, cut off from the wider society for an appreciable period of time, together lead an enclosed, formally administered round of life'.[40] They were an emphatic boundary that marked the difference between life within and life without, and the gateway that pierced it was itself an unambiguous threshold. A prison visitor in the 1960s remembered 'it was "abandon hope all ye who enter here" when you go through that great door clanking behind you. It was designed to impress, impose and, I should think, frighten'. Once they had passed through it, people could not pretend to remain the same as they were washed, searched, deloused and obliged to shed roles, relations and

---

[38] See R. Smith, *Trial by Medicine*, (Edinburgh: Edinburgh University Press, 1981), 32.

[39] R. Evans, *The Fabrication of Virtue; English Prison Architecture 1750–1840* (Cambridge, Cambridge University Press, 1982), 6.

[40] E. Goffman, *Asylums*, (Harmondsworth, Penguin Books, 1961), 11.

the key signifiers of identity:[41] 'you are stripped off. Your clothes and handbag are taken away.[42] You are made to bath, in a cubicle with half doors. You are given a medical inspection. (Later there is an examination for VD.) Then you are locked in a cell for the night'.[43] It is 'impossible', wrote a former prisoner in 1960, 'for people who have not been through the experience to realize what it is like to have nothing of one's own'.[44]

Within the walls, the prison was practically self-contained, 'a little world of its own, with its own news and gossip, its own slang, its own life'.[45] A nursing officer recalled, 'it was like a mini-community, anything that would go on in a small village, if you like, or a small town, was going on there. You had to provide all facilities'.

The seclusion of prisoners was obvious,[46] but so was that of many officers who talked about the repeatedly-traversed triangle of prison, officers' quarters and officers' club, a recurrent round of work and leisure that, until 1967, was spent wholly within the walls:[47] 'poor souls', reflected one officer, 'those that lived in there, they had to have a pass every time, if they wanted to go out for the evening and come back after 10 o'clock, they had to have a pass'. The world outside could sometimes seem a little threatening and insecure (a matter I shall discuss below) and there was safety to be found behind the walls

---

[41] Of course, total institutions are rarely total. They cannot succeed in preventing some portion of the outside entering in: prisoners bring with them associations, habits of thought and identities which resist complete corrosion. And they are especially permeable in the case of busy remand prisons like Holloway with their endless movements of population. For illustrations of the frailty of prison boundaries, see S. Cohen and L. Taylor, *Psychological Survival*, (Harmondsworth: Penguin, 1972) and J. Irwin, *The Felon*, (Englewood Cliffs: New Jersey, Prentice-Hall, 1970).

[42] Removal of handbags was to be one of the most persistent sources of complaint made by inmates to the Holloway Board of Visitors in the 1970's and 1980's.

[43] S. Vincent, 'Inside Holloway Prison', *WM*, 12 November 1966, 24.

[44] D. Crisp, *A Light in the Night*, (London: Holborn Publishing Co., 1960), 69. Women would improvise, making lipstick out of the red bindings of books for instance (a librarian had been puzzled at one point why red books should be so popular). Within a short while, there was a greater liberality of regime. Frances Heidensohn, visiting the prison in 1965, noted that women wore their own clothes and jewellery, made up their eyes and dyed their hair. 'Holloway: September 1965' (unpublished paper). The abolition of uniform for women prisoners took place on an experimental basis in 1965 and was confirmed in 1968.

[45] J. Kelley, *When the Gates Shut*, 19.

[46] See A. Morgan, 'Women in Preventive Detention', *Prison Service Journal*, Oct. 1964, Vol. IV, No. 13, 18–19.

[47] Joanna Kelley reflected that 'the great value of escorts to courts and other places by prison officers is that it gets them out of the prison and they meet other people'.

and in the company of colleagues.[48] Many officers became members of a well-defined, solidary group that outsiders looked upon with some awe, occasionally invoking the language of gangs and tribes to describe what they saw (one, rather unsympathetic former member of staff said 'they are a gang. If you were to spend an evening or two in the officers' club when no-one's on, you'd be horrified . . . '). A former deputy governor said:

by the way the staff's lives evolved, by the way they ran their social lives, in many respects they almost imprisoned themselves, albeit on the periphery. But, by being glued up against the wall and going to and from the staff club and the staff mess, which had been part of the old Holloway as well, they were almost imprisoned by the prison as well, and in some ways, in a sense, perhaps didn't want to be outside the wall.

Second, the internal boundaries formed by the wings and the centre maintained divisions within the prison itself. The organization of the radial prison was deeply imbued with the imperative to order, classify and separate.[49] It kept groups of supposedly difficult and dangerous people apart, curbing their power to influence one another. Classification for men and women alike had been a principle of the Prison Service since at least the 1870s. According to Joanna Kelley, 'it was breaking down in Holloway as being quite impossible to implement when free association was allowed from about 1950 . . . [but] the staff tried hard to implement it. It was still, after all, a standing order'. As late as 1963, Xenia Field could remark of Holloway that 'the contamination of a less criminal type by fellow prisoners more versed and experienced in crime has come to be looked upon as a serious danger, and classification and the division of prisoners into groups has become an important principle in the prison system'.[50] So it was that, in the late 1960s, groups were meticulously categorized and then allocated to different buildings: Wing 'A' housed 'remands, trials and sections'; Wing 'B', 'short and medium term sentenced prisoners requiring strict management'; Wing 'C' was a 'hospital and [had] attached to it Y.P. [young prisoner] remand centre'; Wing 'D' housed the 'stars', women serving their first sentences; Wing 'DX', borstal

---

[48] Frances Heidensohn reported that it was the impression of inmates that unmarried officers were 'man-shy', 'scared to live outside, they'd be'. 'Holloway—September 1965', 19.

[49] See D. Garland, *Punishment and Welfare*, (Aldershot: Glover, 1985).

[50] *Under Lock and Key*, 91.

recalls; Wing 'E', maximum security prisoners; Wing 'F', 'short and medium sentenced prisoners able to accept a more permissive regime'; and Wing 'K', 'babies with their mothers and pregnant women'.[51] Each wing was regarded as autonomous and each had its own distinctive style.

It may be supposed that such partitioning was at once practical, disciplinary and phenomenological, different things being kept securely apart and in their place. The social anthropologist, Mary Douglas, would have looked upon it as a method of controlling symbolic disorder: 'for I believe that ideas about separating, purifying, demarcating and punishing transgressions have as their main function to impose system on an inherently untidy experience'.[52]

Third, the continual work of surveillance reinforced boundaries and demarcations between ranks, identities and functions inside the social world of Holloway itself. The radial prison was built to serve a penal regime, a regime that changed markedly over time, but it seemed always to reflect a close-knit set of spatial, social and power relations. Perhaps its strongest pictorial representation would have been that of an officer on a landing surveying groups of prisoners from afar. Indeed, the spatial metaphor of 'distance' was used repeatedly. Staff were said to be 'firm but distant'[53] with the prisoners, who were distant in their turn (one said: 'how I coped with the staff was us and them really. I kept my distance. They were a row of blue uniforms').

Staff and inmates were required to be somewhat remote from one another. They kept apart, perhaps, as Lucia Zedner has suggested to me, to 'overcome problems of "unhealthy" intimacy . . . a cause of concern even in 19th century women's prisons'. In 1972, *Behind the Times,* an inmate magazine, recorded an interview with an Assistant Governor about to retire after twenty five years in the prison service. When she started work in the late 1940s, it was reported, 'there was a strict no-talking rule between inmates and staff, and only necessary conversation was allowed. Anything other than this could be regarded

[51] J. Kelley, 'The Functions of Holloway', paper presented to the Holloway Redevelopment Project Week, May 1969.

[52] M. Douglas, *Purity and Danger: An Analysis of Concepts of Pollution and Taboo,* (Harmondsworth: Penguin, 1966), 15.

[53] P. Mason and Miss Adkins, 'The Short Sentence Wing—Holloway: An exploratory survey of its problems undertaken at the suggestion of the Governor', typescript, undated, 1.

as familiarity'.[54] And an officer remembered her identical first experience of Holloway at much the same time:

When I first went into the prison service, everything was quite serious. You didn't have much conversation with the women. It was not right to converse. . . . Only work-wise, but you wouldn't dream of going into a cell and talking to a woman. If you did, you'd have to make sure that you had another officer with you. And you had the work parties, and all the women . . . used to have to walk five paces in front of you. . . You were very restricted in your ability then to converse with the women because it was put to you that it was dangerous to have close association . . . They might get you to do things, to post a letter . . . You could be induced to traffic, to get them stuff in and all that sort of thing. You were very strictly told about these sorts of things, and this was one, you have to keep your distance.

The world of the first Holloway was threaded with visible and invisible barriers. One discipline officer recalled that '[staff] knew where they were. There was a line, and I'm not a strict disciplinarian, and never have been, but it doesn't matter whether it's a prison, a hospital, the services, where you get a lot of people together, you've got to have order, and you've got to have rules'. Throughout most of its history, the prison was a place governed by strict propriety (an officer recalled that inmates were told 'be proper, girls, be proper, girls') and by a formality of manners and discourse. In effect, Holloway was regulated by the impersonal etiquette appropriate to potentially antagonistic and irrevocably distinct groups dealing with one another at a public distance[55] in big spaces and under a system of remote surveillance.

That etiquette was old, an entrenched part of the tradition of the place (and of the prison service as a whole). It was described by Lady Constance Lytton in 1914: 'I noticed there was no inflection in the voice when speaking to prisoners, nor did the wardresses look at them when addressing them. . . . it was as if the wardresses wore a mask and withdrew as much as possible all expression of their own personality or recognition of it in the prisoner'.[56] It persisted through

---

[54] 'Personal Interview', *Behind the Times*, no date, 18.

[55] See E. Hall, 'Silent Assumptions in Social Communication', in R. Gutman (ed.); *People and Buildings*, (New York: Basic Books, 1972), 141.

[56] C. Lytton and J. Warton, *Prisons and Prisoners: Some Personal Experiences*, (London: William Heinemann, 1914), 75.

the 1950s.[57] It survived in residual form to the very end: in 1969, said a former deputy governor, there were 'still a lot of staff around who belonged to what was the old school of not speaking to inmates'.

If staff seemed distant from prisoners, governors were seen to be even more remote, their relations tending to be mediated by the officers on the landings who had daily, face-to-face dealings with inmates. It was believed by prisoners that most knowledge about prisoners reached governors at second hand and in edited form: 'governors never do [work out] the measure of the women they've got in there . . . They're not just too distant, but officers won't tell them the truth because that would get them into trouble. Prisoners—they're just too distant from them'.

Staff were themselves stratified and divided. Whilst there might have been familiarity between officers of equal standing who had been recruited at much the same time, there was also a firm hierarchy: 'There was friendliness in your own circle . . . [in] your era of joining, but when I joined there were quite a few old dragons. . . . You were never allowed into the office, the office on the particular landing. Senior officers were in there and you had to wait outside to get your orders'.

The staff had an order of precedence which was confirmed ritually each day: 'We used to call a roll call in those days. I was quite anti this roll call. You had to go and stand to attention and you were in a horseshoe [in the centre] and it started with the people who had been in the service that long and it went to the people who had joined the day before'.

Joy Kinsley, the Governor of the new Holloway in the early 1980s, recalled how, when she had been an officer working in the old Holloway of the 1960s: 'there were hierarchies and old fashioned practices and I was also terrified of being late on parade on the Centre . . . but there was actually a good deal of positive work going on as well'.

Nurses and discipline officers dined apart. Until 1955, nurses did not eat in the officers' mess inside the walls, insisting that they

---

[57] In a strong echo of Lady Constance, an internal history of the prison remarked that until the 1950s, the 'demeanour of the old-style Wardresses in addressing prisoners was by using flat, monotonous tones, carefully looking away as they spoke and never addressing them directly'. J. Oliver, The History and Development of Holloway Prison Prepared for the Governor by Oliver, 'The Head of Works Services', (1990: mimeograph), 26.

needed a change of environment during their meal breaks. Afterwards, they did dine in the mess but, said an officer, 'the nursing
staff and the prison officer staff were separate. I was a prison officer
and it was sort of "them and us" which I thought was really stupid.
You would see them but even in the mess they had their own table to
sit at. The prison officers thought they thought they were a cut above
us, that they were professionals'.

Members of the governor grade were also distant with one another:
'there was more formality. The governors, we used to have very formal
governors' meetings, it was all lists and "madam". One of the things
I abhorred when I first started [in the 1960s] was that I was called
"madam" by everybody, and I constantly told them that madams ran
brothels and this was, I hope, a house of good repute.'

Some Secondary Social Consequences of the Radial Prison

With some hyperbole perhaps, Carlebach said of Jebb: 'before he
came on the scene English prisoners suffered the brutality of total
chaos—after his death they were, for many years, subjected to the
brutality of total control'.[58] The radial prison was designed to dispel
disorganization, but disorganization never wholly disappeared. There
were:

Two prisons going on. One was the formal world which everybody knew was
a bit of a nonsense really. Your magistrates would come round and visit and
people would all go on best behaviour or not, as the case may be, sometimes.
There was this gold fish bowl . . . and then doors would shut and we'd all run
doing ducking and diving, to which the officers mostly turned a blind eye.
They didn't care whether there was extra tea or cheese being taken out of the
kitchen.

Beneath the interlocking, formal disciplines of management and
architecture, Holloway could be a lively, troubled, disquieting place,
with an undertow of violence,[59] disruption and bizarre behaviour.
Women prisoners tended generally to be more frequently charged

---

[58] J. Carlebach, 'Major-General Sir Joshua Jebb, K.C.B., 1793–1863', 29.

[59] One officer recalled, 'in the old place we did have our ups and downs . . . I can
remember one incident when they changed the location—we had borstal girls of course
in those days, and then they put the borstal girls on the first two landings of DX and
put the borstal recalls on the top floor, and that was stupid because, all of a sudden, it
was gang warfare, and I think that was one of the many times that I was absolutely
petrified.'

with disciplinary offences than men,[60] partly, some said, because they were more strictly controlled;[61] partly because they were less well versed in the ways of prison, being more frequently first offenders; and partly because, separated from children and families[62] and often at a greater distance from home,[63] many suffered the pains of imprisonment more acutely.[64] Confinement could be difficult to bear, particularly at first. One newly-committed inmate wrote, 'I experienced the desire to beat the walls and scream—behaviour which puts a large percentage of arrivals at Holloway into padded cells within a few days'.[65]

It was commonplace to remark on the concentration of unhappy and 'disturbed'[66] women prisoners in Holloway.[67] After all, it was the establishment formally set aside to house 'sentenced and unsentenced prisoners requiring psychiatric treatment or medical treatment'.[68]

[60] See M. Eaton, *Women After Prison*, (Buckingham: Open University Press, 1993), 41.

[61] See *Women and Prison: Report of an ad-hoc Working Group*, Women's National Commission, Cabinet Office, 1991, 25. Glennys Howarth has reminded me of how girls' institutions 'tend to rely more on a myriad of petty rules as a means of regulating behaviour'. However, Joy Kinsley, an officer in the old Holloway and Governor in the new, observed: 'women have always been charged with more disciplinary offences than men for a variety of reasons, but . . . not because they were more strictly controlled. It's more to do with the differing reactions of men and women to institutional life and the degree of their disturbance.'

[62] In a special piece of secondary analysis conducted for the Prison Department, the Home Office Research Unit established that, of a sample of 638 women received in Holloway during 1967, 415 women had no children; 223 women had 504 children between them; and 132 of these had their children normally living with them, 285 in total, at the time of their arrest.

[63] The relatively scarcity of prisons for women necessarily increased the probability that their inmates would be incarcerated at some distance from home.

[64] Frances Heidensohn speculated that 'the status of women in our society depends on their role as wives and mothers, and, since prison largely cuts them off from the possibility of performing this, their feeling of anomie is likely to be particularly acute. Even where female prisoners are not wives and mothers, imprisonment cuts them off from the possibility of fulfilling their feminine roles in a way unique in our society: women are nowhere else forcibly isolated from both men and children; women have never been sent to the front line, nor are there female equivalents of the merchant navy or other all male institutions'. 'Prison for Women', typescript, (1968), 3.

[65] J. Henry, *Who Lie in Gaol*, (London: Gollancz, 1952), 29.

[66] Frances Heidensohn was told on a visit by an Assistant Governor in September 1965, 'you'll find all the girls here are mentally disturbed in some way and should be treated, not disciplined'. Holloway: September 1965.

[67] See A. Mandaraka-Sheppard, *The Dynamics of Aggression in Women's Prisons in England*, (Aldershot: Gower, 1986), 9.

[68] *Report on the Work of the Prison Service*, (London: HMSO, 1992), Cm. 2087, 74.

'Many who are here are unstable. They should be in hospital',[69] said a prisoner in 1970.

The inmates were regarded as disproportionately refractory and 'disordered',[70] a theme that I shall enlarge on in the chapters that follow. Dr Knox, the senior medical officer from 1953 to 1967, remembered, 'there were a lot of violent people, young people, people on drugs. A parrot house. There were 120 beds in the hospital full of very difficult people . . . 4 people burnt themselves to death whilst I was there. Lots of girls were banging on the steel doors with their boots'. 'In my day', he remembered, 'it was primarily a matter of maintaining discipline'. His recipe had been to enlist male hospital officers from Pentonville ('I wanted quiet, married, respectable chaps in their 30s') and he then applied 'Broadmoor rules': 'we didn't punish anybody, we put them in a room and then they quieted down. They learned it was no good being a nuisance. It's like being a child. Whilst they 'were allowed to run riot, it was fun, but when they found it wasn't worth it, they stopped.'

Prison regimes are volatile and unstable, swinging from one set of controlling practices to another in the sometimes Quixotic quest for legitimacy, effectiveness, order and security. Holloway was heavily endowed with medical staff and medical tasks and it was inevitable that efforts to exert control turned repeatedly towards medical notions and medical methods (indeed, it is experimentation with a 'medically-orientated establishment' that is the focus of this book). There were periods when social order rested less on physical restraint than on drugs, on what prisoners called 'the liquid cosh'. In 1968, for instance, over 5,000 doses of medicine were issued weekly to some 275 prisoners,[71] and, in April 1969, 6,500 doses were prescribed each

---

[69] In a BBC *Man Alive* [sic] programme on Holloway filmed in December 1970 and shown early in 1971.

[70] See *Report on the Work of the Prison Department 1967*, (London: HMSO, 1968), Cmnd. 3774, 19.

[71] J. Kelley, 'The Functions of Holloway', 5.

week. The heavy use of tranquillizers[72] led some women to retreat into a private haze:

People came out and they were peeing on the floor and walking along. It was the medication. People shuffle—if you've seen films on Broadmoor and Rampton . . . You lived in your own little world surrounded by medication. It's like you had a blanket over your head. You do things like you put food in your mouth and you'd forget to chew it. . . . the huge old-fashioned wings with landings—you can see everybody and everybody can see you, you can see everything that's happening. You could see them but you were so clouded over with drugs, I could never say I met that person . . . because I never remembered because I was so drugged up.

The very appearance of so many shuffling, sedated women could create unease in those around them. Writing in the cinematic metaphor of the day, an inmate described the prison as a snake pit: 'a few women were walking about with pails, and one or two were talking together. They were dressed like myself, but they all looked unkempt, with straggly hair and shiny faces; and they all had the incurious expressions of sleep-walkers'.[73] People looked and behaved oddly. It was never possible to predict quite what might happen.

---

[72] In 1975, the following table was drawn up of daily drug consumption on the different wings:

> *Remand Centre*   (mean number of women = 73)
>   2 litres of Mogadon
>   1/2 litre of Chlorol
>   1/2 litre of 10 milligram valium
>   1 litre of 5 milligram
>   1/2 litre of Largactyl
>   Epineuton and Phenobarbitone for drug addicts and epileptics

> *K Wing*   (mean number of women = 18)
>   2 litres of Mogadon
>   1 litre of Chlorol
>   1/2 of Valium

> *D Wing*   (mean number of women = 55)
>   2 litres of Valium
>   2 litres of Mogadon
>   1 litre of Epineuton and Phenobarbitone (every two or three days)

> *F Wing*   (mean number of women = 55)
>   2 litres of Valium
>   2 litres of Mogadon
>   1 litre of Epineuton and Phenobarbitone (every two days)

Source: L. Dixon, 'Brief general report on my work placement at Holloway Prison during 1975', unpublished typescript.
[73] J. Henry, *Who Lie in Gaol*, 20.

A further consequence of the radial design with its spaces, barriers and boundaries, then, was to provide a measure of mutual reassurance in a disconcerting, tense, volatile and sometimes violent place, a place of strange happenings where everyone could be a little apprehensive. The architecture of Holloway was thought to be structured and secure: it contained few ambushes and ample warnings of danger; it kept people at a safe distance; and it supplied what a former assistant governor called 'comfortable niches':

When people were out on landings, association in the evening for instance, it was possible to observe and have staff posted around the wing who were keeping an eye on what was happening. So, therefore, control and discipline were no problem at all. But at the same time, the prisoners had a feeling of space because you weren't actively policing their activities.

Comfort was not only physical but existential. It could give certainty, order and predictability to experience. A former inmate said:

There used to be very strong boundaries between officers and inmates and there was this anonymous line between us, but you knew a lot more where you stood with them . . . . Whereas now [in 1993] because it seems that there are a lot of younger generations, non-army types . . . and that does have its bonuses, but what I found very strange . . . it seemed to be a lot better knowing where you stood and stuff with these sort of old school officers because the boundaries were very clearly laid out and laid down. Whereas now the chances are that a 30 year old woman is getting told by a 19 year old kid. . . 'now ladies', and that's personally very difficult because now you're also allocated a personal officer even if you want one or not. You're expected to be friends, and I found that all very strange whereas before the only contact you had with an officer, really, was when she was escorting you somewhere or when she was locking you in your cell. Now, there are obviously a lot of good things that have come out of it but in another way it's a bit insidious because, with the old Holloway, there were these very solid boundaries and now they're non-existent to me it seems, and you overstep lines all the time, on a Monday you could do something and that's perfectly okay and then on a Tuesday it could be something else and have a completely different perception of what's good and what not and that, I personally found very, very difficult to cope with.

Routines

The wings had their different routines in the 1960s. For example, in A Wing, the wing housing unconvicted prisoners, time had to be set aside each day for applications to the Governor and for meetings with visiting solicitors, police and probation officers. In B Wing, for 'short and medium term sentenced prisoners requiring strict management', medicine would be served at 8.15 a.m. and 8 p.m. But there was a basic model:

[*Typical Wing Routine*]

7 a.m.	All discharges to Receptions.
7.45 a.m.	All Wings unlocked.
8 a.m.	Breakfast.
8.30 a.m.–9 a.m.	Exercise.
9–11.30 a.m.	Work.
11.45–12.0 a.m.	Dinner.
1.15–4 p.m.	Work.
4.15 p.m.	Tea.
5.30 p.m.	Evening Classes.
	Association.
7.30 p.m.	Supper
8 p.m.	All women checked in.
10 p.m.	Lights out.

The prison day would oscillate between periods spent in 'association' with the relatively large group of people making up one's wing (there was relative freedom of movement *within*, but not between, the wings) and the more isolated and private life of the cells. The public spaces of the prison were large and impersonal, the domain of staged performances and managed fronts, but the cell[74] offered something of an existential release. A prison visitor recollected that 'they were regimented in the big spaces, they would go into meals together or they'd go to workshops or lessons. It was pretty regimented. They could be alone in their cells.' Such were the low numbers of prisoners in the 1960s that there was little need for involuntary 'doubling up', and a cell could become one's own, no longer a cell perhaps, but a 'room' or a 'bedroom' 'because it sounds nicer'.[75] One woman said in

[74] The standard cell measured 13' by 7' by 9' high.

[75] It was only in 1970, with the relocation of prisoners that stemmed from the demolition of the old prison, that there was 'doubling-up' in A Wing. 'In the event', said the officer responsible, 'there was no problem. We had enough room to keep a few women on a single basis so we did not ask anyone to share with the half dozen (out of 70) who in layman's terms seemed most "mad".'

1971 'they say it's homely. I knew I'd be here for quite a long time so I brought the bedspread, I bought the curtains. It's homely'.[76]

Cells were often transformed into 'home territories',[77] the symbolic bases in which women felt that they could preserve some part of themselves,[78] perhaps the womanly part that could be so under threat in a levelling institution.[79] They were cleaned and scrubbed as if to reassert personal control and keep the corruption, evil and dirt of the prison and prisoners away: 'the floors were black, mostly boot polish black, and it was a matter of pride for some to have the best polished floor' said one. Another inmate talked of having a 'black floor that . . . you could see your face in. I put black boot polish, put it on, spit all over it, and then polish it up with a brush and then a buffer. . . . In there, grubbiness is considered a terrible, terrible sin. You have to be super clean, squeaky clean. . . . It was a prevailing culture. Women who were dirty were . . . [it was] a part of not having self-respect'. There would be pin-ups and pictures, curtains and cushions. A deputy governor recalled the 'amazing pictures and all sorts of clutter in their cells that just went with the personalities of the individuals who were there at the time'. And a journalist wrote about how:

no sooner are [women] allocated cells on their arrival, than the little woman takes over. The cell is turned into a nest. They cut out coloured pictures of flowers, animals and babies from magazines, and stick them in neat rows above their beds. They find plastic flowers from somewhere and arrange them in jam jars. Their cells have bright patterned curtains, and every cell door is a different colour.[80]

---

[76] Interview in *Man Alive*, 'Women in Prison', 1971.

[77] See S. Cavan, *Liquor License: An Ethnography of Bar Behavior*, (Chicago: Aldine, 1966).

[78] Accounts of life in men's prisons refer to very much the same processes of domestication. See, for example, Jock of Dartmoor, *Dartmoor from Within*, (London: The Readers Library Publishing Co., n.d.), 93.

[79] With some confidence, Matrix, the collective authors of *Making Space: Women and the Man-Made Environment* (Pluto Press: London, 1984), an analysis of architecture and feminity, assert on their very first page 'Behind every woman is the image of "the ideal home". The ideology of domesticity, which describes how things *ought* to be and *ought* to look, will always affect what we do even when we are reacting against it.'

[80] I. Mather, 'After just THREE HOURS IN HOLLOWAY . . . the questions that haunt my mind', *Daily Mail*, 6 Nov. 1971.

The Inmate World

Within their strong experiential frame, behind their lines, at a protective distance from one another,[81] and within the large spaces of the wings, discipline staff and inmates formed two loosely-coupled worlds. The world of the inmates was heterogenous. Its membership was continually changing. It was fractured, suspicious[82] and occasionally predatory. It was defiling, and I have observed how some women would spend time cleaning themselves, their clothes,[83] and their cells. It attacked and humiliated the self.[84] It was riven, violent and scaring: 'there was an awful lot of very unpleasant violence, very nasty violence . . . you had a lot of alcoholics in prison, a lot more alcoholics . . . prostitute women were put in prison, vagrants were put in prison. We had PD, preventive detention, women in there for years and years who became very brutalised and they were very tough. Very scary women.'

But there were also nets of friends and lovers, and there was a crude, coercive order imposed by the tougher inmates who had been sentenced for longer terms. Stable figures in an unstable world, they were, said Chris Tchaikovsky, the 'caucus who ran the nick. The "governors," in fact, they called them. . . . they were the toughest. Literally physical, the survival of the fittest, Jack the Lad, it all applied. It didn't follow that it was always the biggest, but the nastiest really.'

[81] A former prisoner said, 'the Victorians, the radial [prison], it's the right way. It's so obvious, because you had your centre, all open wires at the top, so the screws had maximum, seemingly maximum surveillance, which meant that the officers were secure, which was much better for the prisoners . . .'

[82] One said, 'I don't really believe friendships are formed in prison . . . you've got everything so screwed down . . . there's so much bragging and so many untruths about your life. . . . there's this whole veneer . . . of hardness. That, and the fact that the injustices you do see constantly, every prison day, you ignore, and that I think, is the great corrosive.'

[83] One recalled her response to the reception area: 'I was in a state of shock. I didn't know who they were and what was going on. It was particularly dirty and messy in there and chaotic, and I remember someone saying to me "you won't be here long. It's alright, it's much better on the other wing". I slept most of the time. Then I remember sort of coming to and thinking, "I've got to scrub my clothes. I've got to scrub my clothes".'

[84] A former prisoner said, 'you couldn't really be yourself in there because you're being treated as a subhuman really. And you resist that. It is true, you don't show anybody, you certainly don't show the officers, and you don't want women blubbing all over the place . . .'

The spaciousness of the wings brought it about that inmates could congregate in numbers, and they could do so in relative freedom and at a remove from the discipline officers. Being thus removed and free, they were at liberty to adapt and modify social order at the margins. Like the inmates of many another total institution, they exerted a limited control over one another and themselves, mediating disputes violently or peacefully, bullying and bribing, and all within the fabric of formal discipline exercised by the staff:

I didn't appreciate what a difference open windows, what light meant, what largeness meant, what ceiling openness was. . . . We used to have 2 officers on D Wing, 40 women, including X, 5 murderers, real heavyweights, Big Bet and Crazy Linda, and we'd have 2 officers on duty, and one officer would go to get the soup and the cocoa with a few prisoners to bring it back from the kitchen. So you'd have one officer on duty. And that's why I say. . . the women socially controlled themselves and the officers were much more secure.

The unspoken rule was that most officers would ignore minor breaches of discipline. Major social control was women with women. Lifers, well not lifers necessarily, but lifers were at the top of the pile, much respected, and then you had a hierarchy. You had your own heavy mob . . . a lot more violence then than now, but the violence was of a different kind, because the 'us and them' was so firmly in place, with of course some crossover, but firmly in place. You'd have a fight with somebody, you could give a time and you'd have somebody watching outside the door, you'd shut the door, have your fight, come out with black eyes, you'd never grass each other, honour would be done and out you'd come.

I described Holloway as heterogeneous, a penal system in microcosm. The inmate world itself was not one but many, and prisoners had to pick their way amongst it. They might elect to be inconspicuous and peripheral, avoiding conflict, the female counterparts to the 'Square Johns' of the American jail system:[85] 'the expression is "keep your head down". That literally means 'do your work and do your time without, you really could do your time, without any violence".' They could become more centrally engaged, choosing (or being forced into) membership of very different groups. At one extreme, there were the discredited alcoholics and vagrants, and the 'negs', women convicted of child neglect. There were the 'real heavies', the tough women and lifers who 'ran the prison'. And there was also a collection of women

[85] See J. Irwin and D. Cressey, 'Thieves, Convicts and the Inmate Culture', in H. Becker (ed.), *The Other Side*, (New York: The Free Press, 1964).

described by many as vivacious, glamorous and interesting, a group that, in the 1960s and 1970s, included members of the proto-anarchist 'Angry Brigade', graduates, fraudsters and women celebrated in the press: 'I've met the most exciting women there . . . there were very special women in there'. An inmate described just such a woman: her 'cell was absolutely wonderful. She used to wear her fur coat and all sorts of things. She was fun and she made me laugh.'

Holloway was not without relief. It could be an exciting place and it sometimes evoked fond memories. Chris Tchaikovsky said:

It's nice to talk about it, it's like a part of your life that you don't often get the opportunity to talk about it in a clear way, not with the 'poor victim' stuff, which is what everybody wants to hear, all the dreadful stuff that happened to me and others, all the agony. We talk about the laughs, the enormous laughs. I think almost everybody. . . said we never laughed as much as in prison. And everybody linked arms in the old Holloway. I don't know whether, I've not seen it in the new Holloway, but linking arms was the common way you walked about. All prisoners linked arms.

Crossing and Blurring the Lines

An ironic consequence of the firmness of the boundaries between 'us and them', between officers and inmates, was the ever-present possibility of slipping across the lines. It was as if barriers so secure could be breached without serious risk. Officers would show kindnesses to inmates. One former prisoner recalled 'a woman officer who, when I was crying one night, and she came and said "here are some tissues". That was a nice gesture'. And gestures were reciprocated:

Inmates looked after each other and they looked after staff as well. I can remember hobbling in on duty on a Christmas morning when I had hurt my toe very badly and one of the inmates rushed off and got me her Scholl sandals so that I would be comfortable. Those are the sort of thing one remembers.

There were friendships, crushes, mock crushes[86] and sexual liaisons between officers and inmates (an ex-inmate recalled 'there was a dynamic that used to happen between staff, relationships happened,

---

[86] The agony aunt's page of the inmate magazine, *Behind the Times*, published in 1972, reproduced a letter from 'Bashful': 'I have fallen in love with the A.G. Is this natural under the circumstances? Do you think you could feel the same way?' 'Dear Bashful', the writer was told, I think it's natural under *any* circumstances. She is rather dishy.'

sexual relationships happened, romantic relationships happened between prisoners and prisoners and staff. Life was lived'). Then, too, there were larger pockets of informality, particularly in the enclaves where a cold demeanour was manifestly inappropriate, in the hospital and the mother and baby unit, for instance.

Most spectacularly, there was the formalized informality of the institutional carnival or *charivari* when, during a limited period of licence, inmates and officers declared what was tantamount to a truce and left the trenches or reversed roles in a joking relationship. Such rituals may be found in the calendars of many otherwise disciplined groups, in armies, schools,[87] academies and asylums, and they can work as a release to make repression and frustration less intolerable. The chief Holloway carnival was at Christmas, a time especially poignant for captive women:

[There was a greater formality] and yet when there was informality it was tremendous fun. I remember a time at Christmas when three of us, very senior members of staff, dressed up and went round singing as 'The Joy-strings, and were treated with the greatest hilarity. I mean, the contrast was so great that everybody did really enjoy it, and made great fun of me being accused of being the drunk on the street, and so on, which would never have happened in the more formal setting.

And a prisoner recalled:

. . . [they were distant] but come things, Christmas, birthdays, they used to volunteer for it, so that we could enjoy that. Now they don't. . . . We used to have things like D Wing versus F Wing, and we used to dress up and the officers used to come in and bring things to help you dress because they wanted their wing to win. We used to come out for a netball match dressed like American football players. The officers said 'Win! Win! Cheat if you've got to win, if that's what it takes. Win! Win! We've got to win!.' The officers were roaring!

More generally and diffusely, the hardness of the lines was softened by what might be called the 'matronly' style of many experienced discipline officers. A prison visitor said 'I expected them to be bullying and hard-faced. They were wonderful, the ones I saw. . . . I marvelled at their patience.' Officers of the first Holloway tended to be rather older than their successors at the new prison (a matter I

---

[87] See I. and P. Opie, *The Lore and Language of Schoolchildren*, (Oxford: Oxford University Press, 1959), 22.

shall discuss below), and they sometimes formed quasi-maternal relationships with their charges. Scarlett wrote about how, in the borstal recall wing, 'the staff are often cast into family roles by the girls—the more senior members frequently being addressed as "mum" or "mama".[88] In late 1965, undertaking fieldwork for a dissertation, Frances Heidensohn noticed the 'comforting motherly—military officers [who] treat[ed] the prisoners benevolently but patronisingly rather like southern white ma'ams with their negro hired helps'. Perhaps, she thought, the '"welfare" and "therapy" aspects of the job are . . . in accord with socially prescribed and valued characteristics of the female role'.[89] In similar style, an inmate recalled of the officers, 'they were older women, single women. . . . A bit like school ma'ams, you know, the dedicated officer, the stereotype. But they were very, they were a lot of them, very fond of the women and the women very fond of them. "Mothers" I called them. And there were a lot of those too, who wound up the girls . . . so that they could mother them'.

Maternalism had a neat affinity with the firm, structured authority exercised by older women officers over the 'girls'—girls being the revealing name used to describe prisoners of any age. It not only enforced subordination but also prepared the way for a more rehabilitative style in the 1960s. Heidensohn noted that 'prison work for many appeared to give opportunity to carry out certain affective and therapeutic aspects of what they perceive as their prescribed roles'.[90]

Modifications and Adaptations

Holloway was modified, adapted and added to over the years. The original radial prison had been intended to sequestrate inmates for the most part. Locked in their cells, free from communication and contamination, it was supposed that they would reflect on their misdeeds in isolation. Jebb had stipulated in 1844 that it would be 'unnecessary for a prisoner to quit his cell, excepting for attending chapel and exercise'[91] (although it should be remarked, as Lucia Zedner has reminded me, that Jebb and 'others had been concerned

---

[88] 'A Therapeutic Community for Borstal Girls in Holloway', 112.
[89] 'Holloway: September 1965'.
[90] Ibid, 5.
[91] Report of the Surveyor-General of Prisons, 7.

that women would not be able withstand the rigours of isolation'). By 1849, the City authorities had trimmed. Their design for Holloway included 'the means of confining the vicious in separate cells; and . . . a sufficient number of workrooms for classified association'.[92] But there had been no provision for education, and classrooms had to be created by knocking two or three cells into one. There had been no provision for dining in association or for associated recreation, as it was called, and there was to be an improvisation of landings or cells which were knocked together. There had been no provision for psychologists, probation officers and education staff, and they, too, had to be housed in improvised cells.

Little by little, practices changed and a new penology came to be conceived within the womb of the old radial prison. In a movement of ideas that I shall explore at length in chapters to come, a movement that stemmed largely from lay men and women in the prison service,[93] Holloway began to employ psychologists, psychiatrists, probation officers and social workers. The first woman psychotherapist was appointed to Holloway in 1939, and the first psychiatric social worker in 1946.

Joanna Kelley was the Governor of Holloway in the late 1950s and early 1960s. She too came to support group therapy, encouraged its introduction into her prison, and praised the manner in which the 'prison service . . . . has been burgeoning with new ideas on the treatment and rehabilitation of offenders, and [the] many brave efforts [that] have been made to try new methods of training and more constructive forms of treatment'.[94] In October 1966, at the very time when the interest in therapy was at its most intense, Joanna Kelley left her post to become Assistant Director

---

[92] 'The New City Prison, Holloway', *The Builder*, 14 June 1851, 576.

[93] It was to be treated with some suspicion by the Prison Medical Service. Psychiatric treatment was not their protegé at all. Consider, for example, the remarks of the Medical Commissioner, Norwood East, on p. 57 of the *Report of the Commissioners of Prisons and the Directors of Convict Prisons for the year 1935*: 'propaganda directed towards the psychiatric treatment of crime, although perhaps necessary and advantageous in some respects, is a dangerous weapon, since it inevitably leads people to believe that benefits will be delivered although failures may be more frequent than successes. . . . Every new cult claims advantages, which too often fail to stand the test of time'.

[94] J. Kelley, 'The New Holloway', *Prison Service Journal*, October 1970, Vol. X, No. 37, 2.

(Women) in the Prison Department, and she took with her an ambition to transform Holloway Prison into an institution which could put the new ideas fully to work.

2

The Prison Department, Women and Criminology

Introduction

The Prison Department to which Joanna Kelley went in late 1966 was itself undergoing radical change in the immediate aftermath of a major security crisis excited by a flurry of sensational escapes. Six prisoners had escaped from Wormwood Scrubs in June 1966. More spectacularly, six months later, George Blake, the spy who had been sentenced in 1961 to a total of 42 years imprisonment, broke out of that same prison in October. In December 1966, another infamous inmate, Frank Mitchell, the so-called 'mad axeman', absconded from a working party outside Dartmoor Prison.[1] A series of dramatic events following one another closely in time can create a stir in government,[2] and the agitated response to the new political problem of prison escapes, and to Blake's escape in particular, had all the appearance of a moral panic.[3] It led to the mounting of the Mountbatten Inquiry into Prison Escapes and Security which reported in December 1966,[4] to the later revisions recommended by a committee chaired by Leon Radzinowicz,[5] to a profound and continuing intensification of safety measures in mens prisons and to a matching restructuring of the Prison Department itself.

[1] See A. Rutherford, *Prisons and the Process of Justice*, (London: Heinemann, 1984), 77–8.
[2] For a discussion of the part played by successive scandals in political life, see E. Sutherland, 'The Diffusion of Sexual Psychopath Laws', in W. Chambliss (ed.), *Crime and the Legal Process*, (New York: McGraw-Hill, 1969).
[3] See S. Cohen, *Folk Devils and Moral Panics*, (London: Martin Robertson, 1980).
[4] *Report of the Inquiry into Prison Escapes and Security*, Cmnd. 3175, (London: HMSO, 1966).
[5] Advisory Council on the Penal System, *The Regime for Long-Term Prisoners in Conditions of Maximum Security*, (London: HMSO, 1968).

P4

The Department had to take on an extra burden of work as it dealt with the reorganization of male establishments. The number of its staff and component units was increased, and, amongst them, a new division, P4, was formed in 1967 with Ken Neale as its first Assistant Secretary until 1970. Neale recalled that 'the male division, with all its heavy security problems was going to have a great deal more work than it ever had. Therefore there was a case for hiving off some of its work into a new division.' The place of the Prison Department within the larger structure of the Home Office is shown in Figure 2.1, and its new organization in Figure 2.2.

P4 was to be responsible for a number of tasks whose chief characteristic was that they did *not* centre on the pressing problems of the adult male offender. Its tasks included women's policy; women's and girls' casework and tactical management; borstal policy;[6] borstal casework and tactical management; detention centre policy;[7] detention centre casework and tactical management; young prisoner policy; young prisoner casework and tactical management; attendance centre policy;[8] attendance centre casework and tactical management; remand centre policy and tactical management; remand and trial casework; assaults by women and girls; assaults by young offenders; assaults by unconvicted, unsentenced civils; commissioning of women's and young offenders' establishments; and the welfare of women and young offenders. It was a small department led by an Assistant Secretary, two Assistant Directors, both with long experience of work in prisons, two seconded senior governors, an architect, and supporting administrative staff. The functions and membership of P4 bear directly upon the theme of this book. Let me explain.

Firstly, a division focussed on policies for women's prisons alone would have been somewhat obscure had it not been for an accumulation of additional duties. After all, women prisoners were few and their numbers seemed to be declining yet further. They did not bulk

---

[6] Borstals at that time were penal institutions for 'juvenile and young adult offenders'.

[7] Detention centres were institutions established in 1952, supposed to deliver a 'short, sharp shock' to young offenders.

[8] Attendance centres were conceived in the aborted Criminal Justice Bill of 1938, and were intended to act as an alternative to the imprisonment of persons under the age of 21. See G. Mair, *Part-time Punishment*, Unpublished Ph.D. dissertation, London School of Economics.

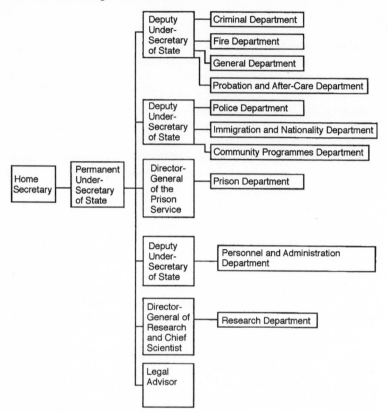

Figure 2.1 *The Home Office in the early 1970s*

large in the politics of the penal system, and particularly in the late 1960s when male prisoners were at the epicentre of interest. Only by assuming additional functions could P4 come to form a sizeable presence within the world of the Prison Department. Neale, its first administrator, reflected that 'as far as staff was concerned, it was a bigger division because of all its other responsibilities . . . [it was] a very big division by Home Office standards'. In the early 1970s, for instance, at a time when the redevelopment of Holloway prison was under way, its staff numbered 36 (24 of whom worked wholly or in part on women's issues), large compared with the 25 of P1 (entrusted with the strategic planning of buildings, the selection of sites, the Steering Committee for Prison Building, manpower planning, the

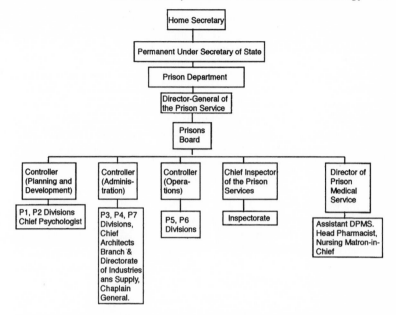

Figure 2.2 Organizational Chart of the Prison Department in the early 1970s

annual building programme and other matters), but quite small compared with the 52 of P3 (responsible for sentenced adult male offenders).

Secondly, P4 could be considered relatively self-sufficient for most administrative and planning purposes. Unlike the divisions responsible for male prisoners, it was able to manage its portion of the penal estate largely on its own, independently conceiving, developing and implementing comprehensive initiatives for women, and its work was the more clearly defined, coherent, concentrated and contained as a result. Quentin Thomas, who had worked in P4, observed: 'because the men's system was much larger, there was a greater division of labour, a division dealing with operational matters, divisions dealing with policy matters, a division devoted to building projects and so on. The women's system, because it was so small, had a privileged position, if it *is* a privilege. The single division brought together a number of those aspects on a day-to-day basis, causing operations to be concentrated in a single division on the women's side.' So it was that the designing and commissioning of new prisons for men necessarily affected many different divisions, but the redevelopment of Holloway prison could be inaugurated, commandeered and planned by just one department. Thomas said:

They were able to capture that building project. On the men's side, it would have been a much greater division of labour. Those issues would have been strung across 4 or 5 divisions. I'm not saying that the result on the men's side would be less coherent or less systematic, the result would have been the same, but in organizational terms it was obviously very much simpler. There was an opportunity there. For example, the project showed a coherence of approach. Whether it was the right approach is perhaps more problematic . . . but there was a thoroughgoing analysis.

Thirdly, a division that was not obliged to consider the problems of adult male prisons and prisoners was doubly free in the late 1960s. The politics of the time made it imperative to submit adult male prisoners to an almost ostentatious attention, discipline, security and control, but no such imperative guided policies towards women. Women's prisons lacked political urgency (although that was to change as the history of Holloway prison itself unfolded). Sir William Pile, Director-General of the Prison Service between 1968 and 1970, reflected that 'the received doctrine was the public will not stand for prisons being soft on men prisoners—post Blake, Mountbatten. The women's problem was different. No public was going to howl about someone going over the wall. No dogs.'

It was certainly to P4's advantage that it had charge of such a small and marginal segment of the penal system. Sometimes, indeed, women's prisons appeared to be on the outer fringe of an organization dominated by male establishments. And, being on the fringe, liable to be overlooked, what was done in and to them might also be overlooked by the politicians, lobbies and the press,[9] a particularly advantageous matter at a time of heightened anxiety about security.[10] David Faulkner stated 'the management of the women's system and

---

[9] See A. Smith, 'The Woman Offender', in L. Blom-Cooper (ed.), *Progress in Penal Reform*, (Oxford: Clarendon Press, 1974), 157.

[10] David Faulkner wrote on 4 January 1995: 'one of the interesting features of Holloway and the Holloway project was the extent to which it was both isolated from and at the same time intimately connected with what was happening in the rest of the service. The project had its origin in the period immediately after Mountbatten, when the service as a whole was concentrating on security and control . . . but a few liberal spirits were trying—and were licensed—to preserve and develop a parallel agenda for both women and young offenders. But that agenda never engaged the energy or commitment of top management or the Prisons Board.'

the management of the young offenders' system which were concentrated in P4 . . . were operating outside the ordinary limits of the adult male system. . . . On the whole, in those, days, people were prepared mostly to leave those in charge of women to get on with it'. In the late 1960s, after all, prisons on the 'women's side' were comparatively inexpensive to run. They were less fraught. They presented fewer problems. They did not have to be bound by what was done on the 'men's side'. Sir William Pile observed that 'the numbers were completely different. It was always an isolated and separate issue . . . more manageable.' P4 could experiment and innovate more freely and cheaply than the men's divisions. In October 1968, it argued in its very first policy study that 'the small and relatively stable numbers of women and girls in custody make their custody and treatment a problem which is well within our capacity to resolve'.[11]

But P4 was also free because women could be defined as different, sometimes importantly so, and it could be claimed that they merited different treatment. I shall argue in this and the next chapter that the exercise of such freedom must be interpreted with some caution. Arguments about gender, and much else, were put reflectively and usually to a purpose. They were politically contingent. On occasion they would be given heightened significance but they could be absent altogether in other places, and it would not do to think that an apparent freedom to make a case necessarily implied stable, deep convictions about what was said.

Yet some matters *were* clear. Women were not only deemed to be less dangerous and less politically visible (matters I shall pursue further in the next chapter). They were also perceived to be heavily invested in child-care and families, and the Prison Department was correspondingly somewhat more lenient in permitting women to wear their own clothes in prison, gave them parole and home visits more frequently, and controlled the receiving and sending of mail less firmly. An official said that there was 'within the system a degree of tolerance as to various procedural rules'.

Fourthly, P4 was a composite division that housed staff (including governors on secondment) who dealt with young offenders, and the treatment of the young tends often to be regarded as a rather more hopeful enterprise than that of the old. The Borstal institutions,

---

[11] *Prison Policy: Women and Girls*, Prison Department, Oct. 1968, 2–3.

especially, had begun as an idealistic movement based on moral training which would 'study the individual lad, . . . discover his trend and his possibility, and . . . infect him with some idea of life which will germinate and produce a character, controlling desire, and shaping conduct to some more glorious end than mere satisfaction or acquisition'.[12] There was cross-fertilization. Some of that idealism of the Borstal movement lingered on as an inspirational force to be transmitted quite consciously from one generation of officials to another. All who had worked in and about the P4 of the late 1960s and early 1970s alluded to the presence of a special reforming tradition. Austin Wilson, Assistant Secretary in charge of P4 in the mid-1970s, recalled that some of the 'idealistic pioneers' were 'still around in my time and there had been within recent memory a director of Borstal administration [who] had been in a sense a professional leader of the Borstal service and almost a sort of father figure for a distinctive treatment-orientated offender-based training regime for young offenders. And the torch that was handed on to me . . . was "you are the successor to this tradition of independence . . . and of therapy rather than punishment as being your theme".' Terry Weiler remembered that the 'whole pre-war tradition which flowed over into the people I was working with when I came in the 60s was that personal influence, staff example and that kind of thing, could still affect young offenders'. And David Faulkner, the Assistant Secretary in charge of P4 from June 1970 to February 1974, also observed that 'the Paterson[13] idea was, I think, pretty well rejected professionally within the service but there was still a strong desire to hold on to the notion that we are actually here to do something more than keep people locked up and stop them escaping and give them the basic necessities of survival'.

A small, late constituent of the tradition of 'doing something more' was the leaning towards treatment inculcated by special courses of 'group discussions' for the governors of institutions for young offenders; these were offered first by the Tavistock Institute of Human

---

[12] Sir Alexander Paterson in *The Times*, 5 Aug. 1925. For a fuller account, see V. Bailey, *Delinquency and Citizenship: Reclaiming the Young Offender 1914-1948*, (Oxford: Clarendon Press, 1987).

[13] Sir Alexander Paterson, born in 1885, was, in Roger Hood's words, the inspirator of the Golden Age of the Borstal system.

Relations in 1964 and continued for some years thereafter.[14] By 1966, 50 governors and staff had attended. They were introduced to the writing of Bion and Balint[15] and to the 'new ideas' that penal institutions for the young should be 'therapeutic and educative rather than custodial and punitive'.[16] One assistant governor recalled how 'we were very involved with organizations like the Tavistock and the Grubb Institute and it was part of our training to go off on these strange groups to sit and shout at each other—the Tavi style . . . I still never fully understand what we were supposed to be doing'. Administrators of the time were a little guarded about the Tavistock Institute, as they were about most enthusiasms.[17] It was supposed that the courses had a variable effect, being capable of impairing as well as sustaining the performance of young governors: 'it was said that it made an enormous difference to some people and that after you could see that they were much better governors; there were a number of people on whom it failed to make any impact at all; one or two for whom it was too much, and that was quite serious'. But the Institute did make its mark.[18]

It certainly offered a bold model and ideology for penal practice. The courses talked about the importance of recognizing 'anti-social behaviour as the result of interplay between a disturbed personality and psycho-social stress' and the inappropriateness of punishing

[14] See D. Miller. 'Staff Training in the Penal System: The Use of Small Groups', *Human Relations*, 19, (1966), 151: 'in recent years a particular attempt has been made to improve the standard of treatment in penal institutions for young people in Great Britain. Adequate training of the staff in psycho-social techniques thus becomes of great importance.'
[15] Wilfred Bion was Chairman of the Executive Committee of the Tavistock Clinic after the Second World War and Director of the London Clinic of Psycho-Analysis from 1956–62. It was said of him that 'applying the rules of individual classical analysis (with a Kleinian emphasis) to the group as a single entity . . . the procedures Bion applies to the study of . . . groups . . . became known as the Tavistock method'. J. Grotstein, 'Wilfred R. Bion: the Man, the Psychoanalyst, the Mystic. A Perspective on His Life and Work, in J. Grotstein (ed.), *Do I Dare Disturb the Universe? A Memorial to Wilfred R. Bion*, (London: Maresfield Reprints, 1983), 6. For Balint, see M. Balint, *The Basic Fault*, (London: Tavistock, 1968).
[16] H. Coplin, introduction to R. Gosling *et al.* (eds.), *The Use of Small Groups in Training*, (no provenance, Codicote Press, no date), 10.
[17] See P. Rock, *Helping Victims of Crime*, (Oxford: Clarendon Press, 1990), ch. 1.
[18] In 1959, for example, the Tavistock Institute was commissioned to study the results of the 'Norwich experiment' in 'humanising relations between staff and prisoners in Bristol prison'. See *Penal Practice in a Changing Society*, Cmnd. 645, (London: HMSO, 1959), 30.

'mental illness'.[19] They talked about the prime importance of 'change situations' and about how unprofitable it was to 'exaggerate differences between the work of the prison and the mental hospital'. They talked about how staff in penal settings 'are more and more being encouraged to regard themselves as caseworkers'.[20] Joanna Kelley herself had attended a Tavistock course in London and a residential course in Leicester, and called them 'the only really useful training I received'.

The older idealism of the Borstal governors and the newer ideas of the Tavistock Institute formed an intellectual amalgam that drifted across P4. It was an amalgam that spread quite far, and especially at the beginning when formal meetings were used to inject cohesion and morale into a new division. David Faulkner remembered of his period as Assistant Secretary in the early 1970s: 'it rubbed off across the division because I tried to run the division as a whole. We did expect ideas across the division and we did have conferences and seminars and so on, and it has always been my . . . style to enjoy bringing people together like that.'

Fifthly, and perhaps most importantly, the very newness of P4 was consequential in 1967. The division at that time could have had no entrenched ways of doing things, no fixed habits of thought or engrained prejudices. Its style and purpose were still to be set. Ken Neale recollected that 'the great advantage we had was its newness. It was a completely new division. Normally, when you take over a division you inherit all the characteristics, but it was a new division and people were taken from here and from there. A completely new head of department.' The division was *malleable*. It awaited new ideas. And especially influential in giving it shape and direction were to be its two most senior officials: Ken Neale himself, that new head of department, and Joanna Kelley, the new Assistant Director (Women).

Within a year, it was Neale and Kelley who came to conceive the Holloway redevelopment project, and, at the very beginning, it was to be their minds, experiences and relations that organized and articulated what was to be done. David Faulkner said 'the critical click or chemistry was the relationship between Joanna Kelley, Ken Neale and Bill Pile [who entered office in 1969, after the conception of the project], and those three . . . made common cause and had a shared

---

[19] D. Miller, 'Staff Training in the Penal System', 155.   [20] *Ibid*, 156.

view'. The early P4 and its first big project were not some disembod-
ied phenomena that flowed inexorably out of the larger politics and
ideology of the penal system in mid-century. They were the personal
creatures of identifiable, influential people working together in a very
special organization.

Ken Neale

Neale had worked in the Cyprus and Central African Offices of the
Colonial Office between 1955 and 1964, rising to become head of the
Rhodesia department during the years of that country's unilateral
declaration of independence. Between 1964 and 1967 he was Assistant
Secretary at the Commonwealth Office and Counsellor in the Diplo-
matic Service. No longer wishing to go abroad and be apart from his
children, Neale transferred to the home civil service, to the Home
Office, and 'the first job I had was the head of P4, which division was
set up at that time and I was its first head'. He remained in that post
between 1967 and 1970 before moving on to other posts in the Prison
Department, becoming, *inter alia*, Director of Industries and Supply
between 1970 and 1975 and Controller, Planning and Development,
between 1976 and 1980.

Neale imported a number of working practices from the Colonial
Service. He had been accustomed administratively to 'out-stations
and the whole notion of a headquarters trying to come to terms with
the problems of people in the field'. Out-stations decentralized the
work of government and decision-making in large, sometimes thinly-
populated territories regulated by a small bureaucracy, and they
entailed much travelling: 'I did a lot more visiting [in the prison
service] than was ever done before because that was what we did
all the time, going out in the Colonial Office, being with them,
working with them, seeing them, and it was in the style to be out
and about a lot more.' Just as he would have made a tour of
inspection in a colony, so he made frequent visits to prisons and
conferences and gauged something of the mind of the governors of
women's prisons.

It would not be sensible to telescope the development of the
argument of this book, but it should be noted that Neale, the
erstwhile colonial administrator, visited Holloway prison itself in
1967, during the first year of his new post, and he determined that
it was 'an affront to civilisation', 'everything about it was disgusting.

. . . I suppose there was a little bit of chauvinism about it, but it was so utterly unacceptable to put women and children in these conditions that it had to go.' Neale and his colleagues came to see Holloway, not as a noble castle, but as a 'Fagin's kitchen, . . . a devilish hole, derelict, run down, dirty and over-crowded'. There was to be a reversal of vision that I shall discuss in greater detail in the next chapter, and some part of it must have arisen out of Neale's transposition of the colonial officer's role. He applied the working injunction to inspect closely what was happening on the ground and assess what he saw there.[21] And, in time, there was to be another extension of the out-station principle in Neale's method of stilling the Treasury's objections to the rebuilding of Holloway prison. He escorted a doubting Treasury official to Holloway itself, persuading her by direct confrontation about the urgency of the case: 'I hit upon the notion, I tried to restyle the whole running of the P4 division in ways which were more akin to the way in which a Colonial Office division had been run rather than a Home Office division. And this included taking the Treasury people who were concerned with these things to see Holloway and say. . . "well, it must strike you as it strikes me".'

Neale brought with him one other, perhaps more general, working practice. He sought to give impetus, cohesion and purpose to the newborn division by fixing on a small number of significant projects that could focus and integrate the efforts of his staff: 'in P4 we identified 3 or 4 major things . . . which we were going to do, and launch and give a momentum to'. The redevelopment of Holloway prison, mooted in the very first year of the division's life, was to be just such a major thing, and 'its manifest success . . . for the whole of P4, the fact that it was pioneering new ideas and new ways of doing the department's work, and involving people very closely in a way that hadn't been done before, it was very good for the morale of P4'.[22]

However, the redevelopment of Holloway prison was not merely an idea that had to be invented in order to breathe life into a new administrative group. It was already being actively championed by

[21] To be sure, other Assistant Secretaries and officials also visited Holloway prison frequently. It should not be assumed that I am arguing that Neale's methods were peculiar to himself.

[22] In due course, when the work on reconstructing Holloway prison had begun, Neale was to write to those who had attended a conference on the project: 'I have no doubt that this conference has done much to enhance the unity of the teams working on this project, and, for individuals, increased their personal interest and commitment to it'. Letter of 14 May 1969.

the prison's former governor, now Assistant Director and a member of P4 working under Neale: 'this one didn't have to be found. Joanna was already there with the idea and it was a question of just endorsing it and saying "yes, this one".'

Joanna Kelley

Joanna Kelley was born in 1910 and obtained a degree in Economics at Girton College, Cambridge. She entered the Prison Service in 1947 and was Assistant Governor at Holloway Prison until 1952, Governor of Askham Grange until 1959, and then Governor of Holloway Prison until 1966. As Governor of Holloway, head of the premier women's prison and occupant of one of the two most senior posts in the women's prison service (the other being the governorship of Styal), she exercised significant institutional authority, an authority enhanced still further when she was promoted to become Assistant Director (Women) until 1974. Those who worked with her observed that she had a commanding, almost daunting personal presence. It may be said that she was a 'remarkable woman',[23] one of those figures about whom stories and myths form in the criminal justice system. Like Margery Fry or Barbara Wootton, she stood out against a somewhat dull background as a strong and intelligent person with an organizing ability to get things done and a capacity to subdue those about her (Neale said of her that 'some of the staff stood in some awe and a little more than awe of Joanna Kelley'). One of her former colleagues, a Senior Medical Officer in Holloway, remarked, 'she was very, very clever. She would stand no nonsense from anybody. The place was quiet when she was there. She was a Mrs Thatcher. She got all the work done.'

Joanna Kelley was not an orthodox moral entrepreneur, fired by single-minded zeal for a cause. She had joined the prison service for practical reasons: 'I wanted a job, and it was offered and I thought to myself "well, take it and don't stay if you don't find it suitable". But you do get rather hooked because you do in fact make an enormous difference to the prisoners in what sounds like very small ways but which matter to them.' She professed to be mistrustful of high

---

[23] This phrase was written of her when she was Governor of Askham Grange by S. Stokes, *Come to Prison: A tour through British Prisons Today*, (London: Longmans, 1957), 203.

aspirations and utopian pretensions (at least in retrospect, looking back over her working life):

It's a thankless task because whatever you do is pretty well wrong. Some people are helped and some aren't. Some escape and some don't. Some come back and some don't. Your regime is to quite an extent influenced by the climate of public opinion. It is to some extent influenced by you. But, on the whole, you are always fighting public opinion in one way or another.

But she was to set herself a task. On promotion to Assistant Director, 'I thought this was a wonderful opportunity. . . I shall spend my time getting Holloway changed and so I did'.[24] She considered the building of Holloway prison to be ill-suited to the application of a scientific criminology and a therapeutic regime. Its design was irredeemably punitive and 'if you are very punitive in your regime you're much less likely to heal minds'. It was quite evident to others around her in the still infant division that Joanna Kelley had arrived with an object[25] and she was formidable enough to accomplish it. Ken Neale remarked, 'Joanna Kelley was the powerhouse of the whole thing and she was a very dominant figure'.

The World of P4

Let me now draw on the history of the Holloway redevelopment project to consider the environment of ideas about women, crime and punishment in which P4 and its staff around 1967 were set, the environment which framed much of their practical working knowledge (and not some other environment of research and thought which *might* have been considered had they been different people, differently placed and differently motivated). Schutz captured the formal character of such a milieu most effectively:

. . . the world seems . . . at any given moment as stratified in different layers of relevance, each of them requiring a different degree of knowledge. To illustrate these strata of relevance we may—borrowing the term from cartography—speak of 'isohypses' or 'hypsographical contour lines of relevance', trying to suggest by this metaphor that we could show the distribution of the interests of an individual at a given moment with respect both to their

---

[24] But she also added: '[but] I didn't do it single-handed. I wouldn't like that impression.'
[25] See J. Camp, *Holloway Prison: The Place and the People*, (Newton Abbot: David and Charles, 1974), 112.

intensity and to their scope by connecting elements of equal relevance to his acts. . . . Distinguishing. . . two kinds of knowledge, namely, '*knowledge of acquaintance*', and '*knowledge about*', we may say that, within the field covered by the contour lines of relevance, there are centers of explicit knowledge *of* what is aimed at; they are surrounded by a halo knowledge *about* what seems to be sufficient; next comes a region in which it will merely do to 'to put one's trust'; the adjoining foothills are the home of unwarranted hopes and assumption; between those areas, however, lie zones of complete ignorance.[26]

Like all life-worlds, the environment of the P4 official was neither simple, static nor uniform. It was an uneven, continually emerging synthesis of different movements and eddies of thought which possessed as many centres as there were individuals to populate it. From the standpoint of any one official, its core would have seemed to consist of a very particular personal history experienced vividly and intensely in face-to-face interaction. About that shifting core, there would have been a more diffuse web of shifting, contingent assumptions about what colleagues and others knew and thought about working problems, a web that would itself have been anchored in the still more general, anonymous and fixed recipe knowledge of the Home Office. And yet even further out, there would have been a horizon of taken-for-granted, universal typifications of institutions and processes based on 'what everyone knew' or was supposed to know.

The world of P4 was always in flux. Home Office staff are moved about with some frequency, and particularly those staff who are taken to be the 'high flyers' ascending to senior positions through a succession of different departments. Assistant Secretaries, especially, were deemed to be successful men and women and they were likely to be unusually mobile. They would work intently for a while on a phase of policy-making before surrendering it to a successor, experiencing the development of a policy in piecemeal fashion and never in its entirety, the past being known only through files and briefings, the present in a welter of intense activity, and the future little at all (officials rarely return to old issues after they have left a department).

Some officials, like Joanna Kelley, were acknowledged experts on

[26] A. Schutz, 'The Stranger', in M. Natanson (ed.), *Alfred Schutz: Collected Papers*, (The Hague, Martinus Nijhoff, 1964), Vol. 2, 93.

women offenders and on Holloway prison above all. David Faulkner, the Assistant Secretary in the early 1970s, called her his 'closest adviser and main *confidante*' in the planning of the new Holloway. She could speak and write with an authority that was based on a direct knowledge of administering prisons and prisoners and an indirect knowledge of research.[27] Ken Neale, too, had visited prisons in the colonies as part of his wider administrative duties. But other officials knew little enough about prisons and prisoners before they entered the prison service. For example, Sid Norris, had had some perfunctory, early dealings with consultations about plans for the new Holloway prison when he had served as Secretary of the Advisory Council on the Penal System at the very beginning of the 1970s. He was to renew his acquaintance with the prison when, in November 1974, some years later, he became Assistant Secretary in charge of P7, the division which by then had assumed control over the redevelopment of Holloway. He recalled: 'I never worked in the prison service until that point and I can't recollect the very early period. From the time I was on the Advisory Council and turning up there (which included a spell in private office) I can't remember anything registering about Holloway.' Officials are allowed little time to prepare themselves for new tasks. All such a one could do would be to brief himself quickly and then swing into action on the basis of what Schutz would call 'cook book' knowledge about prisons and prisoners and a more general working reserve of Home Office formulae for dealing with policy decisions 'in general'.

Any protracted policy would thus be experienced differently in its successive lengths and stages by different officials, and the history of the Holloway redevelopment project was itself to be continually disturbed, renewed and re-invented as diverse officials joined and left the working groups and committees that superintended its progress. Few Assistant Secretaries remained in charge of the redevelopment project team or P4 itself for more than four years. Each encountered distinct problems: one contributing to the planning of the new prison; another implementing planning decisions already taken; and another, Sid Norris in particular, confronting the difficulties that flowed from their implementation. Each would see those

---

[27] When, for instance, Joanna Kelley drafted an article on 'The new look at women in prison, redesigning Holloway Prison', for *The Times* in Dec. 1970, she drew both on her own recollections and on research published by the Home Office Research Unit and by Trevor Gibbens of the Maudsley Hospital.

problems with different eyes and sometimes they would wonder at what their predecessors had done.

Those who came late to P4 would have found that many issues about the treatment of women inmates, in general, and the fate of Holloway prison, in particular, had already been resolved, and, they would have had to assume, resolved for sound enough reasons. Even if the grounds of those earlier decisions were not fully disclosed, officials would have had to believe that their colleagues must have known what they were doing in a past now determinate and closed. After all, it is a necessary part of organizational life that people have a measure of faith in the honesty and good judgement of their colleagues.[28] It would be unreasonable and disruptive to doubt over-much. Consider the position of Terry Weiler. He had had nothing at all to do with the planning of the new Holloway before returning to the prison service in the early 1970s: 'my first tour of duty in the Prison Department was in the 60s which is when I got to know Joanna first and I was establishment officer then so I had nothing to do with anything as creative as new buildings. Then in 1971 I moved out on promotion and in 1971 I moved back again as an Under Secretary and P4 was one of the divisions that reported to me'. By 1971, however, the critical decisions about the shape of the new Holloway had been already taken. They were 'settled before I came . . . It goes back before my advent, but I think that was one of the things that was thrashed out. . . . [The prison] was there being built when I came.' Things already 'thrashed out' and 'settled' cannot be questioned lightly, even by a senior official. It was only when crises come emphatically to dramatize problems that the questioning began. (One may also, however, suppose that crises and dramatization themselves would be contingent features. The very determined do not readily succumb to questioning despite crisis.[29] They may even become more resolved in the face of adversity[30].)

It had to be a durable environment for the most part, steering officials in their everyday deliberations, the context rather than the

---

[28] Simmel said that 'Our modern life is based to a much larger extent than is usually realized upon the faith in the honesty of the other'. *The Sociology of Georg Simmel*, (Glencoe, Illinois: Free Press, 1950), 313. See also P. Manning, 'Police Lying', *Urban Life and Culture*, Oct. 1974, Vol. 3, No. 3, esp. 284; and J. Barnes, *A Pack of Lies: Towards a Sociology of Lying*, (Cambridge: Cambridge University Press, 1994), ch. 10.

[29] See B. Tuchman, *The March of Folly*, (London: Michael Joseph, 1984).

[30] See L. Festinger *et al.*, *When Prophecy Fails*, (New York: Harper Torchbooks, 1956).

focus of problems, treated as more or less objective, 'obvious', needing no justification, the set of ambient shared assumptions that were needed to allow people to get on with their duties. For some it became a matter of great certainty, but for others it was to be a more pragmatic matter. One who had worked with Joanna Kelley said of the case for the special therapeutic needs of women: 'this was Joanna's view. I'm not sure that I was strongly convinced one way or another on that argument and I was prepared to leave the professional judgements about how to treat women to those who had the experience and the responsibility. But what I was trying to do was to argue the case for decent services for women and the best possible share of resources.'

Pragmatics and improvisation are the stuff of policy-making. As I have observed elsewhere,[31] and as I shall observe again in the next chapter, officials must pursue their ends *artfully*. They cultivate their persuasive skills, carefully weaving webs of causality about themselves and their projects, looking for reasons, motives and obligations in the environment around them, translating materials within reach into reasons to be adduced in the pursuit of their goals. Nothing is ever quite what it seems in the official world. It is always amenable to symbolic reconstruction.

The evolution of an environment so constructed would have had its own incremental, self-reinforcing character. Once they appeared to have been settled, its key themes would have been repeated and cannibalized; cited as precedents, mandates and preconditions; employed to shape later decisions; all the while acquiring a history that became its own authority. The papers of the Holloway redevelopment project are replete with phrases used over and over again on the drafting principle that what was accepted once would probably be accepted again, that it was unnecessary to re-invent that which worked.

It follows that it is not worthwhile to be too literal in examining the functions, position, arguments and activities of P4, because they too were material for a measure of sympathetic interpretation and deployment in policy documents. 'Facts' about women and crime were allowed to become rhetorical artifacts, their significance depending as much on the policy-maker's craft as on any 'objective'

---

[31] See, especially, P. Rock, *A View from the Shadows*, (Oxford: Clarendon Press, 1986), ch. 2.

features they may be said to have possessed. Newcomers, possibly wise to the ways of the civil service, if not to the particular substantive problems of P4, might have had difficulty in disentangling what was compelling and what had merely been treated as compelling, what had 'really' prompted certain conclusions and what had been conveniently put for purposes of advocacy. And the insiders who framed those arguments might themselves have become similarly confused. In any event, memories would have been short because the officials who wrote the documents and made the decisions would have moved on after a while.

Those who had doubts in such a climate might well have thought it best to suspend their reservations and concentrate on the tasks at hand. Civil servants rarely issue major challenges to judgements already approved by people more senior than themselves. Nor could they casually reverse policies already in train. Their business is to concentrate on getting things done as efficiently as possible.[32]

I shall show in future chapters that an environment of ideas so constituted and so maintained was actually to prove surprisingly unstable and fickle, liable to sweeping revision, even capsizing, under the blows of apparently minor events that could throw policies and policy-makers severely off course. That net of assumptions about assumptions, beliefs about what everyone else believed, could be quite frail, and particularly so in an interpreted world where things were rarely what they seemed. (In the 1970s, the appearance of a few women terrorists and a modest increase in the female prison population could quite overturn everything that had been said and written.)

It may be said that the environment of P4 was prey to what, in other contexts, Matza called 'multiple shared misunderstandings'[33] and Dollard 'pluralistic ignorance'.[34] Pluralistic ignorance describes the experiences of people who tend privately to entertain one set of ideas but are obliged publicly by the appearance of things to imagine that everybody about them entertains quite another set. Pluralistic ignorance must have been commonplace in the prison service of the

[32] One of Andrew Rutherford's subjects, described as a senior Home Office official, reported of the 1960s that 'we still thought of ourselves as performing functions and carrying out procedures—we did not . . . see ourselves as personally responsible for achieving results'. Quoted in A. Rutherford, *Criminal Justice and the Pursuit of Decency*, (Oxford: Clarendon Press, 1993), 57.

[33] D. Matza, *Delinquency and Drift*, (New York: John Wiley, 1964).

[34] J. Dollard, *Caste and Class in a Southern Town*, (Yale University Press: New Haven, 1937).

late 1960s. It is inconceivable that the mobile and heterogeneous population of P4 and its environs shared a complete and continuing unanimity on all important issues that came before them. Dissenters could undoubtedly be heard saying later that *they* had never subscribed to the consensus about the Holloway redevelopment project (although such *arrières-pensées* are always common enough). Thus, one of the prison's administrative staff said that the claim that female prisoners were mentally disordered 'was an incredibly insulting approach to women offenders', but, she added, 'I certainly wasn't into challenging in those days because I was junior and quite honestly I thought these people must really know what they were talking about, and I guess there were others like me'. It may be supposed that any intellectual universe built on such foundations would be vulnerable, and so it proved to be in at least one critical episode of P4's history.

The Criminology of Women

Most Home Office officials are 'generalists' rather than 'specialists', what Canadian bureaucrats would call 'process persons' rather than applied criminologists and statisticians. They must be able to move smartly from one political problem to another, and their expertise resides chiefly in an ability to deploy the formal, abstract logic of the policy process in the management of different questions, not in their substantive, technical knowledge of any one area. For many a busy policy official, it was inevitable that much criminology and psychiatry should appear to be remote, specialized and perhaps even irrelevant. Academic research was not often couched in the language of the policy process, it did not usually address the political priorities of the moment, and officials would not pursue reports of what it might have to say in every particular. It was a resource available perhaps in principle but infrequently used in practice, known largely at second hand through conversation, the occasional briefing paper (although policy papers rarely allude to academic matters) and conferences.

In considering criminology and criminologists, officials would seek only the reassurance that they were not flouting established academic opinion. Such reassurances could actually be secured quite effectively through the medium of surrogates, through trusted, authoritative specialists known to officials, the sound men and women who could guarantee that what was being proposed was itself sound. The criminology of women could thus take on a personalized guise, and it was the Maudsley psychiatrists, Peter Scott[35] and Trevor Gibbens,[36] who were cited above all by officials involved in the Holloway project. Propinquity was important: those experts were to be found near officials working on pertinent problems at the pertinent time, and they were conspicuous in proportion (Gibbens was mounting a major 10-year follow-up study of 500 women who had come before the criminal courts in 1959[37]). Even so, the officials' references to them were often vague, offered, it would seem, as much for sacerdotal as for scientific reasons. Unexceptional was the remark of one who had been Assistant Secretary in charge of P4: 'Gibbens I certainly remember as a key figure at that time. Peter Scott was influential in that period'. And Terry Weiler observed that 'people like Trevor Gibbens had quite an influence. Peter Scott was another one. They were both psychiatrists who took a real interest in prison and had their feet on the ground, which is the other thing you're always worried about with outside people. They influenced individual administrators.'

The expert knowledge which those specialists mediated was not highly-developed in the late 1960s. There were only the dimmest glimmerings of the feminist criminology that came later to galvanize an interest in the deviance of women,[38] and the empirical work was thin.

To be sure, there was a small body of studies of women offenders and women inmates, each invariably prefaced with a complaint about how slight was the scholarly interest in women, how little work had been done, and how much more needed to be attempted. Typical was

[35] Peter Scott, 1914–1977, was consultant physician at the Maudsley Hospital; Consultant Forensic Psychiatrist, Home Office; member of the Home Office Committee on the Organization of the Prison Medical Service, and the Home Office Advisory Council on the Penal System; and sometime President of the British Society of Criminology.

[36] Trevor Gibbens, 1912–1983, was Professor of Forensic Psychiatry at the Maudsley Hospital; Consultant to the London Remand Home for Girls from 1951; a member of the Royal Commission on Penal Reform, 1964–66; and President, British Academy of Forensic Sciences, 1967–68.

[37] See T. Gibbens, 'Female Offenders', *British Journal of Hospital Medicine*, Sept. 1971, 282.

[38] Perhaps the first important stirring of that intellectual movement was F. Heidensohn: 'The Deviance of Women: A Critique and an Enquiry', *British Journal of Sociology*, 19 (1968), 160–175.

Ann Smith who wrote in 1962 that 'criminological research over the past hundred years has yielded comparatively little information regarding the criminality of women. . . . There is a pressing need for such information; and for further research and scientific enquiry into the whole problem of the criminality of women.'[39] Typical too was Tom Lodge, Head of the Home Office Research Unit, who made much the same charge six years later: 'most criminological research has been concerned mainly with crimes by men, and with male criminals. But crime among women is nevertheless an important problem, not to be studied only as a side-line.'[40]

Most plaintive and revealing of all was the lament which punctuated a brave new series of quarterly Home Office research bulletins on women offenders that appeared first in August 1967. Over and over again it was made plain that the editors of the series were surprised and perhaps even a little wounded by the weakness of the response to their invitation to readers 'to give their views both on the work described and also on problems in which research might be useful'.[41] The second number of the bulletin, published in November 1967, declared that 'all the replies we have received have been complimentary but as they were received from less than 5% of those to whom [the bulletin] was sent, we do not know how to interpret this—are these representative of the other 95%? Or are they the only readers in favour?'[42] In May 1968, yet another editorial deplored the lack of interest shown towards the bulletin: 'we have had few reactions from readers on whether they consider [the bulletin] worthwhile, or whether it is just another piece of paper to be put on one side at some time, a time which will always remain in the future. . . . Owing to the shortage of staff, we are proposing to make the next issue the last, unless there are some strong requests to the contrary.'[43] Despite reiterated threats to close the bulletin unless there was clear evidence of demand, it did survive into the 1970s. But it seemed

[39] A Smith: *Women in Prison: A Study in Penal Methods*, (London: Stevens and Sons, 1962), 3.
[40] Foreword to N. Goodman and J. Price: *Studies of Female Offenders*, iii..
[41] N. Goodman: *Research Bulletin: Women Offenders*, Aug. 1967, No. 1, 1.
[42] *Women Offenders Research Bulletin*, Nov. 1967, No 2, 1.
[43] *Women Offenders Research Bulletin*, May 1968, No 4, 1.

always to be a voice crying out in the wilderness, asking whether anyone read the bulletin, cared for it or wished it to thrive.[44]

It is usually easier to understand why some thing happened rather than why it did not. There were many other criminological areas that could and should have been studied in the 1960s but which failed to attract interest: with hindsight, victims and victimization, crimes against children, the criminology of place and space, the penology of shaming and the workings of informal social control were all deserving matters whose neglect cannot be defended. And one should not be too knowing as one looks back askance at the myopia of one's predecessors. But the absence of a robust and coherent research tradition centred on women offenders in the late 1960s is certainly intriguing.

There does appear to have been the important but tacit criminological assumption that a big intellectual problem must always turn around a big social problem, that there must be some equivalence between the numbers of criminals or the scale and seriousness of crime, on the one hand, and their criminological gravity, on the other. If there were only a few women criminals, and if the crimes they committed were minor, the argument seemed to run, the criminology of women must itself be insignificant in proportion. Gelsthorpe remarks that 'female offenders have always been thought of in different ways from male offenders, as less delinquent, less dangerous, and less involved in criminal subcultures and as a consequence they have less frequently provided a focus for criminological theory'.[45]

In Lemert's phrase, social pathologists, like Custer's men, rode to the sound of the guns. It was only when feminists turned matters on their head to define the *lack* of gun-fire as interesting that the criminology of women began to emerge as an intellectual force in the 1970s and 1980s. Feminists came to ask first why it was that so little work had been done and why women had been so neglected, and that was to be a question for the history and, sometimes more

---

[44] Typical was the article on 'the problem of the future of the bulletin', published in May 1972: 'we reported that, because of staff difficulties and the growing demand for the costing of work, the future of the "Bulletin" was in some doubt. We asked those to whom it is circulated to write to let us know their views on its continuation, but have to date received little response to this. Whilst its future is somewhat less uncertain at the last "going to press" we would still appreciate hearing from those who feel that the Bulletin is serving some useful purpose—and of course, equally from those who don't.'

[45] L. Gelsthorpe, *Sexism and the Female Offender*, (Aldershot: Gower, 1989), ix.

crudely, for the politics of ideas.[46] They then asked why it was that so *few* women committed crime, and that was to be a question largely for the sociology of gender and control.[47]

Before those critical questions of the 1970s had taken hold of the criminological imagination, the absence of gun-fire did little more than suppress interest. Tautologically perhaps, it may be said that the tradition of research and writing was too weak to sustain itself: too few engaging problems were detected in the examination of female crime, there was too little debate, too few big ideas, too little funding and no spirited academic community. In short, there was none of the self-propelling intellectual dialectic that can transform a substantive area into something fascinating to scholars, that encourages them to venture out to explore what may be found there, that leads to a continual definition and redefinition of a terrain, to questioning, criticism, discussion and controversy. The criminology of women in the 1960s was *boring*. It lacked analytic structure, focus, excitement and direction (and the criminology of men was in not much better condition). It seemed to some that it offered nothing solid to grasp or confront. In a piece of intellectual autobiography, Frances Heidensohn wrote that her research on women prisoners in the mid-1960s 'lacked an appropriate conceptual framework. . . . I found no usable criminological perspective. . . . I found a widespread indifference both amongst fellow academics and policy makers.'[48]

As cause and consequence, there was an absolute scarcity of women criminologists prepared to pursue academic research. Men have studied female crime, but those most curious about the area tend inevitably to be women, there being a heuristic and existential affinity between women criminologists and the criminology of women, and

[46] See, for example, C. Smart, *Women, Crime and Criminology*, (London: Routledge and Kegan Paul, 1977).

[47] See P. Carlen, *Women, Crime and Poverty*, (Milton Keynes: Open University Press, 1988); J. Hagan *et al.*, 'The Sexual Stratification of Social Control: A Gender-Based Perspective on Crime and Delinquency', *British Journal of Sociology*, Vol. XXX (1979), 30; and F. Heidensohn, *Women and Crime*, (London: Macmillan, 1985). To be sure, as David Downes has reminded me, Albert Cohen had also asked that question in *Delinquent Boys* (New York: Free Press, 1955). It was, Downes remarks, 'a cornerstone of his theory of delinquent gangs and of subcultural theory in general'.

[48] 'From Being to Knowing: Some Issues in the Study of Gender in Contemporary Society', unpublished paper, 1993, 14.

women criminologists (and, indeed, male criminologists) were not to be found in any large numbers in the universities of the 1960s.[49]

The prime producers of criminological knowledge about women (and men) tended instead to be *practitioners*. They were the growing body of clinical or research psychologists, psychiatrists, doctors and social workers who worked in and about Borstals, prisons and approved schools. It was they who had founded 'a distinctive, indigenous tradition of applied medico-legal science',[50] a science with a close intellectual affinity to the administrative rationality of the radial prison with its numerous classifications and separations, a science that came in time to be extended to women.

Medico-legal science was applied to women in the late 1920s by Grace Pailthorpe. Hers was an investigative and rehabilitative project informed by the question, 'what treatment—using this term in the most elastic sense—would lead to the restoration of these cases [of female crime and delinquency] to the ranks of normal people?'[51] Working under the auspices of the Medical Research Council and supported by M. Hamblin Smith, a psychiatrically-trained prison medical officer who first took the title of criminologist in Britain, Pailthorpe employed a battery of diagnostic and clinical tests to measure the psychology of women in prisons (including Holloway) and in Preventive and Rescue Homes. Her two-hour interview explored a subject's:

reactions to the present situation, her emotional mobility, her moods, the way in which she was disposing of the present situation in which she found herself, viz. by projection, negativism, evasion, &c., her mannerisms (e.g. the childish antics of *dementia praecox*), habit spasms, tremors, blushing, sweating; her affects—self-reproach, self-pity, self-complacency, &c.—and moods were all noted. Her history of depressions and states of excitement were all gone into minutely, with special regard to periodicity and relation to menstruation. The prisoner was seen for two hours at the first interview, and if an easy relationship had been established in the first hour . . . the second was spent in going through the mental tests[52]

---

[49] Supporting material on this theme may be found in my 'Social Organization of British Criminology', in M. Maguire *et al.* (eds.), *The Oxford Handbook of Criminology*, (Oxford: Clarendon Press, 1994).

[50] D. Garland, 'British Criminology before 1935', in P. Rock, (ed.) *A History of British Criminology*, (Oxford: Clarendon Press, 1988), 2.

[51] G. Pailthorpe, *Studies in the Psychology of Delinquency*, (London: HMSO, 1932), 8.   [52] *Ibid*, 12–13.

The work was part of a more general scheme to 'replace the ineffectual niceties of legal punishment by practical technologies involving diagnostic, prevention and curative instruments and institutions'.[53] In an argument that presaged plans for Holloway formulated forty years later, she recommended the replacement of unscientific and irrationally-administered prisons for women by a diagnostic 'central clearing station system' to which 'patients' should be sent in, 'be fully investigated, physically and psychologically, and treatment allocated'.[54]

The beginnings of the psychological investigation and treatment envisaged by Pailthorpe were to become an increasingly prominent feature of the penal system, part of a process that Barbara Wootton, in 1956, called the 'steady encroachment by medical science upon territory till lately occupied by moral judgement'.[55] The first prison psychologist was appointed in 1946 and the discipline was granted establishment as a whole in 1950.[56] By 1955, there were nineteen psychologists and twelve testers on the staff of prisons. They were, according to Professor Gordon Trasler, a psychologist who started his career in the prison service, 'regarded as diagnosticians, the users of tests (and occasionally of interview techniques) for the purposes of assessment'.[57]

Holloway prison itself did not succumb in the 1930s, and no central clearing station system was constructed, but Pailthorpe's ideas did nevertheless make the smaller, direct impact on the prison which I described in the previous chapter, with the appointment, in 1939, of a woman medical psychotherapist and then, in 1946, of a psychiatric social worker.[58] By 1954, the staff included a psychologist and a psychological tester,[59] all receptions being administered psychological tests on admission,[60] and what was done supplied a continual flow of data to be counted and tabulated. In 1972, for instance, it was

[53] D. Garland, *Punishment and Welfare: A history of penal strategies*, (Aldershot: Gower, 1985), 106.

[54] *Studies in the Psychology of Delinquency*, 97.

[55] B. Wootton, 'Sickness or Sin?', *The Twentieth Century'*, 1956, No 159, 433.

[56] *Report of the Commissioner of Prisons for the Year 1954*, Cmnd. 9547, (London: HMSO, 1955), 102.

[57] G. Trasler, 'The Role of Psychologists in the Penal System, in L. Blom-Cooper (ed.), *Progress in Penal Reform*, (Oxford: Clarendon Press, 1974), 129.

[58] See A. Smith, *Women in Prison*, 233.

[59] See the *Report of the Commissioners of Prisons for the Year 1954*, 101–2.

[60] See J. Kelley; *When the Gates Shut*, (London: Longmans, 1967), 107.

reported in a research paper how 'some of the data collected on an ongoing basis by the Psychology Department at HMP Holloway has been analysed. The data—from routine testing and interviewing— relate to 300 women prisoners.' The data included age on testing, scores on Raven's Matrices, scores on Eysenck's Personality Inventory (PI), scores on Lanyon's Psychological Screening Inventory and scores on Foulds, Caine and Hope's Hostility and Direction of Hostility Questionnaire (HDHQ).[61]

Without a 'recognisable conceptual framework' and 'usable criminological perspective', lacking a self-conscious academic community to sustain it, but nevertheless possessing copious statistics, the criminology of women in the 1960s tended to collapse into a small agglomeration of piecemeal empirical studies that fed on the numbers supplied by standard tests. Like the Gluecks, they cross-tabulated all possible factors with delinquency.[62] Of course, there were exceptions. In 1968, Jean Price floated the idea of applying the *anomie* theory of Cloward and Ohlin to young women.[63] But the early research on women was characteristically beset by what C. Wright Mills once called 'abstracted empiricism', the atheoretical, sometimes apparently aimless pursuit of data, and of quantitative data above all.[64] It was 'highly empirical, anti-theoretical . . . ,'[65] driven at times by a demiurge to measure, count and compare, analysing numbers, it would seem, simply because they were there.

The trickle of reports making up the criminology of women would often begin with 'a survey of facts' or of 'characteristics', the positivistic, thing-like traits of people that could be measured, and they would then proceed to record almost everything that could be recorded: the height and weight, acne, physical defects, intelligence, squints, psoriasis and other features of their criminal subjects.[66] Consider Moya Woodside's study of women drinkers admitted to

---

[61] R. Evans, 'Holloway Prisoners: Some Preliminary Results from Data Collected on Subjects 0001–0300', unpublished report, 1972, 3.

[62] See J. Laub and R. Sampson, 'The Sutherland–Glueck Debate: On the Sociology of Criminological Knowledge', *American Journal of Sociology*, May 1991, Vol. 96, 1410.

[63] See *Women Offenders Research Bulletin*, August 1968, No. 5, 2.

[64] See C. Wright Mills; *The Sociological Imagination,* (New York: Oxford University Press, 1959).

[65] S. Cohen, introduction to *Images of Deviance,* (Harmondsworth: Penguin, 1971), 15.

[66] See, for example, P. Epps, 'A Preliminary Survey of 300 Female Delinquents in Borstal Institutions', *The British Journal of Delinquency,* Jan. 1951, Vol. 1, No 3.

Holloway prison during February 1960. Woodside, a psychiatric social worker employed at Holloway, measured many things: the charges on which the women were committed and their previous convictions; their age and employment; their social class and marital status; their place of birth and present address; their intelligence level (ranked from 'very superior' and 'superior' to 'below average'); their preferred drink; and their state of health:

Five had been infested with lice or nits. Six suffered physical deformity or handicap such as squint, tubercular arthodesed knee, alopecia, loss of vision in one eye, congenital malformation of foot etc. Bad teeth or an edentulous condition were common, as also references to anaemia, 'stomach trouble,' past illnesses and operations.[67]

Consider, too, Trevor Gibbens's work on female offenders. It also furnished lists of statistics, reporting, for example, that 25% of a sample of prostitutes received in Holloway in 1967 had a variety of physical deformities and disorders, including ectopic pregnancies, pyelitics, dermatitis, repeated abortions and genital malformations; 25% had attempted suicide; and 25% were alcoholic.[68] He found that, of 500 women coming before 3 courts for shoplifting offences in 1959, 10% had had a major physical illness; 8% had a chronic ill health or permanent disability; 4% had a history of in-patient mental hospital treatment; and 9% a history of chronic nervous tension.[69] Such statistics were almost invariably proffered, one fact after another, as if they were self-evidently interesting and significant, requiring little analytic support, commentary or explanation, and forming part of no clear narrative scheme.

What portraits of criminal women did that little tradition engender? They were shaped by the routine assumptions and methods of the data collection process,[70] being, in effect, the predictable fruits of

[67] M. Woodside, 'Women Drinkers Admitted to Holloway Prison during February 1960', *The British Journal of Criminology,* Jan. 1961, Vol. 1, No. 3, 225.

[68] T. Gibbens, N. Goodman, S. Dell and J. Prince, 'A Medical Survey of Women received into Holloway Prison in 1967', unpublished, 1971.

[69] T. Gibbens and J. Prince, *Shoplifting,* (London: ISTD, 1962).

[70] It should be noted that very much the same criminology generated very much the same typifications of men as well. A prime example is D. West, *The Habitual Prisoner,* (London: Macmillan, 1963). On p. 100, for example, West wrote about how, 'contrary

standardized questionnaires and interviews.[71] They were diagnostic in character, expressed in a language that focussed on pathological symptoms and factors. They were, in short, fragmented lists of clinical components that were categorized, quantified and ranked.

The same dominant typification was presented in study after study. Persistent women offenders were revealed in one report to be below average in intelligence.[72] Wayward girls in approved schools were diagnosed in another as seriously disturbed psychologically (20% showing severe psychiatric symptoms and 32% abnormal personal development or oncoming mental illness).[73] 12% of a sample of female offenders aged between 17 to 20 were reported in a third study to suffer from some form of mental illness and 'a much larger proportion had personality disorders'.[74] A sample of 300 female delinquents in borstal were marked by diseases that included 'a history of psychosis [which] was found in 13 cases (4.3 per cent.; 9 in parents or grandparents, 4 in aunts or uncles). Mental deficiency occurred 6 times (2 per cent.; 1 aunt and 5 siblings). Low intelligence appeared in 7 other cases (2.3 per cent; 4 in parents, 3 in siblings). Epilepsy was found 6 times (2 per cent.; 5 siblings and 1 parent). Alcoholism was said to be present 28 times (9.3 per cent.; 27 parents

to the popular stereotype of a persistent criminal, few . . . prisoners were prone to violence and hardly any were efficiently organized, professional criminals. . . . . The incidence of psychiatric symptoms was much higher than anticipated. Ten per cent were or had been psychotic and a further sixteen per cent had been admitted to hospital or discharged from the forces on psychiatric grounds. Altogether, at least a third had a history of severe mental disorder.' That description could just as well have been applied to women, including the proportions of disorders unearthed by West's survey. It should also be noted that the same portraits emerged out of the application of the same methodologies outside Great Britain. See, for example, C. Robert Cloninger and S. Guze, 'Female Criminals: Their Personal, Familial and Social Backgrounds', *Archives of General Psychology*, Dec. 1970, Vol. 23, 554–8.

[71] One very typical questionnaire was used to 'determine intelligence, personality functioning, neurotic problems, stress situations and the presence or absence of mental illness' in women prisoners. Dr. P. Mason and Miss Adkins, 'The Short Sentence Wing—Holloway', undated report, 3.

[72] See A Morgan, 'Women in Preventive Detention', *Prison Service Journal*, Oct. 1964, Vol. IV, No. 13, 14.

[73] J. Cowie, *et al.*, *Delinquency in Girls*, (London: Heinemann, 1968).

[74] J. Davies and N. Goodman, *Girl Offenders Aged 17 to 20 Years*, (London: HMSO, 1972), 50.

and 1 sibling).'[75] A sample of 264 Holloway prisoners showed 'high extraversion, high neuroticism, and high psychoticism . . . [They were] psychiatrically ill to a marked degree.'[76]

The causes of much of that pathology was held to reside in family 'dysfunction', in quarrelsome homes and broken families[77] or, more rarely, in the mistreatment of women by men, in what Hilary Allen would later call 'the insufferable stresses to which women are characteristically exposed—economic dependence, social isolation, domestic violence, lack of satisfactory status or occupation'.[78]

What makes the studies phenomenologically interesting is that, although it was almost invariably shown that pathological symptoms characterized only a minority of women prisoners, it was nevertheless the symptoms of the minority that were allowed to saturate descriptions of the whole. By a kind of interpretive legerdemain, the 'abnormality' of a few attained much greater significance than the 'normality' of the many (perhaps because pathology was more centrally absorbing to the clinician),[79] and it was abnormality which writers proceeded to discuss[80] amidst what Carlen would much later call the 'mounting academic claims that women criminals are abnormal women'.[81]

At a remove, away from the diagnosticians' and testers' reports, those typifications of women offenders were translated by writers, policy officials, prison staff and others into the vocabulary of a lay

[75] P. Epps, 'A Preliminary Survey of 300 Female Delinquents in Borstal Institutions', 189.

[76] S. Eysenck and J. Eysenck, 'The Personality of Female Prisoners', British Journal of Psychiatry, 1973, No. 122, 696.

[77] Thus 60% of a major study of delinquent girls were found to come from broken homes. N. Goodman and J. Price, Studies of Female Offenders, 8. For a preliminary report, see 'Children appearing before the Greenwich Juvenile Court', Women Offenders Research Bulletin, Aug. 1968, No. 5, 2.

[78] H. Allen, 'Psychiatry and the feminine', in P. Miller and N. Rose (eds.), The Power of Psychiatry, (Cambridge: Polity, 1986), 91.

[79] Nigel Walker warned that 'we cannot . . . exclude the possibility that psychiatrists' diagnoses . . . are being influenced by the very presumption which we are trying to test, namely, that there is probably something abnormal about a woman delinquent'. N. Walker, Crime and Punishment in Britain, (Edinburgh: Edinburgh University Press, 1965), 302–3.

[80] Joanna Kelley wrote to tell me that 'many people, myself included, think that both men and women who are anti-social and break the law, especially of property and of violence to the person, are in some way abnormal and in need of some form of help, by treatment, education, re-education'.

[81] P. Carlen, 'Women's Imprisonment: Current Issues', Prison Service Journal, Apr. 1988, No. 70, 8.

criminology or 'coherence system'[82] that imported expert discourse into common-sense reasoning. The criminological coherence system of P4 talked primarily of inadequacy, defect, damage, disturbance and disorder. The woman criminal was understood to be impaired psychologically. She was unintelligent, immature and incompetent, unable to cope with the vicissitudes of everyday life and forced instead to turn to law-breaking.

So commonplace and established were that criminological coherence system and its vocabulary that it is difficult to find any writers of the time—radicals[83] or liberals, Home Office officials or politicians, insiders or outsiders—departing from them. Whatever reservations people may have entertained about them in private, they seemed to represent the sole conventional public discourse. Oona McCollom Gordon, an assistant governor at Holloway prison in the early 1970s, remembered 'there was a very firm conception and that was that all women that committed offences must have some sort of personality or psychiatric disorder'.

The coherence system's vocabulary was the language of outsiders, those who were neither professionals nor practitioners: in 1963, Xenia Field described women criminals as 'inadequate, unstable, handicapped, or just noticeably dull'.[84] It was the Prison Department's language, repeated over and over again in the stock phrases of official prose. In 1967, the Department alluded to 'the severe personality disorders and emotional disturbances [that] are more prevalent among the women and girls than among the men and boys committed in custody'.[85] It stated in 1970: '"personality defects", "damaged personality", "personal inadequacy", "anti-

---

[82] I have borrowed the term 'coherence system' from C. Linde, *Life Stories: The Creation of Coherence*, (New York: Oxford University Press, 1993), ch. 6. Linde states on p. 163 that 'a coherence system . . . is a system of beliefs that occupies a position midway between *common sense*—the beliefs and relations between beliefs that any person in the culture may be assumed to know. . . and *expert systems*, which are beliefs and relations between beliefs held, understood, and properly used by experts in a particular domain. A coherence system is a system of beliefs derived from some expert system, but used by someone with no corresponding expertise or credentials.'

[83] In about 1974, RAP, Radical Alternatives to Prison, in a pamphlet criticizing the Holloway redevelopment project, wrote of the inmates of Holloway: 'the overriding picture is a sad one. Very few need to be there at all: very few are in any sense dangerous. Often they are there because it is the easiest option available. Many come from very difficult personal and social situations which they are ill-equipped to face.' *Alternatives to Holloway*, (London: RAP, no date), 30.

[84] X. Field, *Under Lock and Key*, (London: Max Parrish, 1963), 22.

[85] *Report on the Work of the Prison Department 1967*, (London: HMSO, 1968), 19.

social outlook", "deeply disturbed"—these are useful terms in which to describe attitudes and to explain resultant behaviour'[86] (but, it continued, 'they do little in themselves to suggest methods of cure and social integration'). In 1972, it claimed that most women in prison 'are inadequate people who have made a mess of their lives'.[87] Next year, in 1973, it asserted that 'many women and girls in custody are social inadequates who have been unable to cope with normal situations in life'.[88] Joanna Kelley herself, the Assistant Director and former Governor of Holloway, wrote about the 'many women [who] come to prison because they are inadequate and inefficient',[89] 'the "damaged personalities"',[90] of the recidivists, the 'very unhappy disturbed Borstal inmates'[91] of Holloway, and the 'damaged personalities'[92] of the prisoners of C Wing.

The criminological coherence system centred on women became one more feature of an environment marked by a freedom from gross political interference, a cohesiveness of approach and a reforming temper. It was material to be deployed in arguments by officials urging change and, in the next chapter, I shall show how those arguments came to a head in the proposal that Holloway should be pulled down and replaced.

[86] Treatment of Women and Girls in Custody, (London: Home Office, 1970), 4.

[87] Draft of *Women in the Modern Prison Service*, unpublished, 1972, 1.

[88] Education in Establishment for Women and Girls, Policy Statement 5, (London: Home Office, 1973), 9.

[89] *When the Gates Shut*, (London:Longmans, 1967), 66.

[90] *Ibid*, 60.   [91] *Ibid*, 40.   [92] *Ibid*, 114.

3

The Grim Fortress: The Condemning of the Victorian Prison

'Worse still, [local residents] are to lose what the chairman of the Islington Society calls their fairy castle.'"[1]

Introduction

In this chapter, I shall try to reconstruct some critical parts of the decision to demolish the old Holloway prison, and it would be useful at the outset to give structural and political context to what was done. Recall that the prison was part of the estate managed by P4, and that P4 had its special features, being new, composite and mildly reformist. The division claimed to occupy an advantageous position, directing a few, uncrowded prisons which had an unusually favourable ratio of staff to prisoners,[2] and whose inmates themselves served short sentences and were not thought to be dangerous, professional or politically troublesome.[3]

Perhaps the cardinal feature of P4 was that it was administratively self-contained and unencumbered with the problems of the 'men's side'. P4 ran its own discrete domain with its own small, special population. It would assert its difference, so much so, on occasion, that it could look decidedly superior to others in the Prison

---

[1] K. FitzHerbert, 'New Holloway?', *New Society*, 25 Feb. 1971, 302.

[2] There was one female officer to every two female prisoners compared with a ratio of one male officer to every three male prisoners in 1972. J. Hall Williams, *Changing Prisons*, (London: Peter Owen, 1975), 182.

[3] It declared that 'there is less public anxiety and fear when women escape from custody, and indeed they escape more rarely from secure conditions' (*Treatment of Women and Girls in Custody*, (London: Home Office, 1970), 2). That was a view with which Joanna Kelley disagreed: 'women were always rather politically hot potatoes because they were always having ban the bombers or suffragettes or something, they made trouble, they didn't mind publicity'.

Department: one who had administered it said 'there was quite a lot of jealousy in the system, an appearance that that part of the system was privileged, and there wasn't a great deal of sympathy for women or borstal training anywhere. . . . There was that kind of skirmishing going on on the boundaries of the division at the time.'

One consequence was that what happened within P4s jurisdiction was liable to be circumscribed politically, open to definition as being relatively watertight and enclosed,[4] without immediate and obvious consequence for the penal system at large. When Holloway prison itself was being rebuilt, an Assistant Secretary of the time said, 'the great mass of the prison service saw it as a rather eccentric, harmless sort of little diversion that we were going into on the women's side and it didn't really have any implications for the rest of the prison service.' Political and administrative insulation was pronounced. In an official centennial history of the prison system of England and Wales, no mention was made of Holloway or women prisoners.[5] And, if they were discussed at all in the textbooks of penology and criminology, women offenders would typically be relegated to a late, omnibus chapter on 'special groups of offenders'.

Being circumscribed, the wider implications and possibilities of the Holloway project could remain open and undeveloped in the late 1960s and early 1970s. It is not entirely clear now, nor, it seems, did it ever appear very clear, how much of what was said and done about female prisoners was supposed to be *sui generis*, and how much applicable beyond the boundaries of the department to the larger world of men's prisons. It is not clear because the division of labour brought it about that it was not an issue that required unambiguous resolution: the business of P4 was to formulate policies for women, not for men, although, as Joanna Kelley remarked, 'the policy. . . . was that we tried out various experiments, which, if successful, could be used as pilot schemes for the men'.

That might have been all there was to say on the matter, but it seems that the larger world of the men's prisons could not be ignored

---

[4] Frances Heidensohn was to write in 1968, 'there is plenty of room to experiment; experiments . . . are particularly suitable for women offenders who are few in number and do not present significant "security" risks'. 'Prison for Women' typescript, 12. See, too, A. Smith, 'The Treatment of Women Offenders', *The British Journal of Criminology,* Oct. 1969, Vol. 9, No. 4, 396.

[5] See A. Edwards, *The Prison System in England and Wales, 1878–1978,* (London: HMSO, undated). To be sure, Ken Neale did refer to the 'women's side' in *Her Majesty's Commissioners: 1879–1978,* (London: Home Office, 1978).

altogether, particularly when it presented so many tempting comparisons to be invoked in the drafting of policy proposals. Like many another argument promoting women's interests, proposals could turn on allegations of difference or similarity, inequality or equality, whenever it appeared useful to do so.[6] Joanna Kelley said 'one was always fighting one's corner and saying the men were much better [off] (and of course they were in a way . . .)'.

So it was that various situated arguments, sometimes complementary, sometimes not, emerged in parallel about the issue of women offenders and their treatment. The case for difference could be made when it was declared that there was such an unbridgeable gulf between the condition of men and the condition of women prisoners that entirely separate penal responses were warranted. Lord Stonham,[7] the Minister of State, certainly made such a declaration when he said in 1969 that 'crime is almost exclusively a man's disease. Generally speaking, women do not commit crimes . . . Since [the] handful of [criminal] women are so exceptional they prompt the serious question, is prison the proper place for their effective treatment?'[8] And, he was to add, in the interests of the family, women should be kept out of prison whenever possible:[9] 'remedial treatment for women should be quite different from that for men'.[10] That was a public statement by a politician giving bold reasons for action.

But Home Office officials discreetly entertained a more practical interpretation of matters. Their argument was not ontological but political. David Faulkner, said that 'I don't think any of us working on the Holloway project wanted to claim that there is something genetically [different] about women . . . . The reason why Holloway was chosen for that sort of [innovative] approach was that the scale

---

[6] See E. Freedman, *Their Sisters Keepers: Women's Prison Reform in America, 1830–1930,* (Ann Arbor: The University of Michigan Press, 1981), 2.

[7] Lord Stonham, 1903–1971, was Labour Member of Parliament for Taunton, 1945-50 and for Shoreditch and Finsbury, 1954–58; Joint Parliamentary Under-Secretary of State, Home Office, 1964-67; and Minister of State, 1967–69. He was described by a very senior official in the Prison Department as a man with a 'very active conscience, a do-gooder, always ready to see the side of the oppressed—"we ought to do this, we ought to do that." In one conversation, it was "we ought to do something about Holloway. Poor women prisoners. Is it civilised to lock women up?"'

[8] 'The Future Treatment of Women Offenders', speech by Lord Stonham to Annual Day Conference, Alexandra Palace, 4 Apr. 1969.

[9] See C. Eade, 'Holloway and old ways will go', the *Guardian*, 17 Dec. 1968.

[10] Lord Stonham, quoted in 'Holloway Prison to be rebuilt', *Daily Mail*, 17 Dec. 1968.

and opportunity were there in a way that didn't apply on the men's side.' Faulkner saw no reason why what was done at Holloway for women should not eventually have been done elsewhere for men. He made the case for similarity: 'I think people would have been very glad if it had been treated as a precedent for men and that a similar approach had been followed for men'. It would however have been more difficult to liberalize the men's prisons, and, 'if it was the right thing to do, you shouldn't not do it for women on the grounds that you might not be able to do it for men as quickly or if at all. Whether that argument actually got into public I'm not sure, but I think that was certainly the way it was seen within that part of the prison service.'

On occasion, the parallel arguments could be rehearsed side by side, uncertainly and without firm commitment. In April 1971, for instance, P4 drafted a circumspect reply to a letter from a Member of Parliament:

The new concepts and approach to treatment of prisoners exemplified in the new Holloway, that of accepting a proportion of those who commit crimes do so not because they are basically bad but because they require treatment of some kind, is not confined to women, though, of course it is much more immediately apparent with them and the decision to provide proper facilities where the necessary treatment can be given in controlled conditions may well become much more widely based if, as we confidently expect, the results from the new Holloway show success in rehabilitation from the commission of offences.

Joanna Kelley herself seemed to occupy something of an intermediate intellectual position, reflecting her own interstitial role as former Governor and present administrator. I shall show in the next chapter that she could argue the claim of difference, the claim of similarity and the uncommitted claim in between.

It is evident that politicians and high officials were drawing different, structurally-embedded inferences about an ambiguous matter in the late 1960s, the politicians electing to use the high moral case and the officials the case of feasibility. And that was hardly surprising. The work of politicians turns on big moral questions designed to be ventilated in public, that of officials to administer practical questions determined in private.[11]

---

[11] There does seem to be a division of labour in such matters. See P. Rock, 'The Social Organization of a Home Office Initiative', *European Journal of Crime, Criminal Law and Criminal Justice*, 1994, Vol. 2, Issue 2.

There was never to be an effective clarification of whether the rebuilding of Holloway and the reform of the women's prison system were considered a special answer to the discrete problems of female offenders or the beginning of a wave of projects that would sweep right across the prison system. Instead, what was done was conceived as an experiment on the women's side that *might* eventually be generalized to men.[12] Ken Neale wrote that 'it was never in my time "vaguely . . . an experiment" but a positive response to the problem as we defined it; nor did I ever think it might be a forerunner of developments on the adult male side. It would, in my case, have been premature to speculate in that way, and tactically, in terms of P. D. politics, damaging.'[13] But Joanna Kelley remarked that 'certainly it applied to men as well but we concentrated entirely on women because we were meant to be testing things out, pioneering if you like. But I think the nearest is the one-off experiment that could be repeated if successful.' And David Faulkner concurred: 'I don't think the prison service ever adopted a policy endorsed by management that that was the way forward . . . all that was endorsed was that this was the right way for women at that time, and some of us were hoping that the men's side of the system would learn from and copy some of the features that were in the new Holloway'.

I shall show at length in Chapters 6, 7, 8 and 9 that the actual response in the mid-1970s to that one-off experiment was to dismiss it as a failure. Its features were not to be copied. And it failed, in part, because it was never put fully to work, the prison and the Prison Department having succumbed to a mixture of local difficulties, a larger loss of faith in the therapeutic ideal and a fiscal crisis that curtailed further building.

It would thus probably be right to claim that the bureaucratic politics of Holloway's reconstruction were more administrative and practical than ideological. The policy-making that undergirded them cannot subsequently be read as an unequivocal revelation of how senior members of the Prison Department defined problems of

---

[12] The Prison Department's expert, Trevor Gibbens, wrote that 'one can hardly doubt that if [the new system at Holloway] works, it will be tried for men; and Holloway might be handed over as a suitable centre for them. For this reason I do not think we should complain about its size. In the past experiments in treating women offenders have often led to their application to men, and this may happen in Holloway'. 'Prisons for Women', undated typescript, 5.   [13] Letter to myself, 24 Jan. 1995.

gender and deviance in the late 1960s and early 1970s.[14] It was too much hedged about, too tentative, open and pragmatic. And there were to be other prisons designed and built for men in that part of the twentieth century that mirrored preoccupations almost identical to those of the Holloway project team. I shall touch briefly on the example of Everthorpe below. What was said about the future inmates of Everthorpe could easily have been said about the women of the new Holloway, issues of gender being quite swamped by the larger enthusiasm for treatment. But my focus is on a women's prison, and it is the treatment of women that I shall discuss.

The Treatment of Women Offenders at the end of the 1960s

Let me proceed by reconstructing enough of the official penology of women at the end of the 1960s to make the Holloway project itself more intelligible. I may have touched on some of its themes before, but it is at this point that it needs to be inserted firmly in place. It should be emphasized again that any official penology is at once a set of assumptions about the nature of the 'objective' world of crime, criminals and punishment, and a set of motivated accounts that works on those assumptions to organize and present arguments for purposes of political and practical action. It is simultaneously a bald recital of things as they appear to the official mind, and a creative response designed to realise administrative objectives, and the two interact continually, checking and shaping each other.

The late 1960s marked the brief, heightened climax of an unusual period which Joanna Kelley described as 'a curious . . . gap in history,

---

[14] Such an interpretation is sometimes put forward, perhaps inevitably so, because the published papers lend themselves to it. Dobash and Dobash, for instance, remark that 'analysing some of the policy documents preceding the opening of these new institutions [Cornton Vale in Scotland and Holloway in England] helps reveal the legacy of past policies and beliefs and explain the modern form of women's prison's and contemporary thinking about the female prisoner. . . . Three linked sets of beliefs have contributed to the importance given to "therapy" in the planning of contemporary women's prison's: the view that women *per se* are more mentally unstable than men; the long-standing assumption that women offenders are by definition mentally disordered, or at least acting out of (stereotypically female) character; and the view, also strongly evident in the nineteenth century, that women prisoners are more "difficult" than men prisoners. R. Dobash, R. Dobash and S. Gutteridge, *The Imprisonment of Women*, (Oxford: Blackwell, 1986), 125, 129.

a certain time in the century when crime was getting less and less, prisons were closing or being discontinued because they didn't have enough prisoners, and there was almost 50 years . . . when rehabilitation was really the policy of the Department. I suppose it started in the '20s really.'

In the 1920s, it will be remembered, Grace Pailthorpe had urged the limited application of psychoanalysis and psychotherapy to women,[15] and psychotherapy did indeed come to Holloway in the 1930s and 1940s to be consolidated thereafter. In 1951 there was to be a modest experiment in which six women in corrective training were housed together and attended group meetings.[16] Five years later, Holloway was reported to be one of three prisons in England and Wales that had 'psychiatric treatment units'.[17] Rose Hacker, a counsellor who worked in Holloway in the late 1950s, remembered how:

I used to run group work with the staff and group work with the girls. [I was there with the staff] to discuss their attitudes, about how they related. This worked out so that we could discuss with the girls when the officers were screws and when they were friends. . . . They were catching on that they didn't have to be just punishing, that they were there to help people, give them rehabilitation and that was creeping in.

Therapy continued to grow in the prison service at large[18] despite early cavils and uncertainties expressed by the Prison Medical Service,[19] opposition from discipline officers who believed that it enabled prisoners to evade the rigours of discipline and punishment, and mistrust from the police, public and magistrates.[20] But it was in the

---

[15] G. Pailthorpe, *Studies in the Psychology of Delinquency,* (London: HMSO, 1932), 92, 96.

[16] See A. Smith, *Women in Prison: A Study of Penal Methods,* (London: Stevens and Sons, 1962), 233.

[17] *Report of the Commissioners of Prisons for the year 1956,* (London: HMSO, 1957), 122.

[18] Roger Hood has reminded me that group counselling was first introduced in Pollington Borstal late in 1957.

[19] See, for example, the comments of Directors of the Prison Medical Service in annual reports of the Commissioners of Prisons for 1950 (p. 81) and 1954 (p. 101) and Sir Norwood East, *Society and the Criminal,* (London: HMSO, 1949), 13.

[20] See J. Morrice, 'Psychiatry and the Penal System, *Prison Service Journal,* July 1962, Vol. 2, No. 5, 2–3.

1960s that it began to come into its own for a little while.[21] At the very beginning of the decade, Howard called therapy 'a dramatic development that has taken place in our prisons within the last year';[22] the Chairman of the Prison Commission, Arthur Peterson, listed the development of group counselling as one of his policy objectives for the future;[23] and plans were advanced to incorporate fifty women in a section of the new prison for psychological and psychiatric treatment at Grendon Underwood.[24]

In Holloway, the Senior Psychologist introduced group counselling in the Borstal recall wing in 1960[25] (Joy Kinsley, later Governor of the new Holloway, remembered that 'I was running the . . . wing in about 1960—as difficult a group as you could find anywhere, but it was a good attempt at a psycho-therapeutic community and in spite of the violence and self-destructiveness . . . the staff/inmates relationships were positive'). Experimental counselling was attempted on C Wing, the short sentence wing, in July 1963;[26] a group for drug addicts opened on B Wing a year later; counselling came to F Wing, the longer sentence wing; and the recidivists' wing became a psychotherapeutic unit. Therapy seemed abundant.[27] A psychiatric nurse who worked at Holloway at the time recollected:

---

[21] *Penal Practice in a Changing Society* (Cmnd. 645 (London: HMSO, 1959) referred to 'new techniques such as group therapy on the medical side and group discussion on the lay side [that] are being developed' (p. 24). Ten years later, the academic journals reflected the growth of penal experimentation. See S. Fisher, 'Therapeutic Community in a Correctional Setting', *British Journal of Criminology*, July 1968, Vol. 8, No. 3, and A. Miles, 'The Effects of a Therapeutic Community on the Interpersonal Relationships of a Group of Psychopaths', *British Journal of Criminology*, Jan. 1969, Vol. 9, No. 1.

[22] D. Howard, *The English Prisons: Their Past and their Future*, (London: Methuen and Co., 1960), 137.

[23] A. Peterson, 'The Next Decade, *Prison Service Journal*, Jan. 1962, Vol. 1, No. 4, 8.

[24] See 'Psychiatric Prison at Grendon, Buckinghamshire', *Official Architecture and Planning*, Nov. 1962, Vol. 25, No. 11, 712. In that same year, it was triumphantly announced that the idea of rehabilitation had become generally accepted in the prison service. See J. Morrice, 'Psychiatry and the Penal System, 2.

[25] *Report of the Commissioners of Prisons for the Year 1960*, (London: HMSO, 1961), 76.

[26] Dr Mason and Miss Adkins, 'The Short Sentence Wing—Holloway', undated report, 15.

[27] In 1964, a review of Xenia Field's *Under Lock and Key* in the *Prison Service Journal* remarked that the book contained a 'paragraph which needs repeating again and again and taken to heart from the Governor to the newly appointed Prison Officer. It is this—"All women (and I would add men) need some help. The problem is to sort out the available treatment and to send the right prisoner to the right source of treatment".' *Prison Service Journal*, Vol. III, Apr. 1964, No. 11, 41–2.

Psychotherapy, drug therapy, behaviour therapy, group therapy. There was an observation unit which was for the very seriously mentally ill and patients were treated as if they were mentally ill within the prison. They were treated then in prison. It wasn't just in the hospital area that therapies went on. There was the mother and babies unit, there were the young offenders, the borstal wing. There was a lot of group work. There was a drug unit and their treatment was very much centred on group therapy.[28]

Prison Policy: Women and Girls

All those transformations of penology fed into policy-making. In October 1968, P4 division issued a formal statement of prison policy for female offenders, the first of a series of 'little leaflets' that were produced by a new division trying to establish its views on various issues. Ken Neale recalled that 'we were talking about what we were doing but there was no document. We collected our own thoughts and put them down so that we could point to them and say "that's what we are doing".' It was making policy 'in the normal course of administrative business', not 'occasioned by operational or policy purposes'. For the first time in a very long while, a division was thinking hard about the problems of women offenders,[29] and it was doing so because it was working within its administrative mandate.

Prison Policy: Women and Girls[30] was drafted under the hands of Ken Neale, the head of P4, and Joanna Kelley, the Director of

[28] A former inmate said: 'the attempts were the drug unit, which was run on group therapeutic lines; F Wing which had some group therapy constantly; and D Wing, which is where I was. We were told we were having group therapy. We were told that it would all be in confidence and we were told we could speak about anything that was troubling us and that officers, who would be present, and an assistant governor, their presence would be conditional on not saying anything outside the room. The officers were terrible gossips. They told everybody about their personal lives, their own and yours. Nobody believed it. Nobody trusted. We used to just sort of sit there and go through the motions. We also had in a psychiatrist from Harley Street . . . . who had weekly therapy groups and, again, that was much more formal. Of course, some women went for the cigarettes. Some women went to unburden. One or two women were severely damaged by that, and a woman, 30 years down the road that I know now, is still on one-to-one counselling. Therapy, therapy, therapy and she is still fixed in the patient role. Never getting out, never, never, never, and still trying to sus out what went on in her childhood.'

[29] In 1968, for instance, an internal document declared about the educational provision for women prisoners that 'the subject is one which in the past never seems to have been studied in any scale or depth'.

[30] *Prison Policy: Women and Girls* , P.D. 4 Study No 1, Prison Department, Home Office, Oct. 1968.

Women's Prisons. It was to be endorsed by the Prisons Board and agreed to by the Home Secretary. It carried weight. With other papers, it framed the 'broad outlines of policy in respect of women and girls'[31] at the very beginning of P4's history. Its themes were to be cannibalized and repeated over and over again in press releases, reports and speeches to come. With its companion policy documents and later glosses, it represents a clear statement of official thinking in the late 1960s.

The burden of that statement was that women prisoners were special. They were special because they could not be regarded as serious offenders (a 'nuisance rather than a menace' is how they were described in an earlier report).[32] 64%[33] of the female prison population in 1965 had committed offences against property; 10% had been convicted of violence and assaults; 6% had committed offences related to prostitution; 3% drunkenness; 2% cruelty to children and 2% murder. Their sentences were short: in 1965 again, some 47% of prisoners had been sentenced for 6 months or less; a further 11% for between 6 months and 12 months; 23% between 1 and 2 years; 8% between 2 and 3 years; 9% between 3 and 10 years; and 2% for 10 years or more. Women prisoners were, in effect, on the margins of criminality, not dangerous, violent or a risk to prison safety. 'Except for a small minority of women prisoners', it was argued, 'the element of security is not so important.'[34]

I have observed that one of the few outsiders to wield professional authority in P4 in the 1960s was Professor Trevor Gibbens, and he gave emphatic support to that stance in his argument that 'clearly great differences in penal treatment are required because (1) [women] commit offences more rarely; (2) are rarely dangerous; (3) respond to punishment or are more easily deterred than men; (4) imprisonment especially is more often counter productive in causing greater damage to the personal relationship with husbands and children on which social adjustment depends more closely in women than in men.'[35]

[31] *Prison Policy: Women and Girls*, 1.

[32] *Report of the Departmental Committee on Persistent Offenders*, Cmd. 4090, (London: HMSO, 1932), 38.

[33] The figures quoted are those used in *Prison Policy: Women and Girls* itself, and they were the most recent then obtainable, being derived from N. Goodman and J. Price, *Studies of Female Offenders*, (London: HMSO, 1967).

[34] *People in Prison (England and Wales)*, Cmnd. 4214, (London: HMSO, 1969), 61–2.

[35] T. Gibbens, 'Prisons for Women', unpublished, undated, ca 1972, 1.

In short, it could be held here (but not in every argument else-where) that women justified an extraordinary response: an official said 'they were a special case in the way that men prisoners were not special cases . . . one point that was very much in people's minds was that female crime and female incidents were relatively rare and were very much the exception'. It was not easy to propound rigorously punitive regimes for a population that seemed to consist in significant measure of young women, naive first offenders, and mothers and children. There were facets of women's prisons that were affecting in a way that the men's prisons were not. Terry Weiler, one-time Controller of Administration, remembered that 'the mother and baby unit, however crude it was, was a more pleasant part of the [system] to go into', and Joanna Kelley herself remembered that 'our problems were quite often different: problems of mothers and babies, problems of family visits impinged more on us, and we didn't have the problems of escapes and very violent prisoners'.

Women prisoners were special because they were so few (Lord Stonham was to call them the 'pitiful few'),[36] numbering only about 1,000 at the end of the 1960s. Their total population had not changed much since 1938[37], and it was expected that they would decline even further. Many were actually 'weak, stupid or lonely',[38] 'muddled, bedeviled women',[39] who should not be kept in prison at all. Women took badly to confinement and restriction[40] in regimes intended primarily for men.[41] They became angry, prone to self-mutilation and violence towards officers (and it was for those reasons, in part, that their prisons were so heavily staffed). With the introduction of suspended sentences under the 1967 Criminal Justice Act and an increasing resort to non-custodial and semi-custodial penalties, it was supposed that most of those minor offenders would eventually be diverted away from the penal system to be treated in the 'community', in 'semi-secure conditions' or at home.[42] Indeed, it was expected that imprisonment for girls under 21 would have ceased

---

[36] See the *Guardian*, 17 Dec. 1968.   [37] See *People in Prison*, 60.

[38] S. Vincent, 'Inside Holloway Prison', *WM*, 12 Nov. 1966, 25.

[39] X. Field, *Under Lock and Key*, (London: Max Parrish, 1963), 21.

[40] This was an engrained, established belief. See L. Zedner, *Women, Crime, and Custody in Victorian England*, (Oxford: Clarendon Press, 1991), 98.

[41] See J. Kozuba-Kozubska and D. Turrell, 'Problems of Dealing with Girls', *Prison Service Journal*, Jan. 1978, No 29, 5.

[42] See H. Jones, *Crime and the Penal System*, (London: University Tutorial Press, 1962, ch. XII.

altogether except 'under very special circumstances' by the year 2000.[43] Louis Blom-Cooper remembered how, when he served on the Advisory Council on the Penal System in the late 1960s, 'we were interested in looking at alternatives to imprisonment for women particularly and, as part of that process, looking at community service orders and deferred sentences and all the other things we covered . . . . I think our whole attitude was "how many of these women do we actually need to put into custodial institutions at all?"'[44]

One last prison at Holloway would certainly have to be retained for the 'difficult hard core'[45] of criminals who were unrepresentative even of women offenders, the deviants within a deviant population, the seriously bad[46] and abnormal cases who could be discovered at the outer limits of the clinicians' measures. David Faulkner said 'the expectation was that Holloway would eventually become the only women's prison in the country and that the women's population would settle down to about 600 or 800. But this is all that it would ever be and I think we were rather optimistic about that.'[47]

However, in the wake of the new penology, the great majority of women prisoners were undergoing progressive redefinition and, it was thought, they were possibly even moving towards eventual decriminalization. Seen through the twin filters of clinical diagnosis and penal reform, they were normal, inoffensive deviants who were not so much criminals, perhaps, as ill, disturbed, lonely, defective or

[43] Group on the Re-development of Holloway: Projected Population of the Year 2000, Note by Secretary, 30 Oct. 1968.

[44] A sub-committee of the Advisory Council on the Penal System was then sitting on non-custodial and semi-custodial penalties. Established in November 1966, it reported in 1970 (Report, London: HMSO, 1970). In the event, the report was to be somewhat pessimistic about the prospects for further reductions in a very small female prison population: 'the scope for reduction of the prison population is . . . much more limited for females than for males, and the difficulties of organizing suitable non-custodial penalties are correspondingly greater, because there are so few offenders in any particular area. We have not found it necessary to recommend any new form of non-custodial penalty designed exclusively for female offenders' (at p. 4). The Advisory Council on the Penal System itself had been established in 1966 with representation from both Houses of Parliament, the social sciences and the police, and its terms of reference were 'To make recommendations about such matters relating to the prevention of crime and the treatment of offenders as the Home Secretary may from time to time refer to it, or as the Council itself, after consultation with the Home Secretary, may decide to consider'.   [45] Prison Policy: Women and Girls, 3.

[46] Those whom P4 described as 'the relatively few women who are imprisoned for notorious crimes'. Prison Policy: Women and Girls, 8.

[47] In effect, it was planned that Holloway, the women's prison, and Grendon, by then exclusively a men's prison, would be twin therapeutic institutions.

troubled people in need of care.[48] Joanna Kelley called them 'all, in one way or another and to a greater or lesser degree, mentally disturbed and deviant from the norm. . . . Their delinquency is a manifestation of malady and therefore requires a remedial rather than punitive treatment.'[49] Minor offenders against property, young offenders,[50] mothers and mentally disturbed persons, drug addicts, prostitutes and drunks, they might be sent to prison for punishment but it was not punishment that they needed.[51] A journalist reflected about the inmates of Holloway of that period that '"punishing" such sick and inadequate women is about as helpful as hanging bells around lepers' necks'.[52] In the medium term, it was asserted, the penal system was moving away from punishment and towards 'the development of non-custodial treatment'.[53] In the short term, however, and for the 'hard core', there would have to be rehabilitation in conditions of custody, rehabilitation itself being defined as the exercise of 'personal influence, hard work preferably of a constructive nature, medical, psychiatric, religious and educational assistance, vocational training, and welfare work.'[54]

If criminal women did indeed need treatment instead of punishment, if therapy was thus sovereign, it seemed that the old antinomies of control were beginning to converge and lose their distinctiveness. Prisons were becoming like mental hospitals and mental hospitals like prisons:[55] Trevor Gibbens observed that 'the heavy load of physical

---

[48] *People in Prison*, 61.

[49] J. Kelley, 'The new look at women in prison. Redesigning Holloway', unpublished, Nov. 1970.

[50] See Goodman and Price, *Studies of Female Offenders*, 14, 23.

[51] The Scottish Prison Service concluded that 'studies of women offenders . . . have shown that by far the greater majority of those who [are imprisoned] are very disturbed personalities or people with severe social problems, so that during their period of deprivation of liberty real efforts at therapy, training and rehabilitation have to be made'. HM *Institution Cornton Vale*, Scottish Prison Service, no date, no provenance, 1.

[52] A. Leslie, 'Fortress of Despair', *Sunday Mirror*, 7 Nov. 1971.

[53] *Prison Policy: Women and Girls*, 8.

[54] *Prison Policy: Women and Girls*, 7. See also *Treatment of Women and Girls in Custody*, (London: HMSO, 1970), 50.

[55] Whilst she was still working at Brixton Prison, a woman who came eventually to work as senior psychologist in Holloway in the late 1960s told a group of Sixth Formers in November 1966, 'there are an awful lot of mental hospitals that are beginning to become like mental hospitals, and really, from a psychologist's point of view, it isn't strictly very important whether the men we deal with are in prison or in hospital'. C. Blackler, 'Talk to Sixth Formers at Basildon' (unpublished lecture), 10 Nov. 1966.

and mental illness and abnormality makes a women's prison into something approaching a secure hospital'.[56] Joanna Kelley herself would certainly have had Holloway become more hospital, less gaol.

Condemning Holloway Prison

Joanna Kelley's complaint about Holloway Prison, voiced in 1967 'that "the buildings have long outlasted the ideas that, prompted their design; today they seem dismal places to both staff and inmates"'[57] had its antecedents. Officials and others had long considered the large, castellated radial prison to be inappropriate for the few, relatively innocuous women who occupied it. Holloway had never been designed for women alone and it was described as overly secure and severe for their containment. As early as 1932, the Departmental Committee on Persistent Offenders asserted that 'in the case of the great majority of women, prison buildings of the fortress type are unnecessary for purposes of security and the effect of such buildings seems to be in many respects worse than on men'.[58] There were plans to take women from conditions of high security in the city to low security in the country where they could become whole again. It was preferable, said Sir Alexander Paterson, having visited female reformatories in America, for women to 'live and work in small units and know neither walls nor wire as an enclosure. The women in charge of these reformatories have the light of heaven in their eyes and their feet firmly grounded in common sense.'[59] In 1938, Lilian Barker, the former Governor of Aylesbury and the first woman Assistant Commissioner and Inspector of Prisons, proposed rebuilding Holloway as a 'prison in a park' on open land near Heathrow, but like many other penal projects, the plan had to be abandoned because of the war.[60] In 1950, it was reported that financial austerity had again led to the postponement of plans to replace Holloway with an institution whose walls would have been only 4 feet high.[61]

---

[56] 'Female Offenders', British Journal of Hospital Medicine, Sept. 1971, 286.

[57] J. Kelley, 'The new look at women in prison', 9.

[58] Report of the Departmental Committee on Persistent Offenders, Cmd. 4090, (London: HMSO, 1932), 39.

[59] S. Ruck (ed.), Paterson on Prisons: Being the collected papers of Sir Alexander Paterson, (London: Frederick Muller, 1951), 71.

[60] Penal Practice in a Changing Society, 21.

[61] B. Townroe, 'English Prisons', The Builder, 28 Apr. 1950, 558.

In April 1962, again, there was to be an informal meeting between staff of the Ministry of Public Buildings and Works and a Planning Officer at the London County Council about the building of a remand centre for both sexes, a hospital and staff housing on the Holloway site. The Planning Officer raised the prospect of Islington Council, the local authority in whose area Holloway was set, resisting any plans to re-build on the grounds that they amounted to a change of use. The discussion was reported to have been inconclusive and nothing more was done. Three years on, in 1965, further new plans were announced to build an alternative prison for women at Theydon Mount in Essex,[62] but again nothing was done.

Proposals to reform Holloway did not die. They were revived once more when, in 1966, representations were made by the Holloway Visiting Committee to the Royal Commission on the Penal System. The committee urged that 'the concept of a female community is basically different from any man's prison and that special and enlightened concessions to women's needs would be well justified'. A high proportion of women prisoners required medical treatment and 'intensive rehabilitation in the form of medicine, psychiatry, religion, education, hard work, individual work, group work and welfare'. They should be lodged in a new secure prison constructed on the existing site of Holloway, composed of separate houses and one very secure block, and supporting a co-operative community organized into 'small groups, flexible in number to allow for experimentation, [that] would learn to live together' freely within a secure perimeter.[63]

Later in that same year, in October 1966, the Home Secretary sought a briefing on the future of Holloway and was reminded that the prison was the only Victorian building still used for women prisoners; that conditions in the prison were inimical to the 'successful development of modern methods of prison treatment and training; and they have in recent years attracted much public criticism'. He was advised that the old prison could not be modernized, that piecemeal redevelopment would be both expensive and irksome, but that redevelopment on site would pose grave problems of relocating staff and inmates. Some part of the prison population might be removed to

[62] See *The Adult Offender,* Cmnd. 2852, (London: HMSO, 1965), para. 30.
[63] 'Memorandum on Women's Prisons to the Chairman and Members of the Royal Commission on Penal Reform', Feb. 1966.

a new closed prison that could be built at Hill Hall in Essex, but it would be inconvenient to transfer women away from relatives, probation officers and the courts, and staff might object to living in a rural area. It was concluded that sentenced women should be sent to a new prison in Essex and that remand accommodation and a group hospital for women and girls should be built on the Holloway site. The rest of the Holloway site could be developed separately for remand, trial and allocation accommodation for men to supplement inadequate buildings in use at Brixton Prison. Once again, nothing was done. Radical Alternatives to Prison concluded afterwards that 'few prisons can have been as universally condemned as inadequate, inappropriate and impossible to run as the old Holloway Prison.'[64] But it required more than condemnation to despatch the old Holloway.

Joanna Kelley had arrived at P4 with a single-minded dedication to act. In 1967, she recalled, 'I remember one of my colleagues saying to me "you can accomplish one thing while you're in this office, but probably not more than one. It will take all your time." And I said it must be to pull down and rebuild Holloway in London.' In the last chapter, I noted how Neale sought to initiate precisely that form of action in order to give focus and drive to his new division. He had anyway come to feel strongly about Holloway: 'I suppose there was a little bit of chauvinism about it, that it was so utterly unacceptable to put women and young girls in these conditions, that it had to go'. Those ideas and that determination were to be injected into *Prison Policy: Women and Girls*.

Joanna Kelley's phrase 'rebuild Holloway in London' is significant. She was convinced that any new establishment must not be built as a 'prison in a park' at Heathrow or Aylesbury or at Theydon Mount near Epping. The one central women's remand prison in the south of England should not be a rural retreat:

The Prison Commission's view at that time . . . was that a prison in the country would be better . . . Epping was one of the places—and that would make a much more formative programme possible, and that it was quite unnecessary to have a closed prison in London. And I, who had been assistant governor at Holloway and then Governor for a period of 12 years . . . I was absolutely certain that you must keep the prison in London, and I really argued that all through, and I think I eventually convinced people. . . . It's interesting to show how times have changed, the idea of reform was that

[64] *Alternatives to Holloway*, Radical Alternatives to Prison, London, no date, 13.

country living is good for people and healthy and in itself the pattern and rhythm of life is good. Which I dare say it is, but of course to transport people for a very short time to those conditions was not particularly helpful. It made it almost impossible for their families to visit them, so it cut out a great many family visits . . . And then, which I think may have been an overriding argument really, that if you were the main remand prison for women, doctors, probation officers, solicitors, having to travel out from London to Epping or Aylesbury, taking an hour each way, madness.

Persuading P4 that the prison should stay in London was Joanna Kelleys opening victory: *Prison Policy: Women and Girls* argued for rebuilding on site rather than at Theydon Mount because North London offered local staff, local medical facilities and easy access for specialist staff, prisoners' visitors, courts and legal advisers.

It was next important to ensure that the new prison would be treated as a special kind of therapeutic institution. *Prison Policy: Women and Girls* offered as its first priority 'the re-development of Holloway beginning with the construction of a central hospital and psychiatric unit'. The new prison was to be a 'larger, comprehensive, versatile and secure hospital'. That phrase was also significant: P4 proposed to turn the old prison on its head. The punitive old fortress with its hospital would become a medical establishment with a carceral appendage.[65] Joanna Kelley wrote to Ken Neale, 'I think we should work on the principle that Holloway is to be a large hospital, treatment oriented, with a small prison, and not as at present, vice versa'.[66] The prison should be redeveloped on site as a collection of sixteen small units, each housing about forty prisoners, each as far as possible a separate entity, and for the most part concentrated in a hospital block and hospital administration.[67]

---

[65] Dorothy Speed, a psychiatrist and medical officer at Holloway in the 1960s, reflected that 'Joanna convinced Ken Neale that women were different in their expression because the mental hospitals were full of women and the prisons full of men'. Joanna Kelley was later to have reservations about the term hospital. She wrote to me in 1995 to say that 'I regret our use of the word "hospital" with its medical and psychiatric connotations. We really had in mind a place of healing, not only of the body but also of the mind and attitudes and education and practice in relationships.'

[66] Letter of 14 Mar. 1968.

[67] Joanna Kelley envisaged that the Hospital Block would include outpatients (X-ray, physiotherapy, dentists etc) and that the Hospital Administration would consist of doctors' rooms, consultants' rooms, a refractory ward, and psychotherapy units for drug addicts, alcoholics, prostitutes, 'those in need of group therapy', the 'mentally disturbed but not refractory etc.' Letter to Director of Prison Medical Services, 16 Apr. 1968.

The new Holloway itself was to take a premier position. It would not only be the hub of the southern complex of prisons in the women's system, but of the national women's system, providing closed prison facilities, including the security wing for the whole country, a psychiatric unit, the hospital for the whole country, a remand centre and the allocation centre for the southern complex.

It was not remarkable that plans for a new Holloway were being drafted in the late 1960s. It was but one potential initiative amongst many. The entire prison system was under review at the time, and building and reconstruction were rife.

The New Prisons

After the tide of radial prisons in the nineteenth century, prison construction effectively ceased. It was as if so much had been done in preparing a unified system of strong buildings that the Prison Commission could continue to work throughout most of the first half of the twentieth century with the materials which Joshua Jebb had supplied. Besides, there was to be a decline in the prison population and a lapse of faith in penitentiaries, prison building had ceased to be a great and admired work of social engineering, and it was always possible to claim funding difficulties. Only one new prison, Camp Hill, in the Isle of Wight, was to be built in the first half of the twentieth century, in 1910,[68] as an establishment for Preventive Detainees sentenced under the 1908 Prevention of Crime Act. The Prison Commissioners became likened to slum landlords administering a dilapidated Victorian estate.

A new economics and a new penology came to change some of that architectural torpor. In the relatively prosperous 1950s and 1960s, at a time of high Government expenditure and confidence in social intervention, the Government started to build prisons again. There was, said Wright, an 'assumption of growth, the expectation that public sector services [would] continue year by year to receive additional increments of resources'.[69] State expenditure rose steadily and continuously for 25 years from 1950 until, by the end in 1975, public spending absorbed some 46 per cent of GDP. The costs of public

[68] See B. Townroe, 'English Prisons', *The Builder*, 28 Apr. 1950, 558.

[69] M. Wright, introduction to *Public Spending Decisions: Growth and Restraint in the 1970s*, (London: Allen and Unwin, 1980), 3.

policy grew by 201% during that quarter-century, faster than ever before.[70] And prisons were planned and built as they had not been for a hundred years. In 1961, John Madge remarked on the 'massive building programme'.[71] There was apparent need of such a programme: after a slump in the prison population before the Second World War, numbers had unexpectedly begun to grow again. Arthur Peterson asked in 1962, 'who would have thought ten years ago that a prison population of 20,000 would grow to nearly 30,000?'[72] Between 1945 and 1970, the volume of prisoners actually increased from 15,000 to 39,000, an average growth rate of 5% per annum.

The new penology was not at home in the old prisons. The 1959 White Paper, *Penal Practice in a Changing Society,* had argued that 'to have to work in prisons which are virtually unchanged since they were built in the nineteenth century or earlier, when the whole emphasis was on security and deterrence, does not invite from either the staff or the prisoners the response to modern methods of constructive training which is necessary if they are to succeed'.[73]

It was inevitable that many of the new prisons of the 1950s and 1960s had to be experiments, their designs solitary prototypes, because prison architecture and planning had stagnated[74] and there were few people experienced in the work.[75] In effect, the post-war building programme was supervised by self-taught architects devising a new generation of institutions to replace what were now thought to be outmoded radial prisons.[76]

By 1954, the Prison Commissioners could report that 5 new prisons were being built and the purchase of 6 properties was being negotiated.[77] By 1956, they reported that 26 new establishments had been opened, mainly by acquiring and adapting institutional buildings,

[70] See K. Judge, 'The Growth and Decline of Social Expenditure', in A. Walker (ed.), *Public Expenditure and Social Policy,* (London: Heinemann, 1982), 29.

[71] J. Madge, 'Trends in Prison Design', *British Journal of Criminology,* Apr. 1961, Vol. 1., No. 1, 371.   [72] Peterson, 'The Next Decade', 3.

[73] *Penal Practice in a Changing Society,* Cmnd. 645, (London: HMSO, 1959), 21.

[74] See A. Blamire, 'The evolution of prison design: a brief history', *MAC TWO,* Feb./Mar. 1975, 16.

[75] See L. Fairweather, 'The evolution of the prison', in United Nations Social Defence Research Institute, *Prison Architecture,* (London: Architectural Press, 1975), 35.

[76] See 'Prison and Borstal Building Programme for HM Prison Commissioners', *The Builder,* 13 July 1956.

[77] *Report of the Commissioners of Prisons for the Year 1954,* (London: HMSO, 1955), 109.

country houses, war-time camps and coastal citadels.[78] There was to be a particularly protracted search for a site for the new East Hubert psychiatric prison that opened eventually at Grendon Underwood in 1962. In 1958, the very first of the new twentieth century purpose-built prisons, the 'permanent security training prison'[79] at Everthorpe, was completed. In language that could have been directed without change at the new Holloway (demonstrating the equivocation and ambiguity of policy discourses which I have discussed), Everthorpe, a prison for *men*,[80] was described as an institution devoted to rehabilitation rather than to punishment, incapacitation and deterrence:

in the last 50 years, an entirely new set of beliefs relating to the function of imprisonment has been growing up. The ideas of retribution tend to be discounted; the idea of penitence is regarded, to say the least, as not enough by itself; the ideas of deterrence and of the protection of the public by immobilizing the criminal retain only a fraction of their former weight. In place of these, the dominant idea is one of rehabilitation. It is recognized today that very many offenders are handicapped as individuals by mental disturbances or are immature personalities, and it is believed that they should be helped towards achieving the kinds of social competence and adjustment towards society that would enable them to fit into normal community life.[81]

Everthorpe was also a prototype and, in time, it came to be defined as yet another victim of architectural and penal inexperience. It was claimed to have been based on a poor design that imitated the discredited nineteenth century prison's it was supposed to have superseded. It was said by an official to be 'out of date before it even left the drawing board'.[82] The design of many of those new prison's was taken to be too amateur and idiosyncratic to be well-regarded afterwards. A senior official remarked:

[78] 'Prison and Borstal Building Programme', 52.
[79] *Report of the Commissioners of Prisons for the Year 1953*, Cmd. 9259, (London: HMSO, 1954), 103.
[80] In the event, it had, in the first place, to be put to use as an institution for young offenders because of the unexpected rise in the number of young men convicted by the courts. Later it reverted to its original purpose, becoming a Category C training prison for some 170 men.
[81] Anon, 'The First New Prison', *The Architects Journal*, 4 Dec. 1958, 814.
[82] L. Fairweather, 'Prisons: A New Generation', *Architects Journal*, 15 Mar. 1989, 27. To be sure, delays between the planning and commissioning of new buildings ensure that *all* new construction is out of date.

In the 60s they were building and they built the most dreadful prisons that you could imagine, the biggest disasters. Everthorpe was one. . . . Blundeston. Coldingley was later and again was a one-off . . . They built them in wings with circular staircases, no observation between the floors, and very difficult to move a prisoner up and down—that kind of thing, which you would have thought, considering all the people who had been on the ground floor in prisons, they would have seen coming.

The Prison Department built for some 20 years. By 1969, it could talk about 'our biggest building programme ever'.[83] The scale of its work was indeed impressive: 4 years later, in 1973, it was administering a total of 69 projects, 26 of which had started work.[84] And then the building programme stalled for a while.[85] The oil crisis of late 1973 led to an economic crisis and an abrupt, temporary reduction in State expenditure in general and of spending on prison building in particular. Estimated expenditure on prison construction decreased by some £43 million over 4 years in 1974[86] and plans for Gartree, Lockwood and Wrabness were abandoned. In 1975, another £40 million was cut, other projects were shed, and major redevelopment was confined to two sites only, Holloway and Feltham.[87] Quite unexpectedly, Holloway was to be left as a lonely vehicle for a penal world-view. But all that was yet to come.

The Final Push

The last great assault on the old Holloway was galvanized by a new department led by determined people responding with wide support to a combination of a new modernist aesthetics, a new penology and a period of brief prosperity in the late 1960s. The establishment of P4

[83] Minister of State's Meeting—24 Apr. 1969, Future of Holloway and Pentonville, Speaking Brief.

[84] The Department was supervising the planning of 3 dispersal prisons, 4 Category B prisons for men, 13 Category C establishments for men, 9 young offender establishments, and 6 remand and allocation centres. It was adapting camps at 7 sites; extending and rebuilding 21 institutions for adults (including Holloway), and 7 institutions for young offenders. It had its eyes on three other sites which it might put to penal purposes.

[85] Rutherford documents how, overall, levels of prison expenditure resumed their rise in the later 1970s. A. Rutherford, *Prisons and the Process of Justice*, (London: Heinemann, 1984), ch. 5.

[86] See *Report on the Work of the Prison Department, 1974*, (London: HMSO, 1975), 10.

[87] *Report on the Work of the Prison Department, 1975*, (London: HMSO, 1976) 10.

led to the institutionalization and focussing of a campaign. David Faulkner said 'there was a lot of internal argument about whether you can keep a prison running while you are doing [reconstruction on site but] there was hardly any planning debate about the principle or the design of the main prison. I think the decision was taken quite easily because the key people were committed to it.'

Aesthetics were important. The prison was Victorian and Victorian buildings were condemned with 'utter revulsion'[88] by many in the 1960s. The Victorian Society, the champion of things Victorian,[89] marvelled at the abiding 'pleasure in destruction which must find its sources in the deepest levels of the collective subconscious'.[90] It was a time, the Society mused later, when 'these [Victorian] buildings had few admirers and were being destroyed with a crass indifference that now seems unbelievable'. The very phrase, 'Victorian conditions',[91] was used as if it were self-evidently critical and it was used often to discredit the prison and point to its obsolescence. Mayhew and Binney's once noble castle had re-appeared as an anachronistic and grim fortress that would never be missed. Even the Victorian Society decided not to remonstrate about the proposal at first:[92] the prison's architect, James Bunning, was not held to be especially distinguished or interesting; the Society was not at that time much concerned with institutional buildings, its focus being on country houses and domestic architecture; and, staffed by a few volunteers, it was obliged continually to forego opportunities to protest.[93]

---

[88] J. Summerson, 'The Evaluation of Victorian Architecture', in The Victorian Society, *Annual Report 1968–9*.

[89] The Society was established in February 1958 by John Betjeman, Hugh Casson, Niklaus Pevsner and others, with the aim, ratified subsequently in its constitution, 'to save from needless destruction, or disfigurement, Victorian and Edwardian buildings or groups of buildings of special architectural merit'.

[90] The Victorian Society, *Annual Report 1967–8,*.

[91] See, for example, a report in the *Daily Telegraph*, 27 Nov. 1969.

[92] I shall show in the next chapter that it was to mount a campaign in the mid-1970s.

[93] The Victorian Society were not wholly opposed themselves to that view of the aesthetics of Holloway in the late 1960s. They were alerted to the prospect of the prison's demolition in Dec. 1968, when a member of the public wrote to enquire 'can anything be done to preserve the picturesque facade of this typical example of Victorian allusive art? . . . Its destruction would deprive me of one my most interesting talking points'. The fate of Holloway was discussed by the Society in Jan. 1969, but the conclusion reached was that 'we do not think we could ever seriously consider pressing for the preservation of such a building if it were ever decided to demolish it, much as we agree that it has an attractive picturesque skyline'.

Penology was important. Officials said without apparent dissent that imprisoning women in such a place as Holloway was brutal. The prison was too heavily fortified for its purpose and too 'forbidding in its appearance'.[94] Built for segregation, security and silence, it was now utterly unsuited to what was being attempted within its walls.[95] 'There have been great changes', Joanna Kelley wrote, 'in the thinking on delinquency and crime, the reasons for it and possible methods for its cure. These have not as yet been greatly reflected in the buildings provided and enlightened, forward looking staff have been greatly hampered in their attempts to improve regimes and treatment methods.'[96] Holloway lacked light, space, facilities, flexibility and freedom of movement and expression.[97] It was out of joint with the new breed of prisons that were being built at home and abroad under the tutelage of a new penology that emphasized guidance rather than surveillance,[98] small therapeutic groups rather than large masses of inmates, and sensitivity rather than harshness.[99] Women would respond better to pleasant surroundings than to the grey, grim, gloomy[100] stronghold of Holloway.[101]

Typifications of Holloway grew ever more stereotyped, the same words and phrases being used so often that they had become 'well-worn . . . part of the Prison Departments own officialese'.[102] Victorian Holloway was ugly, its architecture and adornment 'bizarre',[103] 'grim' and 'bleak'.[104] It was 'a traditional 19th Century prison with fortress type security and a forbidding appearance',[105] one of the

---

[94] Letter from official in P4 to a member of the public, 2 July 1972.

[95] See A. Peterson, 'The Prison Building Programme', *British Journal of Criminology*, Apr. 1961, Vol. 1, No. 1, 307.

[96] J. Kelley, 'The new look at women in prison. Redesigning Holloway', unpublished, Nov. 1970.

[97] See K. FitzHerbert, 'New Holloway?', *New Society*, 25 Feb. 1971, 301.

[98] 'Opening Speech by the State Secretary for Justice, Mrs E. A. Haars, to the Symposium on the Occasion of the Opening of the New Amsterdam Prison Complex', (The Hague: The Ministry of Justice, 1979), 10.

[99] D. Faulkner, 'The Redevelopment of Holloway Prison', *Howard Journal of Penology and Crime Prevention*, 1971, Vol. XIII, No. 2, 122.

[100] The adjectives are Frances Heidensohn's: 'Prison for Women', typescript, 1969, 4.

[101] See Sir L. Fox, *The English Prison and Borstal Systems'*, (London: Routledge and Kegan Paul, 1952), 157.

[102] J. Steele, 'Holloway's soft cell', the *Guardian*, 1 Oct. 1970.

[103] See J. Camp, *Holloway Prison'*, (Newton Abbot: David and Charles, 1974), 10.

[104] *Islington Gazette*, 6 Oct. 1970.

[105] D. Faulkner, notes for the Press Facility on 30 September' Sept. 1970.

'grim early Victorian monstrosities',[106] consisting of 'old grim cell blocks and [a] forbidding castellated gateway'.[107] Its time had passed. With the march of progress, a design once rational and efficient had become transformed into a 'relic',[108] an 'obsolete',[109] 'out-dated',[110] 'unsuitable',[111] 'unimaginative'[112] 'obstacle'.[113] Holloway was 'quite unsuited to the modern methods of treatment that the Prison Service is trained to employ'.[114]

It was at that point that the issue of gender tinged description. If Holloway was a stark, ugly and oppressive place, it was considered all the more disgraceful that it should be used to confine women. The character of the prison excited feelings of *shame* in those who were in a position to make decisions about its future. Officials stated that Holloway was no way to treat women (Ken Neale remarked that 'any self-respecting modern prison system would have to do something about its women'). A knowledgeable member of the prison's Board of Visitors during the 1970s said:

I think that part of the explanation for the rebuilding of Holloway was the fact that people felt quite ashamed of the old Holloway, and somehow shame impacts much more powerfully on that small population of women in custody than it does on large herds of male cattle really. Shame because somehow there is a requirement to treat women better, to be more careful with women. Women are customarily cherished and cared for, and there is a kind of culture which dictates how men should behave to women, which was more alive then than [now]. . . . I think it was not acceptable that women were in such austere, grim, heavy, oppressive, unrelenting circumstances. It was pretty unattractive.

The massive symbolic, aesthetic, functional and physical power of Holloway Prison, the very quality for which it had once been celebrated, was thus turned inside out to become something negative and

---

[106] Minister of State's Meeting: Future of Holloway and Pentonville, Speaking Brief, 24 Apr. 1969.

[107] 'Holloway: planned maintenance in a rebuilt prison', *Buildings Maintenance and Services*, Oct. 1978, 12.

[108] See M. Finnigan, 'My weeks inside Holloway and why I'm glad they're planning to pull it down', *Daily Express*, 18 Dec. 1968.

[109] *Penal Practice in a Changing Society*, 21.   [110] *Evening News*, 5 Nov. 1971.

[111] *Ibid.*   [112] J. Kelley, *When the Gates Shut*, 9.

[113] D. Faulkner, 'The Redevelopment of Holloway Prison', 122.

[114] Speech notes for the Parliamentary Under-Secretary of State for the Adjournment Debate, 14 May 1970.

repulsive. The strength of the old prison was bent back against itself. What had once been powerful became a weakness, a defect and a block to progress. Holloway was indicted by its own expressive force (it was too grim, frightening and bleak to be effective as a place of treatment). Its capacity to classify, segregate and isolate inmates thwarted therapeutic group processes. Its ability to withstand attacks and escape attempts was absurd because its captives were only *women*.[115] It had, after all, never been built principally for women. Joanna Kelley said:

We had always known that—it was practically a *sine qua non* of the service, that Holloway was very unsuitable for women. . . . We thought at the time that it was very, very grim. . . . We thought that barred windows were really very grim and gloomy and dungeon-like. Those long, open galleries with the narrow stone floored cat walks on each side and the wire netting to prevent anyone jumping over from serious injury, we found it very unnecessary. Not just punitive but depressing . . . the endless rows of locked cells and almost no facilities for any kind of recreation in association. It had been a very reformist idea to give them quiet and solitude and a chance for thinking things out. This was being replaced by a chance of meeting together, both for classes, lectures and recreational purposes, and they were allowed to talk . . . [a] really different slant. We thought, yes, it was right to pull down Holloway and build something more.

Economics were important. I have already described the growth in spending on public policy and great building prison programme of the 1950s and 1960s, and I shall show below that Ken Neale and Joanna Kelley came to the Prisons Board with proposals at a particularly favourable economic tide.

Pulling Down Holloway

Like the history of any other documented choice written after the event, official interpretations of the decision to pull down Holloway tend to make use of *ex post facto* accounts, the 'because' motives, that are as much justifications of things known and done as phenomenologically sensitive reconstructions of what was thought at the very moment of judgement, the 'in order to' motives. As a result of much retrospective discussion and drafting, the decision became decked

---

[115] 'There is not much danger of an organised disturbance or an organised attempt to escape.' D. Faulkner, notes for the Press facility on 30 Sept. 1970.

with good reasons and a narrative that was conceived for press releases, ministerial briefings, answers to parliamentary questions and the like. I have myself raided the narrative developed in the late 1960s and early 1970s to write some of this section.

Let me give an example of that narratives use. In 1972, a RAP (Radical Alternatives to Imprisonment) campaign invited members of the public to write to the Prison Department to query features of the decision to rebuild the prison. Officials replied to every letter, and every reply was slightly different, but they also characteristically assorted stock arguments in standard paragraphs. Part of one such reply to a critic recited that:

The present Holloway Prison building has been recognised for many years as an obstacle to progress in the treatment of women offenders. There is a growing recognition that most women in custody need some form of medical, psychiatric or other remedial treatment, and also training to enable them to support themselves in the community after release. Experience has shown that this type of treatment cannot be provided satisfactorily in a traditional nineteenth century building with its forbidding appearance and its emphasis on security, and for this reason the decision was taken . . . that Holloway should be replaced.

Once composed, such a story could be used repeatedly and with only slight modification. It would have been otiose for officials to produce a new argument for every occasion. The effect, of course, was to freeze large interpretations of policy whilst officials got on with their work, and it was be some time before the explanation of what had been done to Holloway was reconsidered and revised. There was an ensuing interpretive inertia that ensured that major policy changes developed in fits rather than smoothly, and those fits had to be induced by crises which challenged the credibility of the old stories and demanded new ones.

It has been easy enough to explain the larger ingredients which were compacted into those stories after the event. It is a little harder to reproduce how matters stood immediately *before* the decision to rebuild Holloway was taken. The confidence of the letter writer of July 1972 was probably not experienced before July 1968, when results were not yet known, certainties reached and authoritative accounts drafted. Observation of other initiatives undoubtedly suggests that policies in the making are emergent and indeterminate processes[116] whose qualities can never be fully recovered subsequently.

The Meeting of the Prison Department Committee

I have argued that proposals to rebuild Holloway were advanced at intervals by people inside and outside the government and prison throughout most of the century. By the 1960s, it appeared to have become accepted that the old prison was effectively condemned and all that remained was to act to bring matters to an end. Even before the foundation of P4 and the entry of Ken Neale and Joanna Kelley into the Prison Department, the replacement of Holloway Prison was a nascent policy whose broad features had been defined and accepted. Although no formal submission had yet been made and approved, Holloway was virtually doomed, and it wanted only a warrant of execution. Joanna Kelley remarked, 'we must remember that, all through the 30s, long before I was in the Commission, they were discussing the disposal of Holloway. . . . So that what I came into was more or less the tail end of that. They all agreed that it was unsuited for women.'

It had not been difficult to get officials to concede in principle that the buildings of Holloway were inappropriate and undesirable. What had been unresolved was just *where* the new secure prison would be set (and thus what kind of establishment it would be); *when* it would be built, and that was a decision that had been postponed repeatedly; and the precise *form* and *structure* that the new prison would take. Kelley and Neale had settled most of those matters by drafting *Prison Policy: Women and Girls* in 1968.

The difficulty lay in the next step, in gaining a firm agreement to commit specified resources within a definite timetable to a new secure women's prison. Terry Weiler said 'there was often a lot of battling for starts . . . If there is only going to be one start in 1968, what's going to have priority? . . . Could you afford to allocate so many million pounds [to the women's system] when the prison population was still rising and we were having great difficulty in containing it?'

It was appropriate that *Prison Policy: Women and Girls*' proposals for a hospital prison first went before the Prison Department's

---

[116] I have dealt with this matter at great length elsewhere, and chiefly in *A View from the Shadows*, (Oxford: Oxford University Press, 1987), ch. 2.

Medical Steering Committee on 19 June 1968 for guidance about future numbers of staff and inmates. They went from there to the Director of Works for 'an analysis of the proposals in relation to the site';[117] to the Prison Department Committee (the omnibus committee composed of some twenty heads of divisions) at its meeting to review the building programme on 22 July 1968; to the Home Secretary nine days later; and finally to Ministers in September.

The proposals presented to the Prison Department Committee were succinct, part of a global submission on the provision of staff housing and new Borstal allocation centres and the redevelopment and replacement of 'obsolete prison service establishments'. There was said to be a particular problem with poor remand facilities at Brixton and Wormwood Scrubs in London: Brixton, founded in 1820, would merit major improvement or complete rebuilding in time.

The Holloway proposals lacked substantial supporting argument, and listed little more than the tentative requirements for a new women's prison on the Holloway site for 400–450 inmates 'mainly in hospital plus nurses' training facilities', a remand centre for 500–550 men, and staff accommodation for both establishments. It was noted in the submission that the programme would have to be planned carefully because women inmates would be in occupation of parts of the prison during construction and security would be very difficult.

Members of the Committee did not immediately accept that the privileged women's system with its uncrowded prisons and unhardened inmates was a prime candidate for a vast new project estimated to cost some £10 million, half the planned budget of the total building programme for a single year. Ken Neale said 'we had to distort some of the priorities, and that's why there was a great battle about it, but it was won'. It was certainly fortunate that planned expenditure on capital projects was growing steeply at that time, rising from £7.26 million in 1967–68, £7.64 million in 1968–69, £15.6 million in 1969–70 to £20 million in 1970–71, 'nearly trebling size',[118] but there was also competition between individual proposals. Neale remarked:

our problem about getting Holloway on to the agenda—everybody agreed it was a deplorable place and in a redesigned women's system it ought to be modernised in order to accommodate more advanced views about its roles—

---

[117] Note by Establishment Division 3, 8 July 1968.
[118] Memorandum from Sir William Pile, 29 July 1968.

but the arguments very strongly in the Department . . . [were] that it would cost so much money. . . that it simply [wasn't] justified in terms of the overall priorities of the system. The prison directors and Chief Director, quite understandably, argued very powerfully . . . that if there was £10m to spare in the development programme, it should be used to do something about sorting out the horrors of the adult male system. . . . And the women's system was thought to be under so little pressure of numbers . . . when it came to allocating scarce money, it shouldn't be spent on the women's system, and that was really the battle that had to be fought.

After all, Holloway was not the only institution to have been criticised at the time. Its fellow London prisons, Brixton, Pentonville, Wormwood Scrubs and Wandsworth, were also deemed to be obsolete nineteenth century buildings that deserved condemnation and demolition. Sir William Pile recollected how he had made a tour of inspection on becoming Director-General:[119] 'I'd never seen prisons and thought I'd better go and see them. I was absolutely horrified as any outsider would be. The real estate was hopelessly out of date—especially the London prisons.' He believed that the London prisons should be rebuilt, not necessarily for therapeutic reasons, but for more straightforward reasons of responsible stewardship. Their state was appalling: 'I wondered whether anyone could persuade ministers we had a bad stock of buildings—irrespective of whether they could be used for therapy'. But there was a legal problem: the male prisons of London were bound by statutes which effectively prevented their redevelopment[120] (the Director-General recalled 'I thought the men's prisons were out of the question—we couldn't sell them for trust reasons').

Holloway was found to be uniquely free of special covenants, and it alone of the London prisons could be safely reconstructed: 'I was persuaded that I could [convince] the Treasury that there was money for Holloway but not the others.' A chance legal and economic factor had singled Holloway out, and that weighed with the Director-General.

But what chiefly won Ken Neale's battle was the special pragmatics of the Holloway proposal. It was argued that spending money on the

[119] Sir William had been Assistant Under-Secretary of State at the Department of Education and Science, 1962; he had worked in the Ministry of Health, 1966; Deputy Under-Secretary of State at the Home Office, 1967–70; Director-General of the Prison Service, 1968–70; He then became Permanent Under-Secretary, Department of Education and Science.

[120] See, for example, the Act for establishing a prison at Pentonville, 5 & 6 Victoriae, C. 29, 1842, s. 4.

women's system would have a disproportionate impact ('it could make a massive difference to the treatment of women rather than men, it was the best use of resources—equivalent investment would have a greater effect' said Sir William); and that there would be less political and public opposition (women presented less of a security risk than men and the public would 'let one get away with reforms of women's prisons but not those of men'). What led to approval of plans for Holloway was the presumption that the women's system could exceptionally be changed by a large gesture: 'if you apply a big force you can shift it but not in the case of the men's prisons' said the Director-General. The Holloway project was to be just such a big force. An official who had worked in P4 at the time argued:

It reflected the ambitions of those responsible for the operational side of the women's system to produce a centre of excellence for the women's system. Obviously, the women's system was very small, and Holloway was the dominant, and remains, I think, the dominant part of it which is not true of any single prison in the men's system.

The Prisons Board was recorded as having endorsed the proposal to reform Holloway prison with some minor reservations about the uncertainty of planning for the future size of the female inmate population. A small group was to be established under the chairmanship of Ken Neale to 'consider the next steps': to draw up specifications for the architect, giving detailed instructions where necessary; consider the timing and basis of the approach to the planning authorities; consider the timetable for construction and expenditure; and the like. The progress and work of that group, meeting for the first time on the very day of the Home Secretary's assent, will be the centrepiece of the chapters to come.

The decision was announced publicly on December 16 by the Home Secretary, James Callaghan, in a written answer in the House of Commons:[121]

Following a review of the custodial arrangements for women and girls, I have decided upon a programme to re-shape the system of female penal establishments in England and Wales. The current total of about 800 women and girls in custody has not varied significantly over the last quarter of a century, and is

---

[121] Although the Home Office had announced publicly in November that it no longer proposed to close Holloway Prison and build at Theydon Mount. The reason given then was that the number of women prisoners was too small. See *The Times*, 11 Nov. 1968.

not likely to change markedly in the foreseeable future. Most women and girls in custody require some form of medical, psychiatric or remedial treatment. The main feature of the programme is therefore to demolish the existing prison at Holloway and redevelop the site by stages. This will permit the building of an establishment that will be basically a secure hospital to act as the hub of the female penal system. Its medical and psychiatric facilities will be its central feature and normal custodial facilities will comprise a relatively small part of the establishment.

The announcement, and the subsequent press conference given by Lord Stonham, received almost universal acclaim and wide newspaper publicity.[122] As is their wont, most newspapers simply reproduced without addition or comment edited portions of the Home Secretary's announcement, Home Office press releases and Lord Stonham's speech. There were exceptions. An editorial in the *Daily Express* of 17 December called the changes 'wise and humane . . . Most women prisoners are not violent, so the emphasis will rightly be on rehabilitation. They should be treated with sympathy and understanding.' And an article by an ex-prisoner in the same newspaper on the following day proclaimed: 'I am rejoicing because Mr Callaghan says they are going to pull it down . . . one must pray that the good intentions don't get watered down before the facilities exist to implement them.'

No one came forward in the late 1960s to question the assumption that women required medical or psychiatric treatment. The only audible critical voice was that of the abolitionists such as Ann Smith and Radical Alternatives to Prison who argued very quietly that, whilst the demolition of the old Holloway prison was to be commended, and the new Holloway's emphasis on rehabilitation was to be applauded, imprisoning women was so ill-advised that there should be no plans for a new establishment at all.[123]

---

[122] There were reports in the *Daily Express*, the *Guardian*, the *Daily Mail*, the *Daily Mirror*, the *Daily Sketch*, the *Sun*, *The Times*, and in local papers such as the *Islington Gazette*.   [123] See A. Smith, 'The Treatment of Women Offenders', 396.

4

The Secure Hospital: Planning the New Holloway

'Hospital instead of jail for girls who break law' (headline in *Daily Mirror*, 17 December 1968)

Introduction

From the first, the Holloway redevelopment project was regarded as a quite exceptional and daunting enterprise marked by an unparalleled scale and ambition. All prison-building is formidable, not unlike the planning and construction of a small town with all its utilities,[1] but with additional requirements of surveillance and discipline unknown to most civil design. The planners not only had to contrive a place with a way of life,[2] an aesthetics, a regime, controls and security, but they had to do so in extraordinarily adverse conditions. *Prison Policy: Women and Girls* had ensured that the new prison would not be constructed in an open position in Aylesbury or Epping but on the congested site occupied by the old prison. The main southern remand prison for women had to be in London and there was no London location to be had apart from Holloway itself. The project entailed reconstructing a prison with its reluctant occupants and elaborate routines *in situ*, promising problems of phasing, safety, order and co-ordination. Ken Neale said 'there were some unique difficulties . . . because never before had the Prison Department ever tried to build a major prison on a constricted 9 acre urban site while continuing to run it'.

No team could possibly have chosen to plan a prison in such a way. 'We were not ourselves anxious to redevelop this constricted urban

---

[1] See J. Kelley, 'The New Holloway', *Prison Service Journal*, Vol. 10, No. 37, 4.

[2] It was observed afterwards that 'the redevelopment of Holloway was seen as a significant penological project, which involved the design not only of a new building, but of a new way of life for inmates and staff'. *Holloway Project Committee Report*, (London: Home Office, 1985), 7.

site and would have preferred a cleared site if there had been any possibility of obtaining a suitable site at the time . . . the Secretary of State was compelled to reach the conclusion that there was no alternative but to rebuild Holloway on its present site despite the problems that that proposal presented', recited a brief in March 1970. The process of reconstructing Holloway would be without precedent,[3] requiring uncommon powers of management as, side by side, the old prison was razed and the new prison erected, inmates and staff were shuffled about, buildings were evacuated and replaced, and temporary security fences and gates were manoeuvred about the site.

The project would be both the first prison specifically built for women in Britain *and* an extraordinary prison in its own right: the plan was for a large, revolutionary establishment at the very hub of the women's system, an establishment that would 'dominate treatment and regimes and the overall deployment in the system of female staff and offenders'.[4] Its bold design would 'embody the most advanced concepts of medical, psychiatric and custodial treatments'[5] in 'one of the world's most advanced and versatile penal institutions'.[6] It would be exciting, innovative and inspiring, its design animated by 'moral values and social merit'.[7] A commentator remarked on the planning team's belief that 'no sacrifice is too great for the New Holloway'.[8]

The project was the first large scheme to be undertaken by the new P4 (Ken Neale had sought just such a big venture to give life, organization and purpose to his division). So grand and complicated a venture would demand co-ordinated action to 'integrate various aspects of the problem and . . . create machinery to facilitate comprehensive and prompt attention to the philosophical and operational aspects of the project'.[9] It would concentrate minds and impart unity and strength to the division. Ken Neale wrote to colleagues in the project group: 'I regard continuity of membership as important in contributing to the development of a loyalty to the group and the project as such. In such a major enterprise it is necessary that the key

---

[3] See D. Faulkner, 'The Redevelopment of Holloway Prison', *The Howard Journal of Penology and Crime Prevention*, 1971, Vol. 13, No. 2, 126.

[4] K. Neale, 'Progress Report No. 1', Mar. 1969, 1.

[5] 'Draft Prospectus to Nominated Architects', 28 Mar. 1969.

[6] *Evening Standard*, 1 Oct. 1970.

[7] Speech notes for adjournment debate on 14 May 1970.

[8] K. FitzHerbert, 'New Holloway?', *New Society*, 25 Feb. 1971, 302.

[9] 'Introduction' to '2nd Steyning Conference Report', 21–24 Oct. 1969, 1.

contributors should feel themselves personally identified with its success'.[10]

In a sense, planning had begun as soon as preparatory work started for *Prison Policy: Women and Girls* in 1968. It had been broadly determined in March that the new Holloway would be more hospital than prison; its organization into small, functional units had been decided by April; and staffing needs had been estimated by July of that year. Formally, however, it was to be in July that the planning of the project was entrusted by the Prison Board to a managing body. Some fifteen to twenty-five people (the numbers varied over the life of the project) called the Group on the Redevelopment of Holloway, the Holloway Redevelopment Project Group or sometimes just the Group, formed the 'major responsible body. . . [that took] the major policy decisions'.[11] They met first on the very day in July 1968 that the Home Secretary endorsed the proposal to proceed, and they met thereafter every month or so, being dissolved only in 1977 when the new prison was commissioned. Their composition, like that of any other official committee, was significant, an icon to be read by those who could understand it,[12] revealing the configuration of institutional interests thought to be affected by the new prison and the kind of establishment Holloway was supposed to become.

The Group reflected diverse interests and purposes. It was chaired by Ken Neale, and it included Joanna Kelley and representatives of other Home Office and Government bodies: the Home Office Directorate of Works, Establishment Divison and Finance Division; the Prison Department's P1 (in charge of the strategic planning of buildings), P3 (adult male offenders) and P4; and, most pointedly, perhaps, the Senior Medical Officer of Holloway Prision, the Prison Department's Chief Psychologist, and members of the Prison Medical Service, including the Nursing Matron-in-Chief, and representatives of the Department of Health and Social Security, the only external Ministry. There were no other staff or groups represented.

The character of the new prison was there foreshadowed, the participation of the medical specialists and the Department of Health clearly signifying Holloway's medical future. From the beginning, the pattern of hospital planning adopted by the Department

[10] K. Neale, 'Progress Report No. 1', Mar. 1969, 3.
[11] Minutes of the Meeting of the Project Team, 10 Sept. 1969.
[12] See P. Rock, 'The Opening Stages of Criminal-Justice Policy-Making', *British Journal of Criminology*, Winter 1995.

was continually before the Group: the Department's planners and architects were frequently consulted; a senior architect, experienced in hospital design, was especially seconded to the Group from the Department; and the one other building project that served as a model for work was not be be a prison at all but a hospital at Greenwich. The Greenwich District Hospital was to provide a template for design, costings and planning procedures, and it became the formal prototype that the Group had in mind when they worked. I shall return to it below.

It had been resolved not to repeat the apparent mistakes of earlier prison projects in the post-war building programme. The cumbersome, lengthy and inefficient process of project planning was attributed in part to the dispersal of decision-making across different committees and divisions within government. There were too many staggered consultations with too many bodies scattered too widely. Neale said: 'one of the things that appalled me was that I looked at various papers of major projects, that it could take 3, 4 or even 5 years before you could actually put a brick on site. And I said this won't do at all. So I devised a completely new way of approaching the project, the project team.'

The new Holloway was to be planned in a new way, employing a 'compact decision-making team to manage the project in all its aspects . . . we aimed . . . at the full integration of all members of the design team with the project administration as a whole. There were no enclaves; every member of the team had access to its papers and deliberations.'[13] The team would achieve more intense, focussed and thorough planning than any hitherto undertaken in the building of prisons. Its work would be continuous and uninterrupted, proceeding stage by stage and at the very same time as the old buildings were being removed and the new buildings were being erected. And, unusually, P4 would itself orchestrate much of what was done, preventing the planning process from becoming too diffuse, ragged and protracted. A senior official recalled, 'P4 went on running the administrative side of Holloway which meant it must have been agreed at the start that it would be different'.

In December 1968, the Project Group gave birth to that slightly more compact, more active body, known as the Project Team, numbering about fifteen, whose function was 'to study how the

13 J. Kelley, 'The New Holloway', 4.

emphasis on therapeutic treatment could best be reflected in the design and management of the new establishment'.[14] The Team would answer to the Group: it was 'governed by the policy laid down by the group . . . [but,] because of its compactness, it afforded a quicker and more effective form for dealing with problems than the group'.[15] It had executive authority to devise and supervise policy in close detail until 1979, and *its* members included policy officials and the Design Team: the Director of Women's Prisons (who was Joanna Kelley until 1974); members of the Directorate of Works and the Establishment Division; the surveyors, engineers and architects of the Design Team (after their appointment in the summer of 1969); a representative of the Department of Health and Social Security; and a succession of Assistant Secretaries responsible for P4 (until November 1974, when P7 took over).[16]

A third body, the Design Team, formed in the autumn of 1969, was functionally independent of the Project Group and the Project Team, but its nominated architects, engineers and surveyors were also a constituent part of the Project Team: 'with their appointment they took over the design initiative and the role of officials changed to one of creating the circumstances in which the Design Team could promote a smooth and continuous operational project on the site'.[17] The Design Team was to be wound up in 1977 with the commissioning of the prison.

The members of that original group of people were themselves taken to be somewhat exceptional. Joanna Kelley was recognised as a powerful woman. Ken Neale (from 1967 to 1970) and David Faulkner (from 1970 to 1974) were the first two Assistant Secretaries to lead it, and they were forceful men, being described later by a senior Home Office official as 'two very go-getter Assistant Secretaries in P4 . . . they both committed themselves'. It was said to be an unusual body that contained 'the eminent names of Prison Department mythology at the time'.

---

[14] 'Press Notice: Holloway Prison to be Rebuilt—New Approach to Women Offenders', Home Office, 30 Sept. 1970.

[15] Minutes of the Meeting of the Project Team, 10 Sept. 1969.

[16] The main function of P7 was to stimulate 'with the assistance of the Directorate of Works . . . in accordance with tactical management and long term plans the development of existing sites and buildings to their maximum potential'. Until 1974, the Holloway Redevelopment Project was explicitly omitted from the list of P7's functions, flagging P4's exceptional role in the first few years.

[17] D. Faulkner, 'Notes for the Press Facility on 30 September'. Sept. 1970.

And that was not all. During the years of the redevelopment project, there was to be a series of *ad hoc* sub-committees formed for specific purposes, the preparation of the architect's brief, staffing, training, administration, security, commissioning and other matters, and each took members from inside and outside the Project Group. The whole amounted to a protracted and complicated venture. It was expected that it would take over three years of planning before the construction of the main complex could even begin. David Faulkner said that 'the size, importance and complexity of the project is as great as any which has been undertaken in this country—it is not only based on a new concept of prison treatment with implications not only for the design but also for the whole method of work within it, but it also involves rebuilding the establishment while it remains in full operational use. This is a formidable task.'[18]

The Project Group, the Project Team, the Design Team and their proliferating sub-committees laboured hard over the years between 1968 and 1985 and they produced a vast spate of decisions and documents. They began their task by considering how the prime functions of Holloway[19] would be built into the new institution, receiving papers from the people who were in charge of all those specialist roles in the prison and the Prison Department: the pharmacists, psychologists, matrons, statisticians, staffing officers, chaplains and doctors. Joanna Kelley herself wrote a master conspectus of the main functions and procedures of the existing prison.

Holloway was to be a cross-breed. In the first instance, it would have to do the standard work of any prison: inmates would still have to be received, assessed, visited, fed, boarded, and escorted to and from the courts. It would be a mosaic of any prison's standard components: the chapels, pharmacy, administrative offices, library, works department, kitchens and the rest would have to be included in the design as they would anywhere else. But it was also to have peculiar features that would make it most unlike any other prison, and the special and the standard had to be reconciled in the one place and the one scheme.

Each planning decision had its attendant meetings and papers, and each was capable of throwing up new problems and further meetings.

---

[18] Ibid.
[19] See J. Kelley, 'The New Holloway', *Prison Service Journal*, Oct. 1970, Vol X, No. 37, 4.

For example, there had to be a revision of the original design when planners were reminded by the Fire Service Inspectorate in June 1973 about fire hazards (and that led to the alteration of central spaces to make provision for fire lanes and the abandonment of plans to install wooden staircases). Police crime prevention officers recommended changes in the design of the staff mess. There were problems about how the efficient cleaning of new windows could be reconciled with economy and security.

The project team visited hospitals, Greenwich, the Royal Northern, the Whittington and St Bernard's in London, and the Withington in Manchester, and what they saw clearly informed their judgement about how the new place should look. They had copious discussions with the Treasury: the project chairman, David Faulkner, noted in March 1970 that the Project Group would 'have a continuous liaison with the Treasury as the basis of the procedures for approval. My object is to avoid having major confrontations . . . arising at key points during the building programme.'[20]

The intricate, detailed and almost obsessive character of a planning process that lasted for some ten years should not be forgotten, but my own description and analysis cannot report the myriad small ways in which all those submissions and deliberations intertwined to affect the design of Holloway. I can dwell on only a few critical subjects and describe them quite summarily by focussing on just one big theme: the evolution of the central character and consequences of the design of the new Holloway.

Architects

If the new Holloway was to be a special place, more hospital than prison, difficult to design and build, it would have to be done well. A prospectus drafted for applicant architects told how the new establishment would be a 'medically orientated establishment' holding 350 women in hospital conditions, 150 women in more normal prison accommodation, and up to 450 male remand prisoners.[21] The old prison would be reformed, renamed, and redesigned so that, 'its outward and inward characteristics should epitomise its advanced

[20] 'Holloway Redevelopment Project: Progress Report No 4', Mar. 1970.
[21] It was to be resolved later at the first Steyning Conference in May 1969, a conference I shall describe, that there would in fact be no male remand prison at Holloway.

role and contribute to the fulfilment of its purposes through the provision of suitable environmental influences'.[22] 'Challenging architectural problems' would be posed by the need to combine a pleasing aesthetics with the 'functional efficiency of the treatment and security requirements'.

A project such as Holloway would require a special group of architects.[23] But the Group lacked faith in the capacities and ability of government design teams of the time: 'there was frustration with the Prison Service building management arrangements . . . prisons took too long to build and they were too expensive and they weren't right when they *were* built'. Desultory talks about the planning of Holloway were held with the Ministry of Public Building and Works in April 1969 and it was reported that the new project would probably exceed the Ministry's resources. Decisions about the choice and appointment of architects were delayed.

In the middle of May 1969, senior officials turned away from these approaches and decided to keep the project within the Project Group. They would commission the very best private architects by looking for a specialist practice capable of a 'really imaginative design' that would make a 'substantial functional and aesthetic impact on the public mind'. Appointing such independent architects, it was argued, would confer a great advantage because they would answer solely to the Project Group and cede sole control and credit to the Prison Department 'without the interference' of other Ministries. It was to be another exceptional arrangement, again without precedent, reflecting the strong sense of property and pride which P4 had acquired in the project.

In the event, the architects appointed in July 1969, Robert Matthew, Johnson-Marshall and partners (known colloquially as RMJM or Rumjum), had no special experience of prison or hospital design. Their expertise lay in planning housing and government and university buildings, particularly the new University of York.[24] They had been known to the Director-General, William Pile, when he had worked in the Department of Education between 1962 and 1966:

[22] 'Group on the Redevelopment of Holloway: Draft Prospectus to Nominated Architects, Note by Secretary', 18 Mar. 1969.
[23] At its first meeting in July 1968, the Redevelopment Group suggested that the Director of Works should consult the Ministry of Health about the selection of architects.
[24] See the obituary of Percy Johnson-Marshall in *The Times*, 19 July 1993.

'they had a good track record of designing educational institutions. . . . It was regarded as a creative thing, a big step forward', he said. Francis Baden-Powell, the RMJM architect involved most intimately with the project, recalled:

At the time that we started all new prisons on green field sites were designed by the PSA [Property Services Agency working within the Ministry of Public Buildings] and the Home Office had the responsibility for looking after all prisons as they were completed. And all the old prisons—if there was the development/redevelopment of a prison on an existing site—that would be done by the Home Office. They hadn't got the resources at the time to tackle this. I don't think they really had the experience of managing something very large, a complex operation. And so they went and interviewed firms who had got experience either of large institutional building complexes, as we have had working on universities in the educational sector, [or] who had got hospital experience because of the hospital connotations.

Steyning

The Prison Board had charged the Project Group with drawing up specifications for the architects. Rather than do so by conferring in London with all its distractions,[25] the Project Group determined to follow a practice outlined by the architect seconded by the Ministry of Health. At a meeting in February 1969, they were told how work on a new hospital had taken place intensively over a week of continuous discussion rather than in months of irregular meetings. The Group superintending the reconstruction of Holloway emulated the hospital planners and adjourned twice to the Foreign Office International Conference Centre at Wiston House near Steyning in Sussex.[26]

Their first meeting, known as 'Steyning I', took place over four days at the beginning of May 1969, and it was the Ministry of Health that prepared its draft agenda. Steyning I was attended by fifteen people, including six members of P4, the Senior Medical Officer of Holloway, advisers from the Establishment Divison, the Controller of Development and Planning, the Chief Education Officer, the Nursing Matron-in-Chief, and the Deputy Chief Architect and Senior Engineer from the Ministry of Health. Their methodology and compos-

---

[25] Ken Neale wrote in July 1969, 'the Holloway project is larger and more sophisticated than anything we have so far tackled and if the timetable which Ministers wish us to achieve is to be kept it is essential that the working project team should be freed for a few days from the day-to-day work of the office'.

[26] Wiston House was a place known to Ken Neale because of his former employment in the Foreign and Commonwealth Office.

tion again showed the hand of the Ministry of Health. Together, they produced a first draft brief and proposals for the phasing and zoning of the project.[27]

A second meeting at Steyning was then held between 21 and 24 October 1969 at which the first brief was considered with the new professional Design Team, the briefing process was consolidated and the Design Team was integrated into the project as a whole.[28] That second meeting, known prosaically enough as Steyning II, was much larger, made up of twenty-eight people. Its core members had attended Steyning I, but it was also joined by the newly-appointed private architects, quantity surveyors and consultant engineers representing firms attached to the Design Team. Like many such conferences, and quite by design, Steyning I and Steyning II generated an intensity of experience which not only led 'individual planners [to] become a team'[29] but fermented a sense of intellectual excitement and ambition. Joanna Kelley, called what was conceived at Steyning a 'momentous decision . . . [that would create] the leading establishment of its kind in the world.'[30]

The Steyning Brief

The two Steyning conferences brought together almost all the personal, intellectual and practical resources that the Project Group considered necessary for the construction of a brief for the new prison.[31] Their participants were recruited from the prison, the Prison Department and the Ministry of Health, and they were treated as self-sufficient for planning purposes. They did not turn outwards to other experts in penology or prison architecture: I have

---

[27] The same procedure was to be adopted for the planning of new P4 establishments at Feltham and Ashford. See J. Mills, 'The new prisons of Feltham and Asford' in *International Prison Architecture*, (The Hague: Ministry of Justice, 1979), 65, 67.

[28] See D. Faulkner, 'The Redevelopment of Holloway Prison', 127.

[29] T. Clayton, 'The Holloway Redevelopment Project', unpublished.

[30] Minutes of a Meeting of the Project Team held on 29 Oct. 1974.

[31] There was a reference library established specifically to support the project week of Steyning I. It included a general brief for a Category C prison (that is, a prison for inmates who, as the Mountbatten Report put it, 'although they lack the resources and will to make escape attempts, have not the stability to be kept in conditions where there is no barrier to their escape'); briefs for new establishments at Full Sutton, Feltham and Coldingley; an Organization and Methods Report on administration of prisons; a report on 'administrative security at Aylesbury'; policy papers on drugs and on suicides in custody; a P4 paper on education policy for women in prison; a site plan of the existing prison at Holloway and other plans of the Islington area; and 'all papers, minutes, etc. so far produced on the Project'.

shown that they had had their misgivings about what passed for expertise in those areas, they relied on their own competence and, anyway, they were not designing a conventional prison but a non-pareil, an establishment more hospital than jail. They did not refer much to experiments in building prisons for women elsewhere[32] (although, for instance, strong parallels could have been drawn between the eventual design of the new Holloway and the structure of a number of penitentiaries for women in the United States).[33]

Of course, the Project Group was, and never could have been, entirely autonomous in its works and deliberations. Before and after Steyning, it had consultations with others, with the Advisory Council on the Penal System[34] and the staff of Holloway itself, for example. (I shall deal with some of those encounters in the next chapter.) But those so consulted claimed afterwards that members of the Project Group behaved as if their minds were already set, all the material decisions had been taken and that the brief was not to be changed in any substantial particular.

The Project Group meeting at Steyning possessed what was, in effect, an experientially-based understanding[35] of what had to be done, a firm practical knowledge that did not require resorting to outsiders and their theorizing. The prospective author of a history of the prison and the project, a man who had been primed by members of the Project Team, said in September 1970 that 'the object of his book was to sell the Project to the public. Ideas would be put to the public as solutions not of theoreticians but of people engaged in the day to day work of the Prison Service.'[36]

[32] The one reference I discovered to the new Holloway's twin sister at Cornton Vale in Scotland was an observation made in 1973 by Joanna Kelley that Cornton Vale proposed to include a hairdressing salon amongst its facilities.

[33] See, for example, R. Flowers, *Women and Criminality*, (New York: Greenwood Press, 1987) and C. Mann, *Female Crime and Delinquency*, (Alabama: The University of Alabama Press, 1984), 192–221. One member did refer to an interest in how women were treated in the Danish prison system, but there is no reference to the matter in any of the papers.

[34] A member of the Advisory Council remembered 'looking back on it now . . . it wasn't strictly within our remit and therefore in a sense Faulkner was coming along, showing us what they were doing, obviously seeking our general approval, but without us having any kind of input into the decision-making. It wasn't within our remit.'

[35] A note for the Leader of the House prepared for a debate in March 1972 recorded that 'When the new Holloway is complete there will . . . be new buildings designed to take account of *all our experience of dealing with women in custody*' (emphasis added).

[36] Minutes of the Holloway Project Team Meeting, 11 Sept. 1970. The author continued, 'there were differences in the incarceration of men and women, but ideas developed through the Project could benefit the whole Prison Service'.

Participants in the Steyning Conferences were confident. Joanna Kelley said of Steyning I: 'I simply think that we all absolutely assumed the therapy—it's unnecessary to say how we all assumed it . . . we were in that climate of absolutely assuming therapy'. The planners were, for a while, *sure* of what they were doing and what they knew, and their knowledge became the basis of the brief. Francis Baden-Powell remembered:

We had psychologists and psychiatrists within the Prison Department. We didn't go outside. There were individual specialists right across the board. The two major elements, I think, in the briefing process were what you might call the security and care side, of which Joanna Kelley, the head of the women's section, was the principal person, and Ian Blyth, who was the doctor [the Senior Medical Officer at Holloway], who was the chief medical adviser on all medical aspects.

The written product of those meetings, known as the Steyning Brief, was formally accepted as the 'basic planning document' by the Project Group at its meeting on 17 February 1970. It provided bold, concrete justifications, specifications and instructions for the work that had to be done. The provenance and legitimacy of the Steyning Brief were taken to be so sound, and its directives so explicit, that it remained in force as a durable master plan and charter for the Holloway project for five years. In this sense, it came to act as the source of a second grand narrative for shaping action. Reference would be made repeatedly to the Steyning Brief as an authority and warrant for action. Indeed, it was only when the world of crime and criminals was thought spectacularly to have changed in the mid-1970s that it was revised. Let me attempt to summarise its ingredients, drawing, where necessary, on the minor refinements and amendments that were added by the project committees and others over the next few months.

The New Regime

The guiding assumptions infusing the new regime were that the large majority of offenders were psychologically or emotionally unstable or socially inadequate rather than criminal; most offenders were young; most would be short-stay visitors; and imprisonment for women might itself be abolished altogether in the future and replaced by attendance centres.[37]

[37] Holloway Redevelopment: Stage C Report, 11 Sept. 1970.

It was said that it would probably be best if such women were not sent to prison at all. Therapy there was always handicapped by problems of compulsion, resentment and an artificial milieu. Joanna Kelley reflected that 'I don't think you can really help them in prisons and I think probably [helping them] should be divorced from punishment really'. In time to come, it was argued, Holloway might well relinquish its role as a prison and be passed over to the National Health Service as a hospital. Its status and function were provisional. It was to be a prison for the time being only.

In the meanwhile, the new Holloway was to be a radical institution that would work in an 'entirely different manner from the present Holloway'.[38] It would supply 'a humane environment for the treatment and rehabilitation of women and girls, in contrast to the mainly custodial purposes of the existing buildings'.[39] Some portion of what was proposed for the new regime was left quite deliberately vague, retaining an indefiniteness that would enable the prison and its Governors[40] to respond to contingencies as they arose, to adapt and experiment, to adopt new methods of therapy or discard old ones,[41] 'allowing for developments in medical and psychiatric treatment that, although as yet undefined, are inevitable in the decades that lie ahead'.[42] Such an experimental and responsive regime required buildings that could themselves be ambiguous and flexible in their appearance and use.[43]

What was certain was that the new institution was conceived as an entity that would operate as a whole to rehabilitate women, its emphasis being 'on medical treatment of all kinds and help with social adjustment and community life'.[44] If women had to be incar-

---

[38] D. Faulkner, 'Seminar on Operational Procedures', Sept. 1970.

[39] 'Holloway Redevelopment: Main Establishment Living Accommodation—Stage D Report', Design Team, Apr. 1971, 1.

[40] In her notes for an undated talk given in 1972, the prison's senior psychologist remarked 'whenever an attempt is made to get to grips with detailed plans for the regime of the new establishment, it is pointed out—usually by the S.M.O. [the Senior Medical Officer] . . . that we have no right to impose on the new Governor . . . a predetermined regime'.

[41] Some forms of therapy were ruled out *ab initio*. For example, in Oct. 1972, the prison's Senior Psychologist was most keen to experiment with operant conditioning in a small trial six bedroom dormitory in the new establishment, but there were humanitarian objections to what was proposed, it being ruled that operant conditioning was artificial, manipulative and disagreeable.

[42] '2nd Steyning Conference Report', 2.

[43] See J. Kelley, 'The New Holloway', 8.

[44] Advertisement for the post of Governor of Holloway, *New Society,* 20 July 1972.

cerated at all, it should not be in a conventional prison that worked to sever its inmates from society, confined them within an authoritarian and hierarchical regime created principally for men, and then controlled their every movement. Holloway would be most unconventional. It would integrate rather than isolate, help rather than punish, restore rather than stigmatise (there would be no punishment block, for instance.[45]) The 'new Holloway has been designed to provide an environment as far as possible related to normal life so as to help women to integrate successfully with the outside community after release'.[46]

Holloway would work constructively around three main themes, attending to them in sequence as the prisoner was drawn stage by stage into the life of the establishment: it would deal first with an inmate's immediate domestic and personal problems by giving medical attention and welfare support; it would next supply remedial education, counselling and treatment; and, finally, it would provide a 'community life where she can form relationships within her group and develop her outlook, interest and skills in a way that will materially assist her to "lead a good and useful life" on release'.[47]

That emphasis on community life was important.[48] Mirroring the Henderson Hospital, it was planned to furnish a community within the walls which would mirror the community without, providing 'an environment as far as possible related to normal life to help prisoners integrate with the outside world on release'.[49] Everything attempted would be subordinate to that end, serving the therapeutic principle by diminishing the crippling differences between prison and society (providing that the modest requirements of a minimum degree of

---

[45] 'Holloway Redevelopment Project: First Brief', May 1969.

[46] Home Office Press Notice: 'Holloway Prison to be Rebuilt: New Approach to Women Offenders', 30 Sept. 1970.

[47] Note on Holloway for Dr Summerskill's forthcoming visit, 13 Aug. 1974.

[48] Looking back, David Faulkner, in charge of the project in the early 1970s, said that 'I was . . . fully committed to—then and ever since—to the ideas of normalisation (linked in later discourse to the concepts of justice in prison and legitimacy), and involvement with the community. The design seemed well suited to the notion of what Woolf later called a community prison' (letter of 4 Jan. 1995).

[49] David Faulkner, quoted in the *Sun*, 1 Oct. 1970.

security were not compromised.[50] Differences between prison and society stigmatized and handicapped inmates and prevented their recovery, they kept the deviant and the non-deviant apart, and they symbolized the magnitude of society's disavowal of the criminal. The new Holloway would work strenuously to erode them: 'the new prison was to indicate rejection neither of the public nor by the public, and its image is to be one of healing and care rather than punishment and fear'.[51] The new Holloway would not be an aggressive, forbidding, frightening or separate place whose very appearance proclaimed how dangerous were the people confined within its walls. On the contrary, its looks would be 'reassuring' (a word much used) and ordinary, a prison that did not resemble a prison: 'the buildings should be as informal, as un-prison like and un-institutional as possible'.[52]

Seen from without, the prison would 'present a pleasant external aspect'. Surveyed from within, 'it is important that the physical outlook from all parts of the establishment . . . should be pleasing and relaxing'.[53] Although there would not be unfettered access from outside—penetration into the interior would be limited, security checks would be in place, and visits would be under full surveillance—the outer community would make much greater use of the prison,[54] and the prison the community, so that the two became more open, trusting and accepting in their relations with one another: 'in this way, the psychological barrier represented by the prison wall may be eroded and an increasing sense of public responsibility for social deviants may be expressed by increasing participation in prison affairs'.[55] So transformed would the public character of Holloway become that it would no longer be a matter of shame to record the prison's name on the birth certificates of children born to inmates in the prison, and, instead of sending women in labour to hospitals

[50] Plans for the new regime were not entirely utopian. For instance, the design anticipated the possibility of women attempting to barricade themselves into their rooms and a prototype window was rejected because it would be too vulnerable to vandalism. The problem of windows was, in fact, to plague the future Holloway. But it had been firmly decided by Jan. 1970 that the ethos of the new Holloway could not bear the provisions of Category A security and Category A prisoners should not be sent there.

[51] Joanna Kelley, 'Note on Women Maximum Security Prisoners and their Containment in the Long Term', 25 Feb. 1974.   [52] Ibid.

[53] 'Holloway Redevelopment Project: First Brief', May 1969.

[54] By participating in programmes and using the prison's swimming pool, for instance.   [55] 'Second Steyning Conference Report', 1969, 2.

outside, it was hoped to install a maternity wing inside the new prison hospital. Some women might eventually have keys that would allow them to stay in the prison at night but work in the wider world during the day. They might be joined by their husbands and families who would live with them inside the walls. It was even hoped that, in time, women would start to come to Holloway voluntarily for treatment instead of being sent there against their will by the courts.[56]

Prisoners would enjoy an appreciable degree of liberty in the prison that was not really a prison. They would be able to move about within a secure perimeter, living in a setting not unlike a small village,[57] having access to their cells, and keys to their doors.[58] Control would be exercised lightly. An official wrote: 'another difference in the proposed regime for this new closed prison will be that free movement within the prison area will be allowed to all inmates except where their physical condition precludes this. There will be the minimum of overt supervision and escorting of individuals and parties from place to place.'[59]

Such free movement about the prison was thought to be therapeutic. A visit to Greenwich Hospital, 'a multi-purpose hospital under one roof', had suggested a contrast: whilst patients were confined in hospital for the 'minimum length of time possible', prisoners were confined in one place for lengths of time that have nothing to do with their health. It would be 'highly desirable to have [them] moving from one place to another through the open air.'[60] Just as a small village might have its shops, streets and meeting places clustered around a common or pond, so the facilities of the new Holloway would be laid out around an open green. Ken Neale recollected:

For exercise people could walk around the little green and Joanna's thought was they need not merely just look at walls but they could look into windows. The shops and the hairdressers and the visitors' room would be round the village green as she called it. And there would be walks with trees, leading to

[56] Joanna Kelley, 'The new look at women in prison', Dec. 1970 (unpublished).
[57] In April 1974, an official made the following marginal annotation to a draft of a chapter of a book on Holloway: 'the aim has been to produce in microcosm as far as possible the community life which exists for example in a small town or village outside'.
[58] See the *Daily Telegraph*, 1 Oct. 1970.
[59] Marginal annotation to draft of a book, 4 Apr. 1974.
[60] 'Holloway Redevelopment: Some Points to Consider', undated.

it so it would be like a little town. And the more was talked about this, the more we felt that it was consistent with the overall approach in a constricted site.

Holloway would thus be transformed symbolically and practically, the classifications, isolations, segregations and activities of the radial prison being transmuted into the organic, natural, fluid and all-enveloping life of a therapeutic community. Take some examples. A swimming pool would be built because exercise was necessarily limited in such a confined site and swimming was therapeutic.[61] Work in the prison would be organized therapeutically, no longer called 'occupational work' but 'occupational therapy' and 'work therapy',[62] and it was therapy, not productivity, that would be its goal. The very word 'prison' might eventually be replaced by the less alienating 'hospital';[63] 'Holloway' itself might be re-named to confirm its new beginning, being called Barnersbury, Chanctonbury or Islington Barners perhaps;[64] cells would become bedrooms or bed-sitters;[65] there would be no use of the term 'segregation unit',[66] no strip cells and padded cells, and bars and heavy locks would disappear. Normal punishment was deemed to be incompatible with the ethos of the new prison and no rooms would be reserved specifically for disciplinary offences'[67] (but there would be a half-section of eight rooms for prisoners requiring separation 'at their own request' or on

[61] A letter from a junior Minister to an MP read: 'the swimming pool is not included as a luxury but as an essential feature of the design. The women and girls at Holloway will need adequate exercise not only for their health but also to prevent them from releasing their energy in more destructive ways . . . It would also enable hydro-therapy to be included as part of the establishment's medical, psychiatric and surgical facilities'. 28 Oct. 1970.   [62] Seminar on Operational Procedures, 5 Oct. 1970.

[63] See the *Evening News*, 30 Sept. 1970.

[64] Those names were proposed at the meeting of the Holloway Redevelopment Project Group, 17 Feb. 1970. In the event, discussions about the selection of a new name petered out without conclusion.

[65] An article in a professional journal noted that 'the word "cell" is no longer used at Holloway, preseumably as . . . a reflection of the new "treatment not punishment" philosophy'. 'Holloway: planned maintenance in a rebuilt prison', *Buildings Maintenance and Services*, Oct. 1978, 13.

[66] Minutes of Meeting of the Group on the Redevelopment of Holloway, 1st Apr. 1969.

[67] On 8 May 1972, the written answer given to a Parliamentary Question about accommodation for disciplinary purposes in the new Holloway was: 'rooms will be available in the hospital if a woman has to be isolated for any purpose. Women in these rooms will be under medical supervision at all times. There will be no rooms reserved specifically for disciplinary purposes.

the Governor's instructions and one unit for 'deeply disturbed and aggressive women').

An authoritarian system that imposed a rank uniformity on its subjects and herded them about in large expanses, would thereby give way to a social order that fostered the independence of inmates who could grow in small personal spaces. Thus the inmates' bedrooms and living quarters would be afforded 'as great a variety of outlook and orientation . . . as possible, to give individuality . . . for each individual'.[68] The notes prepared for the nominated architect's description of the scheme read that the new prison was to be 'organized, but not authoritarian (not symmetrical)'.[69] There would no longer be the radial prison's domineering Centre[70] ('as such'[71]), and, in place of long wings and straight, intimidating sight-lines, there would be a more 'natural' environment of family-like groups living organically in a zig-zag chain of small self-sufficient units housing some sixteen occupants.

A changed building would be matched by a changed moral and social order, the informality of the new architecture being reflected in the looseness of organization that the therapeutic community would impose on the once sharply-defined and rigidly-separate social structures of Holloway. Prisoners once divided by legal status, offence and sentence would be redefined as members of 'psycho and socio-therapeutic groups irrespective of sentence, remand, legal or criminal status'.[72] The former differences between staff, between nurses and discipline officers, professionals and non-professionals, would dissolve within the totality of a multi-disciplinary team.[73]

[68] 'Holloway Redevelopment: Main Establishment Living Accommodation—Stage D Report', 4.
[69] Draft notes for description of the scheme at the Press Conference on 30th Sept. 1970.
[70] Although there would be other rooms, such as a communications room and a regulating office to perform some of the services of the Centre.
[71] Notes to be read in conjunction with the Annotated 'Existing Procedures' Sheets, 1972.
[72] I. Blyth, 'A Regime for the New Holloway', unpublished, 20 Apr. 1971.
[73] Joanna Kelley wrote of a 'bold experiment in staff management, where all disciplines, medical, educational, welfare, psychiatric, nursing and discipline work together as a team under a joint manager'. 'The new look at women in prison', Dec. 1970.

Instead of relying chiefly on direct coercion and surveillance, Holloway would work through the informal mechanisms of a self-regulating community[74] and the mobilization of personal influence, through prisoner helping prisoner, and staff helping prisoner, freely in couples and groups. Joanna Kelley remarked that 'in the design of the new Holloway, we tried to make it possible for people not only to have as many choices as they wanted, as we could manage, but also to have as many one-to-one relationships as we could achieve, because that's the way in which most people are [helped]'. Those helping relationships would themselves be stabilized and anchored in the groups and community constituting the prison, and it was that idea of the group that was to become paramount, the key to the working of the whole.

Groups would be used in versatile fashion: for mothers with their babies; for medical units or the practice of psychotherapy; for work; for community living and 'learning to form relationships'; or for 'more permissive regimes where practise can be given in taking responsibility and behaving in a mature and sensible manner'.[75] The group would be, in part, surrogate family, and 'individual small family groups' would serve as agents of re-socialization, friendship[76] and conflict resolution, furnishing a co-operative milieu in which women, all too often lonely or incompetent, learned how to live with one another again.[77] It was recorded in speaking notes prepared for a press conference in September 1970, that there was a 'need to learn to live in a group and in a community (family—work). So small units and as much freedom as possible, but in secure conditions.'

The prison itself would be rebuilt as a network of groups, some formal, some informal, and some *ad hoc*, of the kind that 'gather immediately on the spot when dispute or fracas occurs'.[78] Function-

[74] It is interesting, for instance, that in a Seminar on Operational procedures held on 5 Oct. 1970, it was argued that, if large numbers of people were to flow freely about the new prison, an appreciable quantity of clocks would have to be installed. Inmates would then freely and individually co-ordinate their movements by observing the disciplines of clock time rather than simply obey orders or follow the movements of officers.

[75] 'Holloway Redevelopment: News Bulletin Number 3', Dec. 1971, 1.

[76] See P. Evans, 'Bedsitters in new Holloway', *The Times*, 1 Oct. 1970.

[77] The model to be followed was that of the psychiatric prison at Grendon Underwood and psychiatric hospitals such as St Bernard's, both institutions having been visited by Holloway staff undergoing retraining.

[78] 'Occupational Therapist's Report', 2 Oct. 1970.

ally, I have noted, Holloway was planned as a sequence of operations, experiences and practices, and the whole was charted as an
interlocking set of regimes to be laid down in all those different
groups. The establishment would be divided roughly between the
greater hospital and the lesser prison which, working together,
would supply the stages and settings of a broad therapeutic career
for prisoners over the length of their sentences. The Senior Medical
Officer proposed the 'setting up of therapeutic units of varying
degrees of rigidity/permissive application, each started by a Functional Group Working Team, so that patients/prisoners requiring a
variety of regimes by virtue to their innate pathology, can benefit
from the appropriate therapy with advantage for their rehabilitation
into society'.[79]

Rehabilitation would take the form of a moral career, a 'progressive flow', from diagnosis and testing; to hospital treatment
only; to day hospital treatment (that is living and sleeping in the
prison but attending the hospital during the day); to a prison regime
only, preparatory to release. The ideal pattern would be a straight
and smooth progression from hospital to prison to outside, but it
was understood that there would be lapses in which prisoners would
fall away: 'the inmate may be unable to cope with the stress in the
prison setting and require the more gentle environment of the
hospital'.[80]

In effect and appearance, then, the new Holloway was designed as
a therapeutic continuum, closely resembling a Monopoly board, in
which inmates would advance unit by unit, square by square, through
treatment suites, alcohol withdrawal suites, alcohol rehabilitation
suites, and all the other units arranged in a chain around the
perimeter until they reached the 'Go' of release or fell back to 'go
to jail' (but of course, being in jail already, it was to hospital that they
would be sent).

[79] I. Blyth, 'A Regime for the New Holloway', 5.
[80] 'Inmate Treatment: Regime and Treatment Objectives—Patterns of Treatment',
undated.

The Prison as Hospital

Holloway would be a hybrid, certainly not a recognizable prison,[81] perhaps more hospital than prison,[82] what was envisaged being standardly described at the end of the 1960s as a 'medically-orientated establishment'.[83] A central part of the new buildings would be a conventional hospital for the treatment of physical and psychiatric ailments but, much more important, it was presumed that the whole edifice would become a therapeutic institution on the model, said Joanna Kelley, of 'the Tavistock and the Henderson—that is really exactly what the patterns in our minds for it were'.[84] Holloway would not only offer group counselling, group therapy, therapy to confront alcoholism and drug dependency, individual psychiatric therapy, electro-convulsive therapy and psycho-drama, but 'psychiatrists are in general agreement that the regime is also a form of therapy in that it conditions the inmate to better habits'.[85] It was said that inmates would require medical care and they would require social retraining, and both modes of treatment would be supplied by the physical and moral structure of the same establishment.

It was quite commonplace to proceed as if Holloway would be a hospital working closely with the National Health Service,[86] exchanging patients with the special hospitals, training nurses for the hospital service at large, perhaps even ultimately being handed over entire and 'with pride'[87] to the National Health Service. Those who administered various areas of the old Holloway took it that they were no longer destined to be the staff of an ordinary prison, and they changed orientation and language as they planned for the new. For instance, amongst many similar submissions listing the future needs of the new institution, the head pharmacist of Holloway wrote in

---

[81] In 1992, the Chief Inspector of Prisons observed that 'the design was similar to that of many hospitals and quite unlike that generally found in prisons new or old'. *HM Prison Holloway: Report by H.M. Chief Inspector of Prisons*, (London: Home Office, 1992), 13.

[82] Joanna Kelley said that the new establishment might well be called Holloway Hospital. See *The Times*, 15 May 1971.

[83] See, for example, *People in Prison*, Cmnd. 4214 (London: HMSO, 1969), 62.

[84] The Prison Department's Principal Psychologist noted in a memorandum of Jan. 1969 to P4 that 'the treatment of individual needs . . . must be carried out within the context of, and with reference to, a general community-based philosophy of treatment (c.f. the treatment of non-convicted sociopaths in mental hospitals such as Henderson and Claybury'.)   [85] '2nd Steyning Conference Report', 1969, 19.

[86] See *Treatment of Women and Girls in Custody*, (London: Home Office, 1970), 6.

[87] Dr Blyth, Senior Medical Officer at Holloway, in *The Times*, 22 May 1972.

April 1969 that he was acting 'on the assumption that the new establishment will be more in the nature of a psychiatric hospital than a prison', and the Deputy Director of Industries and Stores wrote to Joanna Kelley in December 1969 to sat that 'we understand the new Holloway is to be in effect a hospital'.

The Treasury certainly considered Holloway as much hospital as prison. In September 1969, it accepted that, instead of working to conventional prison costings (using Full Sutton prison as a pattern), Holloway's hospital accommodation would be estimated on the basis of the more expensive Department of Health and Social Security prices for hospital construction. So it was that the Treasury permitted the dimension of inmates' rooms to be those of hospital rooms, not of smaller prison cells;[88] and Holloway's heating standards to be the warmer conditions of hospitals.[89] Whenever new guideline figures were negotiated between the Treasury and the Department (and they were negotiated frequently in the inflationary years of the 1970s), they would be automatically applied to the budget for the reconstruction of Holloway itself.

What lay before the planners above all was the example of Greenwich District Hospital, a redevelopment project under construction at very much the same time. Begun in late 1962, with a building timetable of eleven years, Greenwich became a clear precedent and prototype.[90] Ken Neale reported to the Project Group that:

It is appropriate to record the debt which we owe to the senior architectural staff of the design and development group in the Ministry of Health. They have not only provided the services of one of their senior members . . . but have provided much valuable information in a practical way by visits to their own redevelopment project at Greenwich and to Holloway. . . The problems which they have been resolving at Greenwich are comparable with many of those which confront us at Holloway.[91]

Under the guidance of that senior architect from the Minsitry of Health, the larger planning process of Holloway followed that of

---

[88] Ken Neale wrote to the Treasury in December 1969, 'it may be of help if we say that the rooms in the prison were based on the same area, design and construction as those in the hospital to maintain the principle of maximum flexibility'.

[89] Minutes of Holloway Project Team Meeting, 22 Jan. 1971.

[90] Ken Neale recalled that 'we took several decisions. One was that, because it was to be a therapeutically-orientated establishment, we would look at a lot of NHS hospitals, including Greenwich, which was then a new one.'

[91] 'Holloway Redevelopment Project: Progress Report No 1', March 1969.

Greenwich step by step. Both projects involved simultaneous demolition and building, and both were organized into discrete phases that would allow 'the uninterrupted use of the greater part of the [institution] throughout the period of construction'.[92] Both were planned functionally, as were most complex buildings of the time, moving conceptually from use to structure.[93] Both adopted a plan that distributed the main functional areas of the building around the perimeter, leaving open spaces in the centre 'to avoid the possible monotony of a totally internal environment'.[94] Both resorted to the design solution of a principal horizontal thoroughfare, called the 'street', for the physical movement and visual guidance of people and goods around the building. In Greenwich, 'the wards are on the outside walls, and on the first and second floors form a continuous band around the building'.[95] It would be just so with Holloway. And both projects allowed some indeterminacy of design to accommodate unanticipated changes in future patterns of use.

Holloway mimicked Greenwich even in small matters. The design of the staff quarters at the new Holloway was based on that at Greenwich (Prison Officers Association representatives having visited nurses' accommodation at Greenwich Hospital in June 1969); and there was to be discussion about building a day nursery for the children of staff at Holloway on the model of Greenwich.

Designing the Buildings: General Assumptions

1: 'Panopticon gives way to central open space'[96]

The projected numbers and composition of the new prison's population varied from estimate to estimate over the years. At the beginning, it was thought that the new prison would house some 400 women in the 1970s, rising progressively to 560 by the year 2000. Using a working figure of 500 women in the new Holloway, P4 computed that there would be some 180 in the hospital (and 200 prisoner 'outpatients'), 200 in a remand allocation centre and 120 in the prison

---

[92] 'Greenwich District Hospital: A Development Project of the Department of Health and Social Security in Conjunction with the South East Metropolitan Regional Hospital Board', undated, 4.
[93] Minutes of Holloway Project Team Meeting, 10 Sept. 1969.
[94] 'Greenwich District Hospital: A Development Project', 9.   [95] Ibid.
[96] From the architects' slide show on the Holloway Redevelopment, known locally within the Project Group as the 'Child's Guide'.

HOLLOWAY REDEVELOPMENT

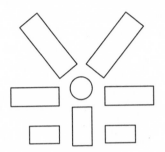

purpose mainly
theraputic not
custodial...

...hence...

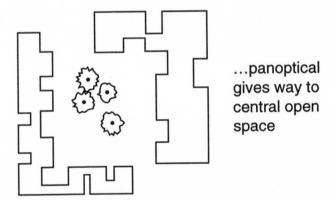

...panoptical
gives way to
central open
space

Figure 4.1 *Architectural Sketch of the Planned Transformation of Holloway Prison*

unit. Of those, perhaps 30 would be members of the mother and baby unit; 30 'borstal recalls'; 60 prisoners in a psychiatric unit; 30 drug addicts and alcoholics; 30 'disturbed patients'; and 30 physically ill patients.[97]

[97] Based on 'Group on the Re-Development of Holloway: Projected Population, Note by Secretary', 9 Aug. 1968.

The architects knew that they had embarked on a venture without clear bearings or precedents: 'the feeling was that we should not be too influenced by what was going on elsewhere, we should reach new solutions . . . a brand new idea, a brand new solution'. And the very largest of those new ideas was that the second Holloway should be a dialectical inversion of the first, a response that would be its very negation, a systematic rejection of the old that turned the radial prison inside out.

The architects designed an institution that would not threaten inmates or public, that would not be custodial but therapeutic, that would not be authoritarian but communitarian ('the traditional prison plan has star shape with dominant control centre. Holloway will have community green as its focus'[98]), and that would be experienced as a place as little 'claustophobic as possible'.[99] They would rid Holloway of the very feeling of a prison ('for instance, the appearance of the Gate which was not like a traditional prison Gate House, there was not a formal facade and the architects had tried to provide a glimpse of the open space and landscaping for people entering the establishment'[100]). And they would further reduce the formal, institutional appearance of the building by breaking down the long lengths of corridor that typified a conventional Victorian prison. In short, theirs was to be prison that was not really a prison, that should not look or work like an ordinary prison, that should not cut its inmates off but would reintegrate them with the world around the walls. The architect principally involved, Francis Baden-Powell, declared:

The idea of the whole thing was to turn the panopticon[101] design inside out and create at the centre of the whole thing space, which represented the . . . therapeutic quality of the whole building. And we were able to do that conveniently because we could actually convert and gradually remove existing buildings on site so that the middle was a hive of activity while we were building around the perimeter.

[98] Holloway Redevelopment Project: Draft notes for [architect's] description of the scheme at the Press Conference on 30 Sept. 1970.
[99] Meeting held at the Nominated Architects with Representatives of the BBC, 13 Aug. 1976.   [100] *Ibid.*
[101] Strictly speaking, of course, the radial design of Holloway was not modelled after Bentham's panopticon at all. But the word 'panopticon' does seem to be employed ever more frequently to refer to any prisons with a strong centre and effective surveillance.

Let me relate the logic of that inversion step by step, employing a number of captions used publicly at a press conference in the architects' own slide show[102] and reproduced here, to explain the principles employed in the design of the project (I have already reproduced the first caption which signalled how the panopticon would give way to central open space). I shall proceed carefully and in the knowledge that this logic was to produce a cluster of features that came to generate very particular problems when the buildings were first occupied. The features will be listed here and their consequences discussed later, in their proper place in Chapter 8.

2: 'Elimination of wall, making buildings in wall where possible and pushing them to the edge of the site.'

Stringent security was not of paramount importance at first. It was not thought to be specially required for women[103] and the old Holloway was to be demolished precisely because its excessive security had become an obstacle to effective treatment.[104] The papers for Steyning I did contemplate a prison population of 120 convicted and sentenced prisoners with a maximum security unit for 20, the minimum viable number for such a unit, but it was concluded at Steyning II that there could not be provision for such a large number of Category A prisoners. The presence of a maximum security unit would have been an irritant that could work only to distort the ethos and management of the new establishment. All that would be retained was a scant provision for a 'special security suite' for four Category A remand prisoners.

Although there would be night patrols, alarm systems and a direct protected telephone line to Scotland Yard (it never having been supposed that Holloway would be an Erewhon), security in the new establishment was nevertheless intended to be slight and unobtrusive. There would be no dogs and dog-handlers, no floodlighting, no closed circuit television and no electronic surveillance at Holloway ('too reminiscent of Big Brother'[105]). With the exaggeration characteristic of hindsight, it was said afterwards in 1974 that 'security was a minimal consideration and the training and treatment of women

---

[102] I shall not necessarily follow the captions in the same sequence as the architects did themselves.   [103] See *People in Prison*, 61.
[104] See D. Faulkner, 'The Redevelopment of Holloway Prison', 122.
[105] See the *Guardian*, 25 Jan. 1971.

prisoners should be broadly analogous to that received in a civilian psychiatric hospital with modern design and modern facilities'.[106]

At the outset, in 1968, the boundary between the prison and the outer world was expected mainly to be 'a protection for the inmates against curious juveniles penetrating the establishment'.[107] Thereafter, the classification of perimeter security continued to be low (it declined from 'minus Category B'[108] in August 1969 to Category C in January 1970,[109] for example). What security there was would be entrusted principally to the close personal supervision and surveillance exercised by staff *within* the perimeter, and to the special position and alignment of the prison buildings[110] *as* the perimeter itself.

Prison buildings formed about half the defensive rim of Holloway. Where no building could act as part of the secure perimeter, there would be a wall, but it would have to be a wall that did not unsettle and displease those who saw it. Consider one section of that wall, a special 'curvy' wall 'built of brick [that] snakes a sinuous path along the boundary and is a marvellous example of the bricklayer's art. . . . Apparently, the curved plan gives rigidity to the wall and, by avoiding corners, is an efficient barrier to would-be escapers. It also is less monotonous to the eye.'[111] Ken Neale said:

We didn't say we wanted it to look like a hospital. We did it rather the opposite way, what we said . . . we want it to look as little like a prison as possible. I remember making a bit of thing about the wall, which is why you've got a curvy wall there. I remember saying to the architects, 'let's think about the perimeter. It's not a high security perimeter. We don't want a prison wall in the ordinary sense and at this stage just think up any solution you can to make a secure perimeter without the wall'.

The architect of that wall, Francis Baden-Powell, said:

Seen from outside [it] was not too threatening—rather like the one at the University of Virginia at Charlottesville—that was for a completely different

---

[106] Note for Chairman of Project Team, 22 Oct. 1974.

[107] Joanna Kelley, 'Note on Maximum Security Prisoners and their Containment in the Long Term', 25 Feb. 1974.

[108] Note of a Meeting held at the Treasury on 7 Aug. 1969.

[109] Minutes of the Holloway Project Team Meeting, 22 January 1970.

[110] See J. Camp, *Holloway Prison*, (Newton Abbot: David and Charles, 1974), 153. That was not an arrangement without precedent. For instance, it was a feature of the design of the Michigan State Penitentiary at Jackson, opened in 1926.

[111] Draft item for *Lovell Link 21*, 5 Aug. 1976.

purpose—but they are a very relaxed idea. If the wall wanders about, you get light and shade on it and it doesn't feel so threatening. Now that is important inside because of the inmate's view of it, but it's also important outside because it makes the people outside feel that it is less of a repressive wall.

The elimination of the high, straight conventional prison wall would work a double effect. By pushing buildings out to the border, it would maximize the use of space in a small site and make the prison that was not really a prison look even less like a prison. To be sure, the perimeter buildings did have to continue to work as an effective barrier. They could not be designed to look as if they were simply part of any familar domestic or institutional structure: for example, they had to be higher than a man (or woman) standing on top of a pantechnicon (the standard specification that had been laid down since Ronnie Biggs's escape); and they could contain no vulnerable windows or doors, no areas shielded from inspection, no hiding places or convenient parapets, no footholds and no canopies on to which women could climb.

3 and 4: 'The road frontage is treated as a linear park which neighbours are encouraged to use.'
'The treatment of the frontage to Camden Road and the gate contains as many indications of normal life as possible: chapels, swimming pool, hall, officers' training centre'

The secure boundary of the prison that was not really a prison was intended to be as reassuring as possible, a boundary that would not mark a great separation between social worlds, but a structure that would act instead to knit them together. Symbolically, it would 'break down some of the traditional barriers between a penal establishment and the ordinary community'.[112] Physically, the main façade of the frontage to Camden Road would consist of an 'informal run of distinct buildings . . . set well back in part . . . [with a] comprehensible sight of "normal" buildings inside'.[113] The recurrent emphasis was on the sheer visual normality of the new façade. Instead of the terror and brute power conveyed by the castellated walls of the grim fortress, the new prison would look comfortably ordinary, unassuming, perhaps almost banal: 'the treatment of the frontage and the gate

---

[112] Draft reply to letter from Member of Parliament, April 1972.
[113] Draft notes for [architect's] description of the scheme . . .

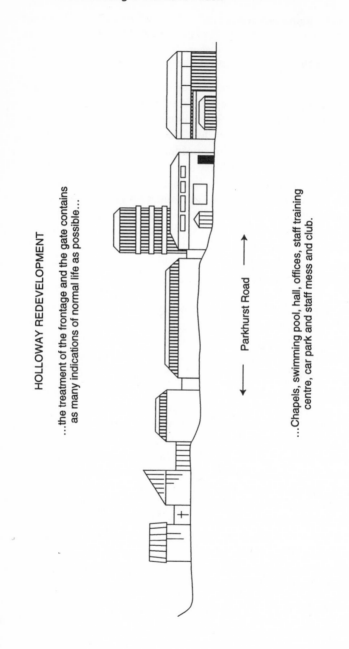

HOLLOWAY REDEVELOPMENT

...the treatment of the frontage and the gate contains as many indications of normal life as possible....

← Parkhurst Road →

...Chapels, swimming pool, hall, offices, staff training centre, car park and staff mess and club.

Figure 4.2 Architectural Sketch of the Planned Transformation of Holloway Prison

HOLLOWAY REDEVELOPMENT

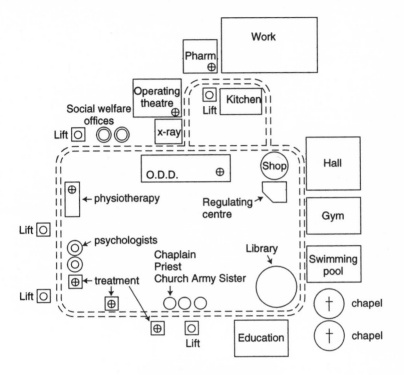

the trolley route becomes the
'village high street': all facilities
used by staff and inmates are
along it, thus everyone becomes
quickly aware of the various
activities and services available

Figure 4.3 *Architectural Sketch of the Planned Transformation of Holloway
Prison*

contain as many indications of normal life as possible'.[114] It was to
'be as informal and reassuring as possible'.[115]

Entry to the prison would no longer be experienced by inmates as a
great passage, a fateful and anxious crossing of a threshold into a

---

[114] 'Holloway Redevelopment: News Bulletin Number 3', Dec. 1971.
[115] 'Holloway Redevelopment', Summer 1972.

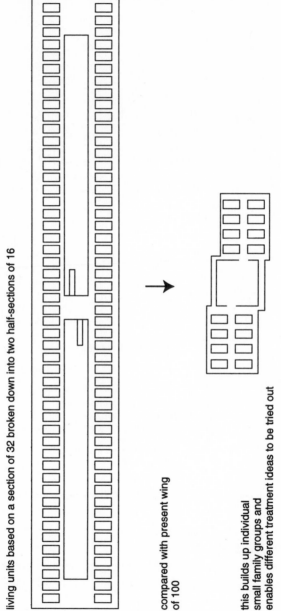

HOLLOWAY REDEVELOPMENT

living units based on a section of 32 broken down into two half-sections of 16

compared with present wing of 100

this builds up individual small family groups and enables different treatment ideas to be tried out

Figure 4.4 Architectural Sketch of the Planned Transformation of Holloway Prison

total institution, but a transition that would be 'un-dramatise[d] . . . pleasant and informal. . . . Some of the tension [would be removed] by giving a reassuring view of the central open space and living accommodation beyond.'[116] The architects even proposed that windows in the prison buildings should not have 'nonretractable' venetian blinds because they would have looked too much like prison bars.

The effect of removing the strong boundaries and clear insignia of a conventional prison was that the prison that was not really a prison did not look much like a prison at all.[117] A journalist wrote in 1982, 'I very nearly missed it altogether. Head down against the rain, had I not chanced to look up and notice a small HM Prison car park sign, I would never have guessed that this low, modern red-brick building was the front to Britain's best known women's prison.'[118]

5, 6 and 7: 'Slope of the site used to give view out from living accommodation, over daytime space.'
'Daytime activities near noisy road, protecting quieter living accommodation.'
'Residential areas specially staff, as close to other residential areas as possible.'

It was recognized that the continual traffic noise flowing from Parkhurst and Camden Roads, the busy streets that skirted the front of the prison, would have troubled the inhabitants of what was a residential institution, and the staff and inmate quarters were pushed back to the quieter part of the site near Crayford and Carleton Roads, the ordinary residential streets to the rear. The quarters were to be placed at the very edge of the site directly abutting those streets, designed to look as little like prison buildings as possible.

The prison was not to be shielded, concealed and segregated, treated as a shameful thing to be hidden away out of sight, as its predecessor had been. Its cells were not to be clustered in the middle of the site, away from the walls and the prying eyes of outsiders. The absence of a high 'forbidding external wall'[119] and the positioning of buildings

---

[116] Design Team, 'Holloway Redevelopment: Phase 4 & 5, Stage C Report, October 1973', 4.

[117] And in that, Holloway was not the only women's prison to be designed to look as if it were other than a jail. See, for instance, Rose Giallombardo's observations about Alderson in *Society of Women*, (New York: John Wiley, 1966), 23 or C. Mann, *Female Crime and Delinquency*, 192.

[118] G. Hudson, 'Behind Prison Walls', *Home and Country*, Oct. 1982, 12.

[119] D. Faulkner, 'The Redevelopment of Holloway Prison', 124.

with normal windows at the very boundary brought it about that staff and prisoners were invited to look out (and, presumably, outsiders were encouraged to look in[120]). There were to be views from the prison's living accommodation on to the surrounding district,[121] and 'across London, not straight onto another prison building'.[122] Francis Baden-Powell recalled:

[There were windows] actually within the residential buildings themselves which were of course entirely within this perimeter wall, so that it meant that within single room where an inmate would be, there was a bay window, and virtually all the rooms had these bay windows, and they could actually sit in the window and feel that they were almost outside but still they would be restrained.

8 and 9: 'Main internal circulation is a ring route used by pedestrians and trolleys.'
'The trolley routes becomes the village high street: all facilities used by staff and inmates are along it'

I have already touched on the village green that would be bounded by the 'high street' of perimeter buildings. The green, planted with trees and shrubs, would convey an impression of openness and freedom at the core of the new prison, an agreeable prospect that negated the very principle of the radial prison, but would yet be subject to close surveillance by officers positioned in the 'regulating centre' near the gate. There would be a happy blend of liberty and discreet control symbolic of the prison as a whole. Women would no longer be imprisoned within great barrack-like wings dominated by a controlling Centre. Their living units would be small and home-like, scattered around a campus[123] in a ribbon of dwellings resembling a familiar, twisting street. Indeed, the campus analogy was close. Recall that the architects had previously designed the University of York, and Lucia Zedner, a graduate of that university, said 'York . . . also used "covered walk-ways" as a circulation route around the campus from one facility to the next'.

---

[120] I shall argue in Ch. 8 that the designers had not considered fully the prospect of the prison being overlooked: an Assistant Secretary noted in Sept. 1971, 'we had thought about inmates looking out but we had forgotten about neighbouring flats now being built looking in. People are always curious about prisons. It could become a peepshow.'   [121] Ibid, 131.

[122] J. Tweedie, 'Prison Breakthrough', the Guardian, undated.

[123] 'Campus' was the word often used to describe the prison.

In the civilian world, people arise every morning and leave their homes to go to work, pray, shop or visit the library. It would be just so in Holloway. Inmates would travel the footpaths crossing the green and along the trolley route as they went about their everyday affairs. The prison rehearsed the routines of civil society in its effort to build a community within the walls. The openness of its design was supposed to convey the openness of the regime. Its domesticity would counter institutionalism. Joanna Kelley said:

We wanted community and we wanted it not to be, as far as we could avoid it, institutional, so the original Holloway which was an institution like a workhouse or a hospital, we wanted to break that down. And yet you had to keep the people contained within the perimeter. It seemed to us that you could best achieve that by having, as it were, a village with a green in the middle, and then different (as you do in a village) very different people living in the different houses, living according to the house and yet, from the security point of view, keep within the perimeter

10 and 11: 'Living units based on a section of 32 broken down into two half-sections of 16. Compare with present wing of 100. This builds up individual in small family group and enables different treatment ideas to be tried out.'
'Units are linked together with buffer zones giving some flexibility of size of unit.'

The accommodation on the village street could be likened to a zig-zag series of paired living units (known as 'half-sections') that followed a serpentine path around the perimeter of the prison. (Indeed, the irregular route of the buildings was to be made more irregular still by the addition of a kink introduced by the architects to make the whole fit into the site when the perimeter had to be adjusted to respond to the needs of a Greater London Council road-widening scheme.) Composed of single or 'four-bedded' rooms, half-sections were the basic elements of the new prison. Groups of sixteen women would live intimately within their small domestic spaces, coming together in the quasi-familial groupings that were indispensable to the practice of therapeutic change.[124]

The village street was to have been laid out as a therapeutic

---

[124] See L. Fairweather, 'Prison Architecture in England', *British Journal of Criminology*, 1961, Vol. 1, No. 1, 359.

continuum, the physical embodiment of a moral career, that took women through 'psycho-diagnostic' units, to psycho-therapeutic units to prison and then, perhaps, to out-patient treatment,[125] the whole being 'joined together to form a continuous string of living accommodation graduating from purely hospital type at one end to entirely non-medical at the other'.[126] David Faulkner recalled that 'the intention was to go from relatively high supervision and low care at one end to low supervision and high care at the other'.

The supervision of each half-section was to be performed by staff moving about or stationed in offices and surveying prisoners through glazed walls. Each section was to be separate and lockable for security purposes and each would be divided from the next by a buffer zone that could be adapted to very different uses. Such intervening, uncommitted space offered useful external areas to which inmates could become attached.[127] They broke up large, possibly threatening spaces into lesser expanses and enhanced the diversity of a potentially monotonous place. Francis Baden-Powell, the architect, said:

The idea was that either as a unit of 20 or 40 it could operate as a separate sort of family group, each of which would have its own nucleus and have a certain range of single rooms. . . . And we wanted to get away from these very long corridors and from the great gallery impression you get in the wings of the existing building. So we designed it so that there were always short lengths of corridor which were staggered in various ways so that people didn't feel overawed by the vast environment.

Conclusion

The design of the new Holloway was original.[128] It was the attempt of experienced penal practitioners and architects versed in educa-

---

[125] See D. Faulkner, 'The Redevelopment of Holloway Prison', 129.

[126] Draft article for *Lovell Link 21*, 5 Aug. 1976.

[127] '2nd Steyning Conference Report', 20.

[128] But not unique: it is interesting that what was done at Holloway was also to be closely followed at Cornton Vale in Scotland, for example. Both charted a therapeutic career, both emphasized small units, (there were units of seven in Cornton Vale to 'enable a family or group atmosphere to be created' ('Report of the Working Party on the Treatment and Training of Female Inmates in Scotland', n.d., 2.). There was a working connection between the design of the two prisons. Joanna Kelley observed 'there was a . . . close relationship between P4 Project team and Cornton Vale. I visited it (or Greenwich) each year, discussed our common areas of concern with the Scottish Office and the governor. Members of the Scottish Office visited P4 and discussed everything about the Holloway project with Ken Neale or David Faulkner.'

tional design to produce the very converse of the old radial prison. The new Holloway was a schematic repudiation of the old. The wings and their centre were turned inside out: where there had been a controlling hub, there would be an empty green; where there had been constraint and surveillance, there would be freedom; where there had been great, intimidating spaces, there would be small, intimate areas; the high, forbidding boundary of the total institution was to become a mundane and reassuring perimeter; what had been separate would become integrated; and where there had been punishment, there would be healing. In short, the terrifying symbolism of the old was to be replaced by the comfortable ordinariness of the new. In the chapters to come I shall examine how that scheme was to work in practice.

5

Metamorphosis I: The Physical Reconstruction of Holloway

'Experience of Holloway highlights the difficulty of complete rebuilding while a prison remains operational and at a time of substantial increase in inmate population. In retrospect it would have been much quicker to build on a virgin site, had we possessed one.'[1]

Introduction

The Project Group's predictions of how long the redevelopment of Holloway might take varied over the years. It was accepted that it would be a particularly difficult and uncertain enterprise, involving not only demolition and construction but all the additional, unforeseen problems that might arise from attempting the two tasks in the one place at the same time. It was evident that the project would resolve itself into a vulnerable and elaborate system of interdependencies. Demolition work on one portion could not start without compensatory construction work on another, and the planners wanted there to be no 'hiatuses'.[2] Lord Stonham said that, 'in scale alone, the project compares with anything so far tackled in the penal field in this country'.[3]

A number of dates for completing the project were aired at the very beginning (1973,[4] 1974,[5] 1975 and 1976[6] were all suggested on different occasions). But the working deadline first generally

[1] Brief for meeting with Minister, 23 Apr. 1980.
[2] Minutes of the Holloway Project Team Meeting, 22 Jan. 1970.
[3] Speech by Lord Stonham at the Annual Day Conference on the Future Treatment of Women Offenders, 12 Apr. 1969.   [4] See the *Daily Express*, 17 Dec. 1968.
[5] That date was given as late as 1971 in 'Holloway Redevelopment—Phasing Moves—Appointment of New Governor', Note by Secretary, 23 Nov. 1971.
[6] Thus, the nominated architect's letter of appointment, dated 2 July 1969, referred to construction ending in mid-1976 and 1976 was the date given by the architects in a number of meetings thereafter (for example, the Minutes of the Holloway Project Team Meeting of 11 Nov. 1970).

acknowledged in the planning of the new Holloway was a decade, the magic number of ten years having been the period fixed for the fulfilment of *Prison Policy: Women and Girls*. Ken Neale wrote in early 1969 that 'the decade in which we set ourselves to complete this project and the full implementation of the new policy for women and girls, of which it is the central feature, expires at the end of 1978'.[7] As time passed and early meetings confirmed what had to be done, the deadline was allowed to fall in 1977, just before the expiration of the decade. 1977, however, was certainly the date that the Treasury was given in a meeting with the Home Office in August 1969, and it was the date most frequently cited thereafter.[8] 1977 became a beacon before the planners.

Phasing

The fall of the old prison and the rise of the new were to be synchronized. There was to be a carefully directed movement, a phased reconstruction, that entailed destroying the old radial prison piece by piece until it occupied half the site whilst the new anti-panopticon grew up on the other half. What was called the 'operating' prison would have to contract, performing all or nearly all of its existing functions within a progressively reducing space, and it would then gradually expand again as it decanted its population of staff and inmates into the new quarters. The architects' own working assumptions in choreographing the project were clear: there could be 'no contortion of final result because of rebuilding problems'; there would be 'interim use to permit new regimes as far as possible', and 'demolition and rebuilding will proceed anti-clockwise in distinct phases'.[9]

It is important to describe the structure of planned phases that came to dominate the future course and character of the project. The record of the Holloway redevelopment project was, above all, a history of its phases. Demolition began in October 1970, but, with greater symbolic potency, the first breach in the walls was made later

---

[7] 'Holloway Redevelopment Project, Project Report No. 1', Mar. 1969.
[8] It was given out in a press notice on 30 Sept. 1970, for example.
[9] Draft notes for [architect's] description of the scheme at the Press Conference on 30th Sept. 1970.

before massed photographers on 11 January 1971.[10] Thereafter, Holloway was to be redeveloped step by step.

At the first, in that opening month of January 1971, it was anticipated that Phase 1, entailing the destruction of the old staff quarters, the jam factory, part of the hospital and a small portion of the perimeter wall, and the construction of new staff quarters, would be complete by September 1973. Phase 2 was to have begun in January 1972 with the demolition of A, B and E Wings, the workshops and the Roman Catholic Chapel and the construction of most of the new prisoners' accommodation by the end of 1974. Phase 3, beginning at the end of 1972 and planned to end by the middle of 1974, involved the demolition of the staff hostel, mess and club and the construction of new education buildings, the chapels and gymnasium and swimming pool. Phase 4, beginning in mid-1974 and scheduled to end in mid-1976, would bring about the destruction of the office block, the gate, F and K Wings, the works and maintenance area and the remainder of the staff quarters on Parkhurst Road, and the construction of the new gate, administration block, workshops, visiting facilities, staff club and mess, kitchen, main stores and car park. Phase 5, beginning in mid-1974 and ending in late 1976, entailed the destruction of D, DX and C Wings, the boiler house, kitchen and hospital annexe, and the construction of the remainder of the living accommodation including specialist hospital accommodation, the reception suite, and medical administration. Phase 6, beginning in late 1976 and ending in early 1977, centred on the conversion of the new buildings which had been used for temporary purposes during the period of reconstruction to their final use.[11] The whole project is laid out in Figures 5.1 and 5.2, the former showing the phasing of demolition and the latter the phasing of construction.

That was the precise pattern mapped out by the planners, but it was not to be accomplished with precision. Successive members of the Project Group, Project Team and Design Team were to become ever more frustrated, annoyed and bewildered as Holloway's problems multiplied and swelled and their timetable failed. A senior member of the Design Team was driven to observe in October 1974 that 'the problems at Holloway are never ending'.[12] The Holloway

[10] See, for instance, the report in the *Daily Telegraph*, 12 Jan. 1971.
[11] Based on 'Holloway Redevelopment Project: Progress Report No 5, Note by the Chairman of the Project Group', Jan. 1971.   [12] Letter to architects, 3 Oct. 1974.

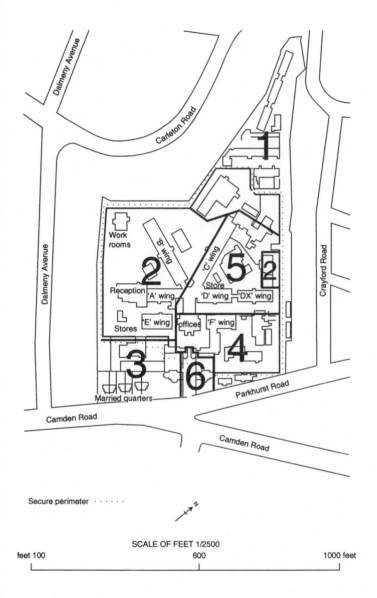

Figure 5.1 Holloway Prison, Phasing of Demolition

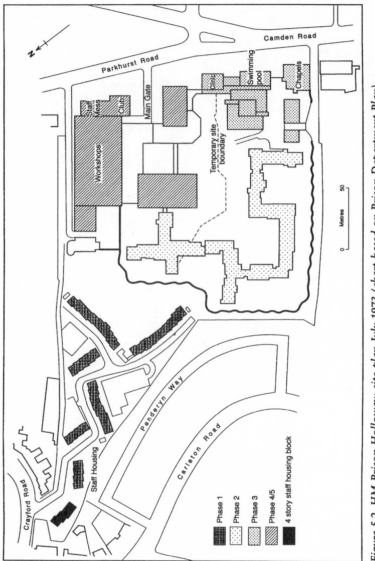

Figure 5.2 HM Prison Holloway: site plan July 1973 (chart based on Prison Department Plan)

project took such a very long time that the rest of this chapter must be an analysis of the nature of delays in the building programme. The next two chapters will examine the effects of those delays.

Delays

The project seemed to be blighted. Almost every affliction that could be heaped on a substantial building and commissioning programme was suffered singly or in droves by the planners, managers and inmates of the new Holloway prison between 1970 and 1985. It was not perhaps the best time to build: the 1970s were a decade of exceptional industrial and economic turbulence which unerringly worked its way to the building site. I shall discuss some specimen examples of those afflictions before I move on to describe how they affected the phenomenology of the new prison, the way in which it impinged on the consciousness of those who lived in it.

Problems of Reconstruction on Site

The cartwheel design of the old prison lent itself well to phased destruction. Insulated wings, each sealed against the rest, could be pulled down one after the other in a great anti-clockwise sweep, concentrating the population in the ever fewer remaining wings. Each phase of that sweep would be managed as a separate programme of demolition and construction centred on a set of functionally and spatially interrelated buildings. In their meetings during the planning phase, in 1970 and 1971, the Project Team were to employ 'activity networks', or 'interlocked time sequence[s] of activities for the guidance of the various departments of the Home Office involved in the Holloway project',[13] to make sense of what they were doing. They plotted how every move in each phase might affect the rest, their planning sometimes becoming so complex that a number of separate 'activity networks' had to be considered simultaneously within the same phase: Phase 3 was to be just such a taxing stage.[14]

In short, the redevelopment project was to be an intricate, contingent, stochastic process; each phase would ease or complicate the execution of the next and future phases in sometimes indeterminate fashion; and the analysis and control of what had to be done became

---

[13] 'Note of a Meeting held on 18 August 1970 . . . to discuss the Phase 1 Activity Network.'   [14] 'Holloway Redevelopment: Phase 3 Network', 11 Oct. 1971.

correspondingly complex. Consider a perfectly typical section of a much longer preliminary examination of the problems of a single phase. It was but one of many such examinations of phases and stages prepared over the years to assist the Project Team. In August 1970, the Team's Secretary reasoned that:

It will provide considerable simplification if the completion of Phase 2 provided the full new living accommodation, for many problems involved in accommodation in later phases will be solved, for practically all inmates can be removed from the old part of the prison into new accommodation at the end of Phase 2, leaving only the problems of providing working spaces and other related necessary activity spaces within the evacuated living spaces in the old prison. Reception, it has been suggested, will have to be moved twice, first to F Wing and then to the Hospital/Remand Centre. If, however, the full new living accommodation can be provided by the end of Phase 2, it may be possible and feasible to move reception into the Hospital/YP Remand Centre building (admittedly at the expense of rather long movements both from the Gate to the Reception and from Reception to the living accommodation).[15]

It is easy to understand how, on occasion, all that proposed activity could get out of joint and members of the Project Team would begin to complain about inadequate liaison and communication between the Home Office briefing architects, the private nominated architects, contractors, surveyors and others. It is easy to understand too, how, from time to time, cascading slippages and delays led to temporary collapses of order and tempo as the planners found themselves unable to 'draw up a realistic programme'[16] for what to do next. On 29 April 1971, for instance, the Chairman of the Project Group was informed by the briefing architect and Project Secretary:

The last part [of Stage D of Phase 2] has been one of frenzied activity and totally insufficient time has been given to the Department by the Architects for comprehensive and deliberate study of the proposals and such consideration that has been possible has revealed several instances where the results of such hurried completion are patently obvious.

Matters were additionally complicated because phasing was not only a way of imparting organization to an elaborate building project. Like

---

[15] 'Holloway Redevelopment Project: Commissioning, Phasing and Reconstruction', Note by Secretary, Aug. 1970.

[16] The specific problem under discussion when this phrase was used was the date of the move into Phase 2/3 accommodation. 'Note of a Meeting of the Working Party Considering the Move into Phase 2/3 Accommodation'. 21 July 1976.

almost everything else in the social world of Holloway, it was given moral and symbolic meaning beyond its mere utility. Phasing was also taken in part to be a statement of precedence, of the importance of groups in the hierarchy that constituted the prison. Waiting reflects on power and authority: those who wait least long are generally the most consequential in any social order.[17] The clearest instance was that of the prison officers who had expected to move into their new accommodation first, before the inmates. That they did not do so was to engender discontents[18] that fed into their later relations with prisoners in the new Holloway.

It had been known from the first that simultaneous demolition, site clearance and construction on a nine acre site would throw up its problems.[19] It could not be a simple operation: it was argued that such a project 'will require exceptionally careful preparation, planning and programming if disorganisation and chaos are not to result'.[20] It was particularly difficult to insulate worlds in such a small area, and the construction project, its workers and their space, on the one hand, and the prison, prisoners and *their* space, on the other, were forever colliding. Joanna Kelley had been prescient when she wrote in 1968 that 'It might take 10 years . . . and the process will be a dirty, dusty and noisy one . . .'[21] Building work had to be regulated to permit life in the 'operating' prison to continue with some semblance of normality: thus, pile-driving was avoided where possible to 'prevent excessive noise'[22] and the Treasury allowed extra money for 'noise suppression'. And that constant propinquity could not but be distracting. It was tempting to be playful before such willing, segregated audiences of men and women, and there were

[17] See B. Schwartz, 'Waiting, Exchange, and Power: The Distribution of Time in Social Systems, *American Journal of Sociology*, 79(4) (Jan. 1974), 841–70.

[18] Noted, for instance in the Minutes of Meeting of Working Party to Discuss the Organization of the Move from the Present to Part of the New Accommodation, 22 Sept. 1976. I shall discuss those discontents below.

[19] One particularly harrowing phase in clearing the site in March and April 1971 entailed the disinterment and interment of the 5 bodies of women who had been executed at the prison. The task was done with propriety and in the presence of a representative of the prison chaplaincy. One who was there recalled: 'being a medical officer, I had to be present when they were doing all this, and the fact that it was done at night made it an even more unpleasant experience'. Another difficulty was occasioned by rumours of the presence of an unexploded bomb from World War II. The Royal Engineers did indeed eventually find fragments of a 50 kilogram bomb on site.

[20] 'Holloway Redevelopment—Phasing Moves—Appointment of New Governor', Note by Secretary, 23 November 1971.   [21] Letter to Ken Neale, 14 Mar. 1968.

[22] Minutes of Meeting of Holloway Project Team, 11 Sept. 1970.

reports of women calling out and performing 'strip-teases' for the construction workers.[23]

More urgently, perhaps, the Prison Department was anxious about security, and especially about the problems of employing a civilian work-force on a prison site when it was at its most vulnerable (belated checks disclosing that some of the workers had criminal records led to their replacement[24]). Temporary security fences were dismantled and erected every time there was a change in the boundary between the areas occupied by the two prisons, and civilian workers were not allowed unsupervised within their perimeter (the fence may clearly be seen separating the two parts of the prison in Plates 5.1 and 5.2). Conversely, officials required permission to enter the contractors site. Bill Avery, the Prison Officer in Charge of Works during that period, remembered:

It opened as it went. It never closed. This was the point, our principal duty was to keep Holloway prison operational, so we had these phase jobs where we came and cut part of the prison off with 17 foot high security fences, and you demolished it, and then you moved from there into the new part. . . It was unbelievable. The job could have been completed in 3 years if they had emptied the prison completely and knocked the whole thing down.

There were limits to what civilian workers were permitted to do. They could not be entrusted with installing locks in the new prison, for example: security locks were fitted only after the contractors had moved out and civilians were not thereafter allowed to return. The obvious difficulty was that such procedures could leave newly-evacuated areas relatively ill-defended until they were once more occupied by staff and inmates, and the compounds that resulted had to be equipped with new security locks and patrolled by staff in the day and by dog-handlers at night. Outside the secure perimeter, there were persistent problems of pilfering, theft and vandalism of materials not yet properly made safe. An earth mover was stolen,[25] the windows of the new boilerhouse were smashed by vandals in January 1976, and, in September 1980, two youths were seen climbing the wall near the building site and the police were called.

---

[23] See the News of the World, 29 Aug. 1971.

[24] See Daily Express, 25 June 1971.

[25] One who had worked on the site remembered that 'one of the contractors did actually lose one of these massive big earth movers. Some lads drove in one Saturday morning with a low loader, went up and saw the foreman, and said "we've come for the earth digger" . . . and they loaded it up and away it went.'

Plate 5.1: Holloway Under Reconstruction (reproduced courtesy of HM Prison Holloway)

Plate 5.2: Holloway Under Reconstruction (reproduced courtesy of HM Prison Holloway)

Problems multiplied as demolition proceeded. The contraction of the old Holloway did not only involve a loss of physical space and consequent possibilities of crowding:[26] it also demanded a conversion of the surviving portions of the radial prison to new, temporary uses as former facilities were lost. Those newly adapted parts of the 'operating' prison had to be made safe and habitable before occupation: when the hospital block was converted into living accommodation in August 1970, for instance, windows were blocked up and chimneys taken down. Yet it was also plain that it would have been imprudent to spend too much money on converting old, condemned buildings and the planners were beset by questions about how much makeshift work could and should be done.[27]

Pari passu, expansion into the new establishment could not simply take the guise of an ever-increasing utilization of the new buildings as they were commissioned: many of those new buildings had also to be adapted to temporary use until the whole was ready and each unit could perform its proper function.[28] In 1970, for instance, it was decided to employ the new swimming pool as temporary accommodation for the kitchen.[29] Yet it was inevitable that many of the amenities considered integral to a fully functioning prison could not be provided until very late, becoming available only when their attendant phases were finished. It was reported in January 1976, for example, that extensive medical and psychiatric facilities would not be ready until Phases 4 and 5 were complete and the whole prison had been taken into use. In some instances, even the temporary conversion of permanent buildings would not do and special makeshift buildings

---

[26] An anonymous 'Report to the Steering Committee to Oversee Redevelopment Schemes' reflected that 'many problems sprung from the fact that the tight urban nature of the site left no room on which new buildings could be erected before existing ones were demolished. The consequential squeezing in of inmates in the remaining limited space and the proximity of building operations with the attendant dust and dirt inevitably lowers the quality of prison life and throws additional strain on both staff and inmates.' 9 May 1975.

[27] For example, it was decided not to convert the windows of the welfare officers' temporary accommodation because installing new windows in the 27″ thick walls of the old Holloway would have cost £1,000 each, a prohibitively large sum to be allotted to a building that was about to be pulled down. The Department acknowledged that 'much of the converted accommodation is not up to the standard that could reasonably be expected if it were to be used for any great length of time or for permanent use'. Letter of 17 Dec. 1971.

[28] And that created additional problems because the original costings had made no provision for the conversion of the new buildings on a temporary basis.

[29] Minute of Meeting of the Briefing group, 27 Nov. 1970.

had to be constructed as part of a new, third group of works (there were to be improvised clinics and a temporary gatehouse for a while).

Each movement of population within and between prisons, and each answering adjustment of the regime and buildings, was likely to be disruptive. A note written by the Project Secretary in December 1971 reflected that 'the phasing of demolition and rebuilding operations has had to be arranged so that adequate accommodation is available at all times to enable the prison to function but, at the same time, ensure that the number of total movements of the "operating" prison are kept to a minimum'.[30] Indeed, work on site had sometimes to be suspended altogether whilst inmates were transferred from one part of the old prison to another (for instance, there was a delay of three weeks in December 1971 because of limitations imposed on the contractor's working area during the movement of inmates from Wings A, B and E). Even so, not everybody could be accommodated on site as the operating prison shrank. I shall describe later the effects of staff being moved into temporary quarters away from Holloway and of some groups of prisoners being diverted away from Holloway altogether as pressure on space mounted.[31]

Industrial Problems

When a project begins to flounder, it is tempting always to cast around for good reasons why delays should not be blamed on oneself but on some other group or, indeed, on impersonal events, and the papers of the redevelopment project are replete with good reasons for delay and inactivity. There were, for instance, the predictable problems of poor weather that would have beset any prolonged works undertaken in the open air (it was claimed that 17 out of 19 working days were lost in March 1975 because of rain, frost and snow[32]). But there were exceptional problems as well and I propose to offer only a few examples of difficulty to illustrate the history of the whole.

The 1970s were exceptionally fraught years for any big building project. They were a time of vigorous construction, labour shortages and industrial unrest, and the project was affected in proportion. The

---

[30] 'Holloway Redevelopment Project: Operational Phasing Movements', Note by Secretary, 1 Dec. 1971.

[31] For example, it was agreed that short-sentence prostitutes would be transferred from Risley to Styal instead of Holloway after 1 Nov. 1970.

[32] 'Holloway Redevelopment: Phases 2 and 3, Report No 23, Report on Progress to 29th March 1975.'

architects reported that they had lost a number of their own staff to other firms,[33] and they repeatedly told the Project Team about how difficult it was to secure labour, and skilled labour above all (there were shortages of bricklayers in December 1971 and May 1972, for example). On 9 June 1973, they informed David Faulkner:

The industry is overloaded with work at a time when industrial unrest had threatened supplies of materials, and prices are uncertain. Labour, particularly in skilled trades such as bricklayers and carpenters, is scarce, and contractors are having to pay premiums to attract and keep tradesmen.

The 1970s in Britain were beset by industrial conflict, and Holloway had its local conflicts too. There was a ban on overtime working on the site between 26 June and 27 July 1972 followed by two weeks of 'strikes, marches etc.';[34] a total strike (as part of a larger national action) between 16 August and 18 September 1972, and lesser stoppages at other times. In the aftermath of building strikes there was an inevitable increase in the demand for labour as contractors everywhere sought to make up for lost time (there were even accusations of contractors on adjoining sections of the Holloway site attempting to poach one another's labour) and workers had to be paid extra incentive payments and bonuses to maintain continuity.

The strikes of the early 1970s threw the delicate planning of the project out of phase: separate contracts could not be completed on time; new contracts could not start because workers, plant and materials were required elsewhere; and costs increased all the while. The consequence was a series of disorganizing ripples that worked their way erratically through the course of the entire project. The project's own News Bulletin reported in March 1973 that 'the Project has been programmed in a series of closely linked phases in such a way that a new phase cannot start until the previous phase has been completed. It follows that delays in one phase must have an effect throughout the Project.'[35]

It was unavoidable too that Holloway suffered the secondary effects of other strikes and emergencies elsewhere. The most pronounced of those external problems were: the energy crisis stemming from the Arab–Israeli war of October 1973; the miners' strikes of February 1972 and February 1974; the Electrical Power Engineers'

[33] Contract progress reports of 27 May 1976 and 23 Aug. 1976.
[34] Architects' 'Diary of Site Meetings and Salient Events on Phase 1'.
[35] 'Holloway Redevelopment Project: News Bulletin No. 5', Mar. 1973.

Association ban on out-of-hours work in November 1973; and all the accompanying power cuts, privations and restrictions, including, most markedly, the three day working week of February 1974. There were ensuing delays and shortages in the production of building materials: bricks were in particularly short supply in 1972 and 1973;[36] but there was also a scarcity of kitchen fittings, steel reinforcements, oil, sanitary ware,[37] concrete blocks[38] and plaster[39] (the Holloway Board of Visitors could not even distribute copies of its agenda in February 1974 because of a paper shortage).[40]

There were other, lesser complicating problems: British Standard paint colours were changed in January 1973 although decoration schedules had been approved 3 months before. All work on the Project moved from imperial to metric standards in February 1970, and there were inevitable confusions about adapting working practices and securing supplies of the correct dimensions. Over-size bricks were delivered in November 1971 for instance. A foreman remembered:

There were two problems. In '72 the building industry went metric, and the job was a metric design, and we all came down as feet and inches men and had to adapt to metric. And in the early days, when we started, we kept on getting loads of . . . although the contracts that we were ordering were metric, we did occasionally, get some imperial ones. So it was a bit of a game.

Damp

The new Holloway was a large project, difficult to design and execute. Not only did it entail all the conventional problems of a big structure, but there were unconventional problems as well. Every ordinary design problem was compounded by the extraordinary nature of a prison. So it was that the buildings were planned to be habitable and useable, but they had also to be made secure against voluntary and involuntary damage, escape, protest, disorder and rescue. Doors were constructed in the expectation that they would receive rough treatment from inmates in the Phase 2 accommodation, and display units for inmates' art work were made 'robust and thief

---

[36] Minutes of Meetings of Design Team, 10 Aug. 1972, 14 June 1973.
[37] Minutes of Meeting of Design Team, 14 June 1973.
[38] 'Quarterly Report No 9', 11 July 1973.
[39] Minutes of Meeting of Design Team, 14 June 1973.
[40] Minutes of Board of Visitors, 27 Feb. 1974.

proof'. Much of the new establishment would have to be maintained by inmates rather than by paid labour. Thirty-six sentenced women were to be assigned to the cleaning party and the Treasury proposed that the landscaping should also be undertaken by prisoners.[41] The Design Team decided in March 1975 that, because no skilled maintenance would be available, all surfaces would be washed or polished, and design should allow for poor maintenance.

It was perhaps inevitable that some parts of such a complex project should go wrong. There were problems with electrical work, for example: work already completed on staff accommodation had to be opened up again and rectified in early 1971. Defects in drainage arose in Phase 1 in May 1974 when a large crane wreaked damage as it was driven over the site. But what was to plague the planners and builders above all was the problem of persistent and seemingly ineradicable water penetration in the windows of the new staff quarters in Phase 1. It is that seemingly small difficulty, more than anything else, which illustrates the delays that could overflow from one phase into another and disrupt orderly planning. Sid Norris became Assistant Secretary in charge of P7 and the chairman of the project in November 1974, just when the problem of damp gave birth to what he called 'the endless saga of the flats and the water penetration'. It was, he said, 'the prime problem of the time'.

Block 1 of the new staff housing should have been ready for handover in December 1972, the remaining six blocks during 1973. The contract had met with what a brief called 'varied and unremitting troubles connected with the shortage of materials, the 3 day working week, the weather, and more latterly electrical faults'[42] There had been delays enough in Phase 1, but what a site foreman labelled the 'total disaster of the staff quarters' was itself postponed because the early summer of 1974 had been dry, and signs of damp did not begin to appear around the windows of the staff quarters until July and August. Water penetration then became an enduring, baffling problem which set the design team against the builders and the Project Group against them both. (An independent consultant and assessor appointed to resolve the disputes between them recounted in 1980 that 'I have taken a great deal of trouble with this item [of water penetration] and I have read many reports and

---

[41] Minutes of the Holloway Project Team Meeting 18 June 1970.
[42] Briefing material for visit, 10 June 1975.

papers on the subject but I am still uncertain about what happened. The narratives of the contractors and the design team have little in common.')

Tests conducted in December 1974 suggested that there were possible leaks through the brickwork. Further inquiries undertaken by a representative of the Building Research Establishment in February 1975 reported incomplete filling of recessed joints with mastic, mortar droppings blocking weepholes and other defects. The prison works staff assembled mock-up windows in the prison workshop to test alternative remedies. The manufacturers of the mastic were consulted and investigated the problem on site. But still the windows leaked. A testy meeting in June 1975 was reported to have been told by Sid Norris, the Assistant Secretary in charge of the project, that:

Phase 1 was a block of flats and 2½ years after the target date for handing over the first block, they were still not finished; the windows leaked and to date 9 months had passed in trying to find the remedy. No one could tell him when Block 1 could be handed over and his last enquiry had left him with the conclusion that, on the most favourable assumptions, it could not be for at least another year.

Further examination undertaken by the Building Research Establishment in July 1975 discovered hitherto undetected weaknesses in the design of the window frames. It was determined that it would be impossible to identify the relative importance of the various defects of each window and that a package of general remedial measures would have to be applied instead to all the new quarters. The builders declared that they were reluctant to carry out additional work without compensation, and the Project Team were reluctant to pay for what they considered to be defective workmanship. There was an awkward stalemate that did not resolve itself until litigation was threatened, resort was made to an independent assessor and the parties came to a settlement in the summer of 1980.

Back in July 1976, however, it was concluded that the programme for dealing with water penetration might take a further two years. And that, indeed, was how long the work took. The problem of damp was not simply a technical matter. It prevented the staff from occupying their new quarters (they had to wait until after the inmates had moved into *their* accommodation). It obliged the Prison Department to find makeshift alternative accommodation for the staff. And it engendered multiple dissatisfactions which thereafter, were to corrode relations between management and staff, and staff and headquarters. I shall deal with aspects of the staff's experience of the project in Chapter 7.

Negotiations with Outsiders

A third set of examples of delay hinges on dealings between the Prison Department and outsiders who came to concern themselves with the project and the fate of the old prison. Plans affecting any large public building in London attract public attention; Holloway was always a symbolically potent institution; and its proposed redevelopment received a response from bodies interested in its buildings, its occupants and its site. I shall again refrain from listing all the negotiations with all the organizations involved in those dealings,[43] preferring to restrict myself to a few cases.

It will be recalled that one of the original instructions issued to P4 by the Prison Board in 1968 had been to consider approaches to the local authorities. The 1960s and 1970s were decades of furious house-building and property acquisition by public authorities. Between 1967 and 1969 alone, 200,000 English and Welsh dwellings defined as unfit had been demolished or closed and, in 1970, it was expected that about 1.5 million new council dwellings would be built in the next six years.[44] The average number of properties controlled by each local authority rose from 1,400 after the Second World War to 14,000 in 1975, the larger authorities becoming the owners of between 20,000 and 30,000 units each.[45] By 1977, 30 per cent of the 17 million dwellings in England and Wales were publicly owned.[46] Islington, the local authority in which Holloway was set,[47] and the Greater

---

[43] In the summer of 1972, for example, Radical Alternatives to Prison (RAP) waged a campaign against the proposed reconstruction of the prison, arguing for its abolition instead. The campaign came to a head with a report published on May 22, a rally on 6 June and a fusillade of letters from members of the public and Members of Parliament. It did not make a discernible impact on the thinking of the Prison Department. It elicited instead replies and defences lodged in the standard narrative of the Steyning Brief. There is little to be gained from giving a detailed history of that and other similar exchanges.

[44] Figures taken from A. Holmans, 'A forecast of effective demand for housing in Great Britain in the 1970's', *Social Trends*, No. 1, 1970 (London: HMSO, 1970), 38, 42.

[45] See A. Power, 'How to rescue council housing', *New Society*, 4 June 1981.

[46] See P. Mayhew and R. Clarke, 'Crime Prevention and Public Housing in England', in M. Hough and P. Mayhew (eds.), *Crime and Public Housing*, (London: Home Office, 1982).

[47] Islington declared that it could have built 300 houses on the site of Holloway.

London Council,[48] the superior planning authority responsible for the larger metropolitan area of London, took it that public housing schemes were of paramount importance, that such schemes should certainly have a higher priority than prison construction, and that any land cleared in inner London should be surrendered to house-building.[49] And they worked in tandem.

In an environment peppered with so much talk about razing the decrepit London prisons, officers of Islington appeared firmly to expect that it would be awarded the site of either Pentonville or Holloway or, indeed, both sites together. In November 1968, the Town Clerk of Islington was reported to have evinced astonishment when P4 announced that neither site would actually be relinquished. Islington Labour Party asked for a formal inquiry. And, two months later, on 7 January 1969, Islington Council unanimously passed a resolution condemning what was about to happen. The Council said it:

deplores the retention of the Holloway Prison site for the new buildings. We once again draw attention to the overcrowded state of the Borough of Islington and to the lack of suitable sites for housing, welfare projects and open space and urge that both Holloway and Pentonville Prison sites be made available for such local needs.

Islington was told that the Home Office knew of the housing needs of the borough but that the custodial needs of women were greater. Indeed, the time would come when Islington would regard the new Holloway prison as a symbol of social progress and local pride.[50] Islington campaigned. It requested meetings with the Minister of State in April[51] and December 1969 (after that first meeting, one

---

[48]   The Greater London Council's own Greater London Development Plan had proposed that the five London prisons should be moved to the outskirts of the capital. At the same time, it had placed Holloway on its supplementary list of buildings worthy of preservation.

[49]   See the *Guardian*, 16 May 1970 and *The Times*, 2 June 1970.

[50]   Letter of 14 Feb. 1969.

[51]   It issued a press release on 21 April 1969 to foreshadow the meeting of 24 April: 'Islington's opposition to the rebuilding of Holloway Prison on its existing site is the logical and necessary manifestation of policy long since declared and recently re-affirmed, to oppose the perpetuation in Islington of two large prisons and to take every possible step to ensure that the land occupied for prison purposes in Islington should be freed to make possible its redevelopment for housing and other essential amenity purposes. That Islington should house one such prison when only five still survive in the whole of London, is considered to be unjust; that it should house two such prisons is in the Council's view totally unacceptable.'

member of the delegation, Councillor Bromfield, observed that 'the needs of the few who have offended against society must not be allowed to prejudice the needs of the overwhelming majority of our citizens, who obey the law').[52] Islington mobilized MPs to protest: and parliamentary questions, and letters to, and meetings with, Ministers followed.[53] On 14 May 1970, there was an adjournment debate on 'the proposed rebuilding of Holloway Prison', the motion having been proposed by a local Member, Michael O'Halloran. The arguments argued in the adjournment debate were those put throughout the political campaign: Islington's desperate need for housing had to take precedence over any claim by the prison and the Prison Department:

the decision to rebuild Holloway jail on its present site in Islington should be viewed and seen to be the public scandal which it is. And that a Labour government should take it makes it worse, it is inhumanity of the first order. Should this plan proceed, it would permanently deprive 1,290 people of a decent home in Islington, and their children of somewhere to play. The opportunity for Islington Council to build homes on land where it has not first been necessary to rehouse more families than will be able to return is the only sure hope that it will be able to solve the many problems arising from its earlier development.[54]

The Prison Department's standard replies were once again almost invariably framed by the master narrative that had grown out of the Steyning Brief. Holloway had to be near locally recruited staff, medical facilities, the courts, visitors and legal advisers.[55] The project was of massive penological and therapeutic importance (Islington was told at its meeting with the Minister of State in April 1969 that Holloway 'is to be the centre piece of the new ten year programme for the treatment of women offenders . . . The new Holloway will provide for the female penal system a central, medically orientated establishment with all the facilities necessary to provide the custodial treatment needed by female offenders'). Whilst Islington might have local responsibilities, it was informed, the Home

---

[52] 'Press Release: Homes or Prisons for Islington—The Next Steps', 29 Apr. 1969.
[53] Members of Parliament wrote frequently to Ministers between 1969 and 1972 about the need to release the site. They wrote again in 1977 when a campaign was waged to preserve the Victorian gatehouse.
[54] Michael O'Halloran's speaking notes for the adjournment debate.
[55] Standard arguments put in a Minister's letter to an MP, Feb. 1969.

Office had overriding national responsibilities to the public and the criminal justice system at large.

After some time, moreover, it could always be argued that too much work had already been expended to turn back. (By May 1970, for instance, it was noted that the consultants had put ninety people to work on the reconstruction of Holloway.[56] Rather less than a year later, in March 1971, it was said 'we are now past Phase 1 and the process is irreversible.[57])

It was thought privately that local residents and politicians would eventually come to value and appreciate the new establishment ('we shall without doubt, receive a number of similar letters from the public, either direct or through M.P.s, until such time as the purpose behind the redevelopment of Holloway is more widely known').[58] The agitation would pass.

But what trumped all else was that, in law, planning permission from local authorities was not required because the site of the prison was Crown property and the project involved no change of use. Islington and the GLC had no authority over the project. The Home Office could pursue its own course, but it chose to do so diplomatically. David Faulkner, the Assistant Secretary at the time, remarked: 'technically it could be argued that the Crown wasn't subject to planning codes in a formal way but . . . as a matter of good practice and openness and good will, [the Office] proceeded according to whatever the circular was,[59] that in effect put us in the same position voluntarily as any other developer'.

So it came to be agreed within the Department that 'the Home Office were in a strong position as the site was Crown land, but the wishes of the local authority should, as far as possible, be respected'.[60] Frequent consultations followed, occurring perhaps every two or three months over several years.[61] Plans for each phase were submitted formally for comment by the local authority's architects. Letters were exchanged. A consequence was that the show of consultation led to occasional changes in the plans. Shirley Williams,

---

[56] Background notes to Parliamentary Motion Adjournment Debate, 14 May 1970.
[57] Draft reply to MP, March 1971.   [58] Minute in file, November 1970.
[59] DOE 80/1971 which arose out of the Town and Country Planning Act, 1968 (it was judged that the circular could not have retroactive effect).
[60] Minutes of the Meeting of the Project Team, 10 Sept. 1969.
[61] And that was a useful point to counter objections that the Home Office had been overly dictatorial in its stance.

the Minister of State, came to promise that there would be a small area of landscaping to soften the line of the new prison (known colloquially within the Department as 'a few blades of grass'). There was talk in January 1971 (talk that was ultimately to be fruitless because of later expenditure cuts) about the provision of a day nursery for local children. And, as I shall show below, there was also to be a willingness to lower the height of new staff housing.

Islington appeared to have been mollified. There was surface protest but, informally, it was reported within the Prison Department, technical co-operation between the Home Office and the local authority proceeded smoothly enough. There were also costs. Every reply drafted, every set of briefing notes prepared, every meeting arranged, consumed the time of officials already occupied with strikes, shortages and the damp in the windows of the Phase 1 staff quarters. They contributed yet more to delay.

Neighbours

Some part of the local authority's and MPs' campaign was ignited by complaints from constituents nervous or indignant about what was planned for Holloway. The more nervous complaints presaged later friction at the boundaries of the new prison that was not really a prison and that was not intended to look like a prison. Not all the community wished the psychological and physical barriers between themselves and the prison to be eroded.[62] In 1976, there were persistent complaints about noise[63] (described as 'two turbo jet engines')[64] emanating from what were variously identified as new boilers and stand-by generators on the site. The MP, Michael O'Halloran, was again active, and the Governor[65] and Ministers sought to reassure him by their remonstrations to the Project Group. Silencers

---

[62] It had happened before. When part of the remaining site of the old cemetery was sold for housing in 1874, the walls of the first Holloway were raised by 3½ feet to deter voyeurs.

[63] The Governor received a letter from a resident in Camden Road in May 1977 complaining 'on behalf of the tenants and myself . . . about the noise from a generator that runs all night this has only occurred since the prison has been rebuilt. If it is possible we would like you to try to quieten this down as it is disturbing our sleep at night.'

[64] 'Minister called in over new prison boiler's, *Islington Gazette,* undated.

[65] O'Halloran had written to the Governor, Megan Bull, in August 1976 and she, in turn, wrote to P7 to say 'copies of these letters should be on your files as presumably you are putting pressure on the designers to remedy the fault in the generator'.

were finally fitted to the generator in 1977, but it was later discovered that it was the boilers that were at fault.

There were complaints about visual surveillance. Residents of Carleton Road wrote in October 1971 to protest at the closeness and height of the proposed new staff quarters: one observed that the adjoining block would 'look straight into my bedrooms and living rooms, and we in turn will look directly into the prison officers' bedrooms, this indecently jeopardizing the privacy of the house occupants and prison officers'. Islington Council's Applications Committee discussed the block at issue, Block 7, in December 1971, and Michael O'Halloran asked a battery of parliamentary questions on the matter between December 1971 and February 1972. In late 1971, the Project Team did accede to Islington's objections and agreed to lower the block by two storeys.[66]

That success prompted a later petition in January 1973 from the residents of houses at 93–101 Crayford Road who complained about how another four storey staff block would 'seriously reduce the amount of light in our house[s] . . . [and] would impose considerably on our privacy and that of other Crayford Road residents which would not encourage community harmony'. But plans were judged by then to have advanced too far and the Home Office refused to introduce any more changes. It was ominously evident that a number of the new prison's neighbours wished to be kept at a safe distance from the new establishment. They would have preferred the buildings to have been kept far away and behind high walls.

Preservation

Some neighbours and passers-by also lamented the imminent destruction of what had belatedly come to be seen again as a dramatic Victorian building in a drab area. I have already noted how, alerted by a letter from just such a passer-by, the Victorian Society had made a lukewarm protest about the project when it was first announced in 1968. By the mid-1970s, concern about the preservation of Victorian institutional buildings, including prisons, had spread. The Director of Works noted in 1972 that there was a growing movement to extend the list of protected monuments and a growing interest in Victorian architecture under the influence of Pevsner and Betjeman. It would appear that architectural aesthetics had undergone another partial

[66] Minutes of a Meeting of the Project Team, 16 Dec. 1971.

volte face: the Victorian no longer excited feelings of revulsion. In its last days, the absurd grim fortress, Lord Stonham's Victorian monstrosity, had become a noble castle again.

The threat from the conservationists might have been a significant impediment, and it was thought important to proceed with demolition as fast as possible before an effective campaign could be mounted. In October 1970, it was therefore decided to follow precedent and not to inform the Royal Fine Arts Commission about the plan to demolish the prison (it was noted that the Commission had no statutory authority). But preservation and historical societies *were* alerted and they did protest.

In March 1971, the London Society asked if, at a minimum, the tower of the old Holloway could be preserved, but they were informed that it could not be so. There were new fears in October 1974 that the Greater London Council (prompted by the Victorian Society) would recommend to the Department of the Environment that the gatehouse should be listed. The Home Office resisted, arguing that demolition was well advanced, that the decision to retain any part of the old prison would seriously interfere with the pace of redevelopment, and that it would be 'quite out of character with the new prison' and an unjustified burden on public funds. The Department of the Environment did indeed refuse the Victorian Society's request[67] four months later and its argument echoed the Home Office's own: 'plans for the demolition of the building have now proceeded so far that no useful purpose would be served in reconsidering the question whether the building should be listed. Much of it has already been demolished and a great deal of the new building is already up.'[68]

Those who had advocated the reconstruction of the prison were largely unmoved by the shift in aesthetics. Joanna Kelley reflected that 'you really must consider the human beings you are holding rather than the beauty of the wrought iron work'.

It was the final May 1977 campaign to save the gatehouse that was to prove the most vigorous of all. In a sad, pleading letter to the Minister of State, the Ancient Monuments Society described the gatehouse as part of a prison 'bedecked in a fairytale Gothic style that had connotations of Damsels in Distress'[69] and called for its

---

[67] The Society had written on 18 Sept. 1974 to the Department of Environment requesting the spot-listing of the gateway and campanile of Holloway prison.

[68] Letter to Sir Hugh Casson, 27 Jan. 1977.

[69] Letter to Lord Harris, 25 May 1977.

preservation. Islington's activist MP, Michael OHalloran, wrote to the Minister of State at the beginning of May 1977 to convey his constituents' dismay at the prospect of demolition. There were meetings on 9 and 10 May between MPs and the Minister, and the Project Group were left in a dilemma (if demolition did not take place, the contractor would have a claim; if it did take place, it would appear that the Home Office had acted hastily). The Minister was advised that the project was too far advanced and too expensive to change, but it *was* agreed to defer the decision for a month in a show of reasonableness.

On 23 May 1977, 49 MPs moved an early day motion in the House of Commons to deplore the destruction of the gatehouse.[70] 70 MPs petitioned the Home Secretary in July.[71] But the Home Office was adamant. It would allow the gatehouse to be pulled down stone by stone and re-assembled elsewhere only if some other body bore the cost and reimbursed the demolition contractor for work lost. On 16 May, the Home Office was told that Islington could not afford to compensate the contractor for delays. A few bits and pieces of the old prison were removed to the Museum of London in June and, on 7 August, the gatehouse was at last pulled down. One who worked on the site remembered, 'I received instructions from the Home Office one morning to get demolition crews in very, very quickly and start swinging the ball before anyone could start and that's what I had to do'.[72]

Eric Moonman, one of the campaigning Members of Parliament, reported: 'the demolition is complete. All we can see now is a row of characterless buildings which could be anything, anywhere'.[73] The Home Office had been successful but, again, it had had to engage in copious correspondence, briefings and meetings, and the project had been slowed down yet further.

---

[70] The motion read: 'That this House, on being made aware that the plans to rebuild Holloway Prison involve the total demolition of the facade, including Bunning's distinctive gatehouse and tower, expresses its concern at the prospect of the loss both to the nation and to the immediate locality of this historic landmark; regrets the effect on the local environment; and calls for reconsideration of the present plans with a view to the possible retention of the most outstanding features'.

[71] See the *Guardian,* 18 July 1977.

[72] In this instance, the *Evening Standard* may not have been amiss when it claimed in an editorial on 19 May 1977 that the lesson 'is the result of a curious fixation with developers that their aim in life is to outwit the conservationists'.

[73] 'How the bureaucrats triumphed in the siege of Holloway "Castle"', *The Times,* 8 Aug. 1977.

Conclusion

All those delays collided and multiplied over time and the project became very long overdue. Phase 1 actually ended with the completion of remedial work in April 1978, five years late; Phase 2 in January 1977, just under three years late; the commissioning of Phase 4 began in May 1979, three years late; and the penultimate phase, Phase 5, was not actually to be completed until the very end of 1984, nine years late. In the next two chapters I shall pursue some of the social, organizational and phenomenological consequences of such a massive lag in executing the project.

6

Metamorphosis II: The Penological Redefinition of Holloway

> 'the pendulum tended to swing between security and rehabilitation. At the time the project started there was a strong emphasis on therapy and rehabilitation, but now due to recent involvement of women in serious crime there is a swing back to the need for more security.' (The principal architect of the new Holloway speaking at a meeting held with representatives of the BBC, 13 August 1976)

Introduction

The delays I described in the previous chapter should not be understood as a simple extension of unchanging practices and experiences through time. To the contrary. They so radically transformed the practices, organization and experiences of the people implicated in the project that the very character of the new Holloway prison was to be altered. If the new prison had been built uneventfully and rapidly on an open site, it might well have been finished when many of its creators were still in control, when ideas about women offenders and prison regimes were still substantially unchallenged, and before the project itself had turned sour. It was to be otherwise and the lapse of time worked a number of phenomenological effects (that is the reason why it is worth considering).

The project group

The fourteen years of this major construction project introduced such a significant hiatus between planning and execution, desire and consummation, that the new prison lost immediate connection with its original authors and inspiration even before it was finished. By 1984 (indeed, by 1977 when the old prison was finally closed but the new prison was still only part-built), all the progenitors of the

Holloway project had retired or had left to fill other posts. David Faulkner (leaving in early 1974), Joanna Kelley (in 1974), Ken Neale (in mid-1970) and William Pile (also in mid-1970) were no longer members of the Project Group. Other founding figures, the Senior Medical Officer of Holloway for instance, had also left (Dr Blyth leaving for a post in Brixton prison in 1976).

That is the way of the civil service and there was some compensation and support in the continuous paper memory of the files. A number of those who had left the Project Group remained in and about the Prison Department for a while. They were not lost absolutely and, indeed, they sometimes had dealings with the project in their new posts. And those who succeeded that founding generation gave themselves to the project just as their forebears had done. But it was not really *their* project as it had been for Joanna Kelley, Ken Neale and David Faulkner. It was work to be despatched competently and without zeal. Some of the inspiration that had infused the original decision had evaporated.

That transformation of ownership was amplified practically and symbolically by two important administrative developments that both took place in 1974. One change was the steady move away from the older model of control over the prison system to an ever greater emphasis on regional managers 'as the service's operational managers, and as the line managers of prison governors; they were keen to extend the authority to the women's service, whose governors' line manager was Joanna Kelley in P4.'[1] When Joanna Kelley retired in 1974, 'the Governor's line manager was a remote male, based a long way further from the prison with no previous knowledge of or feel for the women's service, no background of understanding the Holloway project and responsible for a very large number of men's prisons which always had first claim on his attention'.

The second change was that of the division administering the redevelopment project from P4 to P7. Once work had started on the site, remembered David Faulkner:

it was no longer possible for P4 to handle all its ramifications within its own resources and it needed to rely more and more on the Directorate of Works— who had been deliberately (and some thought insultingly) excluded from any responsibility for the project's development. . . . neither P7 nor the Directorate of Works had any feel for the project's special features or the nature of

[1] The words are David Faulkner's.

Holloway and the women's service, and it was just another project which had no particular priority (until it started to go wrong).

Overall charge of the project moved to P7 in 1974 and Sid Norris, the second Assistant Secretary of P7 to chair the project under the changed arrangement, described a most revealing meeting of the Project Group which he came to chair at that time. It was then that he discovered that the prison's creators had all gone and, with them, the creators' sense of property in the forms and regime of the new Holloway. No one any longer appeared to claim ownership in the new Holloway:

I can remember having a big meeting with the client body saying 'we've got to address this project' and finding that we were in a situation where nobody speaking had any real ownership, which was not the best message you want when you're trying to get a building up. Ownership in the sense of being able to say 'yes, we've always wanted a lecture theatre for this, it's absolutely vital under our training plans for the establishment, or such-and-such'. It had begun to sort of melt away. That was an uncomfortable position in which one was trying to get the building delivered and people were beginning to some-how stand on the sidelines.

By the mid-1970s, the planners' shaping experience of the Holloway Redevelopment Project had ceased to be one of great expectations for a brave new prison and had instead become permeated with irritation at the apparent impossibility of ever getting the building finished. Discontents gathered around the innumerable problems of a project that never seemed to go quite right. Sid Norris was reported to have said at a meeting with the contractors in 1975:

The scheme had been announced with great publicity and . . . as the Design Team's proposals developed and had aroused a great deal of interest. As the project manual put it, it was seen as a prestige and pacemaking project. There was some questioning of the need to hold women in custody at all and the advisability of investing a large amount of money in this one custodial project, but no doubts had been expressed about our ability to finish the project. Now one had to face the fact that however brilliant the conception and design might be it was so far totally ineffective in execution[2]

The prison thus changed significance as time dragged on, becoming less of an exciting experiment than a burden. The work of the Project Group was no longer to achieve great things but simply to bring

[2] Minutes of a Meeting between the Home Office and the Nominated Professionals, 5 June 1975.

matters to an effective and decent conclusion. Sid Norris recalled that, when he had taken over control of the Holloway project in 1974, 'at that stage in the project, your responsibility, as I see it, is to get the project completed and get the buildings up . . . It was rather a distinctive role as being the middle man supplying the building rather then being the client dictating the requirement.'

Perhaps the most momentous consequence of delay was to make the new Holloway vulnerable to changes of intellectual fashion, and that is the theme that will predominate in the rest of this chapter. An over-long gestation had carried the project through a succession of penological eras. Conceived at what proved to be the end of the therapeutic age, the new Holloway was actually to be born in the beginning of May's age of 'positive custody' which took it that 'the rhetoric of treatment and training has had its day and should be replaced'.[3] An official who worked in the Prison Department of the time said simply, 'you could construct an argument that [Holloway] was at the end of a philosophy that had passed its time'. Indeed, a Prison Department report, written in the very year that Holloway was at last finished, stated quite firmly: 'it became clear by 1980/81 that the needs of the female inmate population had changed markedly since 1968'.[4]

Enough time had passed for the still unfinished prison to become defined by many as an apparent anachronism, an ideological relic, ill-suited to the purposes which came eventually to be assigned to it. The bearers of the older therapeutic tradition had moved on and, with them, many of their convictions about crime, criminals and criminal justice. Even those who remained appeared to have lost some of their conviction in rehabilitation: one who had observed them closely as a colleague noted that 'there was [some] continuity of personnel. How far there was any real maintenance of that form of expression of the nature of the regime which had existed when they were first proposing it in the 70s, I don't know'. The frail life-world of the P4 of the late 1960s had proved to be frail indeed (and its successors were also to prove frail in their turn). Looking back, Joanna Kelley said:

When I was leaving in '74 this [idea of a healing therapy] became terribly unpopular . . . It's very interesting, these climates of opinion that go through

---

[3] *Report of the Committee of Inquiry into the United Kingdom Prison Services,* (The May Committee Report), Cmnd. 7673, (London: HMSO, 1979), para. 427.
[4] *Holloway Project Committee Report,* (London: Home Office, 1985), 1.

the whole of the country, isnt it? And I suppose that obviously we must have all felt that we were going too soft on crime, and also that we were being too (which I think we were) too, if you like, patronising. . . . I suppose in a way you found it more difficult to convince your colleagues. It really was a climate of opinion.

The Project Group of the mid-1970s came to find itself in a cold climate that forced its members to alter the design and ethos of the new prison. But the alterations they effected were not simple. They did not at first constitute an utter repudiation of the central traditions of Paterson and P4. To the contrary, they were a series of small and often clever concessions that left as much of the liberal core of the new prison intact as possible. It was as if the last few generations of the Project Group found themselves assailed from within and without by the new penological uncertainties of 1970s. They were no longer convinced, as Neale and Kelley had once been convinced, that women were inadequates who needed treatment. They were surrounded by a larger Prison Department that had lost what trust it may have had in the more radical forms of therapy. But they were not immediately prepared to give ground so completely that the women of Holloway became exposed to the tough new penologies that had supplanted treatment and rehabilitation.

A useful illustration of such tactical defensiveness was a letter written by the Assistant Secretary who was in charge of P4 in March 1976, quite a late stage in the history of Holloway when, as I shall show, major revisions had already been planned in the security requirements of the new establishment. The author, described by his colleagues as a 'deeply moral man', argued the protective case for treatment at Holloway:

I imagine that you will not need me to remind you that the arguments . . . are greatly over-simplified and that, in particular, it is inappropriate and unrealistic to regard 'treatment regimes' and 'containment' as isolated alternatives. As you will know, the tendency in recent years (from 1973 onwards) for women to be involved in violent (especially "terrorist") crime has forced us to reconsider the necessity of providing for a group of women offenders (whose number is extremely difficult to estimate) a degree of secure containment greatly in excess of anything which was previously considered appropriate for females. . . . But the need for containment, although sometimes a factor which can inhibit treatment, should never be seen as an alternative to it. On the contrary, the need to 'contain' brings with it an evermore pressing need to provide appropriate treatment/training regimes within which the

1. Façades of the old and new Holloway Prisons.

2. The Centre and the Village Green.

3. 'Sight lines'.

4. Informal life in Holloway Prison.

often extreme reactions (mental, emotional and physical) of women offenders can be absorbed and even used positively.

In the main, the Project Group were obliged to trim, and the letter of March 1976 is a fine instance of their trimming. They fought little rearguard actions and tactical retreats, trying all the while not to succumb to demands that might have transformed the new prison into a conventional Category A secure prison with no pretence of rehabilitation. And towards the end, it seems, they did so chiefly in the name of what can only be described as decency. An official who had worked in P4 in the early 1970s claimed that the lingering interest in Holloway as a therapeutic institution was probably confined to P4, and that the arguments that were still being put in the name of therapy at that time were 'last ditch, to preserve a decent regime rather than a matter of faith in the efficacy of treatment: better treatment with humanity than no treatment without humanity'. These seemed to be the ideas of a group without uniform or monochromatic convictions. The group had their dissents and uncertainties as any population with a shifting, intelligent membership must have ('I think you've got to recognise that there are cross currents of thought going on . . . with various individuals all the time' said the Chairman of the Project Group in the mid-1970s). Their arguments were shaped by context and pragmatics (being far more emphatic when a case was being put to the Treasury for extra expenditure than in private discussions about difficult matters of policy, for instance.) They adapted and they compromised. By the end, however, there was so little left to trim, so thin was the shell around the Steyning Brief, that the remnants of the original therapeutic conception collapsed in on themselves, leaving the new Holloway a prison after all. Ken Neale observed much later that 'the process seems to have come under strain when the momentum from P4 was lost along with that division's capacity to insulate the project from wider P.D. issues'.[5]

Let me examine how that complicated ideological metamorphosis was accomplished within the very special domain of the women's system. The therapeutic assumptions of the penal reformers had become precarious (and perhaps they had always been so) but they were retained for the tactical moral reasons that I have described. Holloway did not become a woman's Vectis (the escape-proof new

[5] Letter to myself, 24 Jan. 1995.

maximum security prison on the Isle of Wight recommended by Lord Mountbatten) or Alcatraz but it *was* changed piece by piece in negotiations with the Treasury and within the Prison Department itself, and the outcome was a mutant prison that did not (and probably never could) work very well. The new Holloway was stretched and altered to become neither a medically-orientated establishment nor a conventional secure prison, and the forces for change were both internal and external.

The evolution of the new Holloway's purpose and structure was given a triple explanation first by P4[6] and then, borrowing the same terms, by the Holloway Project Committee, the body appointed in 1984 to determine what had gone amiss with the prison,[7] and I shall follow their lead. In doing so, I shall be able to pinpoint the external changes that the Prison Department itself acknowledged in the history of its own affairs. P4 and the Committee concluded that the Holloway Project Group had faced a crisis of adjustment because there had been significant changes not only in the size and nature of the population of women offenders but also in the lengths of their sentences. Women prisoners no longer appeared to be the same, and it was no longer deemed appropriate to treat them as people who required the very particular regime embodied in the original plans of the new Holloway. It was to be a significant shift in the accepted reality of the project and one that was experienced quite differently in the Home Office, with its grand view of the whole women's system, and in Holloway, with its more local view of the prison's particular place in the criminal justice system of the south of England. I shall deal with the first in this chapter and with the second in the next.

The Grand View

(i) The Size of the Population of Women Prisoners

The original planning of Holloway had assumed that the female prison population would not grow appreciably. In what would be an effectively self-regulating system, community penalties, suspended sentences, an increased special provision for the mentally disordered offender and anticipated compensatory changes in legislation would combine to keep the number of women prisoners to

---

[6] 'HM Prison Holloway—purpose and regime', Jan. 1981.
[7] I shall examine the Project Committee and its influence later in this book.

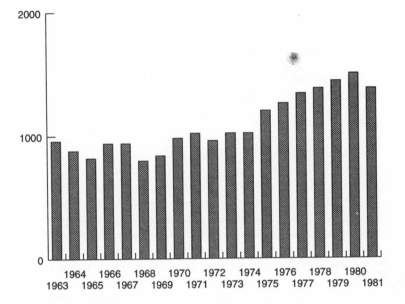

Figure 6.1: *National Average Daily Population of Women Prisoners (source: Prison Department)*

between 800 and 1,000. But the number of women prisoners did begin to rise, and it did so at just about the time that work on the Holloway project had become irreversible. Figure 6.1 shows how small the average daily population of the women's prisons had been when the plans to rebuild Holloway were conceived, and how inexorably and steeply it rose in the years immediately thereafter. By the mid-1970s, there was apprehension in the 'women's side' of the Prison Department that its strategic planning assumptions had been wrong and were in need of revision. Just as the 'men's side' had been long preoccupied with the problem of containing an ever larger and more disorderly population,[8] so, it seemed, the 'women's side' might be similarly beset. What had once been a uniquely protected enclave within the prison system, an enclave with different laws and customs, looked as if it was about to become no different from the rest. A Department report observed in 1977 that

[8] See, for example, reports in *The Times* on 12 June 1969 and 14 Oct. 1970.

between 1938 and 1973 . . . [the population of women prisoners] varied only between about 800 and 1,000. Since then the number of women has increased and in 1975 the average population was 1,219 . . . This rise, although small in absolute terms, represents a significant increase above the general post-war average and is double the rate of increase in the male population in 1975. . . . The larger population is hampering the efforts to build up a comprehensive treatment programme for women.[9]

A relatively sudden increase of 200 prisoners in the mid-1970s represented an unwelcome and unexpected change of trajectory.[10] It elicited alarming forecasts about how future numbers might begin to bear down on the management of the small estate of women's prisons. By 1979, P4 was obliged to conduct a fundamental review of its provision for women. It began to consider introducing mixed establishments, a new building programme and, indeed, the annexation of male prisons.[11] In retrospect, it may be said that the numbers of women prisoners were (and still are) both absolutely and relatively very modest, amounting to no more than 3% of the total. But it was easy enough during a time of indecision in policy formation to attach a menacing significance to large proportional increases in small populations, and, said an official afterwards, 'we were on a pretty nasty upward curve'.

(ii) The Nature of the Population of Women Prisoners

What created that indecision was a merging of events that conveyed the impression that women offenders were becoming not only more numerous but also more dangerous, more criminal, and more like men in their offending behaviour. One event, itself also partly responsible for the disturbing growth in the population of prisoners, was an increase in the lengths of sentence awarded women. Women, it will be remembered, had usually been imprisoned for short terms, but it began to seem that they were being committed for ever-longer periods in the 1970s. P4 reported that 'although all sections of the population have increased, a greater proportion of

[9] *Prisons and the Prisoner: The work of the Prison Service in England and Wales,* (London: HMSO, 1977), 100.

[10] The women's system had long been accustomed to the idea of stable or declining numbers. In 1921, for instance, Ruggles-Brise had commented on the steady decrease in numbers before the first World War. See Sir E. Ruggles-Brise, *The English Prison System,* (London: Macmillan, 1921), 114.

[11] 'Accommodation and regime for female inmates: Note by P4 Division', Mar. 1979.

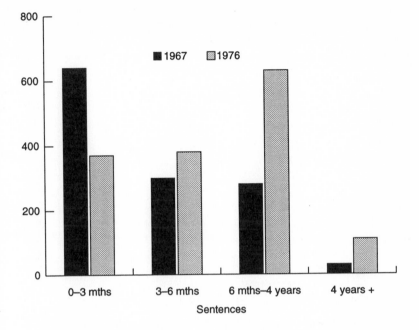

Figure 6.2: Lengths of Sentences for Women, 1967–76 (based on internal Prison Department figures)

women with longer sentences are being received into custody . . . . most of these women have to be held in closed conditions, and there has had to be an adjustment in regimes to cope with them.'[12] The figures from which the division drew that conclusion are presented graphically in Figure 6.2:

It may be seen that the number of women sentenced to long terms had indeed grown absolutely and comparatively. It did look as if women offenders might no longer be what they had been in the past, amenable to definition as naive and inadequate, not really criminal, people unable to cope with the exigencies of life. They appeared more masculine in their statistical profile. Silvia Casale reported that 'the Prison Department in 1980 . . . now recognised the increasing similarities between male and female prison populations, as more women were received to serve sentences for violence

---

[12] 'Accommodation and regime for female inmates: Note by P4 Division'.

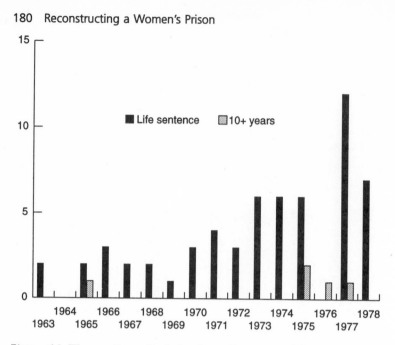

Figure 6.3 Women Committed for Long Sentences of Imprisonment in England and Wales (source: annual statistical reports of Prison Department)

against the person'.[13] By 1979, it certainly appeared to P4 that the behaviour of the female population was becoming more 'normal',[14] more male, and less obviously in need of a discrete policy response: 'in the last 9 years women have become increasingly involved in ordinary crime, and an increasing proportion of our female inmates are simply criminals, and not women in need of some special medical or psychiatric treatment'.[15] P4 concluded with some tentativeness that 'it is now far less clear than it once seemed that a large proportion of female inmates require a high degree of medical attention'.[16] So it

---

[13] S. Casale, *Women Inside: The experience of women remand prisoners in Holloway*, (London: The Civil Liberties Trust, 1989), 18.

[14] It was observed in 1979 that 'women prisoners . . . have shown themselves to be much more "normal" than was expected in, say, the late 1960s'. 'HM Prison Holloway—Purpose and Regime', 1979.   [15] *Ibid.*

[16] *Ibid.* The decline in faith in the medical coincided, as Glennys Howarth has reminded me, with the beginnings of a questioning by 'second wave feminists' of madness in the explanation of female crime. But that questioning did not visibly percolate through to the deliberations of the Prison Department.

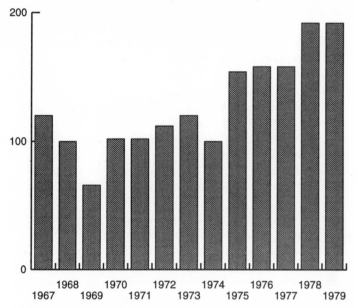

Figure 6.4 Women in Prison for Offences of Violence in England and Wales (source: annual statistical reports of Prison Department)

was that, rather than men seeming to need therapeutic communities like women, women became more like men in their need for humane containment.[17]

Sentencing patterns and committals for violent offences may have changed, but Figures 3 and 4 (drawn from annual statistical reports of the Prison Department) show that, in absolute terms, the changes still remained really quite modest.[18] The numbers of women sentenced to substantial periods of imprisonment continued to be small over the period, but there was nevertheless a distinct and worrying idea growing in the official mind that something was afoot, that women inmates were no longer what they were. What produced that idea was

[17] I am grateful to Glennys Howarth for this point.

[18] By 1993, it was possible for the earlier typification to be restored. For instance, an article in *The Times* of 4 Oct. 1993, reiterated the original description of women prisoners in full: 'most women prisoners are non-violent offenders serving short sentences for property crime. In 1991, four out of five women sent to prison were serving less than 18 months. Only 17 per cent had been convicted for violence, burglary or robbery compared with 37 per cent of men'.

actually more phenomenological than statistical,[19] not so much a reasoned analysis of trend data but the consequence of a sudden and illuminating revelation of female evil that transformed typifications and upset the broad foundation of assumptions on which the Holloway project had rested. The symbolic reality of female crime came to change profoundly.

Such abrupt revelations are not at all uncommon in the criminal justice system. A murder by Teddy Boys,[20] attacks by alsatian dogs or pit bull terriers, the killing of a small child or a young mother, can shock their audience, shatter interpretive frameworks and demand an immediate response. It is as if some portion of the world has been turned violently upside down, and urgent interpretive repair work is required.

The effects of the dramatization of evil can be magnified greatly if a reportable event occurs not once but repeatedly and within a short span of time, if it is made spectacular and horrible precisely in order to be noticed, and if the observing audience is itself already unsure of its response. What shook the Prison Department in the early 1970s was a sudden, melodramatic outbreak of terrorism committed by women who clearly intended to shock and hurt those about them. It was Leila Khaled, a Palestinian terrorist, and Dolores and Marion Price, the 'Price sisters', Irish Republican Army terrorists, who succeeded in upsetting official typifications of female criminals and reversing Home Office policies towards women. Austin Wilson, who was in charge of P4 in the late 1970s, reflected:

Amongst the underpinning ideas for the development of Holloway as a therapeutic hospital was the idea that women prisoners were in a sense intrinsically different from men, and that, although they might have committed some quite serious crimes, they might have committed them rather more for emotional reasons, for reasons connected with physical or mental health, than might be the case for men, and that, by and large, the really 'wicked' crimes were the responsibility of men rather than women. And with that went the belief that you're not providing, you don't need to be providing, Category A type physical security for women prisoners. But into that perhaps

[19] And that was to be a phenomenon world-wide. Francis Allen observed of penology in the United States that the 'modern decline of penal rehabilitationism cannot be fully explained by the persuasiveness of the logical cases arrayed against it'. 'The Decline of the Rehabilitative Ideal', in A. von Hirsch and A. Ashworth (eds.), *Principled Sentencing,* (Boston: Northeastern University Press, 1992), 23.

[20] See P. Rock and S. Cohen, 'The Teddy Boy' in V. Bogdanor and R. Skidelsky (eds.), *The Age of Affluence,* (London: Macmillan, 1970).

comfortable, even complacent thought process, there erupted the problems of female hijackers and female terrorists, and the places where those people could be held within the whole prison service estate were not many.

Leila Khaled, a member of the Popular Front for the Liberation of Palestine, had hijacked a TWA aeroplane in 1969. At the beginning of September 1970, she made a further, unsuccessful attempt to hijack El Al flight 219 bound from Amsterdam to Tel Aviv via London. Soon after the aeroplane's take-off from London, Khaled remembered, 'I threatened to blow up the plane if anyone fired at us. I displayed my two grenades and dropped the safety pins on the floor, hoping to convince everyone we intended business.'[21] Moving to the pilots' cabin, she had then flourished her grenades, and ordered the door to be opened:

I heard . . . shots and the plane went into a spin. Several people attacked me at the same moment. I thought the plane was disintegrating. The firing continued and suddenly I found myself besieged by a pack of wolves, El-Al staff as well as passengers. . . . I was knocked unconscious for a second and was overpowered.[22]

Khaled was arrested at Heathrow Airport, taken to hospital, thence to Hillingdon police station and finally to Ealing police station on 7 September. She was deported from England to Cairo on 1 November 1970. The architect of the new Holloway recalled that 'she created an enormous problem when she was captured and they didn't know what to do with her. In fact, she was held in police stations and wasn't held in prison at all because they didn't think they were secure enough.' The problem of Leila Khaled did not lead to a major and instant revision of penal policy in 1970. The original Project Group were then quite firmly in control of the still infant project and, in 1970, one incident was not enough to jar them. But the emergence of a woman as violent as Leila Khaled, a woman who railed freely at 'wolves', 'Fascist pigs' and 'Zionist liars',[23] did presage change. She was too dangerous to be confined in an old Holloway that was too ramshackle to be secure or in the new, low security Holloway that was being planned. Joanna Kelley observed in 1974 that 'the first cloud on the horizon was the arrest of the Palestinian girl hi-jacker, Leila Khaled. She was retained at Ealing police station and eventually deported.

[21] L. Khaled, *My People Shall Live: The Autobiography of a Revolutionary*, (London: Hodder and Stoughton, 1973), 188.   [22] *Ibid*, 189.   [23] *Ibid*, 195.

There was not thought to be sufficient security at Holloway to keep her there.'[24] There was certainly to be a specific reference to Leila Khaled in December 1970 when the design of a secure remand unit was under discussion. She was cited as an instance of the 'specially risky category A prisoner' that might have to be accommodated.[25]

The Price sisters were arrested at Heathrow Airport in March 1973, two and a half years after Leila Khaled, for their part in an IRA bombing campaign in London. Their bombs had been aimed quite directly at government and the criminal justice system, at Whitehall and the Central Criminal Court at the Old Bailey,[26] and they were lethal, 1 person having been killed and 238 injured.[27] The sisters were arrested on 8 March and remanded at Ealing police station before being transferred to Brixton prison, a male prison, on 17 March, and from there, after a considerable time, to a new secure wing for women in the predominantly male prison at Durham.

The Price sisters embarked on a hunger strike in Brixton in November 1973 to secure their repatriation to Ireland,[28] a strike that lasted 206 days and attracted considerable press attention.[29] The presence of protesting IRA women terrorists in English prisons prompted anxiety about security, an anxiety that was underscored by continued bombings and threats of bombs. Holloway itself was placed on amber alert in February 1973 and there was a bomb scare at the prison in May. Fears were amplified further after the IRA caused an explosion outside the staff mess at Holloway's brother prison, Pentonville, in December 1973, and injured two police officers.[30] Pat Arrowsmith, an English political campaigner, mounted a hunger strike in sympathy with the Price sisters inside Holloway in June 1974, and, with Chris Tchaikovsky, she formed a Prisoners' Action Group[31] in October 1974 (but her protests did not receive press attention).

---

[24] 'Note on Women Security Prisoners and their Containment in the Long Term'.

[25] Much later, in 1995, Joanna Kelley wrote to tell me that 'the case of Leila Khaled did indeed shake the Prison Department who suddenly realised no provision was made anywhere for Cat. A women. The sensible solution would have been the secure unit at Brixton which was small and had originally been the women's wing. But the climate of opinion was changing, we were numbed and the disastrous modifications of Holloway began.'   [26] *The Times*, 9 Mar. 1973.   [27] *The Times*, 8 Mar. 1973.

[28] They were held in Brixton, it was claimed, because there were better medical facilities for women on hunger strike in that prison.

[29] See K. Kelley, *The Longest War: Northern Ireland and the IRA*, (Westport, Conn.: Lawrence Hill and Co., 1982).   [30] *The Times*, 19 Dec. 1973.

[31] The Group was the germ out of which WIP, Women in Prison, was later to grow.

Holloway was itself relatively ill-protected at the time, its walls having been partially dismantled. The Governor reported that 'our perimeter is particularly vulnerable with a security fence separating us from building operations on two sides. . . The recent bombings especially as near as Pentonville have made us feel particularly vulnerable.'[32] It appeared that the lot of women's prisons had changed markedly and 'it must be envisaged the change may be lasting and may increase in scale, whereby more women are convicted of crimes of violence and become a significant danger to the public'.[33] The old and the new Holloway were patently not equipped to undertake the long-term secure confinement of dangerous women. Joanna Kelley reflected that 'security hadn't been built in [to the design of the new Holloway] at first, and when that crept in, in the beginning of the '70s, just before I retired, we were beginning to be aware of the Price sisters—that we simply must have a secure unit—there was nowhere in Holloway secure enough . . . that was the beginning of the climate of change as far as I was concerned'.

The shocking intrusion of women terrorists into the deliberations of the Prison Department came at just that pivotal time when belief in the therapeutic ideology began to waver and collapse.[34] At a distance from the Prison Department, there was a growing volume of reports about the failure of rehabilitation.[35] In 1977, the criminologist, Philip Bean, for instance, pronounced that the rehabilitative ideal had died,[36] the very year that the prisoners of Holloway quit the remnants of the old radial prison for the new anti-panopticon.[37] And the Home Office's own reviews of penal policy in 1977

---

[32] Governor's Annual Report for 1973.

[33] J. Kelley, 'Note of the Deployment of the Forecast Population Women and Girls', 14 Oct. 1974.

[34] Andrew Ashworth reflected that 'the strategy of rehabilitation reached its zenith in the . . . 1960s and then declined spectacularly in the 1970s'. 'Sentencing', in M. Maguire et al. (eds.), The Oxford Handbook of Criminology, (Oxford: Oxford University Press, 1994), 821.

[35] For instance, Sherwood urged the abandonment of rehabilitation and the institution of punishment based on just deserts in 1972 in 'Prison as a Last Resort', Prison Service Journal, Jan. 1972, No. 5, 8.

[36] P. Bean, 'Alternatives to Rehabilitation', Prison Service Journal, Oct. 1977, No. 32, 2.

[37] There was undoubtedly a defensiveness at the time of that move. A draft speech to mark the evacuation of the old prison and the opening of the new on 30 January 1977 stated 'I believe that the idea of the new Holloway will prove realistic and appropriate for the women's prison of the future despite trendy arguments to the contrary'.

deferred openly to the conclusions reached by Robert Martinson,[38] Stephen Brody[39] and others that prison did little to change the offender, that treatment did 'not work' and that the medical model was ill-founded.[40] The Home Office concluded that 'the assumption behind the idea of "treatment"—of offenders as suffering from a social "disease" which is susceptible to cure—is being challenged by evidence now coming to light of the importance of situational factors in the commission of crimes'.[41] Psychotherapy became more and more frequently dismissed as the enthusiasm of a generation now passed.[42] The liberal tradition in penology, the penology that had infused the new Holloway, was proclaimed by the Home Office Research Unit's Stephen Brody to have undergone a 'volte-face . . . with rather astonishing ease and speed . . . rehabilitation has come to be seen . . . as an unrealistic and unrealisable aim.'[43]

The new reality to which the Project Group had to adapt in the mid-1970s, then, was a policy environment increasingly inhospitable to ideas of treatment and preoccupied with rising numbers of women inmates, and particularly of dangerous, Category A prisoners. Projecting numbers forward in time, P4 anticipated a 250% increase in the population of women requiring conditions of high security[44] (see Figure 6.5).

It began to seem quite imperative to change the physical structure and social organization of Holloway in mid-stream, and a major part of the middle history of the project was devoted to undoing some of the earlier design work and tailoring it to the new penological conditions of the 1970s. An official wrote in July 1976: 'it seems clear that some of us now have serious doubts about the validity of decisions taken in the 1960s, and it may be that our successors will curse us for failing to foresee all their needs in the 1980s and beyond. . . . While I recognise that it is often embarrassing to

[38] D. Lipton, R. Martinson and J. Wilks, *The Effectiveness of Correctional Treatment*, (New York: Praeger, 1975).

[39] S. Brody, *The Effectiveness of Sentencing*, (London: HMSO, 1976).

[40] See *Prisons and the Prisoner*, (London: HMSO, 1977).

[41] *A Review of Criminal Justice Policy 1976*, (London: HMSO, 1977), 49.

[42] See R. Prewer, 'The contribution of prison medicine', in L. Blom-Cooper (ed.), *Progress in Penal Reform*, (Oxford: Clarendon Press, 1974), 123.

[43] S. Brody, 'Research into the Aims and Effectiveness of Sentencing', *Howard Journal of Criminal Justice*, 1978, 17, 133.

[44] 250% sounds a large increase, and it alarmed P4, but in practice it was only 15 more places.

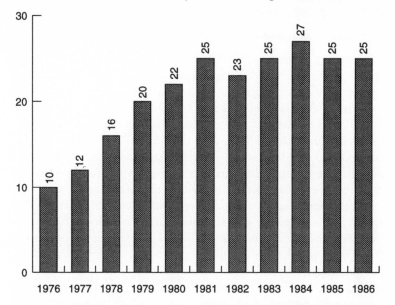

Figure 6.5 P4's 1976 Estimate of Future Average Population of Category A Women Prisoners (based on internal Prison Department figures)

acknowledge that earlier beliefs—sincerely held and strongly argued—have been revised in the light of later knowledge and experience, I do not think we should shrink from the realities as we see them.' It was said that Holloway would have to play its part in the containment of dangerous women, it would have to take larger numbers of more conventional remand and sentenced prisoners, and it would have to shed much of its claim to be a 'medically-orientated establishment'. ('On the psychiatric side,' it was claimed by 1979, 'considerable provision will still be needed to provide the necessary flow of reports to court, and reports for allocation purposes, as well as the support (and where possible, treatment) of disturbed inmates. But the original emphasis on a psychiatrically-orientated regime seems today to be rather over-protective for the female prison population.')[45]

---

[45] 'HM Prison Holloway, Purpose and Regime'.

Design Transformations

(i) Security Matters

The ensuing changes in Holloway's design, and particularly in the Steyning Brief, occurred piecemeal and somewhat reluctantly,[46] step by step, in the copious consultations and negotiations that occupied the work of the planners in the 1970s. They occurred in the meetings of the Design Team, of the security sub-committee that was established in November 1970, and of the Project Team as it discussed costings and plans with the Treasury throughout the length of the project. They were perhaps more a response to external promptings than to inner volition, the drift away from treatment and towards stronger security being spurred on by officials outside P4 itself.[47] The security sub-committee contained representatives from P5, the division responsible for security, and it was chiefly P5, the Prison Medical Directorate and the Treasury that emitted the pressures which altered the specifications of Holloway. The shift away from medicine and towards increased security and larger numbers worked as a single complicated process, and again, instead of detailing every little movement, I shall dwell only on a few of its principal features.

It had been agreed at the beginning that Holloway would be a low security prison with a special, small secure unit for remand prisoners, and that the perimeter buildings and wall would provide most of the protection against escape and attack. Indeed, in February 1974, the new Chairman of the Project Group remarked that the architects had produced a good Category C prison.

The appropriateness of those security specifications was under continual, routine review. Modifications were introduced at each stage of each phase as they came before security advisers for clearance. They were introduced after incidents elsewhere prompted reflection. In January 1972, for example, a parapet wall had to be

---

[46] For instance, Joanna Kelley pointed out in a meeting in February 1974 that only one woman had ever escaped from Holloway and that the new preoccupation with security was misconceived.

[47] At its heart, P4 still attempted to retain rudiments of the older liberal inspiration that had led to the birth of the project. The matter was summarised in March 1976: 'the important change that *has* taken place since 1969 is not in attitudes or opinions about penal treatment, or in the Department's policy towards female offenders—although both are, to a degree, less idealistic than was once the case. It is in the characteristics of a small minority of female offenders and the nature of the crimes they are committing.'

eliminated from the design of the chapel roof and a bay window was installed above the swimming pool building to permit surveillance. The recess formed by an electricity substation on the outside wall was made safe against bombs in September 1973. Doors were clad with metal and fitted with full security locks after the experience of a riot at Bullwood Borstal for girls in January 1973.

But it was in the following year that the security specification of Holloway changed rather more profoundly and schematically. A new head had been appointed at the beginning of the year to the Operations Support Group dealing with security matters and, as is the way of new appointments, he had taken fresh stock of security provisions at Holloway. In the words of the architect:

The key to it was that any design had to be put to the top security person at the Home Office and he would say whether it conformed or not or made certain requirements for it to be altered. And since he changed every year or two, each time the scheme would have to be put to the new one, and he would say 'oh well, we can't have that. I don't mind what my predecessor said, but I say that what we need is such and such, and we need, therefore to change it'.

The new head took office at the very time that the presence of IRA prisoners and the mounting of IRA bomb attacks were having their unsettling effect on official assumptions about prisons and prison safety. Security against the IRA was to become an abiding preoccupation in the Prison Department of the mid-1970s: a senior official said 'I remember one place that was being built in about 1975 and [the security people] wanted us to have anti-tank devices because they reckoned it was perfectly feasible that that was one of the things that the IRA might do, and they had no hesitation in voicing their concern, and obviously people would have been fools not to have taken this into account'.

The IRA also touched problems of security at Holloway. The Steyning Brief, it was said, had been drafted before the phenomenon of female terrorists had made Holloway's requirements similar to those of a high security male prison. Some women in custody now displayed an unprecedented degree of criminal sophistication[48] and 'since 1968 there had been a marked increase in the number of women involved in violent crimes normally associated only with men and the Home Office would have been failing in its duty had it not revised its

[48] Minutes of the meeting of the Project Team, 3 Apr. 1974.

requirements for overall perimeter security at Holloway and for the provision there of adequate accommodation for high-risk unsentenced women'.[49]

By the mid-1970s, however, most of the major planning decisions about Holloway had already been taken and some part of the new prison had been built. Although a comprehensive new security brief *was* produced at the beginning of 1974, it could not but be *ad hoc*, a list of alterations to an existing structure. For example, it laid down that the coping of the walls should be rounded to prevent the use of grapnels; manganese steel should replace mild steel in the bars of windows on the perimeter; the trolley route roof should be strengthened; and boundary lighting should be amplified to inhibit escape attempts. Parts of the prison were fortified, the gate house being made proof against ammonia and its windows against bullets. It was decided that a number of critical walls and doors should be constructed out of more robust materials, no longer concealing their defensive functions (it was noted in a meeting to modify Phase 2 security that attempts to alter the doors 'for appearance sake are not likely to be practicable'). The architect said:

The original idea was to have light security, a wall around the perimeter, and buildings inside it, and, eventually, if it became an open insecure environment, as it were, then that wall could be taken down and just have the buildings standing on their own with their own landscape around them. In the event, progressively from the time we started, we moved from designing buildings within a secure perimeter to designing very secure buildings within a secure perimeter, and the requirements for security became ever more important.

Holloway was thought to be particularly at risk because its entire perimeter was accessible to the public from without and to prisoners from within. There had to be a secure enclave within the prison to accommodate the more dangerous woman. One major proposal made in January 1975 was to provide some 160 square metres of accommodation for women categorized as high risk. The new unit would 'be grafted on to the new establishment, being set high on the fifth floor in what would be called D5 (that is, block D, floor 5, in the new planning language of Holloway), and it would house twelve sentenced and six remand prisoners (admitted to be a 'cock-shy estimate').

[49] Letter to Treasury, Sept. 1975.

Access to the new D5 would be gained by a separate, protected lift; it would be regulated by its own separate control centre; and its prisoners would be given their own secure, rooftop exercise area, closely supervised and observed and covered with mesh to prevent rescue by helicopter.[50] D5, it was argued, would be a departure from 'the Holloway concept as originally envisaged' but it was 'unavoidable'[51] because of the 'outbreak of terrorist actions since Steyning'.

P4 hesitated, arguing that it might be better to abandon plans for D5 and send high security sentenced prisoners to Durham or, indeed, to some new prison altogether. Their hesitation was shared. A working group charged with designing the self-contained secure unit was reported in January 1975 to have become:

increasingly uneasy about the acceptability of making provision on these lines ... it has become very clear that it is even more difficult than was first imagined to reconcile the concept of a secure unit with the general style and purpose of the new establishment; and there are even doubts whether a really secure unit can be sited within a category C prison which is, by design, treatment orientated to the degree that is planned for the new Holloway.

With the support of the Project Group Chairman,[52] the Prisons Board did decide to retain plans for D5 (the unit later becoming C5 and then, in 1978, C1). But, bowing to P4, it determined that it should be employed for remand prisoners only. Eventually, as Holloway evolved, D5-C5-C1 came to be used for the segregation and punishment of sentenced prisoners, being occupied by women described as 'highly disturbed', and it represented a double reversal of the original, Steyning Brief which, it will be recalled, had quite deliberately made no provision for a punishment block.

It is plain that planning had become a little muddled by the mid-1970s, planning for increased security being conducted, on occasion, in parallel with continuing work on the more liberal, therapeutic

---

[50] Rescue by explosives and helicopters was a preoccupation at the time. See, for example, the review by Quentin Hughes of a book on prison architecture in *The Times*, 17 Dec. 1976.

[51] Minutes of special meeting to consider the security provision for Holloway, 11 Mar. 1974.

[52] He observed: 'I took it to the Prisons Board saying "here's the proposal" and the Prisons Board decided they would have it, and the intention therefore was to get oneself out of this situation where one was housing Category A remands in Brixton, and then of course Risley, and it really was a laudable aim to try and get remand accommodation in London which would avoid people being in the sort of accommodation which, with the best will in the world, you couldn't regard as adequate'.

prison described in the Steyning Brief. For example, in October 1974, some time after the introduction of the new security brief, the Design Team presented Stage D of Phases 4/5 with the preface that:

The brief for the whole project has hardly changed since the Steyning Conference in October 1969 when the basic objective was agreed to be to create a humane environment for the treatment and rehabilitation of women and girl offenders and suspected offenders. Minor changes to security have been made during the development of the project that have in no way invalidated the brief but have involved changes in detail to the design approach.[53]

Holloway was in evident transition, its emerging character becoming ambiguous, and there were anxious discussions between P5 and the Project Team about quite how radical and comprehensive the new security provisions were supposed to be. By June 1975, it was thought necessary to submit a paper to the Chairman of the Project Team for a ruling on the extent to which security should be allowed to take priority over other matters in what remained of the planning. And, in July 1975, Sid Norris, the Chairman, did rule, arguing that it would be difficult to change the planning brief in the middle of a project: 'we must exercise restraint in amending the brief for a building which is in the course of design or construction even though we may be developing more exacting security requirements'.

Although Norris may have preserved some of the original design brief, he was not wholly persuaded by the idea of therapy either: 'I wouldn't have wept tears about people being more realistic about the word "therapy" . . . I would have thought that probably various people would have been uneasy about those very "therapeutic" ideas which had inspired the original regime. I would think that even with those who had been involved in devising the idea, the thoughts about regimes had gone by then'.

In tandem with all the other changes and second thoughts that must inevitably accompany a redevelopment project lasting fourteen years,[54] those revised security specifications involved a continual process of redrafting and modification for the Design Team and their contractors. The architects were forever being required to alter

---

[53] Phase 4/5 Stage D Presentation to the Project Team, 29 Oct. 1974.
[54] For instance, insulation standards were improved in 1974 in response to the fuel crisis, and fire proofing standards had to be changed after an inspection.

their plans[55] and the perverse consequence was that a new family of delays and frustrations[56] was fed into the already tardy programme. It was reported by an official in May 1973 that 'we have had evidence from other late changes in the Brief that these have lowered the morale of the members of the design unit at RMJM and they are tending to view the Brief to which they work as suspect and liable to constant change, causing much of their work to be unproductive'. Moreover, because many of the changes in specification led to claims for extra fees, claims that were as often resisted or negotiated, the progress of the project became even further stalled. There were to be recurrent anxieties about mounting costs, lost time and increasing acrimony. A senior administrator remembered:

One of the troubles, if you started building a new prison, it usually took about 5–7 years, during which time security standards would alter, they couldn't possibly have been built into the original plan. If you are using outside architects and contractors, they immediately rub their hands. It's rather like a defence project. If you want modifications, you pay through the nose. And that happened particularly with the establishments they had to convert to be high security, dispersal prisons. They paid millions out for them.

(ii) Money and Medicine

If the revisions to the security brief of early 1974 were the first major catalyst of change in the evolution of the new Holloway, the second was to be a more fitful, running review of costs and the allocation of space. The Project Team may have been continually modifying the Steyning Brief in the mid-1970s, but they had yet to make an unequivocal repudiation of the high hopes of Steyning. That final collapse came after a unremitting series of cuts, modifications and

[55] The principal architect recalled that 'we had a sort of multi-headed client, each responsible for their own particular bit. So we had the prison officers, as it were, on one hand, the governors of the prison, the people who were dealing with security who were quite separate in the organization of the Home Office, and the specialist sphere— organizations like education, the church, psychologists, people dealing with work facilities and so on, and, of course, the doctors and the hospital side of it. So each of them were separate and what we had to do was to try and bring their requirements together as one.'

[56] It was noted, for example, in Oct. 1971 that late changes to the design brief had led to 'a good deal of bitterness among the nominated Architects, who felt we had let them down by not noticing much earlier the implications of the new lay-out they proposed in February'.

changes introduced at the insistence of a Treasury anxious to effect economies.

Holloway was rebuilt at a most difficult time in the economic history of the United Kingdom. The national economy was in the throes of a high inflation that rose to an unprecedented 17% a year in 1974 and to more than 25% by mid-1975. In the latter half of the 1970s, the principal aim of the Government's economic policy was to reduce inflation by curtailing public expenditure. Strict advanced cash limits on 75% of public spending were introduced in 1976, when spending fell by 1.1%, and even larger cuts the year after, when spending fell by 5.5%.[57] Prompted in part by the disciplinary control of the International Monetary Fund, £1 billion was severed from the budget in July 1977 and another £1 billion in December 1977. The Treasury became ever more insistent in its quest for possible savings in public projects. And one such project, the rebuilding of Holloway, was proving to be massively and increasingly expensive. The original estimate for the prison had been between £5,000,000 and £6,000,000; by March 1979, ten years later, it had risen to £11,400,000; and by April 1980, to £12,150,000.[58] The project had suffered not only the effects of incessant national inflation in the construction industry,[59] but also the extraordinary additional financial effects of building on site (agreed by the Treasury in 1969 to be £1,000,000), of rectifying the damp staff accommodation in Phase 1,[60] and of the extra expenditure on increased security after 1974.

The Treasury asked ceaseless searching questions about the requirements of every phase of the design process. The then Controller of Administration, remembered 'there were rows with the Treasury going on. Presumably that was standard during the time on all fronts, wasn't it?' The very first objection the Treasury raised was in 1968 when it disputed the need to dispense with 'slopping out' in the new Holloway, and it persisted thereafter. There were questions about the need for extra security provision, the swimming pool and

[57] See B. Hogwood, *Trends in British Public Policy*, (Milton Keynes: Open University Press, 1992), 41. Spending on 'law and order' as a whole did not fall during that time although items within that budget were affected.

[58] By 1990, the final cost was actually rumoured to be £40 million. *The History and Development of Holloway Prison from AD 1849 to AD 1990*, (Holloway, mimeo, 1990), 21.

[59] In 1971, for instance, there was request to the Treasury for a 17.5% increase in costs for Phase 2, and in 1973 for a 20% 'uplift on costs'.

[60] Estimated finally to have cost some £400,000.

much else. In 1974, it was agreed to lower ceilings and narrow corridors in the new establishment for reasons of economy, a decision that was to have surprisingly profound repercussions. David Faulkner called it the one particular thing he regretted about the design, 'that decision to lower the height of the ceilings and narrow the width of the corridors in order to keep within the cost limits that the Treasury had imposed. We should have insisted on getting the financial limit modified to accommodate higher ceilings and wider corridors.' I shall return to the low ceilings and narrow corridors of the new Holloway in Chapter 8.

In its role as inquisitor, the Treasury was to be the very first body within government formally to challenge the project's continuing (albeit by then somewhat residual and nominal) commitment to the therapeutic ideology of the Steyning Brief. In a letter to the Chairman of the Project Group on 5 March 1976, it conceded the need for expenditure on additional security and then proceeded: 'It is true that opinion on the custodial care of prisoners has changed since 1969. There is certainly a lot of evidence to support the view that "treatment" regimes have produced no impact on the rate of recidivism. If the emphasis has moved towards containment we would expect a reduction in the resources devoted to treatment and, perhaps, recreation.'

The Treasury then mounted a sustained attack at first and second hand on the justifications for those resources. In that month of March 1976, for example, the Senior Medical Officer of Holloway was approached about the wisdom of retaining a male surgical half-unit ('is the development of this accommodation consistent with the development of present policy?'); about the provision of medical officer's rooms; about the delivery suite ('will the Department's policy admit of mothers giving birth within the prison rather than in outside hospital?'), and the outpatients' clinic ('does the Department's experience since Steyning still justify the inclusion of this clinic?'). The Project Group's very mandate was thereby assailed.[61]

---

[61] The Chairman of the Project Group noted on 12 Mar. 1976 that whilst he could deal with the Treasury's allegations about the failure of treatment, it should be P4 that prepared 'an appropriate draft stating the Department's policy towards the penal treatment of women and the regime at Holloway'. The first such draft to appear was actually written in 1979, and by then it was in accord with the Treasury's pessimism about the possibilities of treatment.

In June 1976, after yet more criticism from the Treasury about the rising costs of the project, P7 asked the Project Group to 'look again at every item in the accommodation proposed for Phases 4 and 5 of the project'.[62] Treasury demands were beginning to eat away at much of what had made the original design brief distinctive (the Chairman of the Project Group told yet another meeting held on 13 September 1976 to consider economies in Phases 4 and 5 that 'it would be for P7 to balance the judgement of those who drew up the original Holloway brief with the intention of breaking new ground in penal policy against the judgement of those now asking themselves what was the minimum with which we could get by'). The outcome was that items were indeed shed, an instance of a large loss being a proposed staff training centre, and they continued to be shed for a long while afterwards.

Yet another, major piece of stock-taking was conducted after the discovery that unexpectedly deep foundations would have to be dug on the site for Phases 4 and 5, and that the buildings of those phases would have to be delayed and redesigned in consequence.[63] The Directorate of Prison Medical Services was allowed to 'review the over-generous medical accommodation'[64] in Phases 4 and 5 and, at a meeting held in November 1977, there was a fresh cull, it being announced by the Director that there had been 'changes in attitude since the original plans were drawn up'. The operating theatre, the delivery suite, the mortuary, the pathological laboratory, the male surgical half-unit, and some of the space in the venereal diseases clinic were then lost to the design.

P7 approached the Director of Prison Medical Services once again in August 1978 to inquire what further medical accommodation at Holloway might be pruned ('because of (a) the tight financial position of the Holloway project and Treasury pressure for economies (b) the voluble criticism, currently, of overcrowding problems at Holloway, it is considered essential that inmate accommodation places should be maximised'[65]). And the result was that about twenty extra 'medical'

---

[62] Letter from Assistant Secretary, P4, to Prison Medical Services, 22 June 1976.

[63] It was found after the last portion of the old prison had been demolished that the clay-bearing soil dipped deeply where the remaining living block was to be built.

[64] 'Brief for Mr Weiler's Visit to Holloway Prison on 23rd Feb. 1978'.

[65] Letter of 29 Aug. 1978.

rooms were released for use as ordinary inmate accommodation.[66] Yet more medical rooms were shed in February 1979.[67]

Little by little, the medical accommodation decreased and the inmate accommodation swelled, so that, by early 1979, enough space had been freed to produce a new CNA [Certified Normal Accommodation] of 537.[68] What was left of the therapeutic spaces within the prison then appeared disorganized and scattered, and it was gathered together in one place, a 'hospital area', in a single Block.[69] The hospital had become very vestigial: indeed, so vestigial had it become that the Chairman of the Board of Visitors was obliged to ask the Senior Medical Officer in late 1977 quite what was then meant by the word 'hospital'. The Senior Medical Officer's reply was that 'C5 unit and the Mother and baby unit on B4 landing were generally considered as "hospital" but . . . that occasional use of B3 unit had been made'.[70]

I have observed that a feature of all those meetings was that, by the latter half of the 1970s, it had become clear that no significant person or group claimed property in the new Holloway or wished ardently to defend what had been done at the Steyning Conferences. The loss of medical space had not been contested.[71] Neither had that of the staff training centre.[72] The Chairman of the Project Group in the mid-1970s said:

It wasn't as if this was the way in which everybody was going and all of a sudden a shaft of enlightenment came from outside, or a shaft of disagreement . . . . Given the changes in personnel and the intimation . . . of the

[66] Minutes of the Meeting of the Holloway Project Team, 6 Oct. 1978.

[67] Minutes of 2nd Meeting of Reconvened Commissioning Sub-Committee, 9 Feb. 1979.

[68] Minutes of the Holloway Redevelopment Sub-Committee, 20 Mar. 1979.

[69] Minutes of 3rd meeting of Holloway Redevelopment Commissioning Sub-Committee, 4 Apr.1979.

[70] Minutes of the meeting of the Board of Visitors on 26 Oct. 1977.

[71] The then Director of Prison Medical Services conceded in Mar. 1979 that it was becoming officially recognized that 'Holloway would be a prison with hospital facilities, rather than virtually a hospital, contrary to original expectations'. Note of informal meeting on hospital accommodation, 23 Mar. 1979.

[72] A member of the Medical Directorate informed the Assistant Secretary in charge of P4 in July 1976: 'it is of interest to note the reasons why the advice given in 1969 took the form and direction it did, but only historically so. It seems to me that the arguments used then were built on false premises and aspirations which were as misconceived then as they would be today. Credibility would be more at risk, certainly honesty would be, if the scheme was to proceed without recording the fact that the Medical Directorate no longer sees the need for a Staff Training Centre at Holloway.'

certain lack of ownership, the ownership had melted away, it did not surprise me that, when the opportunity came retrospectively to rethink [after the discovery of the problem of the foundations] things were taken out which obviously people had now decided they didn't want. Mostly medical, probably the whole concept of a hospital and an operating theatre, everybody having their obstetrics and delivering their babies inside the establishment, and so on . . . all these things had gone.

It is never easy to reverse the planning assumptions of a building that is half-finished. The metamorphosis of Holloway had demanded mounting pressure from the Treasury . to achieve economies (although it was a convention that departments did not refer to the Treasury as a constraining influence) and from the Prison Department Committee[73] to provide more accommodation for women prisoners. It had been been accelerated in unanticipated pauses and reappraisals. And it had been eased by the disappearance or half-heartedness of people who might otherwise have been expected to defend the Steyning Brief.

Under all that strain, P4 did finally take stock: there had been 'adjustments in the plans for Holloway', it observed at the beginning of 1979, 'but we have not so far attempted to describe a fresh conceptual basis for the new Holloway, to take account of their change and to replace that which guided the Department in the late 1960s and early 1970s'.[74] That description was to be provided within the frame of a routine annual review of the certified normal accommodation of Holloway.

P4 had set about examining and justifying the proposed allocation of space in the new establishment, and it was then that it disclaimed the past. What the Holloway Project Committee Report of 1985 called a 'revised statement of the purpose and regime', P4's recantation, was drafted first in 1979 and released in modified form in January 1981. Women, it said in arguments rehearsed already in this chapter, were involved ever more frequently in ordinary crime and a higher proportion were being received for longer sentences; they did not need a therapeutic regime and it was no business of the prison

[73] A meeting of 6 Mar. 1979 had determined that 'the lack of places for females meant that the Department would have to take a decision on how to provide more accommodation. It was unlikely that provision for any further new accommodation could be introduced. The regime also needed reviewing.'

[74] 'New Holloway—Purpose and Regime', Feb. 1979.

service to supply the medical attention that was properly the work of the National Health Service:

> These factors, and the realisation that psychiatry has little to offer in the treatment of criminality, have combined to make it impossible to justify the high expenditure and heavy emphasis on medical and related facilities, and have made it necessary to allow for the development of a training regime for a larger number of women.[75]

Holloway would thus be turned on its head once more, being allowed to revert to its original role, its remand and unsentenced prisoners being treated like any other prisoner. It would 'operat[e] under pressure as part of the tactical resources of a hard-pressed part of the prison system; . . . it will operate with a less decidedly medical bias—it will be a prison, not a hospital, albeit a prison with considerable medical support'.[76] A hospital might remain, but its importance would be radically diminished. Only 100–150 women would be patients out of a total population of 550. In the language of the May Committee,[77] Holloway would share with other local and training establishments the:

> objective of providing for the positive custody of its inmates, with education activities and occupational employment provided within a disciplined but caring regime. . . . With the wider responsibilities which it has assumed, the level of security will need to be sufficient to accommodate category A remand prisoners. Provision is also being made for a segregation unit.[78]

In the rest of this book, I shall describe the history of that newly redefined Holloway, exploring how prisoners, management and staff came together in the new spaces that had been prepared for them.

[75] 'HM Prison Holloway—Purpose and Regime', Jan. 1981.

[76] 'HM Prison Holloway—Purpose and Regime', 1979.

[77] *Report of the The Committee of Inquiry into the United Kingdom Prison Services*, Cmnd. 7673, (London: HMSO, 1979).

[78] 'HM Prison Holloway—Purpose and Regime', Jan. 1981.

7

Metamorphosis III: The Social Transformation of Holloway

'Our abiding problem . . . has been to manage a multi-purpose establishment containing all categories of prisoner in over-crowded and uncomfortable conditions with hopelessly inadequate staffing.'[1]

Introduction

At the prison, the announcement in 1968 that Holloway was to be rebuilt was said to have led to a 'period of initial anxiety about proposed change, a period of wild rumours about what was and what was not going to happen, including the rumour that staff were resigning right and left . . . [followed] by a period of feeling that here was a great opportunity to introduce sweeping changes and make Holloway a totally different place'.[2] Yet, after that initial flurry, the project seemed actually to make little immediate impact on most staff and inmates.

Almost nothing would have been seen until 1970 when the phased demolition began. Planning was conducted from afar at 'headquarters', and it involved those at the top of the various hierarchies of the prison: the Governor, heads of sections and union representatives. Consultations between the Design Team and prison were regular and systematic,[3] and they could be intense enough for a time. (One former

---

[1] Governor's Annual Report for 1975.

[2] C. Blackler, 'Symposium on New Institutions: Notes on Holloway/New Holloway', typescript, 10 Apr. 1971.

[3] Thus proposals for Phases 4 and 5 were inspected in 1974 by Joanna Kelley and the then Governor of Holloway, Megan Bull, by the Briefing Group, the Security Sub-Committee, the Medical Briefing Group and, at the prison, by the Holloway Staff Club Committee, the Supervisor of Works, the Senior Foreman of Works, the Organiser of Physical Education and others.

Assistant Governor called it the 'greatest [consultation process] ever done in the prison service. We were shown plans, we were shown models, it was discussed with us and all the theories were put to us.') In May–June 1971, members of the Prison Officers' Association went to Hounslow to visit an exhibition of furniture designed by the nominated architects for the new staff quarters in Phase 1. In 1974, the Design Team displayed their plans for Phases 4 and 5. But it was sensed by members of the prison that the Team came to them as if they were bearing a gift to be admired rather than proposals which could be challenged and amended in discussion. (The position of the Team at that point was that it was *unable* to change the Steyning Brief. David Faulkner said afterwards that 'there was a strong discipline which said that the design brief could not be tampered with without causing unacceptable delay and extra cost (which was true) and this affected the scope both for second thoughts and for consultation (as distinct from explanation)'.)[4] A member of the Board of Visitors remembered 'they were driven by this great sense of . . . HMG establishment generosity: "we're giving you this amazing new prison and it's going to cost £7,000,000!" . . . the culture was sending messages which were "please say 'thank you'", because that's how it was being put. "You're very lucky. There's Brixton, there's Pentonville, there's Wormwood Scrubs. Terrible! But we have singled you out for this amazing new building!"'

The Design Team evidently conveyed the impression in the early 1970s that they had such a firm belief in the good sense of what they were doing that they could not and would not be deflected. A psychiatric nurse working in the prison recollected:

The architects' team came with a model of the new prison and they pointed out how it was going to work, and how it was going to function, and I remember there was a lot from the officers that worked on the landings saying 'with this design, how are you going to see what people are doing, how are you going to observe people, you're going to be in very close proximity with people . . .' . . . They defended it on the grounds that it was more a hospital setting and . . . women who went to prison needed more of a hospitalisation and I feel that it was going ahead regardless of what people said. . . . People get hold of an idea and then everything goes ahead on that idea and nobody wants to see the rights or lefts of it, and I feel that's really what happened . . .

---

[4] Letter of 4 Jan. 1995. He added, 'it also led the staff to question the sincerity of the consultation process in which we genuinely tried to engage'.

although they kind of involved people in it, it was as much as saying this is what's going to happen rather than saying 'we would like your opinions . . . .'

And a discipline officer said:

You see, you've got these people in the top circles who have got these strange ideas . . . [the consultation] was all a farce, wasn't it really? These big meetings went on that you were hard put to attend because you have got all your work to do. . . . We did see drawings and we had these talk-ins about the whole thing and they wanted our suggestions and they were given suggestions but we all knew jolly well that it was just to appease the natives and that they weren't going to take any notice of us!

For the most part, those consultations were brief visitations that did not disturb the prison. Many staff were excluded (one former discipline officer recalled: 'as an officer—my colleagues and the people I met every day were officers like myself—none of them would have been in a position to have looked at the development of Holloway'). Most were too preoccupied with the mundane problems of managing a prison. Immured behind their high, thick walls, they were to remain remarkably untouched even when work started on the site about them in the early 1970s. There was little enough to be heard at first (a former inmate said 'you couldn't get much past those old prison walls. It was a real solid prison'). And there was little to be seen ('the visible sign of the redevelopment was a corrugated metal fence on one side . . . [that] really wasn't particularly visible from the road . . . Certainly it didn't really impinge on what was happening in the old Holloway'). For quite a long time, then, most staff and inmates seemed to be enclosed inside their total institution, sealed against knowledge about events on the building site beyond the walls, concentrating on immediate problems of the here-and-now. One who was then an Assistant Governor said:

The building was going on next door but it really wasn't much of a feature and like lots of staff I didn't take much of an interest in it particularly. We started having organized tours in 1977 to have a look at the redevelopment but, before then, yes, I knew in one part of my brain that it was being redeveloped, but I didn't really take an interest and the site of the prison was undisturbed by that.

And a former prisoner said:

[There was] not much interest. . . We didn't notice it really. There was a lot of dust around the place and I think visits were moved but most things were seen as a possibility for something. There were more places to hide things and more places to secrete yourself.

It was only at the point when half the old prison was actually demolished to clear the site for construction, when, as one who worked on the site said, 'everything was just smothered in dust and muck and so on', that Holloway was disordered for a while. Inmates had to traipse 'with their belongings, bedding, all that kind of thing along the corridors . . . into other bits of the prison'. But afterwards life resumed again within the smaller space that was left: an education officer recalled, 'once it was established as half a building, there was a fence that divided it from the building site and they put in false floors to increase the effective space—not all wings had them but most of them did—it just operated as a half prison but it had all its facilities'.

As I proceed to describe how Holloway then evolved during the years of its redevelopment, I shall pursue trends that carried over from the world of the old prison (operating until the beginning of 1977) to that of the new. A number of significant processes ran continuously through the last days of the old prison and into the early days of the new, and, for narrative purposes, I shall neglect the distinctive part played by the architecture and design of the anti-panopticon until the next chapter.

The Diffraction of Prisoners

The social world of the old Holloway did begin to change after 1970, and one chief catalyst was the quite unforeseen increase in the number of women prisoners that had so alarmed the Prison Department. Despite its straitened character, the reduced 'operating prison' was still the central women's establishment, and, against all the earlier planning assumptions, it was required to take in more women. From 1972 onwards, it may be said that Holloway, once a near-empty prison, was no longer overly large for its population. To the contrary. Figure 7.1 shows that, as its physical buildings shrank in half (reduced to Wings C, D, DX, F and K), so, perversely, its

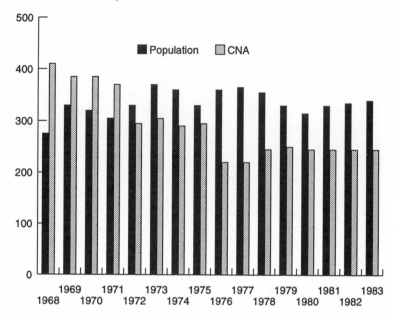

Figure 7.1 *CNA and Average Daily Population of Holloway (based on figures contained in Governors' Reports)*

numbers began to rise,[5] there was 'doubling-up[6] in cells and Holloway became overcrowded[7] with multiple consequences. The population changed erratically, lurching between troughs and peaks. In December 1974, it reached a peak of 387, 30 per cent above capacity.

First among the consequences of the increase in numbers was the decision to resort to a kind of fractional distillation of the population so that many of those inmates who could be despatched safely to other establishments were sent away. In July 1970, the Chairman of the Project Group informed the Treasury:

[5] For example, the Governor's Report for 1974 observed that 'during December, in accordance with the general rise of the female prison population our numbers rose to 385. Since the interim accommodation which we occupy during the current phase of the Holloway redevelopment programme was planned for 300 women, such a high occupancy severely stretches our resources'.

[6] Note of Meeting of Liaison Sub-Group, 24 Feb. 1971. *The Times* (1 July 1974) reported two beds to a cell with no room in between.

[7] See reports in *The Times* of 9 Mar. 1978 and 1 June 1978. In the latter report, the Prison Board of Visitors was reported to have protested formally that with a CNA (Certified Normal Accommodation) of 221, Holloway held 365.

The operational circumstances have changed for the worse as, in common with the male side, numbers have risen dramatically (by about 20–25 per cent since January this year) and although we shall transfer away from Holloway as many women as the rest of the system will bear we shall have to continue to accommodate more people on the site than would otherwise have been necessary.

There was steady diversion: in October 1972, all Borstal girls were transferred to Bullwood (although they returned a year later); in 1975, it was decided to send ordinary convicted prisoners to Styal;[8] within a few more years, many convicted prisoners were no longer even committed to Holloway but were committed elsewhere immediately, and especially to the new women's wing at Drake Hall after it opened in 1975.[9] It was contemplated that remand prisoners might be sent to Pucklechurch.[10] On occasion, Holloway became little more than a kind of penal entrepôt: in April 1975, the Governor reported to the Board of Visitors that 'the numbers remain high in spite of regular transfer to other establishments every week'.

It was inevitable that there was an impact on the composition of the population. A prisoner at the time said 'all my mates had gone except one or two. There were less long-term inmates in Holloway. You were moved quite quickly when you got a longer sentence.' One major group not to be moved was the remand prisoners who had to be within reach of the courts. Another was those women with short sentences whom it would not have been practicable to transfer. And a third was those women defined as dangerous or disturbed whom other establishments could or would not accept.[11] Psychiatric and special hospitals were not under the control of the Prison Department or the Home Office and they were not obliged to receive prisoners from Holloway.[12] After the initiation of what were called

[8] Minutes of meeting of Board of Visitors, 26 Feb. 1975.
[9] Governor's report to the Board of Visitors, 23 Nov. 1982.
[10] Governor's Report to the Board of visitors, 25 May 1982.
[11] It is interesting that whilst the number of women admitted to mental hospital for 'personality and behaviour disorders' rose steadily during the period of the Holloway redevelopment project, rising from 14 to 38 per 100,000 between 1964 and 1973, the length of stay declined markedly during that time, resulting in a reduction from 165,000 average daily occupied beds in mental hospitals for both sexes in 1961 to 109,000 in 1976 and 100,000 in 1979 (source: *Social Trends*). It is evident that more women were being diagnosed as disordered but were staying for less time.
[12] In Feb. 1978, for instance, the Senior Medical Office reported to the Board of Visitors that 'difficulty was experienced in getting admissions into psychiatric hospitals . . . ' Minutes of meeting of 8 Feb. 1978.

'open-door' policies in local hospitals in 1959, leading to the abolition of many security controls, there were to be ever greater problems as hospitals became unwilling to admit 'mentally disordered' offenders who could be defined as difficult or dangerous.[13] Not only was it considered inappropriate for 'scarce medical resources [to be] allocated to people who cannot benefit from treatment',[14] there was growing resistance amongst staff to the reception of potentially violent patients who could be awkward to handle.[15] The matter became particularly fraught after the passing of the Mental Health Act of 1983 which provided in Sections 37(4) and s. 47, that a hospital order could not be made on a 'mentally disordered person' unless the hospital agreed that the offender was one whose condition could be alleviated or prevented from deteriorating.[16] In the mid-1980s, as I shall show in the next chapter, the problem of blockages in referrals was to have an especially deleterious effect on the prison. A prison officer of the time remembered:

I've got vivid memories of people coming from hospitals when we've got a prisoner who shouldn't obviously be in Holloway, and a doctor and a nurse and one other would come to interview her and decided she was too bad, they couldn't take her, not through any fault of their own. They couldn't take her because they hadn't anywhere to go with her. So she was a prisoner.

The problems of incarcerating people thought to be mentally ill were not peculiar to Holloway. They perturbed others at the time. They were to be the central theme of the introductory speech by the Chairman of the Annual Conference of Boards of Visitors on 19 October 1982. 'Let us be quite frank about the matter', he said. 'Transfers of dangerous, chronically mentally-ill inmates are not welcomed by hospital authorities. All kinds of reasons, some sound and some specious are given for refusing them. Psychiatrists don't like them but even when willing to admit a patient find the nursing staff

---

[13] See the Mental Health Act, 1959, s. 60(4).

[14] L. Gostin, *Institutions Observed*, (London: King Edward's Hospital Fund for London, 1986), 14–15.

[15] There were reports of growing numbers of attacks and incidents on nurses and staff. COHSE, the Confederation of Health Service Employees, recorded 48 incidents in 1974, 111 in 1975, 75 in 1976 and 77 in the first 7 months of 1977. *The Management of Violent or Potentially Violent Patients: Report of a Special Working Party offering information, advice and guidance to COHSE Members*, (COHSE, no place, 1977), 2.

[16] For a fuller discussion, see J. Peay, 'Mentally Disordered Offenders', in M. Maguire *et al.* (eds.), *The Oxford Handbook of Criminology*, (Oxford: Oxford University Press, 1994).

objecting to handling them, and faced with industrial action they often give way.'

By the late 1970s, the search for space in the women's prisons became sporadically frantic. A note by P4 in March 1979 observed that the opening of a new establishment at Cookham Wood had 'averted disaster' in 1978 but that there were too many sentenced women in open prison: 'only the most acutely difficult cases can now be found places in the closed prisons'.[17]

Holloway was transformed. It became a receptacle for those whom the staff defined as an ever-growing residue of 'disturbed' women, some linked with drugs offences,[18] many on remand. A prison officer reflected:

We lost the D and Ds, the drunk and disorderlies, we lost the prostitutes as well. We used to get a lot of drunk and disorderlies and a lot of prostitutes, but they changed. They no longer came in prison, and quite rightly in my opinion. But the younger generation, yes it did change. . . . The drug culture in my opinion has increased drastically over the years.

On 31 May 1978, the Holloway Board of Visitors despatched a delegation to the Minister of State to discuss overcrowding, one of the main headings that ordered their discussion being 'too many severely disturbed inmates in Holloway who would be more suitably accommodated in mental hospitals.'[19]

The proportion of sentenced women declined to 50 per cent by the mid-1970s,[20] and to less than 40 per cent shortly afterwards. Figure 7.2 illustrates the jagged growth of remand prisoners and the compensating decline in sentenced inmates (the hospital held both sentenced and unsentenced women, many placed there for assessment.[21]) By the early 1980s it was reported by psychologists working at the

[17] 'Accommodation and regime for female inmates', Note by P4 Division, Mar. 1979.

[18] An undated report showed a six-fold increase in receptions of adult females under sentence of immediate imprisonment for drug offences between 1974 and 1984 (although the absolute numbers were small, rising from 50 to 300). *Silence: Women's Imprisonment*, (London: London Strategic Policy Unit, no date). Of course, as David Downes has reminded me, drug offenders are not the same as offenders with drug problems, 'who are an additional problem'.

[19] 'Delegation of Holloway Board of Visitors to meet Lord Harris—May 31st'.

[20] Minutes of meeting of Board of Visitors, 26 Mar. 1975.

[21] In April 1975, the Governor informed the Prison Department that, at the end of March, Holloway held 191 unsentenced and 205 sentenced prisoners; 53 of the unsentenced inmates were in the hospital, 82 in the Remand Wing and 50 in the Assessment Wing. 29 sentenced women were reported to be in hospital at that time.

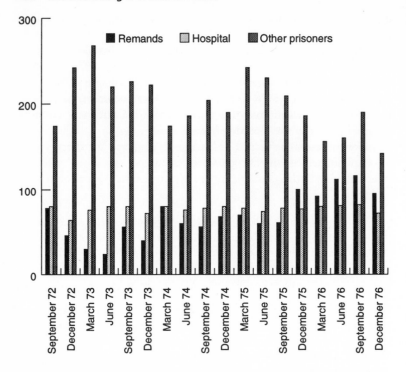

Figure 7.2 Numbers of Inmates in Hospital and on Remand (based on figures contained in Governors' Reports)

prison that 'as many sentenced women as possible are transferred out of Holloway to other prisons, and only those too disturbed to move, those allocated to essential work parties, some mothers and babies, and those selected for the Therapeutic Unit remain'.[22] Holloway became a *de facto* remand prison: 60 per cent of its population were on remand, 37 per cent were convicted and 3 per cent awaited deportation.[23] In July 1978, the Chairman of the Board of Visitors wrote to the Chief Magistrate proposing that the period convicted inmates spent remanded in custody for medical reports should be reduced from three weeks to two weeks. The prison came in time to

[22] C. Stewart and J. Shine, 'Disturbed Women in Holloway', June 1984.
[23] I. Posen, 'A Survey of Stress in Prison Officers at Holloway Prison', 1986, internal report, 5.

be described as a 'transit camp',[24] its rate of population turnover having accelerated so much, and, with it, demands on its staff for escort duties.[25] 1,368 inmates were transferred to other prisons in 1982, for instance.[26]

If it seemed to P4 that there was a growing entropy at the national level and that men and women offenders were becoming more alike, in Holloway it looked quite otherwise. Diversion, distillation and the retention of the non-transferable inmate brought it about that prison's inmates appeared less and less ordinary to the staff. In 1974, the Board of Visitors reported:

Holloway and its patient staff of all levels have burdens thrust on them from all directions without hope of alleviation—from the juvenile courts who commit the young girls whom an ordinary remand home will not take, and from the outside hospitals who sometimes find the conduct of patients sent from Holloway for treatment quite unacceptable and return them to the prison before the course of treatment is completed. On the other side, Broadmoor, Rampton and Moss Side only too often refuse to take women who seem to us to be dangerously deranged and in need of treatment in a medical rather than a penal setting.[27]

Nine years later, the Governor made very much the same complaint:

We received and coped with a number of women presenting very difficult behavioural problems in other establishments. The overriding problem is finding the means to cope with the significant number of highly disturbed women who are often unacceptable to National Health Service hospitals. Sometimes these women have freak mental illness and they respond to medical and nursing care, but all too often they are said to be suffering from personality disorders and do not fall within the narrow definitions of the Mental Health Act, 1959.[28]

It may well be that some of those definitions of disturbance were subjectively problematic. They may well have reflected the general propensity to medicalize the pathology of women.[29] They were certainly an emanation of the special problems faced by women

---

[24] The term was used in a meeting between the Board of Visitors and David Faulkner in Aug. 1981. Minutes of the meeting of the Board of Visitors, 25 Aug. 1981.

[25] That was a complaint made, for example, by the Governor in her annual report to the Prison Department for 1974.   [26] Governor's Annual Report for 1982.

[27] Annual Report of the Board of Visitors for 1974.

[28] Governor's Annual Report for 1982.

[29] See H. Allen, *Justice Unbalanced: Gender, Psychiatry and Judicial Decisions*, (Milton Keynes: Open University Press, 1987).

cooped up in an increasingly congested prison with a young and inexperienced staff, problems that I shall touch on below. Quite what the word 'disturbed' meant at that time was not, and probably could not be specified.[30] It was not used technically[31] (although the Governor of the time, Megan Bull, had a training in psychiatry,[32] she was reported to have claimed that she did not care for the discipline[33]). The word clearly bore twin traces of the diagnostic and the disciplinary: disturbed women being both refractory, a threat to control, and less than rationally responsible for their actions, a clinical matter. One source, *The Oxford English Dictionary* (Second Edition) defines disturbance as 'the action of disturbing', 'interruption of mental tranquillity', and 'interference with the regular or due course or continuance of any action or process'. It seems that the meaning of the word must be referred primarily to the audience which is disturbed.[34]

---

[30] The 'mentally disturbed offender' seems to cover a vast range of behaviour. The Mental Health Advisory Committee of the National Association for the Care and Resettlement of Offenders proposed in 1993 that 'mentally disturbed offenders [should be] defined as those offenders who may be acutely or chronically mentally ill; those with neuroses, behavioural and/or personality disorders; those with learning disabilities; some alcohol and substance misusers; and any who are suspected of falling into one or other of these groups. It also includes those offenders where a degree of mental disturbance is recognized even though that may not be severe enough to bring them within the criteria laid down by the Mental Health Act 1983.'

[31] It does not appear in many of the contemporary standard works of reference where one might expect to find such a technical term (for example, *American Handbook of Psychiatry*, (New York: Basic Books, 1974) or *Gradwohl's Legal Medicine* (Bristol: John Wright, 1976)). The meaning of 'personality disorder' appears to be equally elusive. *Butterworths Medico-Legal Encyclopaedia* (London: 1987), p. 417, states it 'is a difficult term to define'.

[32] She had been appointed medical officer at Holloway in 1967 and was Governor between February 1973 and May 1982. She received her MB and ChB in 1944 and a DPM in 1970. It was taken by many in the prison that the Prison Department's appointment of a doctor signalled the kind of prison Holloway was supposed to be. But one who was on the board that appointed her observed: 'I'd say two things, first of all that she was an impressive woman, not in a flamboyant way but her professionalism, and her balance were very evident on interview. . . . we felt that we saw nothing inconsistent in getting a doctor. Holloway had been governed by male doctors in the earlier stages before Charity Taylor became governor. It was often a male doctor in charge, I suppose removing one of the risks if you've got a male, which has past now, but the slight risk of putting a man in charge of a woman's establishment . . . The other thing, I think I must be fairly blunt, is the other candidates were not terribly impressive'. [33] See *Evening News*, 22 Feb. 1973 and *The Times*, 1 July 1974.

[34] Mental 'disorder' is similarly vague and confusing. Thus the Mental Health Act 1983 s. 1(2) defines it as 'mental illness, arrested or incomplete development of mind, psychopathic disorder and any other disorder or disability of mind'.

But whatever it may have been and whatever it meant, disturbance was undoubtedly a phenomenological reality to the staff of the prison. No reports issuing from the prison during the 1970s (and 1980s[35]) dissented from the view that Holloway was a troubled place peopled by disturbed inmates. And disturbance was a peculiarly difficult state to manage.

Holloway under Megan Bull was to be torn between the imperatives of treatment and punishment,[36] the contradictory responses to the dual facets of disturbance.[37] A member of the Board of Visitors observed:

There was no doubt that . . . there was a very unenlightened view of the role of prison officers, they saw themselves as turnkeys, screws, whatever and they didn't see themselves as treatment people at all, they absolutely didn't, they weren't encouraged to, they weren't resisting anything, they weren't being difficult, the job description for them was you keep them, you hold them, you turn them out, you take the new ones, basically and you do it on a hierarchical basis with a very clear, 'how many stripes have you got, I've got more,' kind of view of your role and responsibility. . . . [Megan Bull's] whole ethos was to interfere with that, which was everybody here is responsible for, everybody here is treating, everybody here who has an impact on and is face to face with a woman who is here in custody is a treatment person, whereupon the discipline staff all said 'no we're not, we're custodial staff, we're discipline staff, we're not treatment people' and she said 'everybody here is because everybody here is having an effect, it may be a negative effect but in the sense that they're treating and we use that positively, okay they may not be treating positively but they are having an effect on the population that's here and to that extent they can't duck the responsibility of being treatment people.' The discipline staff said 'that's giving us more responsibility, we don't want that' and they tried very hard to distance themselves from the nursing staff and the medical staff and there were all these problems about doctors being part time and incomers not being part of the culture.

[35] Even the civil libertarian, Larry Gostin, wrote about disturbance and the problem of C1 in Holloway: 'it houses the most disturbed women in the prison system; three quarters are diagnosed as mentally ill, with a preponderance of schizophrenia, depression and personality disorder'. *Institutions Observed*, 50–51.

[36] For example, it was uncertain in the Manpower Management Interim Report of 1976 whether the new C1 unit for 'highly disturbed women' would be managed as a medical or disciplinary sphere and that uncertainty persisted for years when C1 came into use.

[37] One device employed was to label parts of the new Holloway by block and level (I mentioned D5 in the last chapter). The intention was to defuse the adverse effects of labelling. 'D5' was more neutral than the 'highly disturbed unit', for instance.

The contradiction between treatment and control was thought to have thrown Dr Bull against some of the more disciplinarian officers (an education officer said, 'Dr. Bull kept as much as she could going, she struggled really hard, she's physically tiny and didn't have all this experience but she did stand up to the POA a lot, she kept saying "we're not going to shut those doors, we're not going to do this, that and the other"'). As one who had come from medicine rather than from the ranks of officers and governors, she lacked a measure of legitimacy amongst the discipline officers[38] (but not amongst many other staff and some of the inmates,[39] and certainly not amongst the Board of Visitors[40]). She was expected to manage as a treatment-directed governor in an institution where treatment was on the wane. (A former member of staff said 'poor Dr. Bull had an impossible task because the drive towards the medical model just disappeared when Joanna Kelley went, I don't think anybody took it up as far as I could make out and she was left as governor of a major prison with very little experience, no clout, the officers didn't rate her because she hadn't been on the landings or hadn't been a prison governor and on the day she retired she said to me that she was in despair,[41] she felt that she had not achieved anything, I think she did achieve a lot, she stopped the tide of negativism, she actually held it back as far as one could'.)

The problems and conflict centred on disturbance were substantial, persistent and insoluble and they wore Governors down. They carried

[38] One experienced officer reflected that 'Dr Bull was indoctrinated into this new image of prisoners and even in an interview when she had left she admitted that she had been wrong because every time she took the prisoner's part. The majority of us believed if you were wrong, then you were wrong, and you should be punished because that's the only way to treat people fairly. If one gets punished, they all must. Of course, you must understand that some people are below par and they should not be viewed in the same light as somebody that is all there. Quite often my girls would say "what's wrong with her? She's not been put on report! You've put me on report," and I used to say "you know how many beans make five and you know she does not, and she's only really copying you". I used to tell the girls off.'

[39] She was liked by many of the inmates. (One said, 'I thought she was accessible. Me and ——— a fellow inmate would talk about her—"I should go and tell Dr. Bull about that, she's a very understanding woman" . . . she wasn't inaccessible').

[40] The Board regularly conveyed their admiration for Dr Bull to the Prison Department. Their annual reports referred to her 'humanity', 'intelligence, devotion and informed sympathy'.

[41] Others talked about her sadness at the end. One officer said 'I would imagine as the governor of Holloway during that transition that her hands were full on just surviving day to day as much as the rest of us. She was, I thought a very good governor but I think she ended her career a little disenchanted, which was a pity, but I don't think she felt ever that she'd accomplished what she was either capable of or wanted to accomplish'.

over into the new Holloway and new governorships (more than one governor suffered in health). A counsellor visiting the prison in Megan Bull's period of office remarked, 'it's very hard to be a therapist and an authoritarian. This is a terrible conflict of worlds.'

The Diffraction of Prison Officers

A very similar structural development began to emerge rather later amongst the population of discipline officers, just at the peculiarly difficult time of transition between the old and the new prisons. If the prisoners had been progressively filtered as ever greater numbers entered the women's prison system, so the prison officers of Holloway underwent their own form of diffraction, and their collective composition and character also changed.

Public expenditure cuts had curtailed the hiring of prison staff in the early 1970s, and Holloway itself was reported to be under-staffed (for example, there were 80 basic grade officers in 1974[42] compared with 100 in 1969). In 1976, the Governor reported to the Board of Visitors that the bar on civil service recruitment had left the staff levels 'dangerously low' (it was 25 below its authorised strength of 131[43]) and that, of the 14 women officers then in training in England and Wales, the prospect was that none would be sent to Holloway.[44]

Recruiting resumed in March 1976, Holloway was given 'priority in posting recommendations',[45] and the outcome was that a sudden influx of new officers entered the prison, many of whom were junior, and sometimes very junior indeed, the 'POUTs' or 'NEPOs' only recently trained or still under training at Wakefield. 52 such officers were posted to Holloway in 1977. By September 1977, it was reported that of 102 officers then in post, 69 had under three years experience and 52 under two years.[46] Eight months later, the Board of Visitors believed the problem to be so serious that they complained to the Minister of State, Lord Harris, about the proportions of young staff in post at Holloway.

The demographic structure of Holloway's staff was transformed; a reiterated complaint by managers and the Board of Visitors was that

---

[42] *The Times*, 1st July 1974.
[43] Minutes of meeting of Board of Visitors, 24 Mar. 1976.
[44] Governor's report to the Board of Visitors, 28 Jan. 1976.
[45] Letter from Prison Department to the Board of Visitors, 8 Dec. 1977.
[46] Report of the Governor to the Board of Visitors, 23 Sept. 1977.

the average officer had become quite unseasoned.[47] The Chairman of the Board of Visitors wrote to the Home Office in 1977:

As you will know, the members of the Board of Visitors of Holloway have been concerned for a long time about staffing problems within the prison. We appreciate that the recent increase in recruiting has brought the number of officers to a more acceptable level, but it has meant that the prison is staffed by a high proportion of very inexperienced people.

If there was an inrush of young staff after 1976, there was also a steady loss of mature officers. It was customary in the prison service for experienced officers to be transferred on promotion, and their places were not always filled by people of comparable experience. The second observation made to the Home Office by the Chairman of the Board of Visitors in 1977 was that:

We now find a further problem being created by promotion of experienced officers to higher grades who are then moved to other establishments, reducing still further the number of experienced officers available to us. We wonder whether your department is aware of the serious problems within the prison caused by this practice.

By early 1981, it was reported in a Manpower Control Team review that the prison lacked senior officers: Holloway was short of 24 basic grade officers, 24 senior officers, and 4 principal officers, and 60 per cent of the staff had been in post for under two years.[48]

The third, linked problem was that of high staff turnover (see Figure 7.3). Staff may have entered Holloway, but they left as rapidly. They tended not to stay[49] and they did not mature in post. Thus, the 57 officers who resigned between 1980 and 1983 had served for an average of no more than two and a half years. In 1983, it was reported that 'Holloway tends to have a vast majority of officers who have served under 4 years', 25 per cent having served in the prison for less than two years and 50 per cent for less than three years.[50] The staff body began increasingly to lack cohesion and stability. Resigna-

---

[47] In her Annual Report for 1977, for instance, the Governor wrote about 'very junior staff now representing an increasing proportion of the total . . . We are still very deficient at middle management level'.

[48] Governor's report to the Board of Visitors, 21 Jan. 1981.

[49] In the discussion of their annual report for 1974, the Board of Visitors observed that 'staff difficulties were acute and officers left almost as fast as they joined'. Minutes of meeting, 26 Feb. 1975.

[50] I. Posen, 'Sickness and Resignation Rate of Staff at Holloway', 1983.

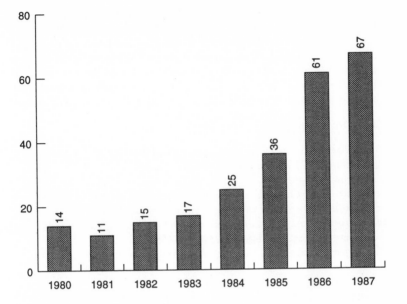

Figure 7.3 Staff Resignations from Holloway (based on figures contained in Gorvernors' Reports)

tion, absenteeism and sickness became identified as endemic to Holloway. There was industrial action.

It seemed to some that the generation of older, experienced, maternal officers who had once ruled in the radial prison was being succeeded by others with a different style. They were, said one former nursing sister, 'the new breed' who came in with 'their book learning they had got at training schools'. It was reported that staff were inept at controlling disturbances and did not seem to understand fundamental control procedures required by Standing Orders.[51] One of the older officers remembered:

We were used to being with the women and all of a sudden everybody wanted their bum on the office table. They didn't want to be with the women, and you're only a prison officer if you're with the women. It's only being with the women that you know what's going on, that you understand what's happening, and who's upset and who's not upset, if there's good news and bad news. . . . Of course, they teach new things in the training school, and one

[51] Manpower Management Interim Report, Jan. 1976, 2.

came back and said 'I never knew my potential until I went to the school', and I said, 'what's that? Potential? Never heard that word before.' And of course they thought I thought they were boasting and I was having a go. A different way of thinking, that they were above all this sort of thing, of being out on the landing, and they all became very far removed from a prison officer and I felt it was a sad thing when the old prison officer was besmirched because we did care, we cared a hell of a lot more.

And a former prisoner concurred:

In the old building they were all old officers and they had seen it, experienced it, 3 officers for 75 women, and occasionally there were fights. If you put that many women together, you've got to expect conflicts of some sort, and they dealt with it easily. It was like 'whose fault is it?'. Nobody said 'it was her fault or her fault'. Nobody said anything so you got 14 days and you knew you were going to get 14 days, it was expected. . . . Then I came back again and I found things very different. . . . I did ask. I asked a few officers and they said its the way they're training them in the school, Wakefield training school.

Damp

It will be recalled that the construction of staff quarters in Phase 1 should have been complete by September 1973, but that the fraught problems of water penetration had delayed completion until April 1978. The staff had anticipated that they would soon move into their new accommodation, and certainly before the inmates who were scheduled to be transferred by the end of 1974.[52] By April 1973, however, it had become evident that it was to be otherwise. Instead of a smooth movement from the old hostel to the new quarters, staff were shuffled around for four years between different forms of makeshift accommodation found for them at varying distances from Holloway. Temporary housing was obtained first at the Police Section House in Stoke Newington, and officers were expelled from Holloway to free the site for clearance in readiness for Phase 3.

[52] In June 1975, briefing material for a visit to the prison observed that 'the staff. . . are becoming increasingly frustrated by the delay, especially as it now appears quite possible that the first of the inmate living accommodation will be ready for occupation before the staff quarters'. When the inmates did make their move, in January 1977, notes for a speech by Terry Weiler marking the event were careful to mollify the staff: 'your private life has been disrupted by the years of delay in completing the new staff quarters. As you know, we are now well on the way to having them ready for occupation, but it is a great disappointment to us that staff were not in the end the first beneficiaries of the new building work.'

The action was not well received. The Governor informed the Prison Department that 'staff were seriously demoralised early in the year by the enforced evacuation of the hostel due to delay in the completion of the new quarters. Considerable anger and resentment still prevails among some Officers.'[53] Problems multiplied. Staff had expected that they would return to their new accommodation after six months but they were balked. More and more POUTs entered Holloway, and they also required housing (forty-five POUTs had to be housed in July 1975, for example). To make matters worse, the Metropolitan Police, finding it difficult to rehouse their own staff, reclaimed the Section House for their own use in 1975. Staff protested,[54] but 'had to endure the upheaval of another move',[55] being evacuated once more to new quarters in Brent, Earl's Court and Hampstead in April 1975. The Governor of Holloway called it a 'disastrous delay'.[56]

Other facets of the planned move were consequently thrown out of joint. Furniture specially constructed for the new prison and held in store had to be used instead by other establishments. There were 'informed parliamentary questions' in the House of Commons in June 1976 and adverse publicity. The acquisition of the block of flats in Brent and the payment of additional rent allowances to increasingly disgruntled officers added to the costs of the project and led to further correspondence with the Treasury (but it also reconciled some officers to living independently, away from the prison, and they became less than enthusiastic about returning.)[57] The matter came to be described within P7 as 'extremely sensitive' and a source of

---

[53] Governor's Annual Report, 1974.

[54] The Deputy General Secretary of the Prison Officers Association wrote in Apr. 1975: 'at the time it was suggested that the proposed accommodation at the Stoke Newington section house would be short stay and block one of the permanent officers quarters would be complete by mid 1974. We are now approaching mid 1975 and as I understand it the work is far from completion. Rumours are now rife at Holloway that the work in hand will take another 18 months to complete and that the accommodation will not be ready for occupation before the end of 1976. If this is true then the short stay accommodation suggested by the Home Office will have been for a three year period which I am sure you will agree is an intolerable prospect.'

[55] Annual Report of the Board of Visitors for 1975.

[56] Governor's Annual Report for 1975.

[57] This was certainly the impression of the second meeting of the Commissioning Sub-Committee of 18 Oct. 1976. A senior Prison Department official remarked 'having built them staff quarters to a standard that had never ever previously been seen in the Prison Department for men or women, then the great fuss was that they didn't want to come back, they rather enjoyed being off site'.

'grave anxiety'.[58] On the officers, the cumulative effect was considerable.[59] They were frustrated, unsettled and resentful. A Deputy Governor remarked:

The rebuilding dislocated them terribly, they were greatly inconvenienced, and their culture—the key bit to their culture was that the staff lived around Holloway in the staff hostel, so there was a well established social pattern in the hostel, in the staff club . . . what was for sure is that when things began to move, the staff were dislocated and they went in 2 different directions, one group of staff went to some accommodation up around Hampstead and the other was Earls Court and so suddenly people were dispersed and had to travel quite significant distances.

The Straitened Prison

The outcome was a kind of lingering implosion. On the one hand, there was a volatile group of short sentence, remand and 'disturbed' prisoners. In her annual report for 1973, for instance, the Governor, Megan Bull, observed of the remand prisoners:

The Remand Wing remains a very difficult area with a large turnover of women of all ages, but usually a high proportion of young girls who find the restrictions and lack of opportunity for physical activity very frustrating. Many of the remand population are very disturbed people who could well be located in the hospital. In fact, because the occupancy of the hospital beds is so high, Medical Remands are regularly located on the Remand Wing where a great deal of very disturbed behaviour is contained, with inadequate medical supervision.

On the other hand, there was a volatile group of prison officers. And the two groups met in a noisy, dirty, crowded prison whose deliverance was repeatedly promised and repeatedly postponed. Preparations would periodically be made to move but they were as often

---

[58] The terms were used in a letter of 12 Apr. 1977.

[59] The Governor reported as early as 1973 'the considerable concern and resentment' caused by the emergency use of temporary accommodation. She wrote 'it is to be hoped that the operation can be completed without serious damage to morale'.

aborted.[60] It was reported that slippages in the Phases 2 and 3 programme and frequent changes in the date for the move had made it virtually impossible to draw up a realistic programme.[61] The staff waited anxiously for news of their transfer to Phase 1 accommodation. What should have been a hard but tolerable period of transition began to prove really quite insupportable.

In late 1971, it had been declared that the operating prison would have to continue 'to function, albeit somewhat uncomfortably, for some years'.[62] By December of that year, David Faulkner wrote to Martin Wright of the Howard League; 'three of the existing wings, as well as some of the workshops and the reception room, have already been taken out of use and partly demolished, and conditions are therefore noisy and cramped for both the prisoners and staff. It can only be difficult to run a prison in these circumstances and tension is bound to develop from time to time.' Only minimum maintenance and modifications were carried out on buildings condemned for demolition, the works staff were employed as much on the new building under construction as in the operating prison, and by 1973 the Governor reported that the prison was congested and in a poor state of repair.[63] Exercise and other programmes declined (in August 1976, when the locking-up figure was 416, even the recreation rooms were used as dormitories).

Prisoners protested: there were reports of rooftop demonstrations in 1971 and 1973, a disturbance in the remand wing in September 1973, window breaking in early 1974, and nine women barricading themselves in the Drug Unit kitchen in July 1976. They were in evident distress: the Board of Visitors were alarmed at 'so much

---

[60] The papers of the prison and the Prison Department are peppered with references to the continual postponement of moves into various phases of the new establishment. For example, a meeting was held as early as November 1971 to give preliminary consideration to the problems of the move from the existing buildings to the temporary accommodation in Phases 2 and 3. A working party was established in early 1972, and quite elaborate detail was discussed (for example, how many inmates might be seconded from Pentonville to assist the move, how the temporary accommodation would be planned, the problem of the steepness of the ramps from the old prison, and the like) but the deliberations of such meetings were massively premature. The working party was to be reactivated after four and half years in July 1976.

[61] Minutes of the Fourth Meeting to Discuss the Organisation of the Move from the Present to Part of the New Accommodation, 21 July 1976.

[62] 'Holloway Redevelopment: Phases 4 & 5', 5 Nov. 1971.

[63] Governor's Annual Report for 1973.

violence and screaming'[64] in the special observation unit. There were fights, assaults and riots.[65] In 1972, the Board of Visitors remarked; 'the growing restriction of space creates difficulties in providing adequate recreational facilities . . . We feel that this restriction is partly responsible for the marked increase in cases of assault . . . which have come before us.'[66]

For a while, still anticipating a properly phased timetable, Dr Bull, the Governor, conceived the operating prison to be a kind of ante-room to the full-blown medically-orientated establishment rising up before her. The difficulties of the cramped old Holloway would be but temporary, and she tried to organize the regime in readiness for the move to the new establishment next door.

The operating prison was treated, in effect, as a therapeutic community in waiting. There was 'occupational therapy for disturbed women'; a drug rehabilitation unit in 1973 ('its regime approximates as nearly as can be achieved in a general prison setting to a therapeutic community'[67]); a group therapy regime run by psychologists on F Wing in 1974; and, on D Wing, 'the main therapeutic endeavour has been to enable . . . by regular and ad hoc meetings with women and staff to learn to resolve the problems of living together as a community'.[68] There were, the Governor reported, 'a large number of visiting Psychotherapists . . . giving valuable help in planning treatment programmes and contributing to staff training'. The prison had 'begun to prepare . . . actively for the new Holloway'.

But the prison oscillated between crisis and calm as numbers of prisoners rose and fell. It teetered on the edge of social disorganization more than once. The fissile combination of staff, prisoners and prison did not lend itself to the orderly preparation of a therapeutic environment.[69] By 1975, the primary goals of containment and discipline had come to eclipse all others. The Senior Medical Officer

---

[64] Minutes of Meeting of Board of Visitors, 26 Feb. 1975.

[65] Noted in succeeding monthly meetings of the Board of Visitors in the early 1970s. Almost every meeting deplored the number of assaults on staff, the overcrowding of the prison, high inmate numbers with, as the Governors' report to the meeting of 20 July 1973 put it, 'resulting stresses throughout the system'.

[66] Draft Annual Report of the Board of Visitors for 1972.

[67] Governor's Annual Report for 1974.   [68] Ibid.

[69] A report of May 1975 for the Prison Department's Annual Planning Exercise talked of 'the squeezing in of inmates in the remaining limited space and the proximity of building operations with the attendant dust and dirt inevitably lowers the quality of prison life and throws additional strain on both staff and inmates'.

alluded to 'problems of overcrowding, doubling up of inmates, the result of the rebuilding. . . . There had been a greater disturbance amongst the inmates and the number of mentally disturbed women within Holloway is increasing.'[70]

There were growing numbers of reports of assaults on discipline and nursing staff, self-mutilation and violence by inmates, and an 'alarming number of cell-fires'.[71] Conditions in the hospital wings were unsatisfactory, 'with a high level of disturbed, aggressive and destructive behaviour' and not enough discipline staff to contain the inmates.[72] It was becoming difficult to sustain any semblance of a normal regime, and staff began to protest that the prison was failing. It certainly seemed difficult to maintain everyday routines. The senior psychologist complained that Holloway remained 'a stressful, frustrating place where tasks, for one reason and another rarely get completed'.[73] And the Education Officer wrote of a struggle to maintain 'a workable routine against a background of constantly changing population, widely dispersed accommodation and transient staff'.[74] In the midst of bad conditions, and working increasingly long hours,[75] the staff were said to have become dissatisfied, more and more frequently sick, and prone to 'personal, sexual, emotional and social problems'.[76] It was, said the Governor, 'profoundly depressing'.

It was in this setting in 1975 that the beginning of the end of psycho-therapeutic aspirations at Holloway came:

Apart from the discomforts of overcrowded living conditions, work areas and visiting accommodation, the modest progress we had made in planning therapeutic regimes on various wings had had to be sacrificed. In order to maintain our numbers at a manageable level we have had to transfer as many sentenced women as places permitted. Our former assessment procedure had to be abandoned in favour of quick decisions on suitability for transfer.[77]

Therapy was abandoned in the face of urgent needs to manage what was seen as a large, unstable and mobile population: 'it is clear that

[70] Annual medical report for the year ending 31 Dec. 1975.
[71] Governor's Annual Report for 1975.   [72] Ibid.
[73] Annual Report by the Principal Psychologist for 1975.
[74] Report by the Education Officer for 1975.
[75] The overtime worked by staff in 1975 amounted to between 16 and 22 hours each week for each overtime grade (including 9 hours a week of extra travelling time allotted to staff because of their residence in temporary quarters outside the prison). Manpower Management Interim Report, Jan. 1976.
[76] Governor's Annual Report for 1975.
[77] Governor's Annual Report for 1975.

overcrowding has meant that belief in the value of treatment for prisoners has gone by the wayside in a sheer effort to keep control of rowdy young girls, who the medical officer has said, are "not treatable".[78] After 1975, it would not be an exaggeration to describe the prison as an institution enduring a sustained crisis marked by a rapid turnover of inmates and a transient staff, by fire-raising, assaults and self-mutilations. At the end of that year, the Governor reported 'our usual high incidence of disciplinary offences, including assaults on staffs, and fires'.[79] There were thirty-three fires in the hospital and a suicide. An interim report by the Manpower Management Team in January described problems of control as 'substantial and continuous'. There had been fourty assaults on staff in 1974. ('This figure', it was noted, 'is only exceeded by a few male prisons all containing more inmates; most far more inmates').[80] The staff were reported to be barely coping with basic obligations.[81]

What probably prevented the completion of that drift towards disorder was the prospect of imminent deliverance in January 1977. The Board of Visitors observed in 1976 that they were delighted that this was to be the last annual report written about the 'old and obsolete buildings of Holloway'. It had, they said, become inappropriate to dwell on the past and the problems raised by the old prison. They preferred to look forward instead.

From July 1976 onwards, officers, members of the Board of Visitors and others began to reconnoitre the new establishment and their apathy and hostility were said by the Governor to be giving way to 'growing enthusiasm for the project and an increasing confidence that the new buildings will be a pleasure to work in and will provide a functional and decent environment for the women'.[82] The promise of the new Holloway was thought by some to allay the misery of the old. The education officer remembered that 'there was always this notion that one day we would move into this paradise'. For the optimistic, the new Holloway would be everything that the old was not: 'I think we were investing and injecting into these pictures. Like you go into a house and think "I'd like to live there, I know what I'm going to do with it"'. Some prisoners talked of the new prison in redemptionist

---

[78] S. Williams in *Building Design*, 9 June 1978.
[79] Governor's Annual Report for 1976.
[80] *Interim Report of the Manpower Management Team*, Jan. 1975, 3.
[81] Governor's Annual Report for 1976.
[82] *Ibid.*

tones too: 'I used to hear about it from ——— [a fellow inmate] . . . and she used to talk about having a light switch and a key and all sorts of those things. It was like dealing with paradise of some kind for ——— and you could almost see it being talked about in a bubble.' Megan Bull was confident that the new building would calm unruly prisoners. It would make things right. The foreman of works recalled that:

I had spoken to the architects and indeed people at the Home Office about the amount of glass that there was in the windows because glass was always being smashed in the old prison and I made my views quite plain about the fact that I didn't like it in the accommodation part and I remember Dr. Bull's words were 'Mr. Avery, when the girls move over into the new accommodation they are going to be going into a different world altogether where they have got their integral sanitation, they've got nice decorations and all this kind of thing and I'm sure there won't be any damage'.

Yet the Holloway about to move at the end of 1976 was not the prison of 1968 when the transition was first conceived. Its staff,[83] prisoners, social structure and existential order had undergone a sea change. The staff were young and some were disenchanted:[84] they had known noise and dirt, rapid turnover, improvised working conditions, long periods on escort duty 'plus fractious inmates . . combined with the gross delay over their own quarters'.[85] The inmates were not those that the original Project Group had envisaged in Steyning: they were no longer preponderantly sentenced for appreciable terms and available for treatment (a former officer said 'there was lots of talk about the need for different prisoners . . . and the total impossibility of getting different prisoners. We did need the prisoners that would match the building'). The penological environment had changed. Local and national management seemed no longer to know quite what the prison was or should be. Too much ideological work had been undone by the sheer practical difficulties of building the new establishment and maintaining the old prison in a time of intellectual

---

[83] The Assistant Governor responsible in 1976 for training the staff for work in the new establishment said that the original high expectations had 'evaporated by then, before we ever moved in'.

[84] The Chairman of the Project Group told a meeting with the Design Team in June 1975 that he feared that delays and difficulties were imperilling the good-will of the staff: 'he feared that through the delay, discontent and disenchantment with the project was setting in'.

[85] Speaking Notes for Party for Holloway Staff on 30 Jan. 1977.

uncertainty and economic constraint. And little could be accomplished whilst the new establishment was not wholly ready. (The new prison, still incomplete, would be used only in part in what was called the 'temporary period'. It was expected in 1976 that the temporary period would end in 1981, but it actually lingered on until 1984.) On the verge of the evacuation of the old prison, the Governor, Megan Bull, warned that:

> Although we feel reasonably confident that we can negotiate the move and function successfully in the new buildings, there is nevertheless a degree of disappointment and even embarrassment that we have constantly to offer an apologia for the much publicised 'treatment' commitment of the New Holloway. It is difficult for the public to understand that for some years to come we shall be a remand centre and local prison, and will hold only a small number of sentenced women . . . the new Holloway will at this stage be a pale shadow of the original concept.[86]

It was resolved that the new prison which opened in January 1977 would have to make do with the resources it had. The first meeting of the sub-committee reconvened to plan the commissioning of the new Holloway decided that 'the regime will be based on the staff available when the move took place in January, as it seemed pointless to plan a regime on staff and facilities which might or might not become available in the future'.[87]

The Move

The population of the operating prison was slimmed down to fewer than 300 to squeeze them into the limited space of the Phase 2 accommodation (although the population would expand again as block after block inside the prison was commissioned). One hundred inmates were transferred out by the end of 1976 and, having a smaller population, Holloway was said to have passed a 'very pleasant and peaceful Christmas without incidents'.[88] Work parties were despatched to clean the new prison before the move, supplies were delivered, seventeen officers were seconded from other prisons to assist the transfer, and on the weekend of 29–30 January, in cold,

[86] Speaking Notes for Party for Holloway Staff on 30 Jan. 1977.

[87] Minutes of the 1st Meeting of the Holloway Redevelopment Commissioning Sub-Committee, 5 Aug. 1976.

[88] Governor's report to the Board of Visitors, 25 Jan. 1977.

clear weather (the chaplain having asked for the help of God in the old chapel)[89], 276 prisoners[90] and six babies were escorted from the old radial prison into the new, not quite medically-orientated establishment. The last act was that 'someone put a notice on the door: "will the last person out leave the key under mat"'.

The move was accomplished without extraordinary incident ('we didn't lose anybody [although] in the midst of packing everybody up, all the prisoners were saying "I don't know where I'm going"—you've got about 50 to 60 people milling around and moaning and groaning and grizzling and you're trying to make sure you've got this, that and the other, and are the store men coming up and what about the meals you've got to organize and the coffee'). But the loss of the structure of the radial prison; the experience of a brief, liminal period in which it seemed difficult for people to adapt; and profound dissatisfaction with the labyrinthine design of the anti-panopticon, worked together to engender an enduring sense of existential insecurity and *anomie* with consequences that I shall describe in the next two chapters.

Epitaph

The last memories of the Victorian prison were described by staff in transcendental language. The word used over and over again was 'eerie'. Terry Weiler, the Controller of Administration, remembered 'I stood in the old Holloway with Joanna Kelley and Megan Bull and we then walked solemnly across . . . It was an eerie feeling there. It always is, I think, to be in an empty prison'. And an officer said:

It was really eerie and all sorts of things . . . Newer staff, like myself, people who joined after me, even, became aware perhaps for the first time, of the true history of the buildings. I think older staff perhaps had a better insight than we did . . . . it really came home to me, standing on F Wing with these

---

[89] Report of the Church of England Chaplain for 1977.

[90] The only member of that group of 276 I spoke to had rather mundane memories of the transition: 'When we moved I was part of the moving party that moved the kitchen. It was disgusting—unbelievable all the rotting fruit and rotting meat—pieces of meat that had lost their shape, their size and you couldn't tell what they were. . . And, of course, in the old building, I still have this awful memory, they served tea up in buckets, metal buckets, and ———— was on teas one day and she said to the officer "look what I've found in this soup"—it was a scrubbing brush—because they used the same buckets for scrubbing the floors. So, she said "what shall I do with it?", she said "put it aside". She said, "no, what shall I do about the soup," so she said "carry on serving the soup!"'

tiny doors, that, yes, Holloway had opened with men, women and children contained here, and for the first time I was fully conscious of the full history of the place and the fact that the stones were really steeped in an awful lot of experimental prison practices that weren't particularly good. . . . I'm not particularly fanciful. In fact, I don't think I'm fanciful at all, and I certainly don't subscribe to theories of ghosts . . . but I was on edge as was everyone else and when someone, very enterprising, went over to the kitchen and made some tea and toast about halfway through the day . . . when she let herself back into the wing, I jumped out of my skin because it really was an eerie place to be.

8

The Labyrinth: The New Holloway and its Problems

'Labyrinth: A structure consisting of a number of intercommu-
nicating passages arranged in bewildering complexity' (*Oxford
English Dictionary*), *Second Edition*

'The Labyrinth was a dungeon'[1]

'I find it easier to find my way through Hampton Court maze'
(former prisoner).

Introduction

I have now assembled most of the pieces which will enable me to
make sense of the final stages of this history of Holloway. The
previous seven chapters have been, in effect, a lengthy preamble to
a description of the chaotic events of the 1980s, setting the scene for
the drama to come.

Consider what had happened. A revolutionary new establishment
had been conceived to transform deviant women, but, little by little,
its creators had departed and those remaining in the Project Group
had not only lost faith in what was being constructed but had found
themselves surrounded by doubters in the Prison Department, the
Prison Medical Directorate and the Treasury. There had been design
changes. Over the years, sections of medical space had been pared
away to make room for an unexpectedly large inmate population. The
indifferently secure Category C prison had grown into a more secure
Category B establishment. There had been the belated addition of C5,
a Category A unit for 'highly disturbed' women. Parsimony had
lowered ceilings and narrowed corridors. But most proposals for
change had come too late in the planning process to alter the
fundamental design of the place, and Holloway remained in essence

[1] *Plutarch's Lives*, (London: William Heinemann, 1948), 31.

a prison that was still not supposed to look like a prison, a place with unobtrusive external boundaries, that overlooked its neighbours and was overlooked in its turn. It was a building with a serpentine rope of small internal spaces joined in zig-zag fashion by short corridors instead of a strong 'Centre'. If Holloway was no longer a secure hospital, it certainly was not a conventional prison. And, waiting to be poured into that singular, labyrinthine place, was a fissile population made up of disenchanted staff and prisoners reckoned to be disproportionately 'disturbed'.

It began badly. Many staff and prisoners feared that it might do so. They were reported to have felt some trepidation before the move at the end of January 1977. An Assistant Governor in charge of preparing officers for the new Holloway said, 'during that time, I began to get awful feelings of doom and gloom, and finding it very difficult to say all the positive things that I was obviously in charge of saying, and believed in at the outset. I got all the objections from the staff, and some of them, of course, one would dismiss as just being difficult, but most of them were from thoughtful, caring people who saw the difficulties coming along.' Staff had forebodings about the small units and their need for heavy supervision, the short corridors and their difficult sight-lines, the dog-leg bends and their threats of ambush, and the windows with their large areas of plain glass.[2] They were nervous. And the inmates were nervous too. A former prisoner remembered that 'there was more frustration. There was tremendous anxiety about the move, about any move. You know, if you move house, they say its one of the top stress levels. So, if you move an institution like a prison, the anxiety is high for everyone.'

Staff and prisoners were justified in being apprehensive. The very beginnings of life in the new Holloway were Dantean:

I just remember a very disgruntled staff and a very disgruntled group of inmates because I was there the day we moved, I got the job of working out the logistics of getting it from one spot to the other and I went around everybody that night to see that they were settled and there were a lot of people crying and there were a lot of people saying this is awful—inmates. Rooms were lovely, bright and clean and fresh, nobody had ever slept in the bed before, that would have thrilled me because that's one of the awful things

---

[2] The matter of the glass windows was discussed in consultations with the Design Team and raised at various meetings of the Board of Visitors, including that held on 28 July 1976.

about prison—that it's not all that clean. But they were very upset, the majority of them. It's hard to explain and they didn't explain. . . . I think they were mostly people who had been in prison before and felt somehow at home in the old building that they didn't feel in the new one. . . . [It was] ghastly. They put plain glass in the windows and the first weekend we were in there almost all the glass was smashed out. . . . And the women were climbing up and hanging out the windows their legs and arms, and screaming at the flats and cutting, not a lot, but enough to really cause a public disturbance, cutting themselves.

There was an initial explosive impact marked by the destruction of hundreds of windows.[3] With some little exaggeration, a former inmate said 'it was all broken up in no time. It was destroyed.' Thereafter followed a sustained period of *anomie* attended by violence, vandalism, assaults,[4] graffiti,[5] fire-setting, barricading and yet more window-breaking. An officer recalled 'there were fires all the time. It seemed to go, if one did it, everybody else did it.' The prison was suddenly and agonizingly revealed to be insecure. Thus, not only were the glass panes of the windows found vulnerable (enlarging risks of damage, assault and self-injury[6]) but, in March, some of the slimmer inmates discovered they could wriggle their bodies[7] and others, less successfully, only their heads,[8] through their bars (a former prisoner said 'we used to get out. I used to go out and visit my mate in the next door cell'). The Governor described how 'it

[3] The most common estimate given by the Board of Visitors and the Prison Department was 300 windows destroyed but the number seems to have been 228 ('Note for the Record—Replacement of Broken Windows at Holloway', 27 May 1977).

[4] In 1978, there had been 20 offences of assault and gross personal violence per 100 women inmates nationally (compared with 6 per 100 in all male establishments) and, of those 20, 10 related to Holloway, 5 to Bullwood Hall and 5 to all other female institutions.

[5] In October 1978, for instance, it was reported that 'the inevitable wear and tear of continuous occupation at Holloway is added to by "at least one incident of malicious damage per week", according to Mr Callaghan [the clerk of works], who has been at the prison during the past five years. "Masses of graffiti, wash basins being torn off and windows broken are the sort of vandalism we get", he said.' 'Holloway: planned maintenance in a rebuilt prison', *Buildings Maintenance and Services*, Oct. 1978, 12.

[6] A psychiatrist working at the prison at the time noted 'what you had is . . . a situation whereby there are lovely new facilities in Holloway and one of the things that these women have the propensity to do is to actually self-harm. So they start to smash up the facilities and use the bits and pieces to self-harm.'

[7] Curiously the specifications of the windows had been based on measurements for the average *man*.

[8] In April, the Board of Visitors reported the growing danger of women putting their heads out of windows and being unable to withdraw them.

became apparent during a very disturbed weekend . . . that it is possible for inmates to get through the windows. I could scarcely believe this.' There were four days of extraordinary disturbance in May 1977: the Governor reporting 'mild hysteria . . . spread[ing] from unit to unit. The incidents of breaking windows has increased and is stretching the resources of the Works Department.'[9]

Viewed from a distance, a great deal of that tension and disorganization were probably not much more than a continuation of the longer history of disorder I described in previous chapters.[10] A troubled population had emigrated into a confusing new habitat where it remained troubled. The senior education officer, Richard Brown, certainly believed that to be so: 'it was always a very disturbed place, Holloway. It's full of very disturbed people . . . and a lot of pain there. It's a place of extremes, of huge extremes. It's full of love and it's full of hate.'

It is difficult to find adequate indices to establish whether the Holloway of the 1980s was indeed a more or less distressed place than the Holloway of the 1970s.[11] It *is* clear that there had been many similar incidents and outbreaks before.[12] For example, window-smashing was not novel: 348 panes of glass were reported to have been broken in a single fortnight in 1972,[13] the damage on that occasion amounting to much more than that done in January 1977; and widespread window-breaking was again reported in January

---

[9] Governor's Report to the Board of Visitors, 24 May 1977.

[10] 'Smashing-up' had a long history. It was common in the women's prisons of the nineteenth century, for instance. See B. Forsythe, 'Women Prisoners and Women Penal Officials 1840–1921', *The British Journal of Criminology,* Autumn 1993, Vol. 33, No. 4, 534. Lady Constance Lytton reported smashing-up in the Holloway of 1914, *Prisons and Prisoners,* (London: William, Heinemann, 1914, 140–1). Continuity rather than discontinuity in disorder was certainly the argument pursued by the Home Office in fielding complaints and parliamentary questions such as one put by Michael O'Halloran in June 1977.

[11] A student sent to Holloway on a work placement in 1975 reported that no record was kept of mutilations and smashings-up unless women were sent on report (L. Dixon, 'Brief General Report on My Work Placement, typescript, 1975), 9.

[12] Disorder at Holloway had certainly attracted adverse press publicity before the move. See, for example, The *Evening News,* 30 Sept. 1970; The *Daily Sketch,* 1 Oct. 1970. Holloway was reported to be more violent than Pentonville in 1970 (The *Guardian,* 1 Oct. 1970). See too 'Holloway: The failure behind the acceptable facade', *The Times,* 1 July 1974, in which it was reported that 'trouble seems to erupt in epidemics. A group went on to the roof in 1972 to stage a protest.'

[13] Minutes of meeting of Board of Visitors, 27 Nov. 1972.

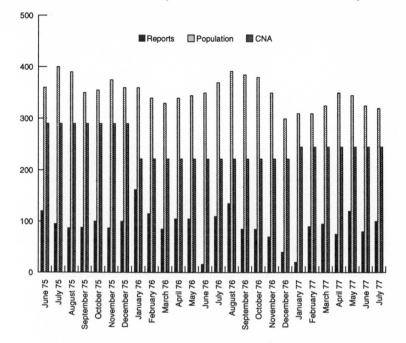

Figure 8.1 *Reports against Inmates at Holloway (based on figures contained in minutes of the Board of Visitors)*

1974.[14] Indeed, an average of 400 windows had been broken each year in the old Holloway.

Figure 8.1 certainly suggests that reports against inmates were not disproportionately high after the move in January 1977, and they actually seem to have reflected the pressures of crowding as much as the consequences of the transfer of population (although it is impossible to interpret the reports without a fuller knowledge of the circumstances in which they were made). Figure 8.2 shows that the most poignant index of all, the number of inmate suicides and attempted suicides, was never to be as high in the new Holloway as it had been in the uniquely crisis-laden year of 1976, the year when the prison was at its most straitened.

The anti-panopticon, it appeared, did *not* offer a new beginning. It was no *tabula rasa*: its physical design did not work to calm inmates,

[14] Minutes of meeting of the Board of Visitors, 23 Jan. 1974.

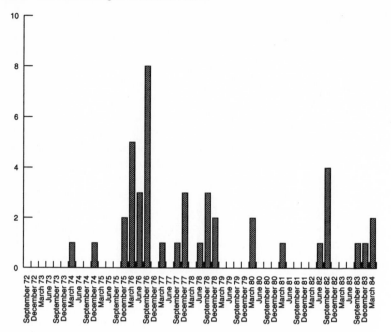

Figure 8.2 Suicides and Attempted Suicides at Holloway (quarterly figures, based on Medical Officer's Reports)

neither did it supply informal social control. To the contrary. It was as troubled as its predecessor had been, and social order within its walls continued to be problematic as before.[15] Month after month, the congestion, disturbance and violence persisted, sometimes subsiding a little, sometimes erupting, often moving in parallel with fluctuations in the prison population, but never so remote that they ceased to haunt the prison altogether. But what also seems to have been the case was that social disorder was made more worrying still by the new and special sense of unease that the anti-panopticon engendered. Officers began to complain loudly about a lack of discipline and problems of morale.[16]

---

[15] On 18 May 1977, for example, the Governor told the Board of Visitors that 'there had been a weekend of disturbances . . . Windows had been knocked out and there had been self inflicted wounds'.

[16] Recorded, for example, in the minutes of the meeting of the Board of Visitors, 18 May 1977.

The new establishment was at first sensed to be disorientating, bewildering and frightening, lacking in architectural structure and discipline. A former inmate recalled 'it was pretty chaotic. It felt that everyone was just finding their feet and complaining that nothing fits. And obviously the overriding worry was all the security. The staff didn't know how they were going to hold security there.'

No doubt, part of the prison's capacity to instil *anomie* may be explained by its sheer newness, and staff and inmates did manage to become accustomed to much of the building after a while. But *anomie* did not wholly decline, it persisted for years, and that was a consequence of some stark features of the building's design to which people could not grow easily accustomed. The new Holloway *appeared* to be a different place. Its disorderliness seemed to have become more acute and dramatic, audible and visible, and that its impact should have been so great is in some measure a phenomenological matter.

I would argue that design, inmate 'disturbance' and staff incertitude in the new prison proved to be an unstable compound. Each of those facets of experience bestowed significance on the others, disturbance becoming more alarming within the context of design, design becoming more frightening against a background of disturbance, and both simultaneously magnifying, and being magnified by, the incertitude of the staff. In effect, each facet was simultaneously a frame through which the prison could be viewed and an object to be viewed itself, and Holloway became transformed into a phenomenological version of a Kline bottle, its faces being at once inside and outside, turned this way and that, giving and receiving meaning. The outcome was a perilously chaotic system of signification which veered towards an ever-greater social disorder and symbolic confusion,[17] a system that manufactured fantastic apparitions and monstrous images. The labyrinth came in time to spawn its Minotaur, and it did so in a fashion that was calculated to make public the problems of the new social reality unfolding within itself.

---

[17] A former prisoner commented that 'I remember writing a poem at that time and it was about chaos and corruption. I picked up that it was chaos. It felt much more overcrowded, much more chaotic than the old building ever had'.

It was a startling baptism for the new Holloway and it awarded the prison a new, strong and disturbing public identity.[18] It was for that reason, because the 'prison is going through a very difficult stage', that it was decided not to grant press facilities to visit the prison immediately after the move. However, within weeks, the London *Evening Standard* reported that '"The Holloway Hilton'—which has been in use for just three and a half months has already been vandalised by the inmates. A party of MPs who toured the prison last week saw smashed windows, damaged walls and key holes blocked with putty.'[19]

Problems attained public prominence as telling contrasts were drawn between the prison's high aspirations and grand appearance, and its sad actuality (after all, no one could have expected much of the old, crumbling Holloway as it awaited its end). They were emphasized by the manner in which design worked physically to amplify disorder: what had successfully been hidden behind the old prison's tall walls and strong, well-placed wings, was to be revealed most starkly by the new anti-panopticon. They were emphasized by the confrontational character of a building with weak boundaries and small spaces.

Let me try to explain how that sense of the *anomie* and danger of Holloway arose and became a public issue. I shall proceed stage by descriptive stage, and, at the beginning, it would be most effective to return to the distinctive properties of the new prison that were flagged by the Design Team in September 1970.

External Boundaries

The Design Team, it will be remembered, had emphasized how the new prison would be marked by its integration with the wider world. Its themes had been:

> *Elimination of wall, making buildings in wall where possible and pushing them to the edge of the site.*

[18] In late 1980, for example, the *Observer* newspaper reported: 'sometimes the neighbours can hear the women in Holloway Prison. They start banging everything it's possible to bang in their cells, and shout and yell out of their windows: the hubbub can be deafening. But that's exceptional. Most of the time the women in prison in this country attract no public attention. . . . [But, the report continued,] the atmosphere in Holloway is stifling, claustrophobic, thick with tension.' J. Watts, 'Walls within Walls', the *Observer*, 5 Oct. 1980.

[19] 'Vandalism—at Holloway "Hilton"', *Evening Standard*, 19 May 1977.

Daytime activities near noisy road, protecting quieter living accommodation.

Slope of the site used to give view out from living accommodation, over daytime space.

Residential areas especially staff, as close to other residential areas as possible.

One of the most important attributes of the new Holloway was that its boundaries were supposed to be unobtrusive and reassuring, not serving to isolate the prison from its environment. Remote, strong, shielded buildings with their small windows were replaced by new living accommodation that pressed up against the margin, and it was accommodation that had been provided with especially large clear windows that were designed to see and be seen. The perimeter had deliberately been made permeable, and I have already described in Chapter 6 how, at quite an early stage, that permeability had come to be recognised as a problem by the Project Group. There had been correspondence and meetings with residents, Members of Parliament and Islington Council about the height of the new staff quarters and the noise of generators and boilers.

In September 1971, prompted by the article in The *News of the World* that had reported how women had been 'staging striptease sessions'[20] for workmen on site, the Project secretary was driven to reflect that:

it has highlighted an aspect of the design of the new Holloway, specifically the windows, which is now due for closer consideration. . . . It is, of course, evident that a window affords two way vision, especially after dark, when lights are in use, but, until now, the accent has been upon providing the inmate with the best practicable outlook from her room, and the surrounding situation of inward visual access has not been given the same amount of consideration. The position is that, on two sides of the Holloway site, there are, or soon will be, high rise blocks of flats which are generally ideally placed to provide inward visual access to prisoners' bedrooms which face towards them and in which we have concentrated upon providing the largest possible areas of glazing. An addition, psychological addition to the problem is that of the attraction of seeing into any enclosed area which contains an unfamiliar activity such as a prison, [or] mental hospital . . . The situation existing at the moment, where the flats have been built after the prison was erected,

[20] 'The Holloway Scandals of 1971: It's the world's strangest strip show', the *News of the World* , 29 Aug. 1971.

arose out of circumstances over which we had little control and the resultant problem was not too severe because of the very small windows in the present prison. However, the circumstances of the design of the new prison to be built on the same site are entirely under our control and a result in which extensive opportunities are provided to existing viewpoints for 'peeping tom' activities (possibly organised and with visual aids) because large windows are provided in the rooms facing the flats forming almost a 'goldfish bowl' situation.

So it was that decisions were taken to hide what would formerly have been revealed. In March 1972, it was agreed to install curtains in prisoners' rooms to avoid 'considerable embarrassment to the inmates and to the prison authorities' (except in C5 where it was considered that curtains would have been a risk). Again, in August 1976, just before the move, it was agreed to replace the large glazed windows in the top sections of the inmate accommodation by 'obscure panes'.

But the new prison could not be hidden.[21] It seemed instead to loom over those around it as groups accustomed to being kept apart found themselves abruptly and rudely thrown close together. And the new unit for 'highly disturbed women', C5, placed atop the mass of the buildings, visible and audible, was especially prominent. Holloway's neighbours were distressed by the new prison that faced them at such close quarters. In particular, the residents of Dalmeny Avenue and the occupants of new flats in Penderyn Way, supported by Islington Council and the MP, Michael O'Halloran, were upset by what seemed to be a new, disagreeable and hostile presence. After January 1977, they made reiterated complaints about what they could see and hear across the wall. The Home Office was told about 'a woman exposing herself' and 'a woman shouting obscenities out of a window at 8 o'clock in the morning'.[22] On 31 March, the 'director of prison administration' was told by the Dalmeny Avenue Tenants Association:

[21] A then senior member of the Prison Department recalled 'you had to take [the complaints] with a certain pinch of salt, I think. In other words, they didn't want the prison there. But inside [noise] had a bad effect on staff and it had a bad effect on perfectly pleasant women prisoners. And, again, this is something nobody had really thought out, and I suppose the old Victorian thick-walled prison had safeguarded against.'

[22] Letter from Western District Officer, London Borough of Islington Housing Department, 17 Mar. 1977.

I would like to lodge a strong protest . . . concerning Holloway Prisoners and the annoyance they are causing. The close proximity of the prison cells to our estate enables us to hear their shouted conversations and foul language. For example, at 10 p.m. on 19th March, 1977. One prisoner was heard calling out that she needed a woman and it wasn't her fault that she was a *lesbian*. After a while another prisoner was heard to call out 'Why don't you F****** shut up, some of us want to sleep.' Eventually the noise subsided, enabling the tenants of Dalmeny Avenue to get some sleep. . . . we have children and elderly citizens on this estate and they are not used to the vocabulary from the prison.

The prison was said to be attracting voyeurs ('the occupants can so easily be seen that there is an attraction for youngsters, and undesirables with the resulting nuisance to people on both sides of the wall')[23]. Women could be seen dressing and undressing ('an unwelcome attraction to the children living in the flats and to outsiders who watch from the access balconies of the flats themselves'). A man was said to have exposed himself to the inmates. Schoolboys would gather to watch the prison at lunchtime and in the early evening. Holloway was becoming a 'peepshow'. 'The women', said a former Chairman of the Project Group, evidently 'didn't behave as they were expected to behave in those original reports that Joanna Kelley has'. The entire situation was described as 'unwholesome'.[24]

The prison management responded by assigning extra staff to control 'improper behaviour' by inmates, but the prime solution accepted in September 1977 was to resort to physical methods. The remedy, adopted unhappily,[25] and after some experimentation with alternatives,[26] was to replace window glass by an 'unbreakable',[27]

---

[23] Letter from Western District Officer, London Borough of Islington Housing Department, 10 June 1977.

[24] 'Use of obscured polycarbonate in window panes of inmate accommodation facing perimeter', 29 June 1977.

[25] The phrase used to describe the Commissioning Sub-Committee's reaction at its meeting of 11 July 1977 was 'not enthusiastic': it was felt 'that, on balance, if this step were not taken, we would be vulnerable at any time in the future to repeated criticism from tenants of the adjacent flats'. 'Use of obscured polycarbonate in window panes of inmate accommodation facing perimeter', 21 July 1977.

[26] There had been an investigation of the effects of treating windows with polyester film, for instance.

[27] In the event, the polycarbonate windows were themselves quite breakable. It was found by October 1978 that inmates had been able to push out over 40 of the new panes.

opaque polycarbonate material[28] (the need to do so had been reinforced anyway by the breakages caused by window-smashing and
'repeated vandalism' by inmates and outsiders[29]). The risk of exhibi-
tionism was to be neutralized by obscuring the windows:

> Since we cannot guarantee that a prisoner . . . may not turn out to be a
> 'stripper' we cannot guarantee that those living in the flats will not have to
> endure the spectacle of a stripper from time to time; more important we
> cannot guarantee that people not living in the flats will visit the balconies
> there to secure a clear view of what they hope might turn out to be a stripper.
> I am convinced that we can neither expect to identify all the potential
> strippers . . . nor exert such detailed control of women's activities in their
> own room as to prevent them drawing back their curtains and exposing
> themselves . . . In these circumstances, given the level of anxiety that seems
> to have developed, I can see no alternative to the PCT's [Project Control
> Team's] conclusion that the windows themselves should be obscured.[30]

By November 1977, over 350 broken window panes had been replaced
by polycarbonate and work proceeded on obscuring the offending
windows in Blocks A, B and C, the blocks that faced Penderyn Way.
The replacement of other windows would wait on the inmates'
behaviour in the new prison.

Patching the boundaries continued as the prison opened stage by
stage. There were, for example, to be hostilities around the staff
quarters. Blocks 1 and 2 of the staff quarters had been placed
immediately opposite D block, the block intended originally for the
hospital in Phases 4 and 5 but released under pressure of population
for use as inmate accommodation. D block was completed finally in
1982 but occupied only in March 1983 as a result of the officers'
refusal to move until various discontents had been resolved.[31] With its
opening, confrontation came to be distributed along the internal
frontiers of the prison itself. Officers and inmates were then able to

---

[28] It was 'reluctantly' resolved by the Project Team that 'unless these measures are
extended to some of the other accommodation, further serious complaints are inevitable. If more opaque polycarbonate is to be installed, now is the time to do it . . .
obscured polycarbonate should be installed in the inmate accommodation which looks
out and is adjacent to the perimeter wall' (letter of 19 Aug. 1977).

[29] Stone-throwing children had broken a number of the outward-facing windows,
including those of the gymnasium and the temporary kitchen. See 'Holloway: Planned
maintenance in a rebuilt prison', *Buildings Maintenance and Services*, Oct. 1978, 14.

[30] Letter of 1 Sep. 1977.

[31] Their campaigns focussed on security, staffing levels and the provision of a day
nursery for the staff's children.

gaze straight into one another's private living space. An officer said 'D wing looked over to the prison quarters, you could see into someone's bedroom, you could see virtually what was under the bed . . . Everyone wants a bit of privacy and they fought for screening of some kind and they actually came up with screens.' And an inmate recalled, 'you can see the prison officers' quarters and they could see you. . . . Why didn't they shut the curtains? We don't do it to give them a thrill or anything. They said "you dropped your trousers" and we said "it's because you were looking straight into our cell. What's the matter with you? Haven't you got a TV over there or a radio? Don't you go out at night? Why do you need to be looking into our cell?"'

Staff and their union, the POA,[32] protested, and the solution adopted was the installation of yet more polycarbonate windows and screens[33] in March and April 1983.[34] It was recognized that the conditions in the newly screened accommodation would be so unpleasant that a special code of practice had to be drafted to cover its use.[35]

Narrowed, barred windows and opaque polycarbonate altered the appearance and internal illumination of the prison. Polycarbonate itself turned out to be less than satisfactory because it deteriorated and became crazed over the years, although no one knew quite why. Some surmised it was prone to damage by ultra-violet light and to atmospheric pollution, others that it was easily scratched (a former works officer observed 'if you're washing the window you've only got to have the slightest bit of material in the cloth and it starts to scratch it'). And crazing rendered an obscure material obscurer still. Superadded to a building that had already been marred by lowered ceilings and short, narrowed corridors, the effect was admitted universally to be brutal. The words used over and over again to describe the new

---

[32] It was discussed, for instance, at the quarterly meeting of the association on 3 Apr. 1980.   [33] The screens were later removed.

[34] The Board of Visitors protested to the Home Secretary about the proposal in Sept. 1983, claiming that the effect would be 'offensive, inhumane and oppressive' to the inmates.

[35] It was agreed in June 1983 that the screened rooms would not normally be used if another was available, that they would be used for the 'less disturbed' inmates, they would be used for short periods for one inmate, and that, if their use did not fall within those criteria, it would have to be approved both by the Senior Medical Officer and the Governor.

Plate 8.1: The New Holloway Prison Seen from Mr. Rush's Bedroom Window (photo by the author)

Holloway were 'claustrophobic',[36] 'oppressive', 'subterranean'[37] and 'depressing'. Members of the All Parliamentary Mental Health Group, visiting the prison in May 1985, observed the 'drab colours, low ceilings and little natural light giving a strongly depressing and claustrophobic atmosphere'. Insiders concurred. A senior probation officer who had worked at the prison called it 'terribly claustrophobic . . . there was the sort of feeling that the ceilings were coming down on you, they were low.' And a former Chairman of the Board of Visitors reflected that 'the staff felt very threatened by the claustrophobia, they loved to go on escort duty [just to get out]'. Most graphic of all was a fellow member of the Board of Visitors:

One of the first things was the colossally oppressive impact of the new building. Far from being this liberating, open, light, wonderful [place], the first impression everybody had was that it was like living in an underground corridor, an Anderson Shelter or something like that, that's how it felt. The ceilings which had been 20–30 feet up in the air were down on top of your head. One had the sense of going around wanting to hold them up all the time. The women, I think everybody, would acknowledge that they suffered from a real claustrophobia. The attempt to have integral security on the windows . . . was the biggest failure in the world. Not only did all the glass go . . . they put in polycarbonate which then scratched . . . It was the oppressive nature of achieving privacy without acknowledging what the price was. I don't think anybody had really estimated the impact of what that was going to be and it was a really significant and serious impact really. I think it affected the way in which people managed each other. Prison officers felt pressed up against the women. They felt they were really pressed up against them. They fought for separation.

As disturbing was the noise emanating from the prison. Holloway had always been a boisterous place,[38] but the radial prison had worked to contain the din. In the new establishment, said an

---

[36] See, for example, *Holloway Project Committee Report*, (London: Home Office, 1985), 22; 'Report on Visits to C1 Unit, Holloway Prison made by Professor Anthony Clare and The Bishop of Stepney', July 1985, 9; and *HM Prison Holloway: Report by HM Chief Inspector of Prisons*, (London: Home Office, 1992), 61.

[37] See The *Guardian*, 3 Jan. 1990.

[38] Charmian Bollinger, the former senior psychologist at Holloway, remembered 'one is so engrossed. You're so engrossed in Holloway. I remember on one occasion I was talking on the telephone to somebody outside . . . who said "what's that noise?", and I said "what noise?", and they said "there's a noise from your end." And I said, "oh, that's just women screaming." And the thing was you just got so used to it, that kind of level of disturbance, that you did blank out women screaming.'

inmate, 'you can't shut yourself off from anything. You hear it all.'
The Governor observed in November 1977 that:

That [noise] never became an issue in the past was probably due to the design
of the old prison whereby cell windows were set high up in the wall and did
not face directly out of the prison. Should the noise reach an unacceptable
level within the prison it was possible to move the offending inmate to a
location where the noise could be minimal. Holloway could control the noise
problem. Since moving to the new buildings the noise of inmates shouting
quickly reached a level which was and is unacceptable to people both within
and outside of the prison. . . . The new design of the buildings and cells
facilitates communication between inmates in different parts of the prison
. . . the contour of the land allows for contact with people outside the prison.
It should be noted that the prison is built on land which slopes down and
away from the adjacent housing estate. . . . People living in these flats and
other housing strongly object to the shouting to and from the prison.

After January 1977, there were mounting complaints about shouting,
banging and the rattling of windows.[39] An officer recalled that 'if you
were a night orderly or even a duty orderly you were absolutely
festooned with telephone calls of irate people that lived around . . .
If you went to one place and shut them all up, and you went to
another, they'd all be roaring and shouting again, you see.'

The Vice-Chairman of the Penderyn Way Tenants Association lived
immediately opposite the new prison (it is the view from his bedroom
that is shown in Plate 8.1) and he kept a detailed log of incidents. His
first entry was made in the first week after the move, on 5 February
1977, ('Shout. Broken Glass') and it continued until 1 June 1978
('another charming day') when, despairing, he gave up. He recorded
twenty-six incidents, including 'calling all night and shouting' in
April, 'screaming at 3 a.m.' in September, 'smashing of windows
and banging' in January 1978, 'shouting and banging all the time'
in March 1978, 'horrible screaming and shouting' in April 1978, and
'shouting, foul language all week—sounded like a mini-riot' in May
1978. He remembered:

We were here before the old prison was knocked down . . . We didn't see a
great deal of it. It used to be more over in that direction because it was like a
centre spike with spokes coming off of it and the spokes came out towards us.
We never got a lot, hardly any noise or anything. No problem really. It was

---

[39] And inmates were reported to have complained about the noise of parties held in
neighbouring houses. See the *Guardian*, 20 May 1977.

only when they built this one. . . . Then when they opened it, that's when we got all the problems with the shouting and the hollering and screaming and banging on windows and such. . . . It was disturbing, when you hear that sort of thing, when you're trying to sleep.

Peculiarly upsetting were said to be the sounds emanating from C5[40], later C1, the unit for 'highly disturbed women'. The Governor remarked that 'the noise caused by a highly disturbed or refractory inmate is comparatively easily managed by day. At night, it takes on a totally different dimension and can be very frightening and disturbing to other inmates, staff and neighbours.' In 1978, C5 was moved down to ground floor level, in C1, below, out of hearing, precisely to 'house the most difficult, disturbed and recalcitrant inmates . . . on a physical level below the outer perimeter wall, thus reducing the nuisance factor caused by citizens calling across from the private sector accommodation adjoining the prison, and also to assist in reducing the nuisance value to neighbours who are increasingly perturbed by the level of noise by day and night coming from the inmates'.[41] But the noise continued. A union official told the local Member of Parliament, Michael O'Halloran, that he had received a letter from a woman whose life 'had been made a misery by the constant screaming, shouting and abuse from the inmates of the Psychiatric Wing . . . Immediately following the building of the wing . . . the tenants whose houses and flats backed on to it formed a tenants' association . . . however the noise continues. Friends and relatives of the inmates congregate on the lawn to hold shouted conversations. Miss ——— is often woken in the middle of the night by shouting and screaming from the prison'.[42]

Much of the discomfort experienced around the perimeter could probably be explained as simple irritation at an unexpected[43] and unwelcome loss of privacy and peace: the Vice-Chairman of the Penderyn Way Tenants Association was a taxi-driver working at

[40]   The Board of Visitors noted the unmanageable 'problem of continual noise and violence' in C5 at numerous meetings, and in its annual report for 1977.

[41]   'Phase 2/3 Accommodation—HM Prison Holloway', 10 Nov. 1977.

[42]   Letter of 10 Nov. 1981.

[43]   The complaints subsided after a year or so. By May 1978, the Project Team was informed that there were no neighbourhood problems to report. The decline may be explained by the efforts made to reinforce the boundaries and by simple habituation. The Vice-Chairman of the Penderyn Way Tenants Association said that, like the noise of trains or traffic, one learned to become accustomed to the sounds emanating from the prison.

night, and he complained principally about lost sleep. But it is impossible not to conjecture that some additional symbolic work was being accomplished as well: the removal of effective boundaries and the enforced, unwelcome proximity of inmates, staff and neighbours brought people together who would rather have been kept apart, safe distances were lost, and the result was experienced as a form of contamination. The prison, it must be recalled, was a world of moral classifications and hierarchies, and the most fundamental oppositions of all were staff/inmate, freedom/control, work/leisure and insider/outsider. Officers did not conceive themselves to be wholly good and the inmates wholly bad, but, in the context of so much disturbance and disorder, in a place where people thought to be wicked were incarcerated, a place whose occupants were accustomed to the spatial separations of the radial prison, it was inevitable that Holloway was riven by a fundamental moral divide.

Fears of contamination were real enough. A former officer argued that discipline staff 'believe that prisoners are evil, that they will contaminate anybody who comes into contact with them. There was a very strong belief around at that time, it's still there I think. Most officers, if you ask them and they're really honest, will say they're evil people.' There was, said a former member of the Board of Visitors, 'the emergence of a knowledge of incest, child abuse, those sorts of things, which were an 80s phenomenon very largely . . . and so here were these women who were damaging their children . . . Killing your child evaporated into a kind of innocent condition in a way compared to some of the other things we became aware of in the 80s.'

One elementary strategy of preserving moral distance and preserving control over oneself and others[44] is to maintain physical distance, to keep apart from things and people unclean. Park once observed that 'in society, we not only live together but at the same time we live apart, and human relations can always be reckoned, with more or less accuracy, in terms of distance'.[45] People like to be able to 'keep their distance' and imposed intimacy can engender unease, especially when the other is regarded as dangerous and evil. Between evil and good, the orderly and disorderly, it is imperative to draw boundaries and insert buffer zones lest one becomes defiled. And

---

[44]   See M. Baumgartner, *The Moral Order of a Suburb,* (New York: Oxford University Press, 1988).

[45]   R. Park, *Human Communities: The City and Human Ecology,* (New York: The Free Press, 1952), 166.

those lines in space attain an even greater importance in places like prisons, mental hospitals and courthouses which were established precisely to define, identify, control and contain morally devalued people, people whose evil has been dramatised publicly,[46] whose very character has been ceremonially degraded and revealed.[47] Lines in such institutions mark out group territories and symbolic spaces that require intense, continual policing.[48] Blurring those lines, transgressing them or eliminating them, attacks the very moral basis of the institution as it is conventionally conceived and defended: 'we attribute . . . great symbolic significance to acts such as trespassing'[49] said Zerubavel.

The radiating prison had been designed expressly to mark out firm lines in space between 'us' and 'them', 'staff' and 'prisoner'. The anti-panopticon with its weak boundaries had eroded them and, in the first instance, it excited sensations very close to those associated with pollution. How else would one explain the use of words like 'undesirables' and 'unwholesome'?

There was to be another effect of the weakening of boundaries. The freedom to trespass across lines and ignore safe zones corroded power in what was an authoritarian institution. The social and physical structures of prisons encase very clear relations of authority. ('in space', argued Markus, 'relations of power are ever-present'.[50]) The lines and directions of power were supposed to be unambiguous: prisoners were people to whom things were done, and those entitled to do those things were the officers, governors and professional staff. Allowing inmates to overlook the officers when they were off stage and in their own private quarters, vulnerable and exposed, looked like a threateningly perverse reversal of relations of authority and power, conferring control on the prisoner. It ate away at the little area in which officers could be at ease, the area mapped out as a home territory,[51] where formality and wariness were not demanded. It

---

[46] See F. Tannenbaum, *Crime and the Community*, (New York: University of Columbia Press, 1938), ch. 1.

[47] See H. Garfinkel, 'Conditions of Successful Degradation Ceremonies', *American Journal of Sociology*, Mar. 1956, Vol. 61, 421–2.

[48] See M. Douglas, *Purity and Danger*, (Harmondsworth: Penguin, 1970), 165.

[49] E. Zerubavel, *The Fine Line: Making Distinctions in Everyday Life*, (New York: The Free Press, 1991), 7.

[50] T. Markus, *Buildings and Power*, (London: Routledge, 1993), 23.

[51] See S. Cavan, *Liquor License: An Ethnography of Bar Behavior*, (Chicago: Aldine, 1966), 205.

threatened the officers' authority and the officers' ability to escape the disciplines of a total institution. Joy Kinsley, the Governor who succeeded Megan Bull, observed 'you could stand in the prison and look straight into the Governor's quarters or into other quarters. That's just bad news. For goodness' sake, when people go off duty, they want to get away.' To be continually alert and guarded was an imposition indeed ('it's not very nice to go out the next day and be told "you looked quite nice in that pink nightie, miss!" When you relax and put your feet up, people were quite upset about that'). A former senior officer said

there is an intense jealousy that builds up and the power issue between staff and prisoners is always there in any prison, and if that's allowed to be fuelled in the wrong direction with an all women society, it can become very unpleasant. Certainly for the prisoners to have the facility to look out and look into the staff quarters . . . they felt their personal privacy and their personal lives were invaded. . . . The panels that were put outside the prisoners' windows, that's so symbolic of the power of the staff over the prisoners . . . I actually think that's appalling. It's an appalling solution.

Internal Boundaries

The Design Team had laid down:

> Living units based on a section of 32 broken down into two half-sections of 16. Compare with present wing of 100. This builds up individual in small family group and enables different treatment ideas to be tried out.

> Units are linked together with buffer zones giving some flexibility of size of unit.

Surveillance

The old Holloway had enabled officers discreetly, economically,[52] remotely and securely to monitor the activities of inmates. Inmates had been allowed to gather in the wings on association, occupying what was practically their own symbolic territory and pursuing their own activities under the distant eye of an officer. A senior probation officer said they 'felt more secure in the old-fashioned wings. . . . the

---

[52] At times, Joanna Kelley recalled, the old Holloway was 'manned by 5–7 officers, all the rest being on leave, sick leave or escort'.

old prison was much better, it was friendlier, it was easier, we could get on better, they felt freer in a way at that time, and I can understand that because when you were locked in a single room or a small dormitory it wasn't the same as having more freedom in an old-fashioned building'.

It will be recalled that the internal geography of the new prison represented an attempt to change that disciplinarian organization and ambience. It would reduce the 'institutional appearance of the building by breaking down long lengths of corridor'.[53] But that new geography came also to pose difficulties of surveillance which were recognized only belatedly by the Project Team (it was laid out graphically for them in April 1971 in the form of a diagram which has been refined and reproduced as Figure 8.3). It was evident not only that staff would have a limited view of what was around them but that they would themselves become conspicuous as they quit their offices to inspect the prisoners. Short corridors, small units, and poor sight-lines would exacerbate the problems of the prison. Instead of the great extended vistas of the wings in the radial prison, officers and inmates would have a reduced space and vision. Where there had been large controlling distances, frontiers and spaces, the new Holloway would bring officer and inmate uncomfortably close together. By early 1971, however, the basic contours of the design had been confirmed and it was acknowledged that the new Holloway would require extraordinarily high levels of staffing, perhaps an additional 20–25 officers, to maintain adequate supervision ('we did not realise that the shape of the Stage C buildings was critical for overall supervision', it was noted in June 1971[54]).

Coupled to a lack of effective surveillance was a feeling of anxiety about the burdensome nature of control in small dark spaces. The problem of the external boundaries was recapitulated within the building itself, hostile groups unhappily finding themselves in close and unwelcome juxtaposition, feeling jostled and contaminated by one another. A former officer deplored 'the fact that it was all open. We had a fear about things, it was going from one extreme really, where you had control to being far more relaxed and open . . . and I

---

[53] Report on Stage D, Phase 2, 29 Apr. 1971.

[54] There was some disagreement amongst members of the Project Team in 1971 about whether they had been fully alerted to the control problems that the serpentine corridors and units would present. It was alleged that drawings had been presented piecemeal and there had been little opportunity for full discussion.

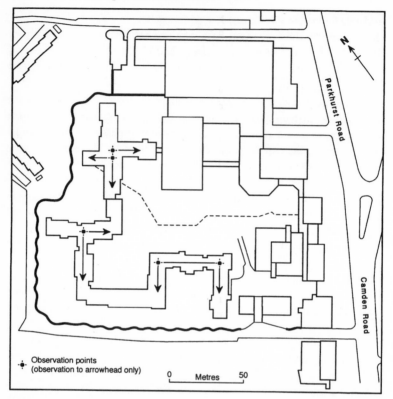

Figure 8.3 *Plan Showing Problem of the Supervision of a Section by One Officer (based on Prison Department plan)*

think that was a fear. We thought we'd lose some of the control if you like.' Dorothy Speed, a psychiatrist who had worked in both the old and the new Holloway remarked 'the body buffer zone . . . doesn't prevail [there which] is very damaging'. Antagonistic groups in authoritarian institutions need to be kept apart. Thrown too closely together, prisoners and inmates began to define their relations as confrontational. The geography of the new prison undermined the comfortable exercise of authority.[55] An officer said

The new Holloway, the immediate problem about actually working on the landings was that you were on top of prisoners and that feels aggressive.

[55] See E. Hall, *The Silent Language*, (Garden City, New York: Anchor Press, 1973), 183.

Because on F Wing, the first wing I worked on, you could see all the activity on landings and the association area from a bridge on the second floor. You were actually physically distant from the nearest possible prisoners by a matter of several feet, and from those downstairs associating watching TV or whatever, you were distant by many, many feet. It gave you every opportunity to make sure you were doing your job and make sure that things weren't getting out of hand . . . but it also left prisoners unaware for the most part, perhaps 'unaware' is the wrong word because I don't think you are ever unaware of supervision, but certainly not feeling oppressive supervision, so that physical distance was a really useful tool. The new Holloway with its cramped corridors, with landings where you actually had to be on a half of that landing to see that half . . . that felt very oppressive.

Confused Space

Those threats and dangers were amplified by the creation of hidden spaces around corners and out of sight[56] where officers and inmates never quite knew what was awaiting them: 'on the new Holloway they built it was all corners and you could be round one corner and then all hell would break loose and someone could be quite viciously attacked and you would be oblivious to that'. The All Parliamentary Mental Health Group reported that 'the high level of ambient noise, the dog-leg corridors and cell design make prisoner observation a nightmare'. Most staff contrasted the old prison with the new, and pined for a lost security and structure.[57] The old Holloway had been unambiguous,[58] certain and intelligible (a former psychiatric nurse said the new establishment 'didn't have a structure to me like I was used to in the old prison'). The confused space of the new Holloway generated fear. In a place housing some very violent women,[59] a place where antagonisms were endemic, the presence of gloomy passages with restricted vision and dangerous turns was calculated to aggravate anxiety, even amongst officers and others professionally inured to risk.[60] And their

[56] See the *Observer*, 5 Oct. 1980 and the *Holloway Project Committee Report*, 8.
[57] See A. Mandaraka-Sheppard, *The Dynamics of Aggression in Womens Prisons in England*, (Aldershot: Gower, 1986), 53.
[58] See the article by a former inmate, Pat Arrowsmith, in the *Guardian*, 21 Dec. 1977.
[59] Megan Bull, the Governor, was reported to have said 'violence is a very serious problem in this prison. . . . Officers are frequently presented with violent aggressive behaviour. We have a lot of disturbed women, and women who have not been violent outside Holloway can be violent inside Holloway'. The *Observer*, 5 Oct. 1980.
[60] A journalist claimed that officers 'hate the new building, with its short, blind corridors'. J. Watts, 'Walls within Walls', the *Observer*, 5 Oct. 1980.

anxiety was not without foundation. Abuse, anger and violence were real enough: officers were reported to have been assaulted 110 times in 1982, 115 times in 1983 and 116 times in 1984. A senior probation officer remembered 'there have been attacks on officers, a very serious one happened, it was in that sort of situation, women were unlocked and it was just around the corner. That was one of the concerns of the prison officers—they couldn't supervise the women.'

Confused space aggravated anxiety amongst prisoners. ('Its sisters here, and screws over there, and they're just following us everywhere, Hiding round the corner, telling us what to do, everywhere you go you'll find a screw. You can't escape they're all around. Creeping about so you can't hear a sound'.)[61] One prisoner said 'there was always an element of paranoia because you can't just, you go in to all different kinds of situations every time you turn a corner, so it is a bit of a jumpy place, definitely'. The new design certainly ran counter to the standard advice given to prudent women (and men) moving about in space.[62] For instance, the assumption on which one group of feminist architects worked was that 'for women it tends to be . . . simple. Spaces where mystery figures lurk, or could easily hide, feel dangerous'.[63] Said a very senior member of the Prison Department, the new Holloway was 'deranged. The architecture that was supposed to calm instead projected an atmosphere of threat.'

The Diffusion of Activity

A fourth consequence of the new anti-panopticon design was the diffusion of activities and populations. Staff and managers lamented the passing of the Centre, the heart of the old Holloway, where officers were wont to gather and talk, and from which they could see the whole prison from afar. Megan Bull, the first Governor of the new Holloway, wrote: 'what everybody misses most is the old traditional "Centre" from which all activities radiate. In fact staff of all disciplines and official visitors comment on the deprivation of casual meetings on the centre which they felt identified them as part of the

---

[61] 'Jenny'. 'A Day out of our lives', 6 Apr. 1990.

[62] For example, the police recommend that women should 'avoid short cuts through dimly-lit, deserted areas'. *Violent Crime: Police Advice for Women on How to Reduce the Risks,* (London: Home Office, 1987), 6.

[63] J. Boys, 'Women and Public Space', in *Making Space: Women and the Man-Made Environment,* (London: Pluto Press, 1984), 49.

institution and at which useful communication could occur.'[64] What had once been concentrated in the 'Centre' was now scattered along the lengths of the units and corridors on their different levels. Staff were no longer clustered. ('There was a greater *camaraderie* amongst staff, you looked after each other, and that sort of thing disappeared with the new Holloway because you became smaller grouped. People could work there 6 months and you didn't know. . . . No Centre.') They were no longer so cohesive: formerly, said an assistant governor, there had been 'greater warmth amongst the staff. The great centre in the radial prison was the meeting place. . . . There was a remoteness in the new one.' Inmates felt less cohesive too: one said 'you can walk along corridors and touch both sides of the walls. It separates the people who live down there to the ones who live round the corner. There's no *camaraderie*. . . . Now even prisoners are alien to one another. If you stick someone round the corner they don't mix with these ones up here. They don't know what the hell they're doing.'

The design of the anti-panopticon thus threw staff and inmates out to the margins where they were spread thin and apart. Lacking a 'Centre', distances between points grew, it was no longer possible to advance smartly from wing to wing; and movement and management seemed to have become more difficult.[65] Support became more remote and uncertain in crisis, and crisis and the threat of crisis were ever-looming ('help used to be a long way away' said a discipline officer). A former Deputy Governor observed 'because it was on a long chain, at each level to go from one end, even into the next unit . . . if there was trouble, there were a lot of doors to be got through and a lot of corridors'. Staff lost their sense of unity, becoming separated, more independent of one another, less able to give mutual aid[66] ('the communications system in the old prison—if there was aggro a bell went and everybody knew about it, it went on the same time, people rushed around, you knew something was going on and felt part of it. With the new system that was implemented, the red telephone system, you didn't necessarily know'). Joy Kinsley, the second

---

[64] Governor's Annual Report for 1977.

[65] In her annual report for 1977, the Governor complained of administrative problems because of the manner in which staff were scattered about the building.

[66] A member of the Board of Visitors remarked that 'the staff at the end of these long wiggly worms were feeling terribly marooned, frightened, unsupported. If you're in a wing that does something like that, and the administration is over here and you're out at the end, and there are only 2 of you on, one there and one half-way down, you feel very frightened down here and there was no sense of being supported.'

Governor of the new prison, said 'the building was depressing. It cut people off from one another . . . they felt isolated, they felt depressed, they felt unsafe.'

Territoriality

Inmates and officers were groups apart that shared features in common: both groups were segregated and enclosed, both lived in some isolation within the walls, both had privy knowledge of the extraordinary underlife of a prison, and both were locked into temporal schedules quite different from those of civilian life. Like the printworkers of the International Typographical Union[67] or the coalminers of the old mining communities,[68] they were solidary, separate, relatively undifferentiated in structure and collectivist in posture. But there was more that made them mirrors of one another. The safety of the members of each group depended on mutual aid in an insecure world; members of each group considered themselves devalued and they looked to each other for esteem; and each group shared an argot, a way of life, and (it was alleged by many) widespread lesbian bonding.

Yet inmates and officers also kept apart (perhaps because they *were* so similar in so many matters)[69] and they formed clearly-defined, exclusive and antagonistic groups. Their difference was maintained by the diffuse insignia and privileges of rank, function, moral standing, freedom, clothing and power. The behaviour of inmates and officers could at times seem almost tribal, military or gang-like, and observers on the scene were apt to describe it in stark and unequivocal terms. One Governor reflected that 'there are all sorts of dynamics . . . but [officers] have gained enormous strength, personal confidence, from being with their own colleagues, other people in the same boat, and particularly with a common enemy, namely the prisoners, so there is a very, very unhealthy structure'. And a psychiatrist remarked 'what there was in Holloway was not just a negative, punitive, racist subculture amongst elements of the staff but there was a very negative gay subculture. [They were] negative towards each other, hostile towards any members of the

[67] See S. Lipset *et al.*, *Union Democracy* (Free Press: Glencoe, 1956).
[68] See, N. Dennis *et al.*, *Coal is Our Life*, (London: Eyre and Spottiswoode, 1956).
[69] See T. and P. Morris, *Pentonville* (London: Routledge and Kegan Paul, 1963) and G. Simmel, *Conflict and the Web of Group-Affiliations*, (Glencoe: Free Press, 1955), 47–48.

staff who were not part of the lesbian community of staff and hostile towards the women.'

Even a voluntary crossing of the lines between inmates and staff was regarded as improper, unprofessional, treacherous, potentially dangerous and possibly contaminating in the early and middle 1980s. Thus, it is revealing that in March 1984 the local branch of the Prison Officers Association voted that female chief officers should return to the wearing of uniform.[70] And much was made of the fact that the second Governor of the new Holloway, Joy Kinsley, forbade staff to have informal contact with inmates and ex-inmates at much the same time. It was, she said, necessary to make 'a painful return to realism',[71] and their intimacy posed a challenge to the controls required in any prison:[72]

There existed in certain parts of the establishment a sort of sub-culture of informal contacts with inmates and ex-inmates, which seemed at times to be near to the media and certainly to go beyond acceptable boundaries. It was almost a corruption of what could be good and acceptable work, if it was all above board, but it was more hidden than that. The Education Officer was very involved in all this—sometimes in good ways . . . but sometimes in defiance of the normal conventions. It had always been the practice that any such contacts by any staff should 'go through the Governor's office'— really for the protection of staff as well as for the good of inmates. There was a need to bring this into some sort of professional order, but the Education Officer presented me with one contact I was not prepared to approve and that caused a reaction out of all proportion.

A probation officer (who would have been transferred by the Department rather than by the Governor),[73] chaplain[74] and education officer were all eventually censured for undue familiarity, for bridging the divide between formally distinct and controlled groups. The Governor's view of the education department, in particular, was that it was 'pretty progressive . . . although they tended to run away with themselves and needed a bit of control'. The education officer was reproved for his casual dress ('I was of the belief that smart casual dress was appropriate because our job was to deal with the inmates

---

[70] Minutes of the meeting of the Prison Officers' Association, 15 Mar. 1984.

[71] The *Sunday Telegraph*, 31 July 1983.   [72] Governor's Annual Report for 1982.

[73] See *The Times*, 18 June 1983. The Probation Department's Annual Report for 1982 asserted that one of its members was summarily transferred beccause he was alleged to be unprofessional in his contact with ex-prisoners.

[74] See *The Times*, 18 May 1983.

. . . and she wanted us formally dressed . . . She wanted to toughen the place up, and she saw me as being liberal'). The education officer was finally barred from the prison altogether for 6 weeks in May and June 1983 for continuing his acquaintance with the former prisoner.[75] The Governor herself reflected that he was 'causing embarrassment to ILEA as well as the Prison Department and his being "barred" was an inevitable result, which we all tried to avoid. I have to tell you there was nothing unusual in my stance on all this. He simply would not conform to the usual professional conventions in prisons.' He was allowed to return only when he accepted an order to refrain from all contact with the former prisoner. (In time, he and others came to form a little network that spread beyond the prison and into the world of politics[76] and the mass media: it was a network that was to have consequence for the evolving public representations of the prison, and I shall discuss it in the next chapter. Joy Kinsley remarked that the Education Officer fought 'me through the press . . . I was subjected to a campaign of character assassination such as few civil servants—of my ilk anyway—have to endure. I was defended in the House of Lords by the Minister . . . but it was a malignant campaign.')

And, amidst that confrontation between opposites, where group was set dialectically against group and self against self, it was as if Holloway was an arena devised just for the manufacture of identities, for the staging of performances and the management of impressions. It was a place of theatrical roles and role-playing. Prisoners would bind their breasts to look lean, tough and 'much more muscular'. They would adopt an aggressive mien ('you had to protect yourself by building up your own image, it's like a piece of armour . . . and you get very, very hard. I was armour-plated by the time I came out'). They would 'never . . . show anyone that prison can get through to you. If a prison is tough it becomes important to prove that you can withstand it, by hiding your real feelings. Of course this creates in the officers the impression that we are hardened, impervious to . . . punishment and separation'.[77] And some officers, in their turn, would cultivate their own hard, combative appearance (one who had worked in the prison talked about a 'gang [being] there . . .

---

[75] See the editorial in the *Guardian*, 25 July 1983.

[76] Lord Longford claimed to have been briefed by the education officer when he spoke in a House of Lords debate about female offenders on 29 Oct. 1985.

[77] C. Tchaikovsky, 'Worlds within worlds', *New Internationalist*, Dec. 1985, 22.

This gang lived in the mess, and used to meet up with the chaps from Pentonville who used to use the mess. I only went into the mess once . . . and I was horrified. They looked like men, drinking beer like men, smoking like men and showing off to the men from Pentonville that they hadn't got a patch on them.') To be sure, most officers looked and behaved otherwise, and it would not do to exaggerate, but the impression was made.

Thus arrayed and so opposed, some officers and inmates were locked together in a relation that can only be described by a vocabulary of anxiety, fear, bravado and antagonism, by the measuring of defeats[78] and the scoring of victories. Like any other agents of control facing a large and potentially refractory population, staff were preoccupied always with the maintenance of their personal and collective authority. There were problems of face, standing and respect. In Holloway (and indeed in other prisons and institutions)[79] theirs was an abiding ambition to ensure that *they* were the group that was manifestly in control, that it was *they* who were seen to run the establishment, and it was *their* writ that ran. Their authority could never be taken on trust. It had to be upheld continually, in big and little ways, practically and symbolically, directly and indirectly. It is in this sense that the screens over the D Block windows were interpreted in the prison as the tokens of a victory won (a deputy governor remarked 'the female staff subculture was very unhealthy and in fact. . . . the panels that were put outside the prisoners' windows, that's so symbolic of the power of the staff over the prisoners . . . There is a rivalry, and part of the rivalry was a kind of resentment about the medical facilities (some of the medical facilities were excellent), the screening'). It is in this sense, too, that one can understand the Prison Officers Association's farewell to the Holloway gatemen in the mid-1980s:

---

[78] For example, inmates complained to the Board of Visitors about the facetious comments made by staff during the opening of their mail—a supreme piece of symbolic triumphalism. Minutes of the meeting of the Board of Visitors, 9 Mar. 1988.

[79] In this chapter, I concentrate primarily on relations between inmates and officers. In the next, I shall discuss governors and officers. In Holloway's sister prison, Styal, many of the same processes were to unfold and at much the same time. There too, the issue was reduced to the question of who ran the prison. See The *Observer*, 23 Feb. and 2 Mar. 1986. See also an account of unrest at Broadmoor in which the POA alleged that the balance of power had shifted too far in favour of the patients: 'Strike threat at Broadmoor as patients get keys', The *Sunday Times*, 3 Apr. 1994.

I can only speak on behalf of all the staff who on numerous occasions have been only to [sic] grateful for the appearances of our gate staff in many incidents. It certainly wasn't the staff here who wanted rid of the gatemen — this decision was out of our hands — but there again it isn't the powers that be, who have to go in and sort the inmates out, and nine times out of ten the mere presence of one of our 'boys' was all that was needed and saved many of us from certain injuries.[80]

It is in that context, moreover, that the social meanings of the new architecture should be appreciated. I have discussed surveillance, boundaries and structure in the new prison, and they are but facets of a larger existential response to space, the sense of territoriality that may be defined as the symbolic appropriation of defensible space by an identifiable group,[81] 'the act of laying claim to and defending a territory'.[82] When adversarial groups are forced to co-habit the same place, territoriality may not be established but actively contested, the subject of competing claims. And space will then be littered with innumerable, sometimes contradictory cues, markers and lines[83] laid down to affirm possession and dominance.[84] Space in Holloway was contested in this way,[85] the subject of competition between officers and inmates. In Keith's words, the 'sense of spatiality mediate[s] antagonism'.[86]

Officers held that it was symbolically and practically important to assert a claim to 'their' place, and the spatial relations of Holloway came accordingly to refract their struggles for authority and power,[87] the human geography of the prison becoming 'filled with politics and ideology'.[88] Take cell searches. Searches were undoubtedly necessary for good order and discipline, but they were also an effective confirmation of the supremacy of official authority, they took control into the very core of the inmate's private space, and they engendered forceful feelings of invasion, subjugation and humiliation. Like raids

---

[80] 'Holloway', P.O.A. Magazine, June 1985, 333.

[81] See B. Poyner, Design Against Crime: Beyond defensible space, (London: Butterworths, 1983), 8.   [82] E. Hall, The Silent Language, 162.   [83] Ibid., 165.

[84] See T. Malmberg, Human territoriality: Survey of behavioural territories in man with preliminary analysis and discussion of meaning, (The Hague: Mouton, 1980), 189.

[85] See M. Eaton, Women After Prison, (Buckingham: Open University Press, 1993), 29.   [86] M. Keith, Race, riots and policing, (London: UCL Press, 1993), 154.

[87] See R. Shields, Places on the Margin: Alternative geographies of modernity, (London: Routledge, 1991), 47.

[88] E. Soja, Postmodern Geographies, (London: Verso, 1989), 6.

conducted by the police in dangerous areas,[89] they could be as much about the maintenance of symbolic domination as problems of contraband, weapons or illegal possessions. One inmate was reported to have said 'It's like having a burglar in your house . . . Just to see them piling into your room—to see the force, the uniform, the authority—its enough to make anyone freak out: and they go through everything in front of you—take the sheets off the bed, the postcards off the board, go through your letters, your things, your dirty knickers.'[90]

The practical ecological solution arrived at in the old Holloway had been to allow inmates a semblance of spatial control under the canopy of the greater and much more effective control of the surveying officer. Crowe observed that 'territorial behavior is demonstrated through both design and use responses. Any area that is well defined by borders and signs says to the user that it is controlled, that it is owned.'[91] The old Holloway had been defined, controlled and owned in a manner that more or less satisfied officers and inmates. It had been mapped out into large areas in which both groups were able to retain some sense of autonomy and property. Its space was at once shared and divided. To be sure, little enough of the old prison had actually 'belonged' to the inmates, but the design of the wings and cells, allied to its characteristically small population, had allowed potentially antagonistic groups to maintain safe separations and distances for the most part. The inmates had occupied 'their' space, the officers, theirs, and between them was a *cordon sanitaire*. The radial prison had been a relatively orderly place until its contraction in the 1970s.

No such ecological solution was practicable in the new prison. It had gone wrong at the very beginning, when the inmates had moved in to take possession of their quarters before the officers could occupy theirs, a symbolic event indeed (a draft speech marking the opening of the new prison observed 'it is a great disappointment to us that the staff were not in the end the first beneficiaries of the new building work'). Ecological problems continued thereafter. The new Holloway was so arranged that it contained many small areas in which it proved

---

[89] See M. Keith, *Race, riots and policing*, 194.

[90] J. Watts, 'Walls within Walls', *The Observer*, 5 Oct. 1980.

[91] T. Crowe, *Crime Prevention Through Environmental Design: Applications of Architectural Design and Space Management Concepts*, (Boston: Butterworth–Heinemann, 1991), 100.

difficult for adversarial groups to separate, draw back from one another and co-exist at a distance proper to formal behaviour.[92] It was certainly difficult to apply the old, successful formulae of the radial prison. In the old Holloway, said an officer, 'the prisoners had the feeling of space because you weren't actively policing their activities . . . normal landing duties in the new Holloway were difficult because it forced [officers] into a situation where they were really confronting prisoners and for prisoners as well because they had no space to call their own. So, difficult, and it began a retreat into offices, which wasn't particularly healthy.'

In effect, the geographical order of the old prison became evident only in its absence.[93] It is often thus, the basis of much social life tending to be seen but unnoticed, clearly visible only in its breach.[94] In women's prisons, wrote Heffernan, 'every form of movement and almost every object . . . has an order of usage and meaning. . . . If undisturbed, the real order may remain almost unseen and unrecognized. However, a deliberate challenge or an accidental assault on the established order by an unsuspecting new inmate or staff member results in verbal or physical conflict.'[95] The new prison did not embody the ecological arrangements of the old. It did not lend itself to the surveillance and controls of the old. Under the model of discipline prevailing in the early and middle 1980s, its spaces were simply too small, confined and confrontational to support a workable division and sharing of territory. In a place where effective segregations were held to be vital, it did not permit distinct groups to remain separate and uncontaminated.

Conclusion

Let me recapitulate. Discipline staff felt unsafe. Inmates and officers were still undergoing progressive filtration, leaving behind a mix of

---

[92] See E. Hall, *The Hidden Dimension,* (Garden City, New York: Anchor, 1969), 21–5.

[93] The Assistant Secretary in charge of P4 between 1974 and 1977 remarked that 'the Prison Officers' Association probably still in my time were developing the theme that there really wasn't much wrong with the 19th century design with its radials because there is nowhere better from which to see down 4 wings than a central point'.

[94] See H. Garfinkel, *Studies in Ethnomethodology,* (New Jersey: Prentice-Hall, 1967).

[95] E. Heffernan, *Making It in Prison: The Square, the Cool and the Life,* (New York: Wiley-Interscience, 1972), 70. One may presume that her observation would apply to men's prisons too.

young, inexperienced staff and transient or 'disturbed' prisoners; and both groups took little comfort from the structure of the new building. There was repeated reference to the staff's sensation of insecurity and danger being magnified by poor sight-lines, blind corners and meagre spaces.[96] (The Prison Officers' Association declared that 'the design of Holloway Prison is a failure . . . "There are too many blind corners." "Too many corners making supervision very hard therefore requiring more staff."')[97] Morale was reported to be at best variable and, in some areas, poor.[98] The Governor's Annual Report for 1982 certainly claimed that staff morale was '"patchy" as one would expect in an institution that is constantly changing and has such a high proportion of newly recruited officers. There are sudden waves of anxiety which have to be relieved from time to time and extra support provided.' Staff experienced exceptionally high levels of stress, sickness and absenteeism: some 20–30 officers certified themselves sick each day during 1984,[99] and the numbers rose to the 40s and 50s in 1985 and 1986. An average of 30 days was lost in sickness for each officer every year.[100]

At meeting after meeting of their association in the mid-1980s, officers voiced grave and diffuse anxieties about their safety: they protested about the exposure of the staff car park to vandalism and theft;[101] they were worried that detonators had been found near staff flats;[102] they were worried about harassment during the time when damp had exiled them from the prison;[103] they were anxious about the activities of former inmates living in a squat near the prison;[104] they were worried about apparently random violence from

---

[96] See the *Holloway Project Committee Report*, 8, 10, and the 'Report of Visits to C1 Unit, Holloway Prison, Made by Professor Anthony Clare and the Bishop of Stepney', July 1985, 10.

[97] *Holloway Prison C1 Unit: A Report by the Prison Officers' Association*, undated, 9.

[98] See *Report on HM Prison Holloway by HM Chief Inspector of Prisons*, (London: Home Office, 1985), 30.   [99] *Holloway Project Committee Report*, 11.

[100] Governor's Annual Report for 1983.

[101] Reported in the minutes of meetings of the Prison Officers Association, 2 Apr. 1980, 12 Nov. 1980, 25 Apr. 1985; and of the Board of Visitors, 22 May 1985.

[102] Minutes of the meeting of the Board of Visitors,14 Dec. 1988.

[103] In late 1980, one officer lived in a council flat next to a number of former inmates from Pentonville and Holloway and she reported being intimidated. Another was shot by an air gun on her journey to work in 1982.

[104] Minutes of the meeting of the Board of Visitors, 28 Aug. 1985.

inmates;[105] they wanted prisoners to be handcuffed on external escort;[106] they wanted all inmates' rooms to be fitted with stronger doors; they wanted discipline officers to be present whenever inmates used tools; they proposed the abolition of Wednesday evening church services because of the 'risk to general security';[107] they refused to open D 'wing' until they were satisfied with its facilities and security;[108] they proposed the establishment of a regular security team; they refused to 'man' C exercise yard until it was 'made safe';[109] they insisted that shields and helmets should be stored in readiness for emergencies;[110] they proposed that the issue of knives and scissors should be controlled;[111] they complained about the lightness of sentences awarded for assaults on officers;[112] and they argued that women should be escorted when moving around the prison at night with the physiotherapist. They even wrote to the Governor in June 1984 to insist on safe staffing levels for the mother and baby unit. In short, on one reading, staff felt defenceless, on another, increasingly repressive, and on a third, they had become very generally, and perhaps indiscriminately, apprehensive, and all were faces of the same beleaguered condition.

Those intertwined responses made them wary, jittery and mistrustful.[113] They shared space reluctantly and fearfully, forever being brought too close to inmates. An officer said there was always a risk of 'sudden confrontation between staff and prisoners, suddenly having to, even walking down a corridor, be absolutely proximate to each other, be just right next door to each other, and that produces . . . confrontations. We all like a bit of space. We can't live on top of each other.' And an inmate said 'in the old Holloway you knew where the boundaries were. I much preferred it. It's not so much because as

---

[105] A published interview with a Holloway officer in 1982 reported her saying that inmates 'can be extremely unpredictable. You can walk straight into an unprovoked attack. There are always officers on sick leave.' 'One Woman's Work', *Ms London*, 1 June 1982.

[106] Minutes of the meeting of the Prison Officers' Association, 8 July 1980.

[107] Minutes of the meeting of the Prison Officers' Association, 26 Feb. 1981.

[108] Minutes of the meeting of the Prison Officers' Association, 25 Nov. 1982.

[109] Minutes of the meeting of the Prison Officers' Association, 15 Mar. 1984.

[110] Minutes of the meeting of the Prison Officers' Association, 18 Sep. 1984.

[111] Minutes of the meeting of the Prison Officers' Association, 10 July 1985.

[112] Minutes of the meeting of the Board of Visitors, 28 Apr. 1982.

[113] And they shared this mistrust with their counterparts in American prisons for women. See R. Giallombardo, *Society of Women, A Study of a Women's Prison*, (New York: John Wiley, 1966), 40.

women we need to be disciplined, but in a totally unnatural environment, you need some sort of rules to go by, you need some guidelines, because it's just chaos otherwise, and that's how I find Holloway now. It's extremely chaotic.' There could be no easy co-existence in confused space belonging to no one.

Chisholm and Smith remarked that geographical space is deeply implicated in practices of social exclusion.[114] The pragmatic alternative to a seemingly impossible co-habitation was for staff to retreat into their offices and for inmates to be excluded from the common parts of the prison, but, having thus been excluded, there was nowhere for prisoners to go apart from their rooms. Conflict was managed by enforced avoidance. Inmates were to be 'banged-up', and it is the effects of locking-out and locking-in that I shall review in the next chapter.

[114] See M. Chisholm and D. Smith (eds.), *Shared Space: Divided Space,* (London: Unwin Hyman, 1990), 9.

9

The Minotaur: Disturbed Women and Monstrous Visions

'Sick women moaned and screamed, mutilated themselves and fought with the staff'.[1]

Introduction

The regimes of prisons are unstable.[2] I have already shown how Holloway itself had moved precariously and rapidly through a succession of political systems, the quest for authority sometimes veering more towards winning the acquiescence of the incarcerated,[3] sometimes more towards the application of force. During the early part of the 1980s, authority was upheld less by compliance-based methods than by a show of power. The creation of legitimacy and consent was never wholly absent from the thinking of managers[4] and officers, but there can be little doubt that Holloway was more transparently coercive in its methods at that time, and force and its consequences came to typify the social organization of the prison.

If one tries to capture the political character of the prison regime in the last years of the 1970s and the first years of the 1980s, one might

---

[1] 'Holloway revisited', *British Medical Journal*, 29 July 1989, Vol. 299, No. 6694, 283.

[2] See, for instance, J. Jacobs, *Stateville: The Penitentiary in Mass Society*, (Chicago: University of Chicago Press, 1977). Jacobs traces at least four distinct stages in the political evolution of the penitentiary: anarchy, charismatic dominance, drift and crisis.

[3] R. Sparks and A. Bottoms would certainly uphold the argument that legitimacy is attainable. 'Order and legitimacy in prisons', paper presented to the American Society of Criminology meetings, 4–7 Nov. 1992.

[4] See the interview with Joy Kinsley, the Governor, in *The Sunday Telegraph*, 31 July 1983. Almost all regimes must attempt to establish what Turk called the 'norm of deference' (A. Turk, *Criminality and Legal Order*, (Chicago, Rand McNally, 1969) 47).

say that it was a time when discipline officers locally and nationally[5] were in nervous ascendancy. Amongst so much chaos, novelty and change, discipline officers in Holloway sought chiefly to re-establish some kind of order. The devastation of the first few weeks had obliged them to do so, and they continued as they had begun. And the Governor during a significant portion of that time, Joy Kinsley, also took it as her task to re-introduce order in what had quite evidently become a turbulent institution.

Joy Kinsley had begun her career in hospital and district nursing, became a Mental Welfare Officer, and then joined the Prison Service in 1966 to serve at East Sutton Park, Holloway (where she worked on the borstal recall wing) and Risley before being appointed Governor of Bullwood Hall in 1972. She became Governor of Pucklechurch in 1977. From Pucklechurch in 1979 she was promoted to develop policies for young offenders in the South East Region. 'When I was in South East Region I became responsible to the Regional Director for women's establishments and finished my service there as Deputy Regional Director. I, therefore, had considerable contact with Megan Bull and Holloway prior to becoming Governor.' From there she moved to become Governor of Holloway between July 1982 and February 1984.

Kinsley's succession to Holloway was taken by some (but not all)[6] to signify an end to medical and therapeutic aspirations in the prison. The Chief Inspector of Prisons observed that 'the present Governor . . . has an orthodox operational background. She had the task, as far as the regime was concerned, of taking the lead away from the medical staff and changing the ethos of the establishment from a prison hospital to that of a prison with a hospital.'[7] Inadequate attention had been paid to security in the past, the Chief Inspector reported, but reforms were being made by Joy Kinsley.[8] She was giving the prison a

---

[5] David Faulkner observed 'a culture of control—rather than normalisation—was steadily establishing its grip on the prison service and the principles and values of the Holloway project were becoming more and more incomprehensible to it. For prison officers, watching television screens in dark rooms became more highly regarded than contact with prisoners. Whether as a consequence of this change or for separate reasons, a climate of fear was becoming increasingly pervasive . . . '

[6] A member of the Project Group attached no particular significance to her appointment: 'We hadn't at that stage got to the point where you could have a male governor in charge of a female institution, and Joy Kinsley had risen to the top of the seniority tree as the next person to be promoted.'

[7] Report on HM Prison Holloway by HM Chief Inspector of Prisons, (London: Home Office,1985), 8.   [8] *Ibid*, 29–30.

'new direction'.[9] She certainly took it, as most of her colleagues in the Prison Department had taken it, that the original ideology of the new Holloway was benign but naive, and she shared their reasons for disbelieving in its promise:

The theory in the '60s was noble, people wanted to do something for this group of women prisoners and there were all sorts of very good reasons for that and it was an area that was small enough to experiment in etc. etc. I have said that what they didn't take account of was the sociological side of things. It was all very well in terms of psychology, to go for group therapy, but sociologically women were changing and they were actually beginning to become more—I don't like the word emancipated—but they were being freed up from some of the constraints and they began to commit crimes more like men, more burglaries and all that sort of thing. They began to behave slightly more like men in criminal terms and therefore they began to get the same sort of sentences . . . . On the other side, from the psychological medical point of view it was, I think, about the time when the psychiatrists were beginning to turn away from group therapy, and saying this doesn't really work after all or it doesn't work as much as we thought it did.

In the early 1980s, Joy Kinsley faced a troubled prison whose inmates, defined as dangerous and disturbed, posed problems[10] of control for an over-taxed and apprehensive group of officers. 'Sometimes', she was reported to have said, 'there is even a tendency to over-sympathize with the prisoner—but, don't forget, our job is also to protect the public. We have mixed-up, unhappy individuals in here, certainly, but we also have some very dangerous people in here indeed. You can't afford to be naive.'[11] Her job was to act firmly, decisively and with realism to restore order to Holloway. Holloway was a prison, and it was mistaken and confusing to proceed as if it were otherwise:

I knew quite well that one of the things that I had to say to people was this has got to be a prison and that was a pretty tough task. . . . I don't think I gave it as a sort of message that you stand up on a platform and say this is what were going to do but I knew and would discuss with senior staff, that that, in fact, was what I had to do, to begin to put some reality back into it and it was a great idea to have a doctor as governor but she was never running

[9] Quoted in M. Dean, 'Holloway's fast lady keeps to her course', the *Guardian*, 25 July 1983.

[10] 'The really hard core of chronic problems—problems that upset society—that hurls bricks through its windows, is drunk in the street and sets things on fire—gravitates to us', she said. *Sunday Telegraph*, 31 July 1983.

[11] G. Hudson, 'Behind Prison Walls', *Home and Country*, Oct. 1982, 14.

a hospital and hadn't had the experience of governing in the way that the rest of us had been trained to do.

Kilsley held that it was wrong to allow the inner world of a prison to converge too closely with the world outside the walls. (I have already touched on the problems posed by probation and education officers[12] having had informal contacts with inmates and ex-inmates. In May 1983, again, a chaplain was warned after giving shelter to a girl who had suffered from an overdose,[13] and, in July 1983, relatives were not allowed to attend confirmation services for prisoners.)[14] It was wrong to allow the formal organization of a prison to become loose, ill-defined and uncontrolled (of the education department, the Governor said, 'they have in the past developed a creative and individualist, perhaps more informal approach to their role than is usual, and required in any prison establishment. The challenge will be to retain the originality and creativity, but to stay within the perimeters required in any prison establishment.')[15] It was wrong to blur formal lines of command and accountability. (A member of the Board of Visitors said 'I can remember when she first came to the prison, one of the things that she said was "there is one person who is responsible in this prison, and it's me. So in order for me to be able to give effect to that responsibility, you have to do your job, which is very clearly set out and defined. Do not step outside that and likewise that happens up the hierarchy"') It was wrong to administer a prison as if it were anything other than a prison. A governor from a later period reflected:

There's no doubt that there were probably issues of security and order that needed to have been dealt with by her. I think staff had felt Dr. Bull was a very nice person, a very kindly doctor, but who had actually not really understood the management of a prison even if it were a prison hospital, I think that that was the view, that she had not really been strong. And of course Joy Kinsley was a very strong person and obviously came into it as a strong governor.

Public depictions of Joy Kinsley were mixed and they changed over time. She was said to be humorous and practical, committed and compassionate.[16] But she tended in the main to be conventionally

---

[12] The Governor had the general support of the Chairman of the Board of Visitors and the Director-General of the Prison Service in the matter of the excluded education officer. See Chris Train's admonitory letter to the *Guardian*, 28 July 1983.

[13] See *The Times*, 17 May 1983.   [14] See the *Guardian* , 25 July 1983.

[15] Governor's Annual Report for 1982.

[16] See G. Hudson, 'Behind Prison Walls' 12.

portrayed as someone committed to discipline, a woman who adhered strictly to the prescribed rules and who supported,[17] and was supported by, the discipline officers[18] (the POA did indeed pass a number of votes of confidence in her in reply to criticism from the mass media[19]). Kinsley proclaimed her backing for the staff generally in their struggle for control over the prison,[20] and specifically in matters such as the screening of D block.[21]

It is inevitable that firm judgements should have been delivered about a firm figure in such a visible and conflict-laden institution. Although, as I have observed, the drift towards officer militancy had started well before Joy Kinsley's arrival and continued for years after her departure, she did come forcefully and personally to epitomize a particular rigour in the politics of Holloway. Those with whom she had had disagreements looked back on her regime as partisan in its shift towards discipline and the discipline officer. One said 'the firm hand ruled. . . Kinsley gave [officers] power. Dr Bull, I think, contained officer power, Kinsley gave it to them and they got more and more out of control. . . . She was an officers' person.' But some officers were less sure of her partisanship. A former member of the local Prison Officers' Association remembered that 'she met us on a regular basis, we had our disagreements, and generally speaking, there would be compromises on both sides'. And Joy Kinsley herself argued that:

One of my objectives at Holloway was to develop professional attitudes and standards, so that positive work with inmates could progress and that *all* members of staff could develop their own professional expertise. It seemed to me that one of the ways to lift the place up was to enhance the role of the officer from mere turn-key to one where treatment and training played equal parts.

[17] Joy Kinsley said that she had 'nothing but praise for staff who were dealing with some very disturbed women'. Minutes of the Board of Visitors, 22 June 1983.

[18] See, for example, *The Times*, 18 May 1983.

[19] See the *Sunday Telegraph*, 31 July 1983.

[20] In her annual report for 1983, for instance, she observed that 'the staff are determined not to be pushed to the limits that they once were. This is not an unreasonable stance and it is certainly not one that can be ignored. However it remains true that Holloway's main strength lies in its staff and their ability to cope with difficult people and that is a very important asset.'

[21] Minutes of the meetings of the Board of Visitors, 22 June 1983, 27 July 1983, 24 Aug. 1983.

'Locking-out' and 'Locking-in'

Let me describe the politics of the prison in the late 1970s and the early and middle 1980s, during the governorships of Megan Bull, Joy Kinsley and, at the beginning, Colin Allen. I have argued that control was exercised somewhat anxiously by a discipline staff who were convinced that they were out-numbered, over-worked and unduly vulnerable to attack in the new and bizarre prison that had been wished upon them (remember that the symbolically-important protective perimeter wall was completed only as late as 1983). Supported by Joy Kinsley as their new Governor, they sought to re-impose order on a weakly-structured prison, to re-affirm its character *as* a prison, and they did so at first by trying to transfer and adapt some of the familiar disciplines of the old Holloway. The new establishment was still described in the language of the old (it took a long while before the word 'wing' was replaced by 'unit',[22] for example) and control was conceived in older style as well. One officer said 'everybody sort of changed when they went through this hole in the wall [in 1977] and went daft, and I felt I was struggling to keep my head above water and saying "we're still the same! We're still the same!" They all had their own ideas how everything should happen, because nobody was really pulling the strings. But I made damn sure I pulled the strings on my wing, I'll tell you that.'

But the units were not wings, the 'Centre' had gone, and the disciplines of the radial prison were ill-suited to the anti-panopticon. Officers found the new prison difficult to supervise: they maintained that they were too few in number,[23] too insecure and too burdened with work such as escort duties to exert full and effective control over prisoners in their rooms, on exercise and in association. By late 1978 they were each working an average of twenty-five hours overtime a week[24] and they said they were 'run ragged'. Their response was to embark on industrial action that centred explicitly on the staffing levels needed to supervise inmates but which seemed to refract all their other discontents as well. Two principal forms of action were practised, 'locking-out' and 'locking-in' (or 'banging-

---

[22] The term 'wing' was still being used in 1983 in the minutes of the Board of Visitors, for instance.

[23] About 10% of the 300 officers in post were 'off sick' on an average weekday in 1984, and some 50 officers were needed for outside staffing for escorts and special watches in hospital. See the *London Standard*, 1 Nov. 1985.

[24] Annual Report of the Board of Visitors for 1978.

up'), and both drew on the officers control over space. In the last resort, they said, it was they who held the keys: 'if we actually locked up, we locked up. They couldn't then get in and out. So we still had the ability to actually lock them up.'

'Locking-out'

In October 1980, the CNA (certified normal accommodation) of the prison was 253, but 286 inmates were in occupation; 167 officers were in post and 86 were available for duty. As part of a wider national campaign,[25] the local POA voted to 'reduce inmate population to the CNA . . . . all inmates presently brought into prison by police, bailiffs and the immigration authorities will be refused until the CNA has been reached'.[26] The women thus refused entry to the prison were lodged chiefly in police cells, and police stations came to act as a kind of sump for Holloway and the other prisons. The POA did eventually abandon their quota of 253 on 17 December 1980, but they replaced it by a new upper limit of 100 above the CNA (that is, a population limit of 350)[27] and it was to that figure to they adhered for years to come.

Despite rising numbers of committals, 350 remained the rule, a rule to which the Governor herself came eventually to acquiesce,[28] and women were locked out month after month. On 27 September 1983, for instance, 25 women were held in outside police custody, and 4 more were held on 22 November.[29] The highest number ever reported was 80 women locked out on a single night in 1986.[30] Inmates destined for Holloway were scattered: trial prisoners being transferred to as far away as Low Newton to prevent locking out in 1985,[31] and the tendency of the prison to filter its population was reinforced yet further. In February 1981, the Governor reported 'this is causing considerable difficulty and embarrassment to S.E.R. [South

[25] The campaign lasted for some time. Of 1983, for example, it was reported by Hugh Klare that 'hundreds of prisoners remanded to custody pending trials had to be held for long periods in inadequate police cells, with only 15 minutes of exercise a day.' *1984 Britannica Book of the Year*, (Chicago: Encyclopædia Britannica, 1984), 575–6.

[26] Minutes of Special Meeting of POA, 14 Oct. 1980.

[27] Governor's Report to the Board of Visitors, 28 Jan. 1981.

[28] Governor's Report to the Board of Visitors, 21 June 1983.

[29] The Chairman of the Board of Visitors protested to *The Times* on 12 Aug. 1985 about the manner in which up to 28 women had been locked out over 6 weeks.

[30] Governor's Report to the Board of Visitors, 30 July 1986.

[31] Minutes of the meeting of the Board of Visitors, 22 May 1985.

East Region] as varying numbers of women still have to remain in police custody. We still have to declare daily the numbers we can accept. . . . We are under pressure to transfer out as many sentenced women as possible.'[32] The 'most difficult cases come to us', the Governor continued, 'the more stable remain in police custody'. The Holloway Project Committee Report noted that, on 26 June 1985, there were 89 women in Styal and 25 in Durham H Wing who had been transferred from Holloway. 18 of the group were serving life sentences, 50 sentences of three years and over, and 46 of under three years.[33]

'Locking-in'

As a second form of industrial action, officers began to rely on an ever-greater suppression of freedom of association.[34] The first POA action in early August 1978 was accompanied by the abandonment of prisoners' evening association.[35] In late March and early April 1979, under a new voluntary agreement, the officers refused to work more than five hours overtime a week, and the consequence was that many women were again confined to their rooms. What started then lasted for a decade, and long periods of confinement became an engrained feature of the prison. Throughout much of the late 1970s[36] and the 1980s, officers refused to undertake substantial overtime work,[37] tasks were dropped,[38] and women were locked in their rooms, isolated and

---

[32] Governor's Report to the Board of Visitors, 25 Feb. 1981.

[33] *Holloway Project Committee Report*, 6.

[34] Bans on staff voluntary overtime and prisoners' association had taken place in the old prison as well. In September 1973, for instance, a staff overtime ban, occasioned by a high rate of sickness, had led to locking-up at lunchtimes on open wings and on Saturday afternoons. The annual reports of the Board of Visitors for 1974 and 1975 also complained about what they called 'unacceptably long periods of locking-up'.

[35] Governor's Report to the Board of Visitors, 22 Aug. 1978.

[36] There were complaints about lack of association due to staff shortages in 1976 and 1977, for example. Minutes of the meetings of Board of Visitors on 28 Jan. 1976 and 27 July 1977.

[37] It was argued frequently that many women officers were married and were less dependant on overtime than their male colleagues.

[38] Thus, in the week 12 Feb. to 18 Feb. 1985, 74 tasks were dropped on Tuesday, resulting in no work and no education all day; 21 on Wednesday, with no work p.m.; 51 on Thursday with no work or education p.m.; 61 on Friday, with no work or education all day; 4 on Saturday and 4 or Sunday; and 33 on Monday, with no work or education all day. (I. Posen, 'A Survey of Stress in Prison Officers at Holloway Prison', May 1986).

inactive, sometimes for twenty-three hours a day.[39] 'Banging-up' became habitual, a reflex response to perceived problems of staff shortage and difficult supervision (a member of the Board of Visitors claimed that 'they were defining their responsibilities as "I don't have to negotiate with this woman. She either does it or she doesn't do it. If she doesn't, she gets banged up"'). Banging-up so accelerated and amplified antagonisms that prisoners, officers and governors became embroiled in a spiralling conflict that threatened to overwhelm them all.[40] Colin Allen, Joy Kinsley's successor as Governor between early 1985 and early 1989, summarized what was to come:

[1979] appeared to mark the first significant female POA action. It seemed to reinforce the negative and reactionary bits in the prison. Staff response to prisoners became sometimes vindictive. The best example of this is that overtime would not be worked if it meant the women would be unlocked for association. In turn the women prisoners reacted badly at being confined when good facilities were available but not being used. Incidents, assaults on staff and vandalism increased. Staff lost confidence and became more nervous and restrictive. . . . A vicious circle was therefore created.[41]

The new disciplinary strategy welled up from, and reinforced, a multitude of stresses, resentments, hostilities[42] and bouts of aggressiveness.[43] The early 1980s were an emotional, difficult time, a time of trepidation, fear and anger. They were symbolized by the 'locked door [as] a norm of Holloway life'.[44] A senior probation officer

[39] See the *Observer*, 5 Oct. 1980 and *Silence: Women's Imprisonment*, (London: London Strategic Policy Unit, no date), 61.

[40] It is interesting, but beyond the scope of this book to explore, that 'banging-up' became a more general feature of women's prisons during the decade. Thus there were complementary reports of women being confined to their rooms in Cookham Wood for very long periods during the same period. See the report of the debate in the House of Lords on 29 Oct. 1985.

[41] 'Governor's Report on the Dispute at HM Prison Holloway', (undated), 4.

[42] The Chairman of the Board of Visitors, a solicitor, wrote to the *Law Societys Gazette* that 'the locking-up of women in their cells for lengthy periods makes them more unsettled and can result in management problems'. The *London Standard*, 1 Nov. 1985.

[43] On 24 Nov. 1982, the Senior Psychologist informed the Board of Visitors that she was developing treatment techniques to deal with the very high levels of aggression in the prison.

[44] S. Casale, *Women Inside*, (London: The Civil Liberties Trust, 1989), 51. On p. 19, she wrote: 'at the time of the research [in 1984], the education department at Holloway consisted of 16 full-time teachers and a part-time budget for 3,000 teaching hours per year. This impressive resource was, however, not in use for most of the research period and it became clear that provision of education depended less on teaching resources than on availability of prison officers to escort women prisoners to classes.'

recalled that 'there was a great fear . . . every door was locked, the bottom of the stairs, the top of the stairs . . . when people are locked up a great deal of the time, then you get violent outbursts and uncontrolled outbursts because there's nothing very much positive going on'. And an inmate remembered, 'doors were locked, we were spending 23 out of 24 in the cells . . . the sinks, toilets, have been smashed, toilets have been kicked to bits . . . People were really angry because they were locked up 23 out of 24.'

Banging-up interfered with the orderly provision of what remained of treatment,[45] education,[46] religious,[47] hygiene, physical training, work,[48] exercise and other programmes.[49] Medical clinics were cancelled.[50] Inmates could not use the library.[51] It was not unusual for the women's day effectively to end with locking-up at 4.30 in the afternoon[52] (and that could be especially irksome during the summer[53]). Problems began to multiply. In 1986, for example, a woman suffered a miscarriage after spending most of her sixteen-hour labour locked in her room.[54] By that time, some prisoners were being locked up without any respite at all and the Chairman of the Board of Visitors wrote to a newspaper publicly to predict that, without association and exercise, without an informal and educational life, there would be riots.[55]

The screw turned and, with each turn, it not only prompted the kind of troubled response that had justified the original banging-up, but it also sustained a greater repressiveness of mood (Colin Allen observed that 'an element among the staff . . . seemed to flourish on

[45] See G. Parker and P. Lowe, 'A5 . . . . The Therapeutic Unit at Holloway', *Prison Service Journal*, Apr. 1983, No 50, 7.

[46] Between 1 Jan. 1984 and 21 June 1985, 45% of planned daytime and 71% of planned evening teaching hours had been withdrawn at Holloway because of 'shortages of prison officers for supervisory duties'. Written Answers, *Hansard*, 24 June 1985.

[47] See *Report on HM Prison Holloway by HM Chief Inspector of Prisons*, (London: Home Office, 1985), 10.

[48] 54% of available time in work was lost in 1981 and 20% in 1982, for example (Industrial Manager's report for 1982). 2,950 hours were lost in 1983 (Industrial Manager's report for 1983).

[49] I. Posen, 'A Survey of Stress in Prison Officers at Holloway Prison', 1986, 6.

[50] Senior Medical Officer's Report for 1983.

[51] Governor's Report to the Board of Visitors, 23 Nov. 1983.

[52] *Hansard*, 18 Feb. 1986.

[53] The problem was mentioned explicitly in the Annual Report of the Board of Visitors for 1980.

[54] See *Islington Gazette*, 14 Oct. 1986.

[55] See his letter to *The Times*, 25 Oct. 1986.

[a] diet of gloom and despondency and actively contaminated young staff joining the prison'[56]). A psychiatrist who had worked at Holloway reflected:

The staff actually . . . don't have the knowledge as to how to actually deal with these people and also the staff start to become frightened of the women, so you begin to have a lock-in culture rather than the idea that the women were not to be on the units, they were going to be on the education department. Then, as in fact the self-mutilation rate rocketed, Head Office did a complete about turn—'what we'd better do now is we'd better put in a regime and make this place into a prison'.[57]

Colin Allen's 'vicious circle' depicted a cycle of repression, reaction and further repression that spun round and round in the Holloway of the late 1970s and early 1980s. It was a circle that bears a close resemblance to what sociologists of deviance were wont to call deviancy amplification, the spiralling process by which social control exaggerates and aggravates the deviant features of regulated conduct; the features so illuminated and enlarged justify the application of yet more severe control; and the process continues in a series of erratic and distorting feedback loops.[58] As social typifications are embellished and consolidated, as social control becomes more strenuously enforced, so deviance itself can acquire an increasingly exaggerated shape, perhaps even coming to embody the very worst fears of those who tried to suppress it.[59] The self-fulfilling prophecies of control have been described in many ways. Karl Weick would say that 'believing is seeing, that powerful groups create the environments to which they respond.'[60] In much the same manner, Lemert would talk about 'secondary deviation', the conduct that ensues when 'a person begins to employ his deviant behavior or a role based upon it

---

[56] 'Governor's Report on the Dispute at HM Prison Holloway'.

[57] It will be recalled that it was in Jan. 1981 that P4s 'HM Prison Holloway—Purpose and Regime' was released. The new policy declared formally the abandonment of psychiatric treatment, the reduction of a medical orientation, and an increase in security. The primary aim of the prison had become the provision of a training regime for sentenced prisoners and remand facilities and services as a local prison for unconvicted and unsentenced prisoners.

[58] See L. Wilkins, *Social Deviance*, (London: Tavistock, 1964).

[59] See J. Young, 'The Role of the Police as Amplifiers of Deviancy, Negotiators of Reality and Translators of Fantasy', in S. Cohen (ed.), *Images of Deviance*, (Harmondsworth: Penguin, 1971).

[60] K. Weick, 'Enactment Processes in Organizations', in B. Staw and G. Salancik (eds.), *New Directions in Organizational Behavior*, (Malabar: Robert E. Krieger, 1982).

as a means of defense, attack, or adjustment to the overt and covert problems created by the . . . societal reaction to him'.[61] Ditton would say that control waves define and animate the deviant phenomena they are designed to attack.[62] In effect, the disorder and repression at Holloway came to give birth to a very special form of deviance, a form that was to be magnified and distorted, and they did so in the very epicentre of all that coercion and chaos, in C1, the subterranean unit for 'highly disturbed' women.

And there might even have been another, more elusive aspect of that dialectic. Douglas once remarked that 'in our everyday lives morality and immorality, respectability and disreputability, the other-worldly and the this-worldly, the sacred and the secular—each term necessarily implies the existence of its opposite for its own meaning and, above all, for much of the force it exerts on our lives'.[63] So too with C1. It was as if there was a symbiotic relation, the highly disordered woman coming to personify the very antithesis of the order that officers wished to accomplish. The more fervently structure was sought, it seemed, the more pronounced did the *anomie* of C1 become.

C1

It will be remembered that C5, the unit for 'highly disturbed' women, had been rendered less offensive and noisy to its neighbours by being taken down below the walls to C1, the lowest floor of all. Physically, C1 was reported to be one of the most oppressive units in the 'most dismal part'[64] of the whole labyrinthine structure of Holloway. Illuminated by slit-like windows that were covered in crazed poly-carbonate, it was subterranean and dark, damp and cockroach-infested, 'claustrophobic and depressing,'[65] dirty, smelly and noisy ('Holloway informants describe C1 as smelling of urine and excre-ment, and say the noise of locked in women banging on their cells is deafening'[66]). Dorothy Speed, the psychiatrist who became Principal Medical Officer at Holloway in June 1986, herself vested with overall

---

[61] E. Lemert, *Social Pathology*, (New York: McGraw-Hill, 1951), 76.
[62] See J. Ditton, *Controlology*, (London: Macmillan, 1979).
[63] J. Douglas, *Deviance and Respectability*, (New York: Basic Books, 1970), 3–4.
[64] H. Bullard and H. Hally, 'Enquiry into Board of Visitors' Concerns about Standards of Health Care', Nov. 1993, 6.   [65] *Ibid*, 6.
[66] Mind/NCCL, 'Crisis in Holloway Prison', undated, 3.

charge of C1, claimed that confinement to so dreadful a place was actually a form of torture which could drive people mad:

What went wrong basically with C1 was that there was no proper hospital, there was a physical area in what was ordinary prison accommodation and there was accommodation for the mentally disturbed, as they called them, on the ground floor level because it was easier to contain them there and it was physically, architecturally, built the same way as on the other levels but it was worse because it was dark, it was on the ground floor. It was damp, there was rising damp because the main drain that comes from the block of flats on the left, not the staff flats, the lie of the land, this would be C wing here, is hollowed away, so it flows down and the main drain into C1, which I used to have to examine, being responsible for the drain. I would find that there was no angle to it, so it was the main flow from the block of flats and there was rising damp everywhere and it smelt of rising damp. There was one rat but they put a plug in the thing so that it couldn't come through, but there had been a rat and of course the girls knew about the rat and it was terrifying for them. It was damp, there were rats and of course the food was thrown down from 5, 4 and 3 and where did it land—on the ground here, and who was happy in the bushes—the cockroaches, that was their home and the nesting and the eggs. So, the ground floor levels, C1 and D1 and worse still D0, which is further on the slope as it goes down, were infested with cockroaches. So the girls would be lying there in the dark on C1 and suddenly you'd feel a bite and people would say 'don't be silly you're hallucinating' . . . . And they'd suddenly become convinced that perhaps they were hallucinating, but they weren't, they were really being bitten by cockroaches because it was dark. So, you could say it was a sort of form of torture, C1.

A 46-bed unit, C1 housed prisoners who were remanded for medical reports (75% in late 1984),[67] or defined as mentally disturbed (73% in 1982–83),[68] suicidal (8% in 1982–83) or disruptive (7% in 1982–83). Being preponderantly on remand, usually for periods of up to three weeks, the population of C1 tended to be transient and unstable in composition. 113 of the 147 women, 77%, received between November 1982 and May 1983 left within that six-month period,[69] 23% having spent less than a week and 70% less than five weeks in custody.

Anthony Clare and the Bishop of Stepney, visiting the prison in the summer of 1985, declared that information about the inmates was sparse, the immediate problems of custody and security overriding

---

[67] See Holloway Project Committee Report, (1985), 14.

[68] C. Stewart and J. Shine, 'Disturbed Women in Holloway', (unpublished), June 1984.

[69] Ibid., 3.

thorough diagnosis and treatment, but 4 out of the 28 women then resident were said to be epileptic, 3 'mentally handicapped', and 6 had 'clear-cut psychiatric disorders although in a number . . . the precise formal diagnosis was unclear'.[70]

C1 was tense and unhappy. A unit without adequate space for association; adapted belatedly and without the advice of the Director of Prison Medical Services; consisting, as the Prison Officers' Association put it, of 'sharply-turning corridors [and] cells that cannot be seen into properly';[71] fraught with 'serious staffing problems'[72] (there were seven officers assigned to C1 in the mid-1980s); it was a place where officers felt 'endangered and insecure'.[73] A psychiatrist reflected 'C1 regularly had a population of some of the most personality-damaged and dangerous young women anywhere in the country. Frankly the staff were terrified of them.' Prison officers maintained that they could not exercise effective control: they said that the women were unpredictable; they did not understand much about the character or management of mental illness, they were disorientated by the noise and confused by the space, and they found it difficult to cope with the aftermath of violence.[74] So disagreeable was it, they said, that work on C1 should only be undertaken by volunteers and tours of duty should be reduced to six months.[75]

The officers made a threefold response to this situation. First was an ecological strategy: the inmates of C1 were banged-up, relegated to their rooms, denied access to territory, recreation and programmes, so that they were no longer free to meet and confront staff in the cramped spaces of the unit. The National Council for Civil Liberties complained that severely ill women were being locked up all day in the C1 of the 1980s.[76] Figure 9.1 shows that, although C1 may not have been the most heavily afflicted unit (C1 was awarded high priority, below 'Searchers' and visits to probation and the chaplain

---

[70] 'Report on Visits to C1 Unit, Holloway Prison, made by Professor Anthony Clare and the Bishop of Stepney', July 1985, 2.

[71] *Holloway Prison C1 Unit: A Report by the Prison Officers' Association*, (London: 1985), 7.   [72] *Ibid*, 7.

[73] Reports on Visits to C1 Unit, Holloway Prison made by Professor Anthony Clare and the Bishop of Stepney, 10.

[74] C. Stewart, 'Progress Report on Training programme for C1 Staff on the Handling of Disturbed Women', 30 Apr. 1982.

[75] Minutes of the meeting of the Prison Officers' Association, 18 Sept. 1984.

[76] Letter to Minister of State, 12 Feb. 1985.

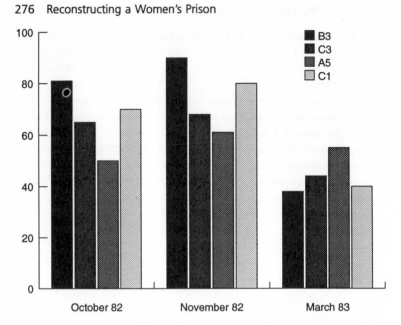

Figure 9.1 *Percentage of Evenings Lost on Association in Specimen Units (based on figures contained in Minutes of the Board of Visitors)*

but above some twenty other tasks[77]), its occupants did undoubtedly lose very substantial periods of time on association. Prisoners were reported to feel despairing and angry, 'claustrophobic and caged',[78] and they turned their anger on others and on themselves.[79] The General Secretary of the National Council for Civil Liberties and the Legal Director of MIND told the Minister of State in February 1985: 'the mentally ill or handicapped person kept in a room, without activity, diversity, qualified nursing care and attention or the space to move about will suffer badly and these women are suffering. Paradoxically the conditions that are in existence for more mentally healthy people in the other wings are much better than those in C1'.[80]

Second was a medical strategy: the inmates were sedated (as they had been in the radial prison). In Holloway as a whole in 1983, 82,140

[77] 'Temporary Task Dropping Priorities', 8 Jan. 1982.
[78] Reports on Visits to C1 Unit, Holloway Prison made by Professor Anthony Clare and the Bishop of Stepney, 9.
[79] See the *Observer*, 25 Nov. 1984.   [80] Letter of 12 Feb. 1985.

doses of drugs affecting the central nervous system were administered,[81] of which 47,866 were anti-depressants.[82] And that very widespread resort to medication, claimed to be the highest for any prison in the country,[83] may well have distorted the behaviour of the inmates, making them even more bizarre in their conduct.[84] They became transformed into sad, sometimes demented creatures, and C1 itself, in the unkind language of the prison, became known as 'the Muppet House'. The General Secretary of the NCCL said that C1 was worse than the Zoo.[85]

Third was a disciplinary strategy: the occupants of C1 were subjected to frequent adjudication and punishment. Punishments available in the 1980s consisted chiefly of the removal of privileges, the loss of tobacco, earnings or a radio, the loss of remission, and the loss of association, that is, solitary confinement.[86] Table 8.1 shows two consecutive days' of Governor's adjudications for the whole prison; these days were taken at random for illustrative purposes (reports do not indicate the inmate's unit and it is not possible to present the adjudications held for those living in C1 alone).

One of the classic organizational dilemmas of the prison was evident in the struggle to control C1's inmates. After the fairly modest range of punishments had been exhausted (punishments which were in any event not much worse than the conditions then prevailing on C1), there was little more that could be done by staff.[87] The Chairman of the Board of Visitors said: 'The real problem were the C1 people who were charged day in day out with assaulting officers again and again, what could you do with them? Take away privileges? If you took away privileges from some of these women, it

[81] NACRO, 'Submission to the Special Project Committee on the Future of Holloway Prison', Apr. 1985, 7.
[82] C. Moorehead, 'The Strange Events at Holloway', *New Society*, 11 Apr. 1985, 42.
[83] 'Crisis in Holloway Prison', MIND Press Release, 26 Oct. 1984.
[84] See A. Mandaraka-Sheppard, *The Dynamics of Aggression in Women's Prisons in England*, (Aldershot: Gower, 1986), 10.
[85] The *Observer*, 31 Mar. 1985.
[86] On 9 Nov. 1983, the House of Lord was informed that 1,251 offences had been subject to disciplinary action in 1980, 1,085 in 1981 and 1,061 in 1982.
[87] It was Gresham Sykes who showed how, in the absence of effective, formal control in prisons, officers and governors would resort to the informal co-optation of prisoners, rewarding them for policing themselves (G. Sykes, *The Society of Captives*, (Princeton: Princeton University Press, 1958, 50–51). That variant was not adopted in the early 1980s but, as I shall show in the next chapter, it was to be adopted in the later 1980s under Colin Allen.

Table 9.1 Governor's and Board of Visitors' Adjudications, August 1983

(a) Governor's Adjudications

23 August 1983

1.	Wilful Damage	Loss of remission 14 days
		Loss of association 21 days
2.	Wilful Damage	Unfit
3.	Wilful Damage	Loss of earnings £1.50
4.	Disobeys Lawful Order	Loss of association 7 days
5.	(a) Offends Good Order	Loss of remission 7 days
	(b) Wilful Damage	Confined to cell 3 days. Loss of earnings, 3 days

24 August 1983

1.	Delivers to other inmate without permission	Stop earnings £1
2.	Wilful Damage Unfit	
3.	Delivers to other inmate without permission	Stop earnings £1
4.	Wilful Damage	Dismissed
5.	Wilful Damage	Dismissed
6.	Assault Officer	Unfit

(b) Board of Visitors' Adjudications (month of August 1983)

1.	Assault	14 days cellular confinement
2.	Absconder	30 days loss of remission
3.	(a) Gross personal violence (amended by panel to charge of assault)	(a) 14 days loss of remission
	(b) Wilful damage to Prison property	(b) Fined £1
4.	Absconder	35 days loss of remission (+ activated 3 days loss of remission award)

made them more difficult. We could put them in cellular confinement, we can fine them so they don't get their money for cigarettes, remission was really for the C1 prisoners—often they were on remand anyhow, so the prospect of loss of remission meant nothing, lack of association that sort of thing. [They were effectively beyond our control.] . . . whatever you did, they were back again and, if they didn't come before us again, they were before the Governor the next morning.'

Punishment may only have exacerbated distress and disturbance, and there was something of a repeated shuttle movement between the segregation unit and the unit for highly disturbed women. Women in 'cellular confinement' could and did damage themselves, and they would then sent back to C1. A medical officer recalled that 'what you would have is this woman on C1, she's not mentally ill, she's just set fire to her cell again or she's assaulted somebody again, she knows what she's doing, she should be punished, put her on governor's report, the woman then goes from C1 and goes down to the segregation unit, seen . . . on adjudication, but then, whilst down on the segregation unit, woman cuts wrists, tries to hang herself, identified as a suicide risk, has to be admitted back to the medical unit'.

Mentally disordered women were being punished rather than treated,[88] and, some argued, they were being punished for breaches of rules they could not understand and could not keep.[89] The Board of Visitors found it difficult sometimes to justify its role as a quasi-judicial body. As early as 1977, it declared its alarm about adjudications emanating from C1's precursor, C5: inmates were being passed as medically fit, the Board stated, but 'we feel that they understand little of what is going on or how to conduct their case'.[90] There was said to have been the application by medical staff of what was called the Styal method of adjudication: inmates were not treated with special consideration unless a medical report indicated that the offence was a specific symptom of their condition.[91] In 1982, the Board of Visitors pronounced again on the difficulties of adjudicating on disturbed inmates.[92] The Chief Inspector of Prisons himself expressed particular anxiety about 'the use of disciplinary proceedings against prisoners who appear to be disturbed or mentally disordered'.[93] It was wrong to discipline them as if they were normal,[94] he said, yet, of 40 women who had been certified as fit and tried by the Board of Visitors during one period in 1985, only 8 were 'mentally normal': 'the remaining 32 had a wide range of

---

[88] T. Maden *et al.*, 'Psychiatric disorder in women serving a prison sentence', unpublished, 1993, 2.

[89] See V. Stern, *Bricks of Shame*, (Harmondsworth: Penguin, 1987), 28.

[90] 'Board of Visitors' Annual Report for 1977'.

[91] Minutes of the meeting of the Board of Visitors, 28 June 1979.

[92] 'Board of Visitors' Annual Report for 1982'.

[93] *Report on HM Prison Holloway by HM Chief Inspector of Prisons*, (London: Home Office, 1985), 2. [94] *Ibid.*, 20.

conditions including brain damage and mental impairment'.[95] A former deputy governor remarked that there has:

> always been an issue about women and prison and about how they behave, and is this mad behaviour or bad behaviour and are they in control and should they be on adjudication and dealt with through the disciplinary procedures or should they be on treatment?

The Home Secretary was informed by the charity Women in Prison that in the first six months of 1984, over half the women on C1 had been punished for such offences as offending against good order and absenting self without leave: 'we ask you to consider whether any other unit for the mentally ill and distressed would punish patients for wandering off without first asking permission'.[96]

At numerous points in the early 1980s, the Senior Medical Officer was asked by the Board of Visitors to explain how it was that inmates from C1 could be ruled fit for adjudication.[97] It seemed to the Board that those who were manifestly unfit were being presented repeatedly for judgement and punishment.[98] It was a comparative matter, the Chairman of the Board reasoned: in the midst of so much manifest pathology, it was easy enough for a psychiatrist to change frame and perspective to normalize the abnormal. The quite mad could begin to look 'fit' enough:

> if you have dealing with psychiatric patients for years and years, you some-times forget that there are people who are perhaps not exhibiting quite such severe symptoms, but who are nevertheless to the man in the street and to the person on the Board of Visitors adjudicating, are very sick indeed. . . . We often had arguments about it with the [medical officer], we would often invite him to stay, but he never did.

And the other prime disciplinary authority, the Governor, Joy Kinsley, said:

> The great criticism is these women haven't done anything bad enough to take them in to custody but it was really because there wasn't any other answer

---

[95] Quoted in N. Davies, 'Mentally ill "on trial" in Holloway', the *Observer*, 10 Nov. 1985.

[96] Letter to the Home Secretary, 26 Oct. 1984.

[97] At the meetings on 16 Dec. 1981, 26 May 1982, and 23 June 1982 for instance.

[98] In May 1982, the Board of Visitors recommended that the Senior Medical Officer should attend a mock adjudication exercise.

and it was a protective thing and then you had to set about trying to do something about it and the medical staff at the time were very reluctant to unfit these women for adjudication [i.e. to deem them to be medically unfit to be disciplined] so that I was forced into the position of trying to adjudicate on very disturbed ill people, it's extraordinarily difficult. . . . I did the best I could and sometimes I had some very fierce arguments with the doctors.

It is evident that there was a profound ambiguity at the core of C1: could a unit for the highly disturbed properly fall under a broad system of control that presupposed responsibility and intentionality, and, indeed, should it be the therapeutic or the disciplinary, the nursing staff or the disciplinary staff who held sway in the place?[99] It was an ambiguity recognizable in almost all organizations that are bent simultaneously on control, reform and rehabilitation:[100] most criminal tribunals assume deliberateness of intention but those wedded to treatment assume that nonconformity is a consequence of emotional disturbance; most criminal tribunals assume the universalism of law, but those wedded to treatment, the individualization of response.[101] Indeed, an insoluble contradiction was built into the very idea of 'disturbance':

The phrase 'disturbed' was double-edged. It was seen as referring to both psychiatrically ill women AND those whose behaviour or mental state was clearly disturbed, as evidenced by the difficulties they presented the prison in the management of their persistently disruptive behaviour, but who were not considered to be suffering from mental illness.[102]

Yet something had to be done. Staff faced (and probably contributed to) a disorder that could not be ignored. There were persistent

[99] The ambiguity and conflict had not been confined to C1. In Nov. 1974, for instance, there had been correspondence between the POA and the Governor about a new doctor's unwillingness to certify women fit for adjudication.

[100] See D. Cressey, 'Limitations of Organization of Treatment in a Modern Prison', *Theoretical Studies in Social Organization of the Prison*, (New York: Social Science Research Council, 1960). In 1961, Galtung claimed that the functional incompatibility of retribution and therapy was the most frequently studied topic in penology. J. Galtung, 'Prison: The Organization of Dilemma', in D. Cressey (ed.), *The Prison: Studies in Institutional Organization and Change*, (New York: Holt Rinehart and Winston, 1961), 122.

[101] See J. Jacobs, *Stateville*, 206.

[102] C. Stewart and J. Shine, 'Disturbed Women at Holloway', 1–2.

complaints by the POA and occasional complaints by the Governor[103] that inmates alleged to have assaulted officers were not punished appropriately, that the Board of Visitors and the Senior Medical Officer were too lenient, and that their authority had been undermined.[104] On 10 November 1982, at the suggestion of the Governor[105] and the discipline officers, the Holloway and Pentonville Boards of Visitors held an 'adjudications exercise' that was designed to remedy matters, but one member of the Holloway Board declared afterwards that she was 'sorry that the summary seemed to point to the Board the need to be supportive to the discipline staff rather than being an impartial body weighing up the facts as set out to them'.[106] A member of the Board of Visitors who elected to report on the problem in 1983, stated that:

an adjudication can take on a special significance for the prison officers and inmates. It is seen as the opportunity for justice to be seen to be done and an appropriate award meted out. This in itself can lead to difficulties for the Board because mitigating evidence, usually about the fitness of the inmate who made the assault, can result in relatively mild awards being made even when serious injuries have been caused.[107]

The Norwegian criminologist, Galtung, might have argued that the structural ambiguity of C1 could have been settled by a territorial compartmentalization of the prison into discrete therapeutic and

---

[103] In one instance in early 1984, an inmate who had been charged with two offences involving a 'very serious assault' on an officer was awarded 14 days and 28 days cellular confinement by the Board. The Governor informed the Board that she was unhappy at such an award and the general principle in such cases should be to make an award of loss of remission: 'to award Cellular Confinement to———meant very little, as she was kept locked in her cell most of the time, because of her behaviour. The Governor also informed the Board that there was very little confidence in the way that the Board of Visitors dealt with their adjudications'. Minutes of the meeting of the Board of Visitors, 22 Feb. 1984.

[104] Cf. the correspondence referred to in n. 99 above.

[105] She remarked that 'it was a problem that their adjudications lacked credibility in the prison. This was also at a time when judicial reviews were beginning to crop up and it was important—for all concerned—to get things tight.'

[106] Minutes of the meeting of the Board of Visitors, 25 Nov. 1982.

[107] J. Ward, 'Assaults on Prison Officers by Inmates', July 1983.

disciplinary spaces,[108] that the attempt to maintain a semblance of the two regimes in the one place was destined to be fraught.[109]

Instead of compartmentalization, however, there were multiple confusions in C1. Nursing staff and disciplinary officers vied ceaselessly with one another for dominion over treatment, space, standing and control. The unit may formally have been placed under the control of a forensic psychiatrist and two visiting psychiatrists in the mid-1980s, but there was no clear management structure,[110] C1 being practically administered by an admixture of different hierarchies[111] with two 'chains of command';[112] there was no clear ideological structure; no clear disciplinary structure; no clear areas of responsibility; no machinery for resolving disputes;[113] and there was no clear territorial structure.

Most of the C1 nurses were recruited from a local agency on a temporary basis, and the disciplinary staff tended rather to disparage their competence. Three of the five nurses working on C1 in 1985 were agency nurses and prison officers repeatedly declared their opposition to working with women whom they said were ill-versed in the problems and routines[114] of the unit.[115] And matters were exacerbated by racial tensions between nurses and uniformed officers and between West Indian and African nurses.[116]

Disciplinary staff strove continually to maintain their symbolic and practical supremacy over the medical staff: nurses were said to find it difficult to work in C1 because they had to be escorted by uniformed officers,[117] they were not allowed to work without the presence of discipline officers, and discipline staff refused to recognize nursing

---

[108] It had been Joanna Kelley's original intention that the conventional role of the discipline officer would actually disappear. Francis Baden-Powell, the architect of the new Holloway, reflected that she 'introduced the idea that if security was no longer important, what then were the prison officers going to be doing? And her idea was that they should in effect retrain as caring officers, so that their role would be to take over the kind of social caring—they would be the opposite numbers to the nurses, the nurses were the specialists in the medical side and they were the equivalent of nurses'.

[109] J. Galtung, 'Prison: The Organization of Dilemma', 127.

[110] See the Home Secretary's reply to a Parliamentary Question in the House of Commons, 17 July 1985.

[111] See The Holloway Project Committee Report, 23.

[112] Report on Visits to C1 Unit, Holloway Prison Made by Professor Anthony Clare and the Bishop of Stepney, 8.

[113] See Report by HM Chief Inspector of Prisons, 1985, 19.

[114] See Holloway Prison C1 Unit: A Report by the POA, 1985, 7.

[115] Thus the POA passed resolutions deploring the policy in Jan. 1981 and again in Jan. 1983.   [116] S. Casale, Women Inside, 91.   [117] Ibid.

staff as 'unlocking officers'.[118] Nurses were 'marginalised',[119] 'infan-tilised' and 'second class citizens'.[120] A governor said 'the nursing group were completely disempowered and the alienated group and deskilled'. The Chief Inspector of Prisons concluded that morale had been damaged by conflicts between the operational and the medical departments.[121] NACRO called the atmosphere in the unit punitive rather than therapeutic, seclusion and restraint having become ende-mic features of the place,[122] and, indeed, in May 1985, an occupa-tional therapist resigned in protest at conditions in C1, arguing that the regime was dedicated primarily to containment, that therapy had been foregone.[123]

The disciplinary having gained a tenuous supremacy (a nurse said 'prison officers were ruling the roost'), C1 was managed practically as if it were a part of the prison (albeit a wayward part) to be organized very much like the rest. A nursing sister remarked that 'people were sent to C1 to work who had no interest in the needs of the mentally ill. They saw the C1 patients in the same light as other inmates and put people on report. . . . The regime was very strict, very oppressive, they treated the unit as a part of the prison to be treated like any other. They felt if someone was sent there it was a soft option.'

Being part of the prison, C1 could not be allowed to lapse into chaos, dirt and disorder. Joy Kinsley observed:

One of the things that I saw as an ex-nurse, if you like, was that prison nursing is often not as clinical and hands on as nurses want it to be, it's a different sort of nursing. . . . the staff who worked on C1 in terms of discipline staff were really very caring and very dedicated people and they wanted to help these women tremendously but saw the nurses as not being as helpful as they thought they ought to be. The nurses saw the staff as interfering but it came as a great eye opener to me because I had been years away from my nursing, but I discovered for instance that nurses saw it as no part of their job to get the women to keep their rooms clean, so the place was filthy and if they thought the staff told them to clean it up, that they were being punitive, so there were all sorts of conflicts going on and a lack, I think, of clear medical lead.

[118] Minutes of the meeting of the Board of Visitors, 24 Sept. 1980.
[119] Report on Visits to C1 Unit, Holloway Prison Made by Professor Anthony Clare and the Bishop of Stepney, 8.
[120] Senior Medical Officer's Annual Report for 1982.
[121] *Report by HM Chief Inspector of Prisons*, 1985, i.
[122] 'Submission to the Special Project Committee on the Future of Holloway Prison', Apr. 1985, 11. [123] The *Guardian*, 22 May 1985.

Locked up, drugged and frequently punished, the inhabitants of C1 were unruly. There were high rates of vandalism,[124] damage,[125] barricading, floodings,[126] arson and violence against other inmates, staff and the self[127] (50% of the occupants of C1 were declared to have suicidal tendencies[128] and 7% inflicted injuries on themselves in 1985)[129]. Five women died in the unit between 1981 and 1985.[130] Waves of disturbance would pass through the unit; these were particularly intense in 1985, when the number of remand prisoners was at its peak, when twenty incidents of self-mutilation were reported in a four week period in June and July alone,[131] and twenty-four incidents in just under three weeks in November.[132] The injuries sustained could be quite 'gruesome':[133] using information supplied to the press by WIP, NACRO reported how, in 1984, a woman had gouged out an eye and another had attempted to cut off a breast. Josie O'Dwyer, once an inmate in C1, recalled how 'people just sit there. They howl or they scream or sit there and bang their heads against the wall. I felt like I was going off my head when I was in there: everyone is screaming and banging so in the end you start banging yourself.'[134] One inmate I interviewed recalled how 'I remember hearing a big

[124] The BBC television programme, '10 days in Holloway', broadcast in 1986, showed graffiti and the strip cell walls gouged out by hair brushes, for instance.

[125] On 26 Jan. 1983, the Governor announced to the Board of Visitors that £60,000 was being spent on strengthening and improving C1 and A1 in the wake of damage caused by inmates.

[126] See the statement made by Lady Ewart Biggs in the House of Lords, 13 Dec. 1985.

[127] T. Maden et al., 'Psychiatric disorder in women serving a prison sentence', 2.

[128] Although rates of suicide tend generally to be lower amongst women than men prisoners. See *Suicide and Self-Injury in Prison: A Literature Review*, (London: Home Office, 1990), 22.

[129] *Holloway Project Committee Report*, 22. That high rate of self-mutilation persists. J. Wilkins and J. Cold, for example, reported 7.6% of remands in Holloway over an eight week period in an unspecified year had a history of self-mutilation. 'Self-mutilation in female remanded prisoners', *Criminal Behaviour and Mental Health*, 1991, 1.

[130] The dates, causes of death and coroner's verdicts were: 9 February 1981, cardiac asthma—natural causes; 12 July 1982, traumatic cerebral haemorrhage—death due to misadventure; 13 Feb. 1984, subdural haemorrhage—open verdict; 29 Apr. 1984, bronchopneumonia renal failure—natural causes; and 16 Oct. 1985, self suspension—accidental death caused by lack of care.

[131] 'Cuckoo's nest at Holloway', the *Observer*, 21 July 1985.

[132] See 'Violence of jail women', the *Observer*, 25 Nov. 1985.

[133] 'Developments at Holloway', NACRO briefing, Feb. 1988.

[134] Quoted in N. Davies, 'Protests grow over Holloway horror wing', the *Observer*, 16 Sept. 1984.

thump and about several minutes later, another thump, . . . and I could see . . . this woman was actually sitting on the radiator and putting her arms behind her back and going forward and smashing her head on the floor'. And, behaving thus, prisoners in C1 were taken to merit even firmer supervision. Women so disturbed could not be trusted to conduct themselves responsibly. They were an evident danger to themselves and others.

C1 became known as a terrible place, to be described almost surrealistically, in the language of dream and nightmare. On 19 September 1985, a woman wrote to Women in Prison about her first experience of the unit: 'I lay down on my bunk listening to the deafening screams, the banging and the confused tormented stutters of the mentally sick. I wept and wept.' One who had worked in the unit described how 'the smell on C1 hits you first. Pungent, choking, thick; a clinging assault on the nostrils. Next the cries reverberating along tunnel corridors. Shouts and screams, banging and wailing. Pale, wide-eyed faces, disorientated and vaguely inquisitive protrude from hatches in cell doors. . . . Often distraught, sometimes deranged, always alone these women sit in cells for 23½ hours out of 24.'[135] Visitors to the unit might be met, as was the local MP, Jeremy Corbyn, by 'continuous screams from a woman banging her head on the brick and plaster walls of her cell'.[136]

And in the bowels of that dark, terrible place, amidst all that noise, it was easy to imagine that there were monsters. Outsiders certainly searched for them. A nursing sister remembered that 'people came in with expectations, they expected mad people and clanging doors. Once a woman shut a door quietly with two hands and a BBC woman was upset because she hadn't clanged the gates when she was being filmed.' And monsters could be supplied. Harry Wisebloom, the maker of the BBC '40 Minutes' programme, '10 days in Holloway', broadcast in 1986, said 'there was so much that was extraordinary. A woman from the medical side 'phoned me to say they had a woman who was a vampire. She would cut herself and drink her own blood. The staff were saying "look at the kinds of people we have!"'

---

[135] Letter from former student social worker at Holloway, the *Guardian*, 29 May 1985.   [136] 'Women in Prison', Nov. 1983.

Holloway Prison as a Public Problem

Holloway was well placed to become a public problem. It was exceptional because it was one of the very few prisons for women, and such institutions attract the public gaze[137] (and particularly the gaze of those who are fascinated by exposés centred on scandals such as lesbian relations:[138] Jeffrey Bayes, a Chairman of the Board of Visitors in the 1980s, said 'Holloway was and always had been a voyeur's delight as far as the media are concerned'). The prison was set in a densely populated section of the capital, near Fleet Street and the television studios, and was peculiarly accessible to reporters (a home affairs correspondent observed that 'Holloway will always be a story because it's both prisons and women and there is something special and unusual in that [and] it's to hand, it's down the road').

And the new prison was made more accessible by design. To be sure, there were occasions when the press were denied entrance: it was the view of the Board of Visitors in the troubled year of 1976 that the best way to manage relations with reporters would be comprehensively to ignore them,[139] and they were banned again during the disturbances following the move into the new prison in 1977. But the more general policy was to encourage openness. The Director-General of the Prison Service had determined in 1976–77 that prisons and their Boards of Visitors should make themselves more approachable to the media.[140] Colin Allen reflected that 'prisons had not been open to public scrutiny by the media until the very late seventies. The policy had been to keep it in house and suddenly there was a change. Governors were exhorted to build relationships with media representatives to explain what was happening inside.' The Holloway Board of Visitors themselves sought to be more open, being one of the first to circulate their annual reports to the press and to make their members available to reporters. (One member said 'it arose out of

[137] There was, David Downes reminded me, a popular television series called 'Within these Walls' between 1974 and 1977, in which Googie Withers played the governor of a women's prison and drew attention to the inner workings of a Holloway-like institution.

[138] See, for example, the report of an affair by a prisoner and an assistant governor in the *Sunday People*, 13 May 1979.

[139] Minutes of the meeting of the Board of Visitors, 21 June 1976.

[140] A letter of 20 Sept. 1976 from the Prison Department to the Board of Visitors laid down that restrictions would not be placed on the making of public comments in the media but the privacy of prisoners and the security of the establishment should be respected.

a view that people who were in the position of members of the Board had a duty to the outside world in terms of externalising information about closed communities basically, and that had to be good and had to be responsible and had to be acceptable. It may be unattractive and it might reveal things people preferred not to know, but that was what accountability meant and that's what we ought to be doing'.) The Board even invited a *Guardian* journalist, Malcolm Dean, to join them in April 1978 (he was invited, said the woman who proposed him, 'because we wanted a press person, we wanted to have a control over own voice in the press'). As a professional matter, he did not write about the prison whilst he was a member, but he was to do so quite frequently afterwards.

And that was not all. Several television programmes were made in and about Holloway, even when it was at its most riven.[141] The cumulative effect of all that greater transparency, Malcolm Dean concluded in 1994, was to make prisons more interesting to journalists:

In the last decade, prisons've become much more prominent and more accessible, so the two things probably feed each other because you can now, every time there is a prison story there is something in the library of the BBC or ITN which shows you prisoners, there was never any of that 20 years ago. . . . If all prisons became higher profile partly because of the way disputes create news stories, then there was an opening out which has regenerated interest in prisons.

Little informal political networks are forever coalescing in and around the criminal justice system. Composed of policy officials, journalists, academics, practitioners and politicians, they come together in universities, conferences and dinner parties, at public meetings and seminars, on the boards of journals and in television studios. For a while, one such loose network came to form about the emerging public issue of Holloway. It was organized, as all such groupings are, by the numerous and diffuse connections that were mobilized as the issue took form. For example, Richard Brown, the embattled Senior Education Officer at the prison in the mid-1980s, had been at Oxford University with Malcolm Dean, the *Guardian* correspondent and they came together over Brown's expulsion from

[141] A member of the Board of Visitors called Holloway 'a sad and cruel place' on a Thames Television programme in early 1981, for instance. Minutes of the meeting of the Board of Visitors, 25 Feb. 1981.

the prison ('he was quite good at taking an awful lot of flack before he had ever bothered to call me, to be honest. It was sometimes other people calling me and saying "Richard is in a real mess". He didn't actually do that in fact. I think people on the Board [of Visitors] spotted things. I got a couple of leaks from them'). And Nick Davies, one of the first journalists to report conditions in C1, learned about prison conditions in part because his mother, a prison visitor, was a member of a Trust promoting art in prisons, and it was her link with Clean Break, a theatre group made up of former prisoners, that led him to WIP, Women in Prison.

The network focussed on Holloway contained four principal groupings who made occasional use of one another. One was composed of Prison Department officials distressed at what was stirring in the prison. Another was politicians identified with penal matters. A third was journalists, and chiefly the home affairs correspondents of the *Guardian*, the *Observer* and *The Times*. And a fourth was a larger congeries of activists occupied with penal reform. They transmitted and reported information, they campaigned and they lobbied, and their methods were often discreet and oblique. Important knowledge could travel quite anonymously and quietly on occasion. A journalist remembered 'I was home affairs correspondent. There were HO officials who were ringing to say "can you run this story for us?" They said "you are our liberal conscience".' Robert Kilroy-Silk, founder and Chairman of the Parliamentary All-Party Penal Affairs Group, at that time an MP asking frequent questions in Parliament about conditions in C1 and Holloway, said of his liaison with officials:

It was always very discreet and very subtle and very hesitant because they were afraid of compromising themselves obviously, but they were good men and decent men and women, who wanted to share with you their knowledge and hope that you might take the same view of it as they did and might do things about it. . . . I always in the end had to exercise my own judgement. What they were doing was they were pointing the way and it was a matter for me whether I went down that path or looked at those things or even regarded them as a priority, because their priorities wouldn't always necessarily go hand in hand with mine.

He remembered too how he had known journalists, Nick Davies of the *Observer*, Peter Evans of *The Times* and Malcolm Dean of the *Guardian*:

There would be a two way channel of communication between them. They might say to me 'have you heard?', because they couldn't get Parliamentary action, and I'd also keep them informed of things. And you knew they were sympathetic and they would write stories you could get stuck into a newspaper because they knew you were speaking with authority and knowledge. . . . I can see Malcolm saying 'have you heard?' and he might have mentioned things and not said 'put down a question', but 'why don't you do something about it?' And you would. So there was two way in that, but it wasn't formal and you might not speak to them for weeks.

What chiefly triggered the transformation of Holloway into a public issue was the work of a group of former Holloway inmates who had banded together in March 1983 as Women in Prison. WIP was a 'support and campaigning group for women prisoners'[142] whose prime mover was Chris Tchaikovsky, an ex-prisoner herself, and then a member of the Greater London Council Women's Committee.[143] In September 1984, alerted by fellow ex-prisoners about a succession of deaths in Holloway, WIP began to protest, and its protest was directed especially at the press. The first palpable response to WIP was an article written by Nick Davies on the 'Holloway horror wing' in the *Observer* on 16 September 1984 (Chris Tchaikovsky remembered that 'I had called dozens of journalists before speaking to Nick and they weren't in the least bit interested in what was happening to the women on the unit. One journalist told me that a woman putting out another woman's eye is news, but a woman putting out her own eye isn't'[144]). Davies himself recalled that he had been placed 'in touch with Chris Tchaikovsky who spoke to me. . . . I got into Holloway—it was difficult to get in—I may not have said that I was press—and I met a woman who had cut her breast' and, he added, 'there were people in the Home Office who wanted the story done. They wanted money, publicity and resources to do things at Holloway'. The article recited how:

There is growing concern over conditions in Holloway Prison's psychiatric wing—known to inmates as The Muppet House—where there has been an outbreak of self-mutilation among the women prisoners. [C1] has a troubled history: two women have died there, one by setting fire to herself, the other

---

[142] Women in Prison, no date.

[143] See C. Tchaikovsky, 'Worlds within worlds', *New Internationalist*, Dec. 1985, 22.

[144] She continued, 'it is an important point because most media interest in women's prisons is prurient and it is still difficult to get anything that isn't salacious reported'.

from a haemorrhage after repeatedly banging her head against a door. . . .
The women on the wing—and even some of the staff—. . . complain that the
regime on the wing breeds desperation and that the atmosphere has deteriorated in the last few months. . . . The pressure group Women in Prison
appealed for help to the local borough council, Islington, and to the Greater
London Council.

It was that article above all that awarded national prominence to the
problems of Holloway.[145] It mobilized what Richard Ericson and his
colleagues would call 'pack journalism', the mass pursuit by reporters
of a story illuminated and given authority by their own activities.[146]
Holloway became the centre of media attention for a while, and
reports about it were published almost daily[147] in the *Morning
Star, The Times*, the *Guardian* and the *Daily Telegraph* and again
in the *Observer*. Holloway had become interesting not only because it
was palpably troubled but also because other newspapers and journalists attested to its importance.

WIP organized demonstrations outside the Home Office and the
prison in 1984 to demand an enquiry into conditions in C1, demonstrations that were combined, in part, with protests mounted in
sympathy with women from the encampment at Greenham Common who were imprisoned in Holloway.[148] WIP was joined by MIND
and the National Council for Civil Liberties,[149] by NACRO,[150] the
Prison Reform Trust and the Howard League. Orchestrated questions
were asked in both Houses of Parliament about the state of C1.
Ministers began to wonder whether Holloway might not be labour-
ing under the difficulties of too complicated a role.

It was determined that there would have to be a new beginning. Joy
Kinsley would become Governor of Brixton Prison from February
1985, and her successor would be a young man, Colin Allen, then

---

[145] See V. Stern, *Bricks of Shame*, 26–7.

[146] See R. Ericson *et al.*, *Representing Order: Crime, Law, and Justice in the News
Media*, (Toronto: University of Toronto Press, 1991).

[147] See J. Morton, 'Inside Holloway', *Solicitors Journal*, 10 Apr. 1987, 45.

[148] Those protests had started in Feb. 1983 and continued for a considerable time.
They were joined in July 1983 by former inmates.

[149] Representatives of MIND and the NCCL visited the prison in Jan. 1984 and a
statement was released in Oct. 1984 that talked generally about a 'crisis in Holloway
prison', and specifically about the isolation of prisoners in poor conditions. MIND
Press Release, 26 Oct. 1984.

[150] NACRO had learned about Holloway from the articles by Nick Davies in the
Observer and from the personal connection of Jill Matthews, a member of its staff,
with Chris Tchaikovsky of WIP.

Governor of Maidstone Prison.[151] And, in December 1984, the Home Secretary announced his decision to establish a committee to review the function and structure of Holloway.

The Holloway Project Committee

Like so many formal enquiries, the decision to found the committee (which became known as the Project Committee) was the concatenation of internal and external pressures put to good use (and indeed nursed) by those who came to the view that Holloway needed imposed change.[152] There had been the 'glare of publicity under which Holloway operated during 1983 and 1984',[153] a glare that had been supplied in part by worried officials and members of the Board of Visitors. WIP claimed that the decision was an answer to all its campaigning, and the Committee certainly acknowledged the part that WIP had played.

There had been a critical report prepared by the Chief Inspector of Prisons in February 1984 which had deplored the lack of morale in Holloway and the conflict between operational and medical departments. In his prefatory statement, the Home Secretary noted how the report showed the prison to have 'undergone constant disruption caused by the ten year redevelopment programme, and . . . its difficulties have been exacerbated as a result of the change in the role envisaged for the prison'.[154] 'Partly in the light of [the Chief Inspector's] findings',[155] the Home Secretary decided to assess Holloway's regime and future development.

There had been the informal judgement of the short-lived Control Review Committee set up in September 1983 in the aftermath of the riot at Albany Prison in May[156] 'to inspect conditions and restore confidence in the system' (as a member phrased it.) There had been extensive visits to dispersal prisons by teams of experienced officials[157] to 'see what was going on'. The Committee did not report

---

[151] Colin Allen was then 42. See *The Times*, 7 Dec. 1984.

[152] *The Holloway Project Committee Report* certainly acknowledges the role of WIP on p. 2.   [153] *Holloway Project Committee Report*, 3.

[154] Statement by the Home Secretary, *Report on HM Prison Holloway*, July 1985.

[155] *Ibid.*

[156] See R. King, 'Order, Disorder and Regimes in the Prison Services of Scotland, and England and Wales', in E. Player and M. Jenkins (eds.), *Prisons After Woolf: Reform through Riot*, (London: Routledge, 1994), 47.

[157] See A. Langdon, 'Control Review Committee', *Prison Service Journal*, January 1985, No. 57, 8.

on the female prison system,[158] and made no formal inspection of Holloway, but an unofficial visit had led to the judgement that the Prisons Board should be advised that 'something ought to be done about an unsatisfactory situation [at Holloway]'.

P4 itself had responded to the persistent, irritating and wasteful problem of 'locking-out' in a prison with unused capacity. One who had worked in the division at the time said:

The Holloway issue started to build at the latter part of 1983 when the prisoners began to be locked out in police cells and the issue that burst Holloway onto the political scene was that Holloway had a lot of unused empty accommodation which was newly built and had never been occupied and that empty accommodation was standing, a lot of officers were being recruited and posted in, so the number of women officers was increasing dramatically and the real urgency was prisoners in police cells, including women prisoners. A lot of staff, empty accommodation, where was the return? And of course the political embarrassment of locking prisoners up in police cells was on Leon Brittan's desk for a very long time. So, from then on Holloway was a big thorn in the side of the Prison Department and it was, as that grew because the pressure groups became very interested, there was so much activity from pressure groups and MPs that eventually the Holloway Project Committee was set up and sat in January to June '85.

All those diverse communications worked their way to the Prison Department and then up to the Prisons Board where they met with a sympathetic response. A key member of the Prisons Board, one who has been credited with some share in the final decision to recommend the review of Holloway, observed of the prison, 'it was a mad-house: the staff thought that they didn't know what the prisoners were doing; they kept them locked up all the time; there was a heavy-handed governor at the time. . . . the whole situation was deplorable'.

In what a Holloway governor came to call a 'classic Home Office, Prison Department ploy' it was decided to mount a departmental inquiry. The Project Committee was announced on 12 December 1984 by the Home Secretary. It was to be a 'small operational group with modest representation from headquarters, a group that included the Governor designate, a Governor from P4, the Director of the Mental Health Division of the Department of Health and Social Security, and the chairman of the Board of Visitors. There was no POA

---

[158] See *Managing the Long-Term Prison System: The Report of the Control Review Committee*, (London: HMSO, 1984), 1.

membership and neither they nor the Governors' Section of the SCPS submitted written representations to it.

The Committee's terms of reference were to prepare a plan for the development of Holloway Prison as the main local prison for women in the South of England; assess the numbers and composition of the population that should appropriately be held in Holloway; at the instigation of the Directorate of Prison Medical Services,[159] to identify what specialist functions might be better performed elsewhere 'having regard to Holloway's role as a local prison' ('we are trying to simplify the tasks of Holloway and make it more manageable' it was noted); and 'to consider the regimes that may best be operated in Holloway Prison, with the aim of enabling the prisoners to spend the maximum time possible out of their cells and to have access to a variety of activities'.[160] At the outset, it was not quite sure what the functions of a local prison actually were ('it is desirable to have this degree of freedom and flexibility at the beginning' observed the official who drafted the terms of reference). Neither was it sure what numbers should be recommended: the prison had been planned for a theoretical maximum occupancy of 556, but that would only have been feasible with staffing at an intensity that might not now be judged affordable. The committee would have to decide whether to leave expensive accommodation unused or commit large resources to the recruitment of officers and, it was conceded, staff appointed in the past had not actually been managed properly. At the outset, too, it was recognized that the future regime would have to bear some realistic relation to the resources likely to be available 'so as to avoid perpetuating the mistakes of the past'. The centre of political and media attention had been C1 and the assumption was that it would also have to become the centre of the Committee's attention. C1 would need wholesale reform: it was thought that there would have to be a clarification and definition of its roles (the core role was the psychiatric assessment of remand prisoners but, it was stated, other functions had been aspired to); and management should be allowed to reflect that definition, with an elevation of the standing of the medical officer in charge. From the first, it was thought probable that

---

[159] The suggestion was that a reference should be retained to the functions of a local prison rather than to the needs of the women incarcerated in Holloway.

[160] 'Role of Holloway Prison to be Reviewed', News Release, Home Office, 12 Dec. 1984.

it would be impossible to continue to look after disturbed women in the present building and that a brand new unit would have to be built.

The Project Committee Report

The Committee sat between January and July 1985 and its report gave the familiar history of the redevelopment project and the aspirations that had infused it, aspirations that were eventually confounded not only by changes in ideology but by the nature and size of the women's prison population and the lengths of sentences that women served. The 1981 review of purpose and regime, coupled with copious management and staffing difficulties, had led to 'an impoverished regime with limited access to association, education and other activities'.[161] Holloway had been beset by ensuing problems of self-injury and the possible use of drugs for control purposes. Growing public concern about the 'care, treatment and conditions' of women in Holloway Prison, and in C1 above all, had led to calls for an inquiry and the Committee was the formal reply that the Government had chosen to make.

The Committee proceeded methodically through a list of problems. It reviewed Holloway's future *population*, touching on the history of locking-in and locking-out. Locking-out of numbers over 350 was so 'unacceptable and so costly', they reported, 'that we think planning should reflect the need to cope with maximum peaks rather than average populations'.[162] The Committee recommended that the prison's operating capacity should be increased rapidly to at least 400 and, on the completion of building, to 500.

The Committee reviewed the *design* of the building, marking how therapeutic desire had exceeded performance. The building had too few single rooms; it was bedeviled by poor sight-lines and a sprawling layout; by weak security; and, lacking a centre and no big spaces, by the need for high numbers of staff. 'It is a sad irony', the Committee observed, 'that a building designed to foster a high level of care for inmates is having the opposite effect'.[163] But very little could be done to alter an unsatisfactory design, and there could only be slight physical improvements within the existing structure.

The Committee reviewed *staffing* matters. Holloway was characterized by a high ratio of staff to inmates that stemmed both from

---

[161] *Holloway Project Committee Report*, 2.   [162] *Ibid.*, 6.   [163] *Ibid.*, 9.

unusual problems of supervision and surveillance, and from the need constantly to second officers to escort women inside and outside the prison. As many as seventy-five officers might leave the prison every weekday to accompany prisoners to courts across the breadth of south-east England. Many staff were stressed and sick, and absent from the prison. It was recommended that a manpower review be initiated promptly and that inmates should be afforded greater freedom of movement within the prison itself.

The Committee reviewed the problems of *'mentally disturbed'* *prisoners* in Holloway. Those women tended largely to be unsentenced and therefore ineligible for transfer to hospital under the various Mental Health Acts: only about half the prisoners recorded as disturbed could be deemed to be in 'urgent need of treatment'. The remainder 'cannot be transferred to hospital, although they are suffering from psychopathic disorder or mental disorder because, being unsentenced prisoners, the [1983] Act does not give power to transfer them'.[164] Neither could prisoners be transferred if their condition was 'untreatable'. The outcome, the Committee said, was that a number of difficult and disturbed women were destined to remain in Holloway although 'to a lay person they may seem every bit as "mad" as those who meet the criteria for detention under the Mental Health Act'.[165] The prison service would have to continue to bear the responsibility for disturbed inmates whom it could not turn away.

The Committee reviewed the specialist *functions* of Holloway. Medical facilities had to be retained because it was the only female prison with comprehensive medical cover and the capacity to treat remand and sentenced prisoners. The mother and baby unit should be retained. A unit for women with drug and 'dependency problems' was to be closed, in part because it had not coped well with the transient and rapidly changing population of Holloway. The Committee was less certain about what could be done for Category A prisoners and suggested that there should be a full review of the nature and characteristics of the female prison population. (It was noted by the Prison Department that the Committee were not enthusiastic about the effect on the regime of introducing Category A prisoners to Holloway.)

The Committee reviewed C1 at unusual length. The bulk of inmates in C1 were on remand for medical reports and there was nowhere else

---

[164] *Holloway Project Committee Report.*, 14.   [165] *Ibid.*, 16.

for them to be sent in southern England. But its *building* was poor, not unlike a dungeon. What little free space there was tended to be confused and difficult to control, and the staff felt insecure. The judgement was that C1 was manifestly defective but that it had to remain, re-sited elsewhere in the prison: 'it is impossible to care properly for disturbed women in the environment created by the present buildings. We therefore recommend that a new purpose-built unit should be built to replace C1.'[166] Any new structure should combine what the Committee called 'safe space', maximum observation and minimum intrusion. In the meantime, C1 should be made more habitable and secure, its more dangerous features being removed and some of its spaces being enlarged by the removal of walls.

The organization of *staffing* in C1 was confusing, conflicting and contradictory. Treatment was administered by visiting psychiatrists and nurses and discipline by governors and discipline officers. The greatest source of friction was said to be unlocking: the discipline officers appeared to have lost confidence in the capacity of nurses to control inmates, and they insisted on being present when inmates were unlocked. For their part, a frustrated medical staff claimed that discipline officers were exaggerating problems of security and control. The Committee took it that C1 was not working as its planners had intended; there was little teamwork and little multidisciplinarity; but the Committee appeared uncertain what reforms to recommend. The medical side were said to propose total nursing cover but acknowledged not only that discipline officers would cavil at surrendering control but that there were too few nurses of calibre effectively to superintend the unit. Nurses could be trained to discipline officer requirements, but too few would be likely to come forward for training. Nurses could be recruited as hospital officers but the medical staff were again pessimistic about attracting sufficient numbers.

The *regime* of C1 was condemned as inadequate. Women were closely confined for excessive periods of time, they lacked work or recreation, and self-injury had become a common response. The Committee declared that it 'deplores the fact that inmates spend so much time locked up and inactive, without means of diversion or occupation'.[167] Selected women should be allowed to take work back to their room or dormitory.

---

[166] *Ibid.*, 23.   [167] *Ibid.*, 25.

The unit was recognized by the Committee to be part simultaneously of the hospital and of the prison, and for the time being, the recommendation was that it should be managed jointly by a senior medical officer and an officer of governor grade. A task set the senior medical officer would be to devise a new regime for the 'care and treatment of disturbed women' in the unit.[168] In addition, a new principal medical officer should be appointed to oversee the general medical care in the prison and in other female establishments.

Draft reports were discussed at meetings within the Prison Department in late June and early July. It was concluded by one senior official that the report's 'implied and overt criticisms of the situation at Holloway are all perfectly sound. . . . there is now such a wide— and generally accurate—understanding of what has gone wrong there that it will not be politically possible to do much less than the report recommends . . . in human terms something no smaller than the report's package is needed to care properly for the inmates at Holloway (and particularly those in C1).' But the proposals would be expensive and would require 'careful brokering'. There was some trepidation about the prospect of increasing the CNA: it would take a lot to break the POA grip on Holloway some thought. There were other reservations about proposals for a joint management structure on C1: tension could arise between the assistant governor and the medical officer placed in charge of the unit and it might be better to insert C1 firmly in the medical management structure. It was not clear to members of the Department that the Committee had been right to accept that Holloway was under-staffed, but the recommendation to carry out a full manpower appraisal was welcome.

The report went to the Prisons Board on 10 July and was approved as a 'sensible and well written document'[169] under 'any other business'. It went to Ministers and to the Home Secretary five days later. Ministers were told about the unforeseen increases in the size of the women's prison population and the changing assumptions about treatment which had resulted in a 'wholly unsuccessful attempt to graft the functions of local and training prisons on to a secure hospital framework'. Holloway's buildings were described as 'inherently inconvenient, claustrophobic and highly staff-intensive'. A fortress mentality had developed amongst the staff. In C1, espe-

---

[168] *Holloway Project Committee Report,* 27.
[169] Prisons Board Minutes, 10 July 1985.

cially, life was 'well-nigh intolerable' for the most highly vulnerable section of the women's prison population. The Home Secretary was informed that the Committee's diagnosis had come as no surprise.

In their turn, ministers agreed that the report was positive and that their response should be positive too. The report would be published and it would be implemented. On the day of its publication, 17 July 1985, it was met by an arranged written parliamentary question and a prepared Government response in which the Home Secretary gave very general approval to the Committee's recommendations. The report was, he said, 'a valuable analysis of Holloway's difficulties. I very much welcome the committee's positive programme for an urgent increase in the prisons remand capacity, the development of its regimes, improvements in management structure, and ways of reviewing staff deployment to ensure that the prisoners get more time in association and more access to Holloway's extensive facilities'. The Home Secretary, Leon Brittan, said further that special attention would have to be paid to remedying the problems of C1 whose physical state was wholly unsatisfactory and whose management structure was unclear ('urgent action is needed to rectify its deficiencies'). C1 should be rebuilt in a different part of the prison, and 'immediate steps will be taken to improve conditions on the unit'. Particular attention would be paid to improving the liaison between the nursing and the discipline officer staff, and the 'need to create an environment conducive to the assessment and treatment of disturbed inmates'.

Conclusion

The Prison Department acknowledged that it faced a dilemma after July 1985. Holloway was admitted to be an 'open sore' but surgery could not be too 'intrinsic or entrenched' because the prison's confidence required rebuilding. Capacity would be allowed to increase to 400 in the first instance and to 500 thereafter, following a full P6 manpower review, but the increase would have to be handled with skill by management because of anticipated difficulties with the POA. The Governor in his turn would have to be given administrative and political support in tackling the main staffing issues. The DHSS would be approached about the recruitment of good quality nurses. There would be an urgent search for a new Principal Medical Officer and a new Senior Medical Officer for C1 ('C1 needs a new broom', it was thought. The unit had to be organized anew under medical direction and action could not be taken without medical help).

The new Governor, Colin Allen, himself a member of the Committee, afterwards held that the chief elements of the report were that 'the unused accommodation should be opened up to receive prisoners currently in Police cells; there should be a Manpower Review. . . ; the regime should be opened up; a new building should replace C1 and in the meantime extensive interim improvements should be made and a caring regime should be created in the Medical Units'.[170] The report had stressed the importance of a lack of middle management, he was to tell the Board of Visitors.[171] But the main conclusion he drew was that the Project Committee represented a 'new start' with clear objectives that had received the full support of Ministers and Prison Department.

[170] 'Governors Report on the Dispute at HM Prison Holloway', 4.
[171] Minutes of the Board of Visitors, 23 Apr. 1986.

10

Theseus: Colin Allen and the Reformation of Holloway

'[He] ma[d]e his way through the intricacies of the Labyrinth, [and] he slew the Minotaur . . .'[1]

By 1985, it seemed as if a benign but ill-conceived design for a revolutionary penitentiary had foundered on the brute realities of staff and inmate conduct. That might have been all that there could have been said about the redevelopment project: its epitaph would have to be that it was a bad idea that had failed in practice. But that was not quite all. There was to be yet another twist in the tale that obliges one to reflect not only about the relations between architecture, planning and behaviour, but also about the nature of causality in social life.

Holloway after the Report

The Project Review Committee had declared that Holloway had to change. Officials were conscious that the Department and the prison would be under renewed pressure from the press[2] and politicians in the Autumn of 1985 when the new Parliamentary session opened and that there was a clear political need to demonstrate progress. Indeed, there were to be repeated admonitions from the Parliamentary Under-Secretary of State, Lord Glenarthur, that pressure was mounting in Parliament about the lack of progress made and, particularly about delays in the structural work on C1. The Minister was being harried

---

[1] *Plutarch's Lives*, (London: William Heinemann, 1948), 37.

[2] The Prison Department held that there would be some advantage in arranging for a considered media portrayal of Holloway at some point the future, but matters of timing and opportunity would have to be judged carefully. In the event, it was Harry Wisebloom's BBC documentary, '10 days in Holloway', that was to be filmed in April 1986, the first time that cameras were allowed into the new prison. It will be recalled from Ch. 9 that it was Harry Wisebloom who was offered the monstrous vampire.

in the House of Lords[3] (particularly after the suicide of a middle-aged woman in C1 in November 1985),[4] his colleague was being harried in the House of Commons[5] and the Director-General of the Prison Service was harried in his turn. Officials were reminded that they had to remember the political sensitivities of the Holloway problem.

Colin Allen

The new Governor, Colin Allen, the man who was expected to deliver the change, had started his career as a borstal housemaster, had been Deputy Governor of Feltham between 1971 and 1977, Governor of Huntercombe between 1977 and 1981, and then Governor of Maidstone Prison until February 1985 when he assumed his post at Holloway with a clear mandate to implement the recommendations of the Project Review Committee when it reported in July.

I was Governor of Maidstone at the time that I was called to a promotion board. At that time, if you were successful you waited until a senior position came up and for the department to tell you where you were going. Someone rang me up and said 'are you sitting down?' and I said 'no', so they said 'well, you had better, because we are sending you to Holloway'. I had never been inside a female prison at that point but gradually I realised the reason for my appointment. A major problem was that only part of the prison was open, largely because the POA were refusing to use more of the accommodation. The POA were saying there were not enough staff, yet the department had been throwing staff at the prison without it making any difference to the regime. Because it was not open plan as the old Holloway had been, the POA were saying that staff were far more insecure. The dilemma was clear. The POA kept the women locked up because they said there were insufficient officers and the more they locked up the women, the more aggravation they received. The more aggravation, the more assaults against staff took place and the more anxious they became. It was a classic kind of circle. That was the major problem, but another significant issue was the hospital, C1, which had had a terrible reputation. A woman had gouged her eye out and there was a high level of self abuse. Women were depicted on television as banging their

---

[3] There had been a debate on C1 in the House of Lords on 13 Dec. 1985 during which Lord Glenarthur had had to report that 'progress is being made but one simply does not achieve results overnight: they have to be planned carefully'.

[4] Lord Glenarthur had been obliged to tell the House in Jan. 1986 that changes in C1 so far had amounted to an assessment of 'the condition of the fabric in some detail before planning the changes that can be made'. NACRO Briefing; 'Developments at Holloway', Feb. 1988.

[5] Ten parliamentary questions were asked about Holloway between 18 and 20 Feb. 1986 alone.

heads against walls and the Home Secretary was being asked questions in Parliament about what was being done about it. I was conscious of a huge head of steam growing outside the prison. The previous governor had been in dispute with the education officer over his alleged association with former prisoners as a result of which the education department had been sent into exile, beleaguered in a little portakabin in the middle of the grounds. I could see that the Prison Department had reached a stage where it felt that it needed to have a change so they moved Joy Kinsley to Brixton and sent me to Holloway, almost entirely ignorant about women prisoners and prisons.

Organizational change is often accomplished most effectively by new leaders,[6] and it was just so with Colin Allen. He was what organizational theorists would call a 'transformational leader',[7] a charismatic man who came inevitably to personify the new order and assume an importance commensurate with the magnitude of the transition through which he had to steer the prison. He was the creature of dramatic events he helped to create. An outsider who made a television programme about Holloway in his time called him 'tremendously straight. There is a strong religious feeling, a humanitarianism.' The Chairman of the Board of Visitors in his time, Jeffrey Bayes, said 'I think that one of the few things the Home Office actually got right was the inspired choice of Colin Allen as the Governor'.

The prison that the new Governor inherited remained insecure, volatile and unsettled.[8] It continued to diffract inmates and staff who remained in uneasy relation with one another. Colin Allen told the Prison Department at the outset that Holloway was 'desperate for staff',[9] and the Department responded by recruiting the majority of new entrant women officers from all over the country[10] for the prison. Arriving at Holloway itself, however, those young officers

---

[6] See K. Cameron and R. Quinn, 'Organizational Paradox and Transformation', in R. Quinn and K. Cameron (eds.), *Paradox and Transformation*, (Cambridge, Mass.: Ballinger, 1988), 9.

[7] See A. Levy and U. Merry, *Organizational Transformation*, (New York: Praeger, 1986), 65.

[8] Holloway retained its notoriety after the Project Review Committee Report: in Aug. 1985, a Marylebone magistrate refused to commit women to what he called such an 'uncivilised prison'. *Islington Gazette*, 16 Aug. 1985.

[9] Letter from Governor to Regional Director, 7 May 1985.

[10] There was some apprehension in Headquarters lest that vigorous recruitment be read as a premature endorsement of the POA's argument that Holloway was radically under-staffed. Officials would have preferred to wait for the findings of the Manpower Review.

tended to encounter serious accommodation problems and moved on. A Chairman of the Board of Visitors said 'the percentage of officers who have been here for any length, it's very, very low because it's always had a history of taking nippers as they call them, the ones straight from college, who don't really want to be down in the south east . . . if they come from the north or wherever, it's difficult to find housing down here, it's expensive, their families are up north, so they will be waiting to have a transfer as soon as they can, so the percentage who have been here for longer than three years I would suspect is really very, very small'. The officers were still predominantly inexperienced and transient, nervous about conditions in and about the prison, anxious about matters such as vandalism in their car park[11] and insecurity within the walls, 'worried, quite understandably about their safety',[12] and they frequently absented themselves, claiming sickness[13] or stress.[14]

Prisoners were still being transferred and locked out, leaving the more 'disturbed' women behind. Mentally disturbed women were reported in 1986 to be 'constantly . . . admitted to Holloway Prison, often because there [was] nowhere else for them to go'.[15] And the staff continued to use their keys to control refractory inmates. There was task-dropping[16] and locking-in as there had been before,[17] programmes were being shed[18] and prisoners were being confined to their rooms, and the reaction to the experience of repression was more disturbance and waves of what the authorities called 'hysteria'. Prisoners were locked up for as much as twenty-three hours a day in November 1985,[19] and, in C1, a concomitant was

---

[11]   Minutes of the meeting of the Board of Visitors, 22 May 1985.

[12]   Colin Allen speaking in '10 Days in Holloway', BBC, 1986.

[13]   The Governor's report to the meeting of the Board of Visitors of 27 Nov. 1985 began 'there is currently a large staff sick list'.

[14]   Noted, for instance, in the minutes of the meetings of the Board of Visitors, 27 Aug. and 27 Oct. 1986.

[15]   T. Turner and D. Tofler, 'Indicators of psychiatric disorder among women admitted to prison', British Medical Journal, 8 Mar. 1986, Vol. 292, 653.

[16]   Education was one prime casualty. Minutes of the meeting of the Board of Visitors, 23 Apr. 1986.

[17]   See the letter from the Chairman of the Board of Visitors to The Times, 12 Aug. 1985.

[18]   In Sept. 1985, for instance, the Board of Visitors were told about the closure of the prison's workshops. Minutes of the meeting of 25 Sept. 1985.

[19]   See 'Jail's plea in lock-up crisis', the London Standard, 1 Nov. 1985.

fifteen cases of self-mutilation,[20] two major fires and 'many flood-ings'.[21] Disciplinary reports mushroomed ('a particular group of disruptive inmates account for the majority of these'[22] said the Governor) and so did Board of Visitors' adjudications, although Jeffrey Bayes, a solicitor and the Chairman of the Board, was once more reported to have observed; 'I would say more than half the women who came before us are suffering mental disorder. We have complained repeatedly about it. Many of them cannot have a grasp of the proceedings.'[23]

After the publication of the Project Review Report, meetings were held inside the Prison Department and between the new Governor and the Regional Director. It was agreed that the Governor, P4 and the Regional Director should continue to meet informally and reg-ularly and that they would require Ministerial support for whatever they resolved to do. It was also agreed that the Governor should not be constrained by very precise stipulations about how each of the Report's recommendations should be applied. It would not have done to place him in 'such an inflexible position'. It was for the Governor and the Director jointly to 'sort out the tensions' in Holloway.

Chief amongst the Prison Department's priorities in late 1985 was the need to end locking-out by increasing the prison's capacity to 400 as soon as possible, with the longer-term aim of gradually increasing to 500. To make that possible, the immediate programme would be to conduct a review of current staffing by the South East Region man-power unit, although difficulties were anticipated because commit-ments about an operational capacity of 350 had been given by Joy Kinsley to the local POA Branch Committee in the past. The Regional Director would write formally to Colin Allen to request him to revise the CNA according to the accommodation that was then available: there was unused capacity at the prison and it was thought that there was no reason to suppose that the figure of 350 was 'not negotiable'. The Governor would also be invited to produce a regime plan by early November for submission to the Manpower Team so that they could

---

[20] More generally, there had been 82 attempts at self-injury, 1 attempted suicide and 1 suicide between 1 Aug. 1985 and 17 Jan. 1986. Written Answer, House of Commons, 21 Jan. 1986.

[21] Debate on Holloway Prison C1 Unit, House of Lords, 13 Dec. 1985.

[22] Minutes of the meeting of the Board of Visitors, 27 Nov. 1985.

[23] N. Davies, 'Mentally ill "on trial" in Holloway', the *Observer*, 10 Nov. 1985.

start their own review in mid-November for completion in a month.[24] The CNA did begin to rise progressively (and always with the acquiescence of the POA), growing to 415 in March 1987 and to 447 two months later, although fits of locking-out reduced the numbers from time to time.[25]

In the matter of C1, there would be a search for psychiatrically-trained nurses or appropriately trained hospital officers; plans would have to be drafted for a new purpose-built unit; and a search was reported to be under way for a Principal Medical Officer and for a Senior Medical Officer. The Governor said he was reluctant to pursue other recommendations until those appointments had been made: the overseeing of C1 had been entrusted to an Assistant Governor in the interim but precipitous action without clear medical direction would 'only give further leverage to our critics'.

The Manpower Review

By the end of 1985, Holloway had been subject to the Manpower Team appraisal promised by the Project Review Committee, and it was proposed that the prison should be treated as three separate units: a local prison with court commitments, a training prison and 'an area for disturbed women and hospital'.[26] Holloway should be staffed by 264 basic grade officers (the recommended staffing level at the time was 269, and the actual number in post were 249) and the number of senior and principal officers should remain unchanged. No more than 40 officers were to be involved in court or outside hospital commitments each day, and staff would have to be redeployed so that they did not supervise the activities of inmates so intensively. The 'bottom line,' Colin Allen informed the Board of Visitors, 'is that Management want an open regime for Holloway at all times'.

The Reforms

Unlocking

Colin Allen had not entered Holloway with a clearly-conceived strategy. Unaccustomed to the political and social organization of

---

[24] The Manpower Appraisal did indeed arrive by the end of November. Governor's report to the Board of Visitors, 23 Oct. 1985.

[25] In Dec. 1986, for instance, the staff declared that they would lock out numbers above 365 until their car park was made secure (minutes of the meeting of the Board of Visitors, 17 Dec. 1986).

[26] Minutes of the meeting of the Board of Visitors, 25 June 1986.

women's prisons, he had at first found it difficult to decipher the structure of Holloway and propound formulae for change: 'I had never been inside a female prison before . . . [and] all my previous experience was as nothing here because I wasn't getting the kind of feedback . . . . So it took some time for me to get any degree of confidence about what I was doing. . . . [But] I came in on the back of the Holloway Project Committee's recommendations which were to open the establishment out, to make use of the terrific facilities that are there and to make the regime humane.'

The Governor appointed a group of senior staff from across the prison to look into possible ways in which the prison might develop. All staff were asked to put forward their ideas. A preliminary period was spent in drafting plans with senior colleagues away from the prison, in Muswell Hill, north London, in what came inevitably to be known as the 'Muswell Hill Group'. A member of that group, the new Deputy Governor, recalled that 'one very specific question, and in a sense that is the central question, [was] about how you interpret women's behaviour, and given that there were a lot of assaults and the fear of the staff was very high about the level of assaults, the level of self-harm among the women, that issue was really acute'. Particularly important too were early discussions between departments to promote the idea of a 'multi-group working, team working to break down barriers', and the barrier between nursing and disciplinary staff above all.

The new Governor worked on bodies outside and inside the prison, deliberately exposing the inner workings of Holloway to inspection so that its original and continuing problems could not be neglected by those who were pressing for reform. He needed others to create the objective reality that would give urgency to his own efforts to reorganize Holloway. The Chairman of the Board of Visitors remembered that 'there was far more openness and far more public discussion. They let people come in.' In January 1986, for instance, the Governor made an unprecedented public appearance at a meeting organised by the Islington Council Women's Committee.[27] BBC television was invited to make a programme about the prison in 1986. (Harry Wisebloom, the producer, recalled that Colin Allen 'didn't believe what he was seeing as the first male governor to run a prison run by a set-up of women. He believed the public should

[27] See the *Caribbean Times*, 31 Jan. 1986.

know. Ann Hair [the new Deputy Governor] and Colin Allen were appalled at what was happening, appalled at what was going on in their own prison. . . . His ideas was "let's bring things to a head. Let's bring people in"'.) I shall show how, during the great strike or lock-out of 1988, in particular, Colin Allen employed the press to expose conditions in his prison as a means of exerting pressure on himself and on the others who might place pressure on him (Nick Davies, a key journalist, remembered that 'he was intelligent enough to see that I was useful as an ally rather than as an enemy. In a sense, we worked together'). The Governor was, as Weick would say, busily creating the environment to which he would be required to respond.[28]

After security training, members of the Board of Visitors were given their own keys (once a symbolically potent matter) instead of having to be escorted about the prison by officers. Colin Allen, said the Board's Chairman, 'was quite ready for the Board of Visitors to be a partnership'. The Board was freed to inspect the prison and report on life there, and its annual reports were distributed to the press for the first time, acting as yet another exterior stimulus for change. After all, the Board's strength was that it could speak to the press as the Governor could not: 'we deflected media attention . . . whereas the Governor couldn't go on telly or answer frequent questions on the radio, I frequently did. I had a large number of appearances and we published our annual report.'

Little by little, the prison began to change. Unlike some other governors whose 'heads were full of security', said a member of the Prisons Board, Colin Allen was a confident man who recognized that women prisoners were not 'much of a threat'. The Governor had been charged by the Department to 'open up' the prison and the unlocking of Holloway was what he set out to accomplish. In parallel with Fresh Start (which I am about to describe) and the Manpower Appraisal, Allen initiated an 'open door regime', freeing his managers to consult with the POA 'without pressing too hard about staffing levels'.[29] There was an insistence that change would have to be introduced gradually, in consultation with the POA and in step with increases in staffing.[30] Colin Allen said 'I did not set out to do battle with the culture of the POA full frontal. I didn't do that. For 3 years Hollo-

---

[28] See K. Weick, 'Enactment Processes in Organizations', in B. Staw and G. Salancik (eds.), *New Directions in Organizational Behavior*, (Malabar: Robert E. Krieger), 1982.

[29] Governor's Report on the Dispute at HM Prison Holloway.

[30] Governor's Report to the Board of Visitors, 22 Jan. 1986.

way's managers worked very purposefully with Prison Service head-quarters, South East Regional Office and the POA to introduce changes. There was a *quid pro quo* arrangement. It gradually loose-ned, and the effectiveness of it was astonishing. A small number of managers (Chief Officers, Principal Officers and Senior Officers) worked very hard to open up the regime with much success.' The POA did agree to renegotiate the reserve task list and task dropping with the Governor but, they insisted in July 1986, 'there must be two officers on a landing for any women to be unlocked and that if for some reason one member of staff have to leave the unit, women will be locked in'.[31] Later, in February 1987, they revised that figure to a minimum of three officers being present in a unit during full associa-tion,[32] and three officers became the POA's norm thereafter.

Work on the physical fabric of the new building was completed at last in 1985. No longer having to adapt and improvise the uses to which space could be put, Colin Allen (working with Dr Speed, the Principal Medical Officer, when she was finally appointed) was free to redistribute units so that those performing like functions were placed next to one another on the same levels (and those that were unlike were removed elsewhere: the 'hospital' on the fourth floor and the treatment rooms on the second were relocated, for example). So it was that the fifth floor was dedicated to sentenced prisoners; the fourth to convicted remands and those awaiting sentence; and the third to remands; and, performing these functions, they permitted what was, in effect, the lateral integration of space. No longer obstructed, no longer composing such a mass of confused space, units on the same levels could be opened up to one another and a new system was initiated, 'free flow', the lightly escorted mass move-ment, four times daily, of women to their various occupations. The Education Department, swimming pool and the gymnasium began to work properly for the first time.

By 1986, an open regime had indeed been established on most living units during weekdays from 7.30 in the morning until 7.30 in the evening. The Board of Visitors recorded in their annual report for 1986 that their earlier complaints about lack of association 'no longer applied'. An unlocked prison centred on 'free flow' and light super-vision reduced the power of the officers, increased the independence

---

[31] Minutes of the quarterly meeting of the POA, 22 July 1986.
[32] Minutes of the meeting of the POA, 25 Feb. 1987.

of the inmate, and alleviated some of the experience of repressiveness and conflict. Doreen Yardley, then a senior probation officer at Holloway, reflected:

In the beginning security was the biggest word that was around. Things relaxed because the women were allowed an Education Department which functioned fully, people weren't always escorted individually as they used to be, all these things took staff and made it more confrontational really. If you can't go anywhere without a member of staff and they have got what they call the free flow when the doors were open and people took themselves to work or to their education or to probation without . . . there were officers around, the whole prison was flowing about at particular times, but there was a sense of you were taking yourself.

What was to be of special importance was that the apparently incomprehensible building that had posed so many difficulties for the staff and inmates began finally to make sense. Staff had been trying in vain to apply the controlling strategies appropriate to a radial prison, but the unlocking of Holloway transformed it into something resembling the Project Group's original conception of how the prison should have worked. The Deputy Governor said:

We changed the whole way we used the building. Instead of thinking of it vertically, because of course vertical organisation made it difficult to go upstairs and downstairs all day long and have a relationship at that level, . . . in that period we rearranged it so that the functions (when I say the functions I mean the remand women, the convicted women and the categories) we actually deployed them laterally, horizontally through the building, so that you organised the institution according to levels rather than vertical slices because it made people more accessible to each other.

And Colin Allen said:

One of the great things that happened and one of the things that pleased us was that as we began to open out the regime and to unlock the women, encourage them to education, to the gym and workshop, the residential units ceased to be places where they lived all the time and began to be used as intended for sleeping, eating and association. Of course, suddenly the building began to make sense. Up to that point, the prison had been run traditionally with vertical house units. It was a year before I realised that the prison had been designed laterally rather than vertically, and a key to progress was to enable prison officers to get used to the idea. Objectively, staff had a strong point. If you are supervising inmates, it is much safer from a control point of view to have an open area where you can see other staff. It gives a much greater feeling of security and there are much better designs for prisons than Holloway, but not in that small space. There is no reason why the culture of Holloway should not be conditioned in such a way as to make it entirely comfortable to run the prison with that design. However, for that to happen, you had to have capable staff operating professionally, led by capable managers who know what they are doing in giving inmates sufficient space and opportunity to express themselves legitimately. If all these features existed, there would not be the tension that was created in the building.

There was to be a sustained decrease in many of the indices of the older problems of Holloway. In C1 alone, 'non-fatal self-injuries' declined from 55 in 1986–87 to 24 in 1988–89.[33] It was to be Dr Speed's particular pride that there were no deaths by suicide at all at Holloway between 1987 and 1990, the last year for which she had data. By 1992, the Chief Inspector of Prisons could comment that 'it is difficult fully to appreciate the extent of all the changes that have occurred at Holloway in the past five years'.[34] He reported how self-mutilations had declined from some 1,000 a year to 150 in 1990;[35] there were fewer assaults and attempted suicides, and no suicides; and the number of adjudications had dropped so that the level of offending at Holloway had become lower than the average in female prisons.[36]

C1 and the Hospital

C1 assumed an especially emblematic importance in the reorganization of Holloway. It had been identified by the press, Department and Ministers as representative of all that was wrong at the prison. The Project Review Committee had assigned the greatest attention to it. And the reforming administration of Colin Allen and his colleagues took it that C1 had a special didactic significance: if the hard case of C1 could be redeemed, the rest of Holloway should follow. Dr Hindson, the new Senior Medical Officer, said 'we consciously set out to show that if C1, with its population of the most difficult and

[33] 'Holloway Revisited', *British Medical Journal*, 29 July 1989, Vol. 299, No. 6694, 283.
[34] *HM Prison Holloway: Report by HM Chief Inspector of Prisons*, (London: Home Office, 1992), 127. [35] *Ibid.*, 1.
[36] *Ibid.*, 57. The links between association, freedom and low levels of disciplinary offences has also been noted by J. Sparks and A. Bottoms, 'Order and Legitimacy in Prisons', paper presented to the American Society of Criminology meetings, 4–7 November 1992, 18–9.

damaged women on serious charges such as arson and GBH, could be unlocked all day with staff working with them, then that could be the norm for the rest of the establishment. We were intent upon not conceding a different regime for the segregation unit and the medical units, as compared to the rest of the prison. That was what the POA wanted, but we were not going to agree with it.'

The Principal Medical Officer, Dr Speed, was appointed to take overall medical charge of the prison in June 1986, and she and Colin Allen proceeded to re-organize the prison between them: 'it was a marriage of minds because my office, the PMO, was literally opposite the Governor's office and I was in and out of his office'. The regime and structure of C1 and the medical units began to shift under her general management and the local management of the new Senior Medical Officer, Norman Hindson, appointed in April 1986.

The organizational structure of the medical units was reformed. Four permanent appointments replaced a proliferation of fifteen part-time doctors ('doctors were coming in from all over the place, everybody was interested in women, it was bedlam' said Dr Speed) and medical procedures were simplified (there was, she said, too much 'over-doctoring' at Holloway, women were being seen too often and by too many visiting medical staff.[37]) Each of the four doctors was placed on call at night: 'so that there was continuity for the night staff, there was the same doctor, so we did receptions each, we each had the same night, and we each knew who came in'.

The physical structure of the medical units was reformed as part of the wider redistribution of space. It will be recalled that the units had been left somewhat haphazardly about the prison in the aftermath of the many financial cuts of the redevelopment project. When Dorothy Speed arrived at the prison, 'there was no hospital, there was no proper segregation unit and there was no mother and baby unit'. There were scattered units on B2 and D2 ('psychiatric'), B4 ('Hospital: physical'), C4 ('mother and baby unit') and C1. By January 1987, as Figure 10.1 shows in highly schematic form, she had gathered all the medical units together under medical management and set them down in the one continuous place in C1 and D1 with a combined occupancy of ninety beds ('Colin Allen and I decided we couldn't have all this moving up and down. It was absolutely crazy'). Mothers and babies were placed in separate new quarters in D0 under

---

[37] Minutes of the meeting of the Board of Visitors, 27 Aug. 1986.

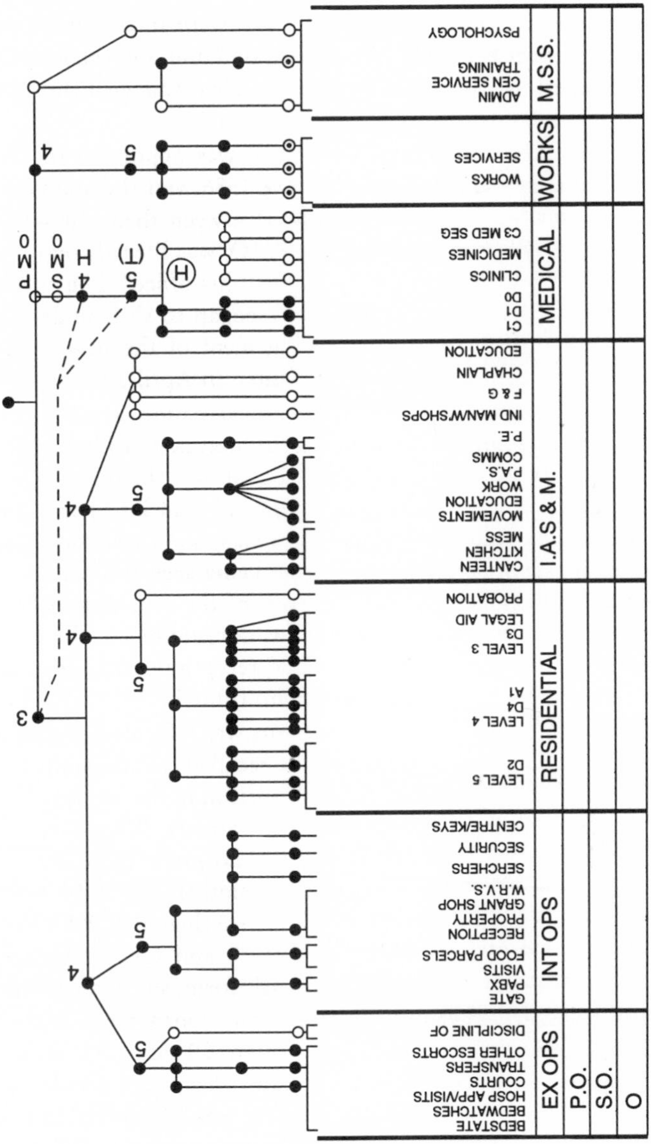

Figure 10.1 HM Prison Holloway Management Structure (based on Governor's Report)

a governor grade ('it wasn't a medical unit. Pregnancy is normal'). In effect, Dorothy Speed applied Galtung's formula by carving an independent hospital area out of the prison and placing it firmly under medical control ('there was a medical officer in charge here, C1, a medical officer here, D1, and an obstetrician in charge on D0.')

Without a hospital we *had* to have a Medical Area, designated and dedicated for medical continuity. . . We had to get the nurses managing the medical areas . . . and this restored a modicum of peace as we allocated directly from Reception following medical assessment which was done in continuity, on a roster, by full-time medical staff. Followed by regular twice weekly case conferences with all 4 MOs, and after the Matron retired in July 1987, with Senior Nurses and myself pending the arrival of the Health Care Manager.[38]

And Colin Allen observed:

The key to managing women prisoners, particularly those in C1, was to achieve a harmony between the doctors and other managers so that there was proper treatment of the needs of the women, whether they be medical or other training, custodial needs. The important thing was to have an agreement that one woman needed to be taken to the hospital because at that time she needed some special nursing care because of her medical state, while another woman did not need that; she could go into normal location and be handled in a different way.

Working as a complement and counterweight to the hospital area, A1, a new segregation unit, a place for punishment, was established 'because the place was being run as a prison with the staff expecting to put people on report and expecting an adjudication, and the Board of Visitors were running it in the same way'. The consequence was a reduction in moral and structural ambiguity and a restoration of orderliness. In place of a prison whose occupants were diffusely and uncertainly treated as 'disturbed', pathological and unpredictable,

---

[38] Letter, 1 Dec. 1993.

there was a return to a neat segregation between the medical and the custodial, the therapeutic and the punitive.[39]

The Senior Medical Officer, Dr Hindson, would examine the profiles of inmates to assess 'whether or not they are patients, and when they go to court, should they be sentenced or should they be going to psychiatric hospital?' Women needing medical care were placed under the doctors;[40] no longer to be run 'by discipline staff with nursing staff pushed aside'. The other women were consigned to the prison proper. 'We made it work by having taken out the canker', said Dorothy Speed, 'the medical canker, which was everywhere. We had localised it.'

The Prison Department acceded to the appointment of ten new nurses in January 1986[41] and work started on the modification of ten cells in C1 a month later.[42] In August 1986 a new association area and dayroom was provided adjacent to the unit. C1 'began to take on major improvements', marked by a 'caring' rather than a punitive atmosphere, with the nurses in the ascendancy. Women were spending an average of 15.6 hours locked in their cells in 1987 on C1, compared with 21 hours in 1986.[43] The Board of Visitors observed that the dayroom had 'considerably increase[d] the time that [women] are out of their cells. This in turn release[d] tension and create[d] a more relaxed atmosphere.'[44] To confront the specific, central problem of self-injury and attempted suicides, probation officers and doctors brought in volunteers, including former prisoners such as Chris

[39] It was a return because that had been the practice in the old prison. A former assistant governor remembered that 'in the old Holloway there was a clear distinction between the medical and non-medical areas . . . Whenever one of the "mad" women on my wing misbehaved, was put on report and was made "unfit" for adjudication, I would negotiate with the hospital for her to be taken in as a patient. Usually the hospital claimed they were full, and would only take the woman in question if I would take another back. . . . There was no treatment for them in the hospital and the officers used to joke about whether or not they had been "cured". They accepted this situation, but it was important to maintain the position that if someone could not be disciplined by being put on report they would become a hospital patient, at least temporarily.'

[40] A nursing sister said 'Colin Allen accepted that the unit was [under medical control] but if C1 was functioning and out of the *Guardian* and the BBC, it was alright'.

[41] Governor's report to the Board of Visitors, 22 Jan. 1986.

[42] The work included replacement of sanitary fittings and plumbing arrangements, the recessing of light fittings and radiators, improvements to observation within the cells, and redecoration in suitable colours. (Oral answer, House of Commons, 20 Feb. 1986).

[43] 'Developments at Holloway', NACRO Briefing, Feb. 1988.

[44] Annual Report of the Board of Visitors, 1986.

Tchaikovsky of Women in Prison, and the Samaritans, to visit inmates, starting in C1 and then branching out elsewhere. Chris Tchaikovsky recorded that 'Colin's open door policy was remarkable. He agreed to the request of a family of a woman who had died on C1 to visit her cell. They said it was important to them to be able to place her somewhere to ease their shock and grief. . . . [This was an] example of Colin's accessibility to the women and their families.' By July 1986, the Governor reported that the medical management of C1 had improved dramatically.

Firm criteria were laid down for judging the fitness of women for adjudication: 'if an inmate has been assessed by the Court as needing medical treatment . . . it follows that they will be unfit for Adjudications'.[45] A nursing sister who had worked on C1 remembered:

Dr Hindson changed the adjudication process—'don't submit for adjudication people who were mentally ill.' Instead, we sat down and talked to them, where we thought they would listen and understand. The practice of calling women prisoners by their first names, a tradition in the female service, had been lost. We reintroduced it.

There was a general attempt to work *with* rather than against the women incarcerated in C1, Dr Hindson persuading inmates to work with the nursing and medical staff:

When we went in the situation in the medical units was so bad that we literally sat down and said to the women 'you've got us beaten. Can you please tell us what we need to be thinking about, what we need to work with you about, so that you no longer need to try to hang yourselves, flood your rooms, set fires, cut yourselves, punch people and carve your wrists open. What together do we need to think and talk about?

And he tried to persuade the nursing and medical staff to enlist the co-operation of the inmates:

[We encouraged] the staff to have some confidence in themselves, getting them to believe that they could come to work and do a job working with the women and not against the women. Achieving relationships on a positive footing so that staff were less likely to be assaulted, the women less likely to self mutilate. Giving the staff the confidence to interact with the women and to identify the boundaries involved. Gradually we won both the staff and the women over.

[45] Senior Medical Officer's report to the Board of Visitors, 23 Ap. 1986.

In effect, Dr Hindson and his staff transformed C1 into a place governed more nearly by the etiquette and manners of civil society: 'there were simple things like when you come to work in the morning, the first thing you will say when you unlock somebody is "hello, good morning, how are you, how were you last night?" And that was a lot for the staff because they were still getting a lot of verbal abuse from the women and there was a lag before the women started to change their behaviour.' Life began to be regulated by little maxims. There were, for example, what Dr Hindson called the 'E' words, 'I enjoy coming to work now, I actually feel empowered by being able to sit down and talk to inmates on a one-to-one basis, rather than feeling threatened by it'.

Images of Women

An important consequence of the transformation of C1 was a companion transformation of structured definitions of disturbed women. It was as if the prison in its different phases and regimes revealed different glimpses of its captives. In the new regime in C1, staff believed that they were beginning to learn more about the women who had been consigned there. Instead of constituting problems of control to be despatched to the solitude of their rooms, or cases to be assessed briefly for forensic purposes, women started to talk to nurses and doctors. They appeared to have talked quite candidly on occasion, and the nurses and doctors listened. Just as, in a very different setting in Bristol in the late 1960s, when penal reformers allowed themselves to hear, perhaps for the very first time, the anguish of victims of crime,[46] so the staff of C1 began to see more clearly the women in their care. They learned about life-histories. They learned about past sexual abuse. It was a revelation. Dr Hindson recalled:

Over a period of time the women actually started talking to us and we got the most enormous amount out of it . . . . All the issues about their early life experiences. There were many accounts of serious sexual abuse, both as children and adults, both in the community and in institutions. We were able to identify that for some inmates opiate misuse in late teenage years was a marker for sexual abuse in early teenage years. Just everything flooded out . . . We eventually realised that many of the inmates were powerless when in the community, they were social class 4 and 5, their families had already

[46] See P. Rock, *Helping Victims of Crime*, (Oxford: Clarendon Press, 1990), ch. 3.

broken up, etc. They had histories or careers of criminal damage, or breach of the peace, drunk and disorderly and being remanded to Holloway. When, however, they came into Holloway and were up against the uniform and authority, many of the personality disordered women were undergoing a catharsis by acting out aggression and violence against others and/or themselves. They had never had the opportunity to resolve all their earlier experiences of loss, physical abuse and sexual abuse. Over a period of time, individual women had the confidence to talk and give their individual stories. Over a 5 year period, we profiled the C1 population on the grounds of virtually everything, serious physical abuse 90%, serious sexual abuse 70%, drugs and alcohol . . . The adage that men externalise violence, women internalise violence, became too simplistic a dichotomy once we had a clearer understanding of the women's feelings, thoughts and actions.

And it began to seem that it was unhelpful diagnostically to think of many of the women in C1 as mentally *ill*. It was evident instead that chaotic lives had produced chaotic people: 'we started to clarify the confusion. The articles published in the press about these women were incorrect. Many did not suffer from any mental illness. If they were suffering from any disorder it was varying degrees of personality damage.' One may presume that Joanna Kelley's and Francis Baden-Powell's plans for the intimate spaces of the units might have begun to work after all, that they did lead to a diminution of social distance.

The Changing Politics of Holloway

Power began to change shape within the prison. Colin Allen had brought in a new team of managers (one of his colleagues remarked 'the building was finished, the new broom was in, and we were going to get on with it'). In December 1985, he appointed a new deputy, Ann Hair, formerly attached to P4 and the erstwhile Secretary of the Project Review Committee. The Board of Visitors were given keys and allowed to inspect the prison virtually at will, no longer subordinate to the discipline officer's power to unlock.[47] The press were allowed a greater freedom. Male senior officers were posted to Holloway for the

---

[47] One member recalled that, before being given a key, she had had 'to plan your visit quite carefully. For instance, if you were visiting 3 people, you had to try and get to the furthest point to start off with, so then you could actually ask an officer to let you through a door, and you could travel that way to the next point of call, and then you could often, and it was quite often, you could get stuck at the bottom by the trolley route waiting for someone to come past to let you out'.

first time in March 1986,[48] joining a male Governor[49] and a male Chairman of the Board of Visitors, and joining them, in part, to break up what was considered to be a solidary and reactionary group of women officers, a mass that contributed to a 'very, very unhealthy structure'. By 1987, staff were moved from block to block every twenty weeks. The Governor began to investigate closely the claims of officers on sick leave in an attempt to curtail absences and, indeed, one officer was dismissed in consequence.[50] Colin Allen, said a colleague, 'by allocating different duties, by promoting and sacking, he managed to dispel that group'. But there were conciliatory gestures as well. A fence was erected around the staff car park, an important act in an insecure world, because prisoners and ex-prisoners had, as Ann Hair put it:

throw[n] things and vandalise[d] the staff cars and they felt that the unsafety of their cars almost symbolised *their* unsafety and by putting this fence with a gate and a combination lock . . . once we gave them the fence, they actually felt cared for and they felt they were getting something for *them*.

The Governor thought that he could detect few signs of transformation at first: 'apart from the replacement of Senior Medical personnel and interim structural alterations on C1, very little happened in the first 12 months after the Report was published to change the main regime of the prison. Fundamentally this was because the POA had achieved a very powerful position and resisted any change which in any way appeared to benefit the women'.[51] But the Board of Visitors reported 'a considerable improvement of the regime'.[52] And the POA themselves sensed that they were no longer the political figures they had been under the governorship of Joy Kinsley.[53] 'The Governor did not go through the [POA] Committee to arrange anything', one

---

[48] It had taken some eighteen months to persuade the Department to allow male officers on to the landings. It had been an 'anathema at first' said a governor.

[49] Colin Allen was widely supposed to be the first male Governor of Holloway but, in fact, he merely resumed a tradition of the place. The first seven Governors between 1852 and 1947 had all been male. The first woman Governor was Lady Taylor between 1947 and 1959.

[50] Minutes of the meeting of the Board of Visitors, 26 Nov. 1986.

[51] Governor's Report on the Dispute at HM Prison Holloway.

[52] Annual Report of the Board of Visitors, 1986.

[53] In the lesser realm of C1, a nursing sister said, 'once Norman [Hindson] established that the medical side was in charge, strong POA people, their noses were put out of joint. They wanted to be in charge. Their authority was undermined.'

member protested at a meeting on 28 October 1985.[54] The POA sensed that 'the inmates are ruling the prison. There is no moral [sic]', and asked 'is it not time we put our cards on the table, and showed who does run the prison?' With no contrary votes and only 2 abstentions, the meeting of 138 passed the motion that 'this branch ballot the membership in accordance with regulations to take a vote of no confidence in the managerial structure and techniques at this prison'. Two weeks later, at another special meeting, the POA declared by a vote of 96 to 13 that it was prepared to take industrial action falling 'short of strike action' to prevent the implementation of 'recommendations contained within the Holloway Project Committees Report without full and proper negotiations with your elected representatives'.[55] The *Guardian* newspaper drew the premature but prescient conclusion that 'relations between prison officers and the governor of Holloway women's prison have broken down'.[56]

Hostilities

The Hostilities of 1986

Episodic locking-out and locking-in at Holloway were part of a much wider pattern of national militancy that came to a head in early 1986 and persisted for years thereafter. It was a time made dramatic by well-publicised threat and counter-threat, hurried meetings peppered with resounding declarations from the Prison Officers Association and Government, an omnipresent (and somewhat concocted) sense of crisis and the enduring prospect of a full-blown strike. The POA were generally on the march in the mid-1980s to protest against financial cuts in the prison service and against reductions in manning levels at a time of unprecedented overcrowding in the prisons (there were nearly 47,000 prisoners in England and Wales in early 1986, the highest the population had ever been, some 3,000 more than in 1984–85 or 1983). *The Times* reported how the prisons were approaching 'a crisis' with the working of extensive overtime, widespread 'banging-up', and much talk of ballots on industrial action,[57] the first time that a full strike had ever been publicly mooted by

---

[54] Minutes of Special Meeting Re: Industrial Action, 28 Oct. 1985.
[55] Minutes of the meeting of the POA, 18 Nov. 1985.
[56] 'Advice on mentally ill in Holloway "ignored"', the *Guardian*, 11 Nov. 1985.
[57] *The Times*, 2 Apr. 1986.

prison officers.[58] The Home Office, in its turn, maintained that it was not for the POA to determine staffing levels:[59] troops would be sent in to run the prisons and camps would be opened if the officers did withdraw their labour.[60] The issue had become charged, openly political, ideological,[61] a trial of strength about what the Prime Minister[62] and the Home Secretary[63] both came to describe, in the new, more general language of industrial relations that was emerging during that period, as 'management's right to manage'.

It was a turbulent time. Inmates rioted when the Governor of Gloucester Prison, attempting to introduce new staffing levels in April 1986, suspended thirteen officers for refusing to undertake court duty.[64] Prisoners erected a barricade on B5 and smashed up two dormitories[65] when staff took industrial action at Holloway itself on 26–27 April 1986. A national ban on overtime instituted by the POA on May 1 led to a wild day and night[66] during which there was a riot that 'wrecked' Horfield Prison in Bristol,[67] a disturbance at Lewes Prison, a fire at, and escapes from, Northeye and a fire at High Point.[68] It all illustrated, said the POA as they announced the cessation of the ban, that 'prisons are extremely dangerous places and our members are deserving of the very highest degree of protection, regardless of the financial implications'.[69]

Fresh Start

'Out of the ashes'[70] of the 1986 dispute, there arose 'Fresh Start', a grand review of the staffing and management of prisons. In what was called the 'most radical change the Service has seen since the Gladstone Report',[71] two task forces were set to study working practices and management structures in the summer of 1986, make recommendations by December 1986, and translate them into instructions by

[58] *The Times*, 28 Apr. 1986.   [59] *The Times*, 12 Apr. 1986.
[60] *The Times*, 8 Apr. 1986.
[61] The Adam Smith Institute mooted the privatization of prisons as a reply to the POA. *The Times*, 16 Apr. 1986.   [62] *The Times*, 16 Apr. 1986.
[63] *The Times*, 28 Apr. 1986.   [64] *The Times*, 30 Apr. 1986.
[65] Minutes of the meeting of the Board of Visitors, 28 May 1986.
[66] See the report of the Chief Inspector of Prisons, *Report of an Inquiry into the Disturbances in Prison Service Establishments in England between 29 April and 2 May 1986*, HC 42, (London: HMSO, 1986).   [67] *The Times*, 1 May 1986.
[68] *The Times*, 1 May 1986.   [69] *The Times*, 2 May 1986.
[70] B. Hughes, 'View from the Chairman of the Prison Officers Association at Gloucester', *Prison Service Journal*, July 1988, No. 71, 34.
[71] 'Comment', *Prison Service Journal*, July 1988, No. 71, 1.

early 1987.[72] New staff contracts based on a unified grading system were to be issued in September, and Fresh Start itself was planned to come into force in October 1987. Members of the Prison Department called it an attempt to purge the prisons of 'Spanish customs'. The central principles of Fresh Start were to limit the number of hours worked weekly by discipline officers to thirty-nine, substantially reducing the amount of overtime that they worked; and to transform governors into 'managers', affording them much greater freedom in the flexible redeployment of officers. Staff were to be paid a basic salary, freeing them from what management regarded as their excessive dependency on overtime pay.

Fresh Start was debated, contested and fought locally and nationally by the POA, the Association coming eventually to the opinion that the Home Office had failed to provide adequate numbers of staff to enable the new working arrangements to succeed.[73] The prisons were again beset by overtime bans, lockings-out (1,300 prisoners were locked out and in police cells in early October 1987)[74] and new threats of strikes.[75] A special POA delegate conference meeting in London on 30 October 1987 proposed a ballot 'for action over new working systems'.[76] There was renewed talk about the army being drafted in to staff the prisons should officers strike.[77]

At Holloway itself, the local POA at first declared its willingness to accept Fresh Start in May 1987 (insisting however on the assignment of three officers to a landing during 'full association'[78]) but then it wavered, rejecting the new system in September,[79] just before its implementation,[80] and finally, after 'months of discussion within departments and between management and the POA in order that the new staff and work structures would be understood and appreciated',[81] it went uneasily over to the new system on 1 November 1987.

---

[72] See R. Evans and P. Shapland, 'Lessons from the Literature', *Prison Service Journal*, July 1988, No. 71, 23. Documents linked to Fresh Start actually started to appear towards the end of 1986.

[73] The POA declared that 950 extra staff were needed nationally to implement Fresh Start. *The Times*, 30 Oct. 1987. [74] *The Times*, 20 Oct. 1987.

[75] *The Times*, 27 Oct. 1987. [76] *The Times*, 31 Oct. 1987.

[77] *The Times*, 24 Oct. 1987.

[78] Minutes of special meetings held concerning task lines, 9 Feb. and 25 Feb. 1987.

[79] At almost the very last moment, at their meeting of 14 Sept. 1987, for instance, the local POA had voted by 128 to 1 that the Fresh Start proposals were unacceptable.

[80] Minutes of special meeting of the POA, 14 Sept. 1987.

[81] Report of the Board of Visitors, 1987.

The Hostilities of 1988

The pattern of industrial relations I have described persisted almost to the end of the decade. An alternating pulse of threat, counter-threat and hurried meetings continued until matters intensified climactically in 1988. In January of that year, prison officers across the country were balloted and voted 'overwhelmingly' (by 9,385 to 3,700) for a bundle of loosely-specified forms of industrial action over the proposed new manning levels.[82] Only 2 out of 135 local branches were reported not to have supported sanctions. Officers, the Prison Department was warned, might 'work to rule', 'walk out', ban overtime or engage in 'all out' strikes, and there were renewed emergency talks between the Association and Department to prevent action being taken.

At Holloway, the conflict was mediated by the focal issue of unlocking. Locking-in had come to condense and symbolize all the wider discontents about power and authority, territoriality and insecurity, freedom and control, that had accumulated in the prison since the redevelopment project had first been mooted. It 'has all the ingredients of Holloway's difficulties over the years'.[83] An officer said 'you need to have some back-up. It's a difficult job. You need to feel that you've got somebody around sometimes . . . it was totally unacceptable to us to unlock while you were on your own.' Control over space had come to represent authority and security, and it was contested on two fronts, one between inmates and officers and the other between officers and management. Colin Allen summarized the management view on one of those fronts: 'the question to be resolved is does the Governor have the authority to say two staff should unlock up to 32 women or should it left to the whims of the staff. . . . it was imperative that this was established, or there is a chance in the future of Holloway reverting to where it was some time ago'.[84]

The growth in CNA faltered: a proposal by the Deputy Governor to increase the CNA by 8 to 487 was rejected in February 1988[85] and it was decided not to open new units until more staff were appointed.[86] Little skirmishes were fought between management

---

[82] *The Times*, 2 Jan. 1988.
[83] Governor's Report: Board of Visitors Meeting, 8 June 1988.
[84] Minutes of the meeting of the Board of Visitors, 8 June 1988.
[85] Minutes of the meeting of the POA, 24 Feb. 1988.
[86] Minutes of the meeting of the Board of Visitors, 24 Feb. 1988.

and officers about the POA norm of three officers unlocking a unit. On 3 March, for instance, two officers refused to unlock their units until three officers were present. Their action was repeated four days later, and the two officers were charged formally under the Code of Discipline, being admonished when they appeared before the Governor at the end of the month. The local branch of the POA, meeting without its chairman on 14 March, re-affirmed their support for what its members had done, voting again not to unlock inmates for evening association with fewer than three officers. On 26 March, another officer refused to unlock unless three officers were present and a formal charge was again brought.

A crisis threatened, the local branch invited the Chairman of the National Executive Committee of the POA to address them in April, and the complaint was made that since the inception of Fresh Start, there had been no agreed manning levels and that the Governor was 'refusing to talk or listen to local POA'. Officers voted once more to adhere to their mandate of 14 March.[87]

The Governor took it that the Chairman's speech 'was very much "A Call to Arms" where those attending the meeting were told that their safety and indeed their lives were threatened by Management's policy on unlocking',[88] and his reply was a memorandum to Heads of Department re-emphasizing his policy that under normal circumstances only two officers should normally unlock:

The subject of most interest . . . has been the staff required to unlock the living units. . . . since Fresh Start in November 1987, there has been an open regime in the Residential and Hospital areas. This has been achieved by adopting the practice of two staff normally being required to unlock each of the small units. It has worked perfectly satisfactorily and the open regime has contributed enormously to the improved atmosphere both for prisoners and for staff. In the past month there have been four incidents where members of staff . . . who do not normally work on a residential area refused to unlock without three staff being present. The Managers in the Residential areas have tried to persuade the staff concerned but without success and as a result, formal disciplinary proceedings have been taken on four occasions. The local branch of the POA put a proposal to me that a minimum of three basic grade Officers should unlock for evening association per unit, except the Medical Wings and D Zero which would need additional staffing. I have not accepted that this is necessary and have reinforced through Line Management that the

---

[87] Minutes of the meeting of the local POA, 14 Apr. 1988.
[88] Governor's Report on the Dispute at HM Prison Holloway.

normal requirement is for two Officers to be present when a Unit is unlocked except in exceptional circumstances where the staffing requirements will be judged and decided upon by the Grade VI or Grade VII. *It is a Manager's decision and not one in which all staff should be able to use their own discretion.*[89]

The reverses at Holloway were both unanticipated and somewhat inexplicable to management. All the previous reforms, the growing liberalisation of the prison, the opening-up of the regime, were at risk of collapse in the face of what appeared to be a root anxiety about accelerating change, imminent losses of power and the rejection of assumptions on which many prison officers had worked for decades. It seemed to management as if officers might actually have a secret hankering after the adversarial, the crisis-laden and the repressive:[90]

I had underestimated the degree of disturbance, as it were, within the subculture of staff. What happened was there was a tremendous and quite unexpected, as far as I was concerned, reaction to the improvements that had taken place. Quite suddenly, it became a national POA issue with male POA officials from outside Holloway being involved. The whole thing became a national issue over the very small and reasonable instruction that 2 staff under normal circumstances were sufficient to enable groups of 32 prisoners to be unlocked in the evening. That's how it became sort of world war time. . . . There was a substantial group of staff, who appeared to be only comfortable at an unconscious level when there was trouble in the prison.

The local branch of the POA informed the Governor that if he did not meet them, there would be an escalation of action, and a meeting was indeed arranged for 25 April. But, at the very outset, the branch insisted that there could be no further discussion unless it was agreed that three officers should unlock units. That, said the Governor, was unacceptable.

There was an *impasse,* Colin Allen wrote to the Regional Director to report on the position,[91] and another meeting, a 'Cubbon meeting',[92] attended by powerful outsiders, the Chairman of the POA

---

[89] Governor's Report to the Board of Visitors for Apr. 1988, emphasis added.

[90] A psychiatrist working in Holloway at the time reflected that there was a 'fear of how the regime is going to be, the staff are intending to implement a regime that is far too liberal and will put us at risk'. The following quotation is from 'Governor's Report on the Dispute at HM Prison Holloway'.

[91] His letter was subsequently to be copied and read by the POA, creating a rift between the management of the prison and the region.

[92] Named after Sir Brian Cubbon, the Permanent Secretary at the Home Office at the time.

National Executive Committee and the Deputy Regional Director, resolved that there should be a three days 'stand-off' in which the local branch would call their own meeting to 'review' their mandate and management would agree for a while to suspend their insistence on two officers unlocking.

When it did meet, the local branch remained adamant. It would hold to the norm previously agreed and proposed only that it would discuss safe manning levels with the Governor.[93] The Governor, for his part, was determined not to negotiate about the levels: 'I am absolutely convinced that this is a vital issue for the long-term well-being of this prison'.[94] The Regional Director told Colin Allen that officers who were redeployed after refusing to unlock with two staff should not be paid during their redeployment and, emboldened, the Governor informed the staff that the 'present situation where staff were refusing to abide by his reasonable policy could not continue'. Lines of battle were drawn.

Quite consonant with the wider pattern of threat, counter-threat and negotiation, a meeting at Prison Department Headquarters on 17 May then ceded ground once more and gave the POA until 24 June to 'review their Mandate' on unlocking. The stopping of pay and disciplinary action against nine officers were temporarily suspended. Colin Allen reported that 'up until that point I had naively thought that the Prison Service was serious about introducing the changes at Holloway, and it was only when it came to the fore at [that meeting] where I realised they were actually bringing pressure on me to withdraw'.

The Governor and his staff took it that the Department was nervous in the face of an impending POA national conference: 'the current position reflects the Department's ambivalence about how management and the POA are expected and allowed to function'.[95] Managers at Holloway were said to be demoralized: 'Senior Officers and Principal Officers on the Residential Units felt even more undermined and their authority was being mocked by some staff on the units'.[96] The POA were acting as if they were 'victorious', Colin Allen told the Board of Visitors, who placed themselves behind him to

---

[93] Minutes of the meeting of the POA, 3 May 1988.
[94] Governor's report to the Board of Visitors for the month of May 1988, 11 May 1988.   [95] Governor's Report: Board of Visitors Meeting, 8 June 1988.
[96] Governor's Report on the Dispute at HM Prison Holloway.

remonstrate to the Parliamentary Under-Secretary of State, Douglas Hogg:

A new regime and a new attitude has developed. By the time Fresh Start began, inmates were having a more constructive life and being given a considerable amount of association. The Board was delighted to observe a more relaxed and cheerful atmosphere. . . . [However] The Board are alarmed and concerned that . . . they heard that the Department had reversed the policy they originally supported and rescinded the charges laid under the Code of Discipline and withdrew the letters about reduction of pay. This undermined the authority of the Governor and his Managers in a crucial way. To be seen to hand back power to the POA can only jeopardise the proper running of the prison.[97]

By 24 June, the arrangement agreed in May had lapsed and the POA undertook tentatively ('as an interim measure and without prejudice to the outcome of further discussions'[98]) to allow two officers to unlock but only 'according to the circumstances'. But their tentativeness evaporated within days and the POA determined once more that it would 'take what steps were necessary to ensure . . . safe staff manning levels'. It threatened members with action if they did not conform to Association policy. Subsequent adherence to the conflicting norms was uneven, some units being unlocked by two, some by three officers. A newly-formed sub-committee of the Board of Visitors, established expressly to liaise with the warring groups in the prison,[99] reported on 13 July 1988 that it had conducted two tours of the prison and found that most units were being unlocked with two officers 'but that the officers regard this action as going against POA advice, but they are doing it for the inmates'.[100]

On 29 July, the Governor was told formally by the local branch secretary: 'anyone under the guise of Management attempting to unlock any units with less than 3 staff, the whole prison will be secured'. An urgent meeting was held with Regional officials, P8

---

[97] Letter from the Chairman to Douglas Hogg, Parliamentary Under-Secretary of State, 10 June 1988. The Chairman was informed that 'the outcome . . . was a formula designed to preserve the Governor's position and at the same time offer an acceptable way for the local POA Branch to adjust its apparently intransigent stance' (letter of 12 July 1988). However, mistrust was again incited because the Board of Visitors was subsequently informed that a copy of her letter had been passed to the POA.

[98] Minutes of the meeting of the POA, 13 July 1988.

[99] The sub-committee was formed on 8 June 1988 to talk to staff, the POA and middle management.

[100] Minutes of the meeting of the Board of Visitors, 13 July 1988.

representatives and local and national POA officials, and, to the Governor, it seemed that Department wished again to avoid confrontation and that the POA were treating Holloway from a 'national issues stand-point'. Negotiations 'broke down'.[101]

The Great Strike (or Lock-out) of 1988

Industrial action began on the evening of 29 July: four staff were withdrawn from their post, the officers began locking-out, and three women delivered in police vans were refused admission at reception. Senior staff and the Governor (who was then on leave) returned to Holloway. The next day, 235 discipline officers walked out, having been instructed to withdraw to what the POA called a 'safe area' in the D2 spur,[102] thirty officers remained, and the prison faced what management called a strike and the POA a 'lock-out' (a member of the POA branch committee said 'for me it wasn't a strike. We were locked out. They refused to give us keys and you can't go into prison without keys'). The nurses had not been called out, but elected as a group to work normally, and they, the governors and the non-striking officers, stayed in post to staff the prison whilst the strike lasted. A working officer said 'that was a sad day. I never thought I'd see the see the day when prison staff would just walk out.'

From the first, the strike was somewhat confused and confusing. Ostensibly, it centred on unlocking and control over the landings and inmates, but it seems to have condensed so many of the diffuse and sometimes inarticulate discontents that had gathered in Holloway that the unlocking issue was more than a little expressive. It embodied a status politics that enveloped groups in competition over tokens of symbolic supremacy in a small, confrontational institution. Participants and observers now[103] find it difficult to describe what the precise *casus belli* could have been at the time. Not untypical was a nurse who said 'I had no idea what the strike was about. . . . I still don't know what it was about. Colleagues tell me now that they don't know.' Not untypical too was a governor who

---

[101]   Board of Visitors Chairman's Report, undated.

[102]   The local branch POA maintained that they were in the safe area in a state of readiness should disorder break out in the prison. A member of its committee said 'we never left the premises. We always staffed the premises in case of difficulties. We made that absolutely clear but they brought in people from outside.'

[103]   That is, in 1992–4, the period when I conducted my fieldwork.

said 'I think that underlying it was that there was nothing to have a power battle about, the thing had been put back on to what might have been a more acceptable balance of where each group should have been at, and perhaps there was a feeling that that couldn't actually be tolerated'.

In the very first few days, it was inevitable that there should have been some uncertainty about how long the strike or lock-out might last[104] and how behaviour and patterns of allegiance would unfold within the prison itself. A member of the Board of Visitors said: 'I think that from the point of view of the governor and those who were in the prison it was tense because we didn't know what was going to happen next and we didn't know to what extent there might be trouble and again, we didn't know how things were going to pan out'. Skeleton staff on Level 4 and other parts of the prison maintained what Colin Allen called a 'normal as possible a regime' but gate and reception officers tried to turn eight receptions away and they were relieved by senior Holloway staff. The hospital had been covered by deployed discipline officers during the day but they were withdrawn by the POA in the early evening, leaving C1 and D1 to be managed solely by the nurses and doctors. It seemed to the Governor as if the POA were toying with the management by 'gradually peeling off their members from various parts of the prison'. Only three night discipline staff appeared initially for duty that first night. The Governor had an agreement with the local police authority that women police officers could be drafted in at short notice to patrol the landings if he felt it was necessary. In the event, he judged that the mood of the prison was so calm that the night staff were confident that they could handle matters. Colin Allen and his Deputy toured the prison at 11 oclock and pronounced that the 'atmosphere among the women . . . was excellent'.[105]

Despite some intimidation of working staff on the second day, the Governor reported, 'the routine settled down today': 'it was amazing what a small group of capable staff could do. There was almost a euphoric atmosphere.' An abortive attempt was made to persuade the catering staff (who were not POA members) to join the strike, but they continued to work, and the inmates were described by the

---

[104] A member of the Board of Visitors said, 'No one never knew how long these things were going to last for. We thought it's just a flash in the pan, it's only going to last for a short time and of course it did go on for weeks.'

[105] Governor's Report on the Dispute at HM Prison Holloway.

Governor as unusually 'expansive in their compliments' about the food. Staff were supplemented by volunteers composed largely of 'Governor grade detached duty staff' who were personal friends of the senior management. At the Governor's request, too, the Board of Visitors maintained a watchful presence throughout the strike, their members keeping a detailed log of incidents.[106]

Managers then attempted to plan a new regime that could be sustained with the merest of skeleton staffs. Colin Allen said:

We just worked from hand to mouth [in the first few hours]. How are we going to get through the night? And then it was the next day. . . and we realised that we didn't want to run it in the way that it had been run before anyway because there had been far too much unnecessary supervision given to women. So we evolved a . . . sensible way of operating with the staff that we had got. We used visitors and helpers and anybody that we felt could assist us.

In retrospect, thought Colin Allen, the second day was the crucial day of the whole conflict. It showed that the prison could continue to operate. The only activity that the group running the prison could not perform unaided was the escorting of prisoners to the courts. Indeed, the Governor was summoned before two courts to explain why he could not produce prisoners. The best that he could accomplish eventually was half the normal number of escorts.

Of course, management was obliged to manage in a time of strike, to keep the prison running, to admit receptions, and feed and care for the inmates. But its fulfilment of that obligation was commonly interpreted as more than instrumental. It became a highly charged, symbolic matter of demonstrating publicly that the managers could succeed in 'facing down' the striking officers. The strike was quite transparently a theatrical culmination of all the lesser opening skirmishes about authority, the control of space and the dangerousness of inmates. It could lead to victory or defeat, to a vindication of one side or the other. The competing rhetorics of management and union were being put to the test. Colin Allen said 'it wasn't that we were trying to make out for ourselves. We were simply interested in retaining the improvements in the place for the good of the women and the staff.' Pitted against one another were the rival discourses traced by Adler and Longhurst in their study of the Scottish penal system. One discourse, centred on 'normalization', emphasized the

---

[106] They were supposed to do so anyway under procedures nationally agreed under Circular 38/1981 of Aug. 1981, well before the Holloway strike.

'prevention of negative effects of prison' and the treatment of inmates as if they were 'normal' individuals who should be confined with minimum security. The other, the discourse of control, stressed the importance of regulating disruptive individuals, good order, discipline and the protection of prison staff.[107]

For Colin Allen and his colleagues, it was imperative to show that it was possible to preserve an open regime that was intact, peaceable and workable. For the POA, it was vital to demonstrate that the prison was a dangerous place that could not survive without ubiquitous restraint and tight surveillance ('the union says staffing has been cut to the extent that it is no longer safe to unlock cells'[108] said a Times report on the dispute). One woman officer from Askham Grange who travelled to London to support the Holloway strike was reported to have stated that 'there is no such thing as a "safe" job for a prison officer'.[109] And that competition between penal realities was how the conflict was read by many insiders at the period. One who worked in prison at the time observed, for instance:

Colin was very unlucky in that the strike had to happen. I think the power of the POA had to be broken, and he did that. He didn't want to, and he resisted it for ages, but when it came he stood firm. . . . Somebody had to take them on because they were just unbearable. Officers in there were just disgusting in the way they behaved.

What was remarkable was that management, non-striking officers, nurses, members of the Board of Visitors,[110] volunteers[111] and

---

[107] M. Adler and B. Longhurst, *Discourse, Power and Justice: Towards a New Sociology of Imprisonment* (London: Routledge, 1994), 41. It is interesting that Adler and Longhurst's third style of discourse, the rehabilitative, the discourse of Joanna Kelley and the Project Group, was held to focus on improving the deviant individual by socializing her back into society through the provision of training and treatment.

[108] *The Times*, 3 Aug. 1988.   [109] *The Times*, 9 Aug. 1988.

[110] A member recalled that 'it was very unusual—the Board of Visitors were serving meals and doing all sorts of things—virtually unheard of in those days for a Board of Visitors to be so active'.

[111] One prison visitor recalled 'I came back very late at night and found this message on the answer machine from the RC sister here saying could I please ring her, it didn't matter how late, and I thought there has to be something up. Basically what she wanted was as many prison visitors as possible who would be able to help her run the visits because the governor, Colin Allen, wanted to make sure that the visits continued and that the women weren't going to suffer in any way. He wanted to make sure that they got to education, that they had social visits, legal, everything. Clearly, it meant that the volunteer force, if you like, were going to have to run the visit side, and that included the police and customs.'

inmates, supplemented later by groups of governor grades from other establishments, did more than cope against adversity. A prison shorn of most of its discipline officers, lacking the threat of force that officers can bring to bear, is a most vulnerable and precarious place. Jeffrey Bayes, a member of the Board of Visitors, observed that 'it was the first example to my knowledge of a prison being run without prison officers (and run well, and without any disasters)'. Yet all reports suggest firmly that, in the absence of most discipline officers, the prison was in many ways an easier, happier, more relaxed and less repressive institution.[112] Holloway during the strike became, in effect, a self-conscious, co-operative and positive experiment in how to administer a prison regime with only the slightest of supervision. The education officer even called it 'a golden age. We had no officers there but the women themselves did the check in and the check out and there were none of the hostile officers around.' To be sure, it is not easy to attach proper weight to what happened in the six weeks of the strike. In the melodramatic conditions of the time, the strike was very much like a carnival, a brief, exciting, extraordinary respite from the normal *longueurs* and rigours of prison life (a member of the Board of Visitors said 'they thought it was quite fun really—here they were, they had a bit more freedom, they were unlocked all day but they didn't on the whole, I can't remember them abusing those privileges'). And the response by inmates and working staff could not but represent something of an act of defiance against a visible opponent, a tangible gaining of ground in the territorial wars of the landings and units. The education officer was himself uncertain about how permanent the golden age might have been: '*I* think there was a change of behaviour. The only significant question is how long it would have lasted and some people allege that things were already beginning to get worrisome and dangerous. I don't know what evidence there is for that. It seemed to me to work very well.'

But, for all that, the mood of the prison was quite clearly exceptional. Consider the very first entry in the Board of Visitors' log. It is

---

[112] It is interesting to note similar reactions on the previous occasions when the officers of Holloway took unofficial action. In April 1975, the first time such action was taken, the Governor reported that the effects were 'rather enjoyed by the inmates as a change in routine'. Governor's report to the meeting of the Board of Visitors, 23 Apr. 1975. A similar report was made to the meeting of the Board of Visitors on 22 Oct. 1980.

worth reproducing literally and virtually in full because it succeeds so admirably in capturing the character of the prison under siege:

31 July 1988
I visited the prison today at the request of the Chairman in view of the industrial action. On arrival at 10.50 am I met Miss Hair who told me that chapel had taken place as usual and that normal visiting is expected this p.m. Mrs————reported no problems in the kitchen and I later saw an excellent lunch served on the wings.
A & B & Cs 3s, 4s, 5 + D3. All the women were out of their rooms and I was told by officers & inmates that they had been most of the morning. All connecting doors were open. Officer presence was minimal. The atmosphere was excellent and there was no trouble whatsoever. Many inmates commented on the following lines:
    'The prison is much more relaxed with so few officers—but then we have excellent officers on B4 anyway'.
The officers present were a group self-selected for good motivation. One said:
    'Of course things are going well. The only officers in the prison are those who want to do the job—though I fear that any trouble will catch us short-handed.'
Another:
    'I'm the SO here and I know when it's OK to unlock. I object to a basic grade coming onto the unit and telling me we can't.'
Another:
    'I'm a POA member but probably not for much longer. I get bloody well paid to do a job and I'm going to do it. My conscience would not let me walk out on the inmates.'
Another:
    'I'm not a POA member—that's why I'm here—but I sympathise with them. We feel we're being trampled on by management. But I don't think I'd leave the inmates to stew.'
In the afternoon I visited D1 & C1. Patients were in their rooms (1.30 pm). No discipline staff present. Nurses reported no problems.
I went to the visits area at 2.10 pm. Visits were in full swing. Miss ____ told me there had been no difficulties or delays.
I have been thoroughly impressed by all the officers in prison at their duties today. The governor was determined to outface the POA on this occasion and only hope that the politicians have the backbone for it. From today's example of a prison being run with minimal discipline staffing the POA have disproved their own case. But today is today, and at present the situation is a novelty to the inmates, who appear to be co-operating. Indeed, several officers praised the helpfulness of their wings. We shall have to wait and see what . . . tiredness and the weekdays bring.

Despite the caveats and uncertainties, the pattern of that first day held. Day after day, members of the Board of Visitors and others described a pacific prison whose inmates were on full association, who were being educated, fed, exercised and visited. The Board Chairman's own personal report on 1 August, for example, recorded that 'everyone was coping magnificently'. Three days later, the Board of Visitors' log recited:

Atmosphere remarkable. Prison life seems remarkably peaceful. Obviously staff are working very long hours, & fatigue has become an increasing problem. The inmates are extremely cheerful—& many have said that the atmosphere is much better than usual. They are very relaxed—so relaxed in fact that the food tastes better & there have been as many compliments to the kitchen as complaints!

Formal social control had ceased to be problematic. Inmates worked *with* the governors and with those officers who had remained. Colin Allen remarked that 'during the dispute, and the dispute went on for 6 weeks so it wasn't a 2 hour wonder, there were times when there was just 1 member of staff supervising 120 women on level 5 and he had no difficulties. He could have been left there permanently and would not have had a single bit of trouble on that unit because he had the respect of the women. He knew what was happening.'

And, during that brief equipoise, during the amity of the strike, images of women changed again. The viability of the emergency regime hinged crucially on the co-operation of the women, and the women co-operated indeed. Colin Allen said:

we thought . . . unless they actually force us . . . and the only thing that could have forced us was the behaviour of the women, if the women got out of control, then we were obviously going to be in problems. . . . The first week was very anxious because we didn't know what [would happen]. Then, gradually, we realised after the first week [that] what we *hadn't* reckoned on was the effects of the difference that treating the women would have on the way they behaved inside, and it was clear to us that we could survive.

It was as if there was a new social contract in the prison. Women were, as a member of the volunteer visitors reported, treated as collaborators in a common enterprise: we wanted to 'treat people with respect, to treat people as equals, as being capable of doing things and they responded positively'. The women now began to appear rational, reasonable and responsible. The senior probation officer working in the prison during the strike or lock-out recalled:

The strike showed a great deal of what could be done and that you didn't have to be terrified of women who are all going mad . . . because women who are given responsibilities for themselves, for doing things that had all been regarded as sacrosanct, the women were expected to help, and help each other and help run the place.

And Dorothy Speed, the Principal Medical Officer, concurred:

When the staff walked out . . . we secured the gate and [Colin Allen] brought in 15 governor grades to assist, male mostly, and of course, for the women, this was absolute bliss because it was so normal. We had practically no adjudications at all. In fact, I don't think there were any.[113]

In even the most problematic units, C1 and D1, supervised during the strike wholly by nurses,[114] it was reported that there was 'particularly good morale . . . there was a great feeling of confidence in both inmates and staff'. The units were opened up and managed as if they were any other secure unit. Dorothy Speed remembered that 'the medical bit couldn't have been better . . . we established a proper regime. They were unlocked. They went out on exercise. They had their meals out. They had a secure period locked in. We ran it like a secure unit so that, because they weren't being pushed back and locked in, they weren't banging, howling, scratching, setting fire, and these were the most difficult people, these 90.' Colin Allen observed that 'the Nurses in C1 and D1 particularly were able for the first time for many years to see themselves and be seen as Officers of the prison with all the responsibilities and esteem flowing from that position'. And one of those nurses herself recalled:

The inmates got more responsibility during the strike and they responded well to it. I said to a group in C1, 'we know what to do to live'. I never saw a group who at the time was thought to be inactive behaving so well. I never saw so much peer pressure.

The POA may frequently have warned that social order was in danger of imminent collapse, but order did *not* collapse. Instead, as the Board of Visitor's log recorded mechanically every day, it was 'all

---

[113] Of course, as Jeffrey Bayes, a member of the Board of Visitors, sapiently observed of reports, 'the reason they went down was because there were no prison officers to report them and members of the Board of Visitors weren't going to—weren't able really to make reports about prisoners when they were going to have to hear the cases'.

[114] Dr Hindson, the Senior Medical Officer in charge of C1, recollected that 'we didn't have a single report. They were quite remarkable and they didn't do it by toadying up to us. They just kept their distance.'

peaceful'. The adjectives most routinely applied by visitors to the prison were 'relaxed', 'peaceful' and 'cheerful'. Indeed, and perhaps not so remarkably, the Board of Visitors' entry for the 6 August concluded 'I have never seen so many smiles on inmates' faces'.

Former inmates from WIP visited the prison throughout the strike, and, reflected Chris Tchaikovsky, 'the change was really amazing. Striking officers tried to imply that there were more drugs in the prison but WIP workers reported that the women were less drugged than usual (and they can tell). I visited many times and the atmosphere was entirely different. Visits went on for as long as the visitors wanted to stay.'

For management, the chief practical problem, reported again and again, was the sheer physical strain of keeping a prison in operation with reduced staff and in straitened circumstances. There could be no effective system of shifts and reliefs when 90% of the discipline officers were absent. On the 3 August, for instance, the Chairman of the Board of Visitors noted that 'I was still concerned . . . about the level of fatigue of everyone, especially the officers on D3'. A colleague, visiting C1 on the same day, recorded in her log 'the nurses particularly tired'.

The Holloway strike was fought simultaneously on different levels. It was, of course, as a member of the Board of Visitors put it, 'basically, as always . . . the POA versus the governor'. There were sporadic attempts between the two to resolve the dispute, but they were alleged to founder on POA objections to the presence of striking officers at meetings and the demand that the POA norm of three officers to unlock a unit should remain in force. There was an uneasy relation between prison and Prison Department. Management's continuing complaint was that the Governor received little support and understanding. It was as if they were obliged to fight alone. A governor remarked that 'the difficulty was actually for headquarters to understand what to do about a women's prison that was striking about issues to do with the treatment of women. That was so beyond their comprehension.' Governors described themselves as 'extremely paranoid' about their apparent isolation and desertion: 'the Governor was left feeling very much that the actions of Headquarters were demonstrating that the Holloway strike belonged to the Governor and Senior Staff of Holloway and not the Prison Department'. The Chairman of the Board of Visitors remonstrated to the Regional Director and, on 5 August, directly to the Minister, Douglas Hogg:

'I said we were very concerned about the lack of support given to the prison and that, apart from the visit of the regional Director no-one from the prison department [had come] and that the Director of Prisons or his Deputy should visit'.[115] Senior officials did manifest themselves publicly at the prison thereafter. On 16 August, the Director General himself visited Holloway.

The politics of those relations were sometimes transacted quite noisily. The Holloway strike was followed avidly by journalists who had been made ready by their prolonged coverage of the general conflict between the prison officers and the Home Office and of the specific problems of Holloway itself. It was followed by journalists, moreover, who had been assiduously primed by insiders. The management of news had become a strategic objective for strikers and management. The Governor commented that:

It was clear from the moment the strike began that the way in which the media reported what was going on at Holloway was going to be very important. . . . We offered open-house to the press early on in the dispute and this was without doubt an unqualified success. We remained open to the media and gave numerous television and radio interviews.

The strike was quite critically mediated and constructed by its public reporting. On 3 August, Colin Allen wrote that 'press interest continued and the main news again gave coverage to the matter'. If Colin Allen himself was unable to deal directly with the media, the Board of Visitors were able to do so, and they did so repeatedly. On 2 August, for example, the Chairman of the Board was interviewed on Capital Radio, on 3 August on BBC radio, and on the following day, by the Press Association, the *Guardian*, *The Times*, and *Independent* newspapers. On 8 August, members of the Board were interviewed on Woman's Hour, ITN, BBC News and Thames Television.

From the start, the strike was the subject of propaganda and counter-propaganda disseminated to the press, it was interpreted through the lenses that commentators brought to bear, and it took on multiple, pointed political meanings. Thus, a number of Conservative politicians understood the strike to be focussed on a contest between union and management power. Michael Mates, the Chairman of the Conservative Members of Parliament Home Affairs Committee, was reported to have said that 'prison officers are the

[115] Board of Visitors' Chairman's Report.

last of the old union diehards. I hope the Home Secretary will take a robust line with them. It is for management to manage the prisons.'[116] The striking officers portrayed Holloway as a dangerous place plummeting out of control, rife with weapons and drugs, requiring firm discipline:[117] 'From our window we see them passing syringes. The management must be finding it very difficult .'[118] An officer was reported to have said 'we can't guarantee enough safety for inmates if the prison is unlocked. If a major incident occurred, we might not be able to handle it . . . How can a prison be expected to run smoothly with inadequate staff searches? It is leaving the prison wide open for our safety and the safety of the prisoners.'[119] The chairman of the Prison Governors' Association was reported to have called for firm control to be restored, for troops and the police to be sent in to relieve Holloway.[120] Colin Allen himself took it that the strike was exposing 'the myth that Holloway needs vast numbers of staff for it to run effectively'.

Those warring, highly motivated accounts were accompanied by sets of quite contradictory images of what might actually be happening behind the walls. Striking prison officers were reported to have 'mocked claims by Mr Colin Allen . . . that Holloway was running smoothly with the help of deputy governors from other prisons and non-striking officers'.[121] Those who talked in the discourse of normalization depicted a smoothly-functioning institution, those who talked of control, a prison in disarray, a place that was 'no longer safe'.[122] It was a pivotal matter, a test to determine what might happen to a prison when the bulk of those responsible for formal surveillance and coercion had been removed. The battle of political representations was resolved finally by the Governor's decision to invite the press, radio and television to tour the prison on 9 and 10 August and to enter the prison thereafter.[123] The argument would be settled by the mass media playing the part of arbiter.

---

[116] *Observer*, 7 Aug. 1988.

[117] The Governor reported that 'POA lies and black propaganda continued to come with increasing regularity, all sorts of rumours about guns and drugs in the grounds were pushed out to the news media'.

[118] *Observer*, 7 Aug. 1988.

[119] 'Defiant staff talk about drug dangers', *Daily Telegraph*, 16 Aug. 1988.

[120] 'Call in troops, says goal governor', the *Guardian*, 8 Aug. 1988.

[121] *Daily Telegraph*, 16 Aug. 1988.

[122] See 'Prison staff take crisis into dispute', the *Guardian*, 4 Aug. 1988.

[123] The Chairman of the POA called it a 'cynical use of inmates by the Department'.

The outcome was unequivocal and laudatory. For instance, the *Guardian* reported 'inmates enjoying a changed atmosphere . . . the atmosphere was relaxed'.[124] And under the headline 'Governor deserves medal, say inmates', *The Times* reported on 10 August that 'few staff were on duty at the prison, but the inmates were well-behaved and the atmosphere was calm and relaxed. The prisoners were enjoying time off from the usual supervision. . . . [One inmate said] "Most of us are on the governor's side. . . We think the prison officers are being a bit silly really. I don't think they need any more staff. There's never been any aggro here. It's going to be pretty tense when they return back to work." . . . [And another said] "We're doing fine without them. It's better than before. The atmosphere is easier." Most telling perhaps was an article by Robert Kilroy-Silk, an influential man, the former MP, member of the Parliamentary All-Party Penal Affairs Group and the Home Affairs Select Committee:

The prison officers taking industrial action at Holloway Women's Prison say that they are primarily motivated by concern about security. Perhaps that is true, though I doubt it. More likely it is power and money. What is true is that the prison is functioning without them. In fact it is running better. Nor does there seem to be a problem with security, despite the fact that there are some 200 fewer officers supervising the locking of prisoners, and that the inmates are actually being allowed to move freely about the jail. According to Press reports, the prisoners are well behaved. That is corroborated by accounts given to me privately by discerning and experienced prison visitors. There do not seem to be the problems that the warders feared. On the argument that lies behind their industrial action we should now be seeing vicious attacks on staff and mass break-outs. Neither has occurred. . . . The child-like pleasure that the women display at being allowed to associate with each other and participate in common household tasks is, itself, a condemnation of the regime that exists when the officers are working normally. They should never be allowed to work normally again.[125]

The strike sputtered on for weeks: an exhausted working staff supported by governor grades continuing to run the prison; pickets and working staff fitfully challenging one another in their daily encounters at and around the gate; desultory talks being held between strikers and management; recriminations being levelled

---

[124] 'Freedom behind Holloway's bars', the *Guardian*, 10 Aug. 1988.
[125] 'The Holloway eye-opener', *The Times*, 12 Aug. 1988.

(for instance, by the POA against the Board of Visitors for their alleged partiality); and threats being proffered by the POA to extend the dispute nationally (seven other prisons had taken action in sympathy with Holloway).[126] But, internally, the reports were always the same: the inmates were 'cheerful and co-operative' ('even on the medical units'). On 13 August, for instance, the Governor recorded that the 'prison was running beautifully; the cleanliness was marked and inmates generally were taking a pride in what they were doing'. And the prison's senior probation officer talked of the prison being more free, more 'comfortable' and less threatening.

On 20 August, the local POA voted to go back to work, the planned date of return being 25 August, but such was their insistence on the hazards of Holloway and the need to restore symbolic supremacy over space and people that they demanded that they should tour the building to search for weapons. The dangerousness of Holloway had always been a central theme in the POA case. They had claimed persistently that inmates required comprehensive vigilance and control, and the threat of weapons came powerfully to epitomize the risks they faced.

A member of the Board of Visitors reported that working officers were apprehensive about the prospect of their colleagues returning, 'some on behalf of the women, others for themselves'. But the strikers did not return on 25 August. It seemed to management that the POA had been under the impression that 'when they returned to work all the things they had demanded and gone on strike for would be acceded to'. Governors maintained that the new levels of staffing stipulated by Fresh Start must remain unchanged, and the branch POA decided to resume the strike.

To the Governor in those last few days of the strike, it appeared that the Department was desperate to settle, and that talks were being conducted in his absence. He was, he said, 'paranoid' about the encircling departmental politics of the dispute. Although he 'affirmed that there was no reason for anxiety about the reaction of prisoners to staff returning from strike', the Department appeared to concur with the POA that there should be full and vigorous searches of the prison and prisoners on the resumption of work.[127] The officers themselves declared their anxieties about the presence of potential weapons such as scissors and knives:[128] the chairwoman of the branch POA said 'we are worried about the safety of our

[126] The *Guardian*, 8 Aug. 1988.   [127] *The Times*, 23 Aug. 1988.
[128] *The Times*, 29 Aug. 1988.

members. If they go back without satisfactory searches, how do we know that a pair of scissors or a knife is not going to end up in somebody's back?'[129] The Governor saw no such threat.[130] He recorded on 2 September:

The Department were desperate to avoid national industrial action. It was another day of heavy pressure. . . . [it] is clear that the NEC were desperate to get the Branch back to work. Further attempts were made to get the Governor to change his policy on searching and create a maximum number of women who could be supervised by a member of staff. On both counts he refused to move. . . . Back in the prison, the Governor noted that he could never remember a better atmosphere in any penal establishment which he had visited or worked in.

The Aftermath

The end of the strike was declared on 9 September. It was, reported the Governor, an enduring enigma why members of the local branch should have so changed their minds (the POA themselves seemed to have believed that they were returning because their terms had been agreed). Officers returned on 13 September amid rancour,[131] disgruntlement and 'non-communication'[132] (one striking officer said 'agreements were struck they never adhered to'). The aftermath was described by the Board of Visitors as 'unhappy and somewhat bitter'[133] and by the Governor as 'bleak': there were 'masses of delinquent behaviour from the oncoming strikers and enormous patience displayed by working staff and managers'. There was said to be 'anarchy' in the medical areas on the second day, the principals vying with one another again for control. Officers claimed they were too few in number to unlock, the inmates petitioned the Principal Medical Officer not to let the officers return,[134] Colin Allen decided to dispense with the officers altogether for the 'sake of the women patients', the officers refused to receive prisoners from the nurses, and the POA withdrew their members.

It was as if the wars of the landings were about to be fought all over

[129] 'Holloway weapons fear', the *Guardian*, 29 Aug. 1988.
[130] *The Times*, 13 Aug. 1988.
[131] The local branch POA meeting of 5 Jan. 1989 expelled those staff who had worked during the strike and passed a vote of no confidence in the POA NEC.
[132] The word was used by a member of the Board of Visitors.
[133] Annual Report of the Board of Visitors for 1988.
[134] Senior Medical Officer's Report to the Board of Visitors, 14 Sept. 1988.

again. The Governor recorded that 'managers spent two days absorbing the delinquency and patiently giving people the opportunity to
adjust. It was then a question of re-asserting management's authority
unless anarchy[135] [was] going to be allowed to prevail.' Officers did
not report for work. They claimed to be sick ('the sick rate seems to
be orchestrated by the POA' thought a governor). They withdrew
their labour piecemeal and according to their own assessment of
risk. They sought to show that they were once more unambiguously
in command ('once they came back in', said a member of the Board of
Visitors, 'they decided to apply the prison rules very strictly'). On 17
September, there were problems with unlocking on the '3s'.

The Governor issued a general order threatening disciplinary
action on 24 September, officers were disciplined (two officers being
temporarily relieved on the 22nd, one being suspended for disobe-
dience on the 29th, five being suspended on the 30th) and the branch
POA threatened a day of protest. On 27 September, there was said to
be a hostile atmosphere on the '4s' and '5s'. The returning strikers
themselves described how:

Shambles was the order for the day. The Governor allowed six officers to
search the prison, for those of you that know Holloway you'll know that the
place is enormous. Wednesday PM we were now searching with two officers,
the Governor was satisfied so searching ceased. We were far from satisfied at
this point we were missing (still unaccounted for) a hacksaw, pliers and
scissors. Since our return, we have found that a 'patrol state' does not
exist, we are being ordered to unlock during dinner patrols, needless to say
once again we are upset, none of our agreements have been honoured,
minimum staffing levels are being ignored so we applied patrol state. Further
orders followed, we began working only conditioned hours, no contract
hours, on Thursday 22nd September after six days conditioned hours only
worked we returned to normal working, during dinner patrol that same day
an officer was temporarily relieved of her duty, the vast majority of staff were
attending a branch meeting with the NEC present. We think, at this point, we
were supposed to withdraw our labour however, just to confuse management,
we returned, having decided at this time its better to fight from within than
from without.[136]

The Chairman of the Board of Visitors informed the Home Secretary
in a letter of 24 September:

---

[135] Of course, as David Downes observed, 'anarchy' in a different and better sense
was more or less what had occurred for several weeks during the strike.
[136] 'Jottings', undated.

I see from a report in today's *Times* that you consider the dispute at Holloway Prison to be settled. I wish it were. The situation is that, although the officers have returned to work, a state of continual disruption exists. The atmosphere in the prison is giving the members of the Board of Visitors, who have visited daily since the dispute started, cause for considerable concern. It appears to us that a proportion of the officers returned to work with the idea of disrupting the regime and disobeying the orders of the Governor.

Holloway seemed slowly to be gyrating towards its old antagonistic spiral, leaving one unstable equilibrium for another. By 2 November, 11 officers had been suspended for refusing to 'breach the security manual' and 100 had asked to be transferred elsewhere.[137] Staff were reporting sick, 34 in the second week of December alone, and coupled with the shortages caused by suspensions, there was a pretext again to reduce the length of time which inmates could spend on association. A barricade was erected by prisoners in December.

In November 1988, the Prison Department announced that Colin Allen (described in the press as 'the beleaguered governor')[138] would be transferred from Holloway to the Prison Inspectorate and, on 16 January 1989, he did indeed leave the prison. A working officer claimed that 'the loser out of it was Colin Allen. He was moved on and I think he was made a bit of a scapegoat for it, but I think he handled himself very well'. It was thought that Allen had to go because he had become an embarrassment, one who had 'unwittingly stepped in between the Prison Service and the Prison Officers Association'. But it was perhaps an inevitable move in the choreography of relations between prison officers, Prison Department and management, a political opportunity to start again, representing as a later Chairman of the Board of Visitors put it, a 'new beginning, so nobody lost face'.

---

[137] Yet it should also be noted that other officers liked what they saw of the changed regime and declared that, if they had known what would happen, they would have gone back much earlier.   [138] The *Guardian*, 22 Nov. 1988.

11
Conclusion

'At Holloway, more than ever I have experienced, it is not the
facts of how things are that is important, it is how people feel
and imagine things are that is important' (Colin Allen)

It is tempting to look upon Colin Allen and his colleagues not only as
some sort of collective Theseus who vanquished for a while the
monster of madness in the bowels of Holloway (a monster that
proved to be hydra-headed) but as a latter-day Pinel. Pinel, it will
be recalled, was born in 1745, died in 1826, and is linked forever in
the mythology[1] of asylum reform with the liberation of the inmates
of the Bicêtre. It was he who was supposed to have broken the
lunatics' manacles and treated them benevolently as rational, responsible beings. To Pinel belonged the 'immortal honour of having
practically established the superiority of kind over barbarous methods of treatment'.[2] A madman so freed was reported to have undergone a 'sudden and complete' change. He who had once 'cr[ied] . . .
in the exuberance of this own self-inflicted anguish, or writhed under
the terrors of some self-created misfortune' could be 'restored . . . to
tranquillity if not to sanity'.[3] Of one particular lunatic, it was said,
'no sooner was he liberated than he became obliging and attentive'.[4]

Like Philippe Pinel, Colin Allen and his staff demonstrated that it
was possible to reverse the vicious dialectic of locking-out, locking-in,
insecurity, disturbance and conflict.[5] The reversal might have been

---

[1] It seems that Pinel never did actually strike the chains in the manner that was so
heroically portrayed. See A. Scull, *The Most Solitary of Afflictions*, (New Haven: Yale
University Press, 1993), 377.

[2] D. Tuke, *The Progressive Changes which have taken Place since the Time of Pinel
in the Moral Management of the Insane*, (London: John Churchill, 1854), 13.

[3] W. Browne, *What Asylums Were, Are, and Ought to Be*, (Edinburgh: Adam and
Charles Black, 1837), 137.   [4] D. Tuke, *op. cit.*, 15.

[5] Gregory Bateson would have called that dialectic 'schismogenesis', intending to
convey the self-reinforcing behaviour that amplifies conflict through a negative reinfor-
cing cycle of increasingly extreme reactions. The term has been applied to organizational processes. See R. Quinn and K. Cameron, 'Organizational Paradox and
Transformation', 6.

temporary, it was certainly unstable, it reflected the short-lived triumph of inmates and managers in the 'face-games' of the prison,[6] and it did not reassure the striking prison officers who continued to worry about *their* loss of symbolic and spatial authority. But it could be accomplished,[7] and it could be accomplished, moreover, in the labyrinthine regions of a Holloway which had been condemned as quite unmanageable.

The reversal revealed, too, how the effects of space can be mediated rhetorically. It is clear that physical space embeds and symbolizes experiences of sovereignty and identity, that, in Soja's phrase, it 'concretizes social relations'.[8] But it is also clear that people are capable of distancing themselves from those 'concretized relations', of interpreting, appraising and working on them. Indeed, Simmel has reminded us that social life is a ceaseless dialectic between the alienated forms of consciousness and the creative power of consciousness to respond to those selfsame forms and amend, replace or evade them. Seemingly objective conditions can be transcended. So too with Holloway. The prison might have been full of frightening spaces and dog-leg bends, but there was no tyrannical and immediate causal link between its architectural design and the behaviour and ranking of its occupants. To the contrary, although the experience of the physical structure of Holloway did amplify fears and anxieties, although it engendered a particular form of power relations and a specific imagery of women, the period of unlocking and the subsequent strike did demonstrate that old experiences could be surmounted by new practices. Casale argued baldly of C1 that 'ultimately the problem is not one of architecture. It is a problem of philosophy.'[9] And she was right. All the governors and professional staff who lived through the great strike of 1988 were of a mind that the prison's

---

[6] The Chairman of the POA NEC had objected during the strike to inmates being interviewed about conditions in Holloway: 'are we being asked to accept that prisoners should now advise the general public on how prisons should be run?', he asked. The *Guardian*, 10 Aug. 1988.

[7] The subsequent history of Holloway consisted of movements swinging ceaselessly between the repression and liberation. The 1991 Annual Report of the Board of Visitors, for instance, recorded another end of locking out and a more humane, open and secure regime. But Holloway has never been stable and there have been more recent reports of locking-in and disturbance.

[8] E. Soja, *Postmodern Geographies: The Reassertion of Space in Critical Social Theory*, (London: Verso, 1989), 7.

[9] S. Casale, *Women Inside: The experience of women remand prisoners in Holloway*, (London: The Civil Liberties Trust, 1989), 98.

building and its terrors were of lesser importance than its culture. One, Dr Hindson, said simply that the building 'wasn't the primary problem', and a senior probation officer said that 'the new building was terribly claustrophobic but I think it depends on what's going on within a building. If there's plenty going on and it's free then it doesn't matter so much.'

Alan Gewirth once observed that there are no iron laws of sociology because there is no imaginable law that cannot be broken by someone somewhere who chooses to exercise his or her will. It is thus with architecture. Its influence could also be resisted. The strike did seem to have constituted a decisive turning-point in the history of the prison. It was a revelation of possibilities. The regime after the strike was never as oppressive as before. A former assistant governor said in 1993:

I'm fascinated going back to Holloway now to see how staff compensate for that sort of forced intimacy by free flow association and movement of the wings with the doors open. It's wonderful to see all of these annoying doors that we had to keep unlocking and locking again and now they're standing open. That's great stuff!

The development of Holloway also conveys something of the organization of knowledge about criminal women. Holloway looms large in the criminal justice system and it played an important part in shaping public experience. After all, it is the principal prison for women in England and Wales, being set in the capital, with the largest number of female inmates, near Whitehall, Parliament, and the national press and television. It is a remand prison and its testers have worked ceaselessly to manufacture data about its occupants. Its reconstruction was a conspicuous experiment in social change. It is hardly remarkable that the prison should have been attracted much of the political, criminological and media gaze on criminal women in the 1960s and 1970s.

The transformations of typifications of female delinquency had their greater and lesser histories. I have already recounted how it was that much understanding was structured by the quiet, steady activity of psychiatrists, medical officers and psychological testers, by unexpected changes in the rate of population growth and sudden, explosive occurrences that transfixed the political mind. The testers and the terrorists affected the practical work and design of the prison. But I have also shown how that work and design had, in their turn, a social momentum that was only loosely coupled to the larger ideo-logical changes. Work and design evolved, passing through different states which I must simplify and exaggerate for purposes of analysis.

Three principal models of relations were visible at different phases in the recent history of the prison, each with its own, distinctive structure of control, social organization, space and imagery. First was a configuration based on the large formal spaces of the radial prison, a formality of social relations and an impersonality of style. Formally, the deviant woman in the first Holloway was disciplined and controlled, but, informally, she enjoyed a measure of freedom and independence within strong bounds. There was an imagery of inade-quacy, of the half-trained, unintelligent and usually docile woman who lacked a vicious criminal will. She was what Dorothy Speed, the Principal Medical Officer, might have called the 'sad' woman. It was only when the radial prison was half-demolished, when space was compressed and the population had grown, that it became difficult to sustain the old disciplines and the old imagery and the problem of disturbance, always latent,[10] acquired a prominence.

Second and third were the models formed by the contrasting uses of the anti-panopticon, the 'normalizing' and the 'controlling' techni-ques described by Adler and Longhurst, or the 'kind' and the 'barbarous' techniques of Tuke. Methods that 'opened up' space seemed, if only for a while, to reduce confrontation, reward inmates for compliance and supply an image of the reasonable (or at least the 'reasoning') woman amenable to perusasion,[11] the woman whom Dorothy Speed might have called 'bad', the one who could choose her fate. Those methods that restricted space seemed to punish and seclude, exacerbate conflict, and supply an image of the disturbed or 'mad' woman. The one tended to emphasize the normal and the rational, the other the abnormal and irrational. One generated possibilities of co-existence, the other exclusion. One exacerbated feelings of fear, insecurity and a sense of the dangerousness of place. The other depressed them. And the components of those

[10] Earlier accounts of women prisoners are replete with references to disturbance. See, for instance, descriptions of disorder in Griffiths' history of the Millbank penitentiary. A. Griffiths, *Memorials of Millbank*, (London: Henry King, 1875), Vol. 1, 121, 268–9.
[11] See, for example, the case history of very different regimes in the development of a federal penitentiary. M. Colvin, *The Penitentiary in Crisis: From Accommodation to Riot in New Mexico*, (Albany: State University of New York Press, 1992).

equations were interdependent. They justified and reinforced one another: a compliance-based strategy brought about an enlargement of the space occupied by inmates and staff, encouraged association and promoted a moderate independence amongst the women, whilst a control-based strategy diminished them. The matter may be depicted as in Figure 11.1.

Three Models of Equipoise

Model I: *The thinly-populated radial prison (before 1970)*

Variant	i.	'Docile' or 'sad' women → formal control → formal relations → big spaces
or	ii.	Formal control → formal relations → big spaces → 'docile' or 'sad' women
or	iii.	Formal relations → big spaces → formal control → 'docile' or 'sad' women
or	. . . .	

Model II: *The 'locked-in' or 'banged-up' prison (1970–1986)*

Variant	i.	Small spaces → tight control → insecurity → exclusionary practices → 'disturbed' or 'mad' women
or	ii.	'Disturbed' or 'mad' women → tight control → insecurity → small spaces → exclusion
or	iii.	Tight control → 'disturbed' or 'mad' women → insecurity → small spaces → exclusion
or	. . . .	

Model III: *The 'opened-up' prison (1986–)*

Variant	i.	Light control → open space → assimilative practices → 'reasoning', 'reasonable' or 'bad' women
or	ii.	Open space → assimilative practices → 'reasoning', 'reasonable' or 'bad' women → light control
or	iii.	'Reasoning', 'reasonable' or 'bad' women → light control → assimilative practices → open space
or	. . . .	

Figure 11.1 *Three Models of Equipoise*

To be sure, the models were never exclusive: there were pockets of disturbance (and 'mad' women) in the old radial prison, for example. And it would be glib and naive to suppose that Pinel and Allen had solved forever the conundrum of how to rule prisons fairly and effectively. There can be no simple and invariant solution to all problems of order and legitimacy. Prisons are mercurial institutions, and there are many times when they cannot be managed with normalizing strategies (the inauguration of the new Holloway was not a propitious period, for instance.) But, for a little while, and for reasons that are quite transparent, Holloway did become a much more civilised and peaceful place. Jeffrey Bayes, former Chairman of the Board of Visitors said:

It showed that a prison could be run, at least short term, first of all without the prison officers—in a much wider sense it showed that a relaxation of the regime could have a beneficial effect and I think that this was something that the Home Office ought to have learned and mirrored that in other establishments. Relax the regime. It's much better.

And Colin Allen himself concluded that:

The women prisoners at Holloway were given responsibility for themselves, other prisoners and staff in a way that they had not been given before. This liberated them in a quite extraordinary way, making for very responsible behaviour from women who had been anything but responsible. Behaviour between prisoners and staff and between prisoners and prisoners improved consistently during the dispute. This was because prisoners were treated less like children and more was expected of them.

Epilogue

The plot of this narrative ends effectively in the late 1980s with the departure of Colin Allen, but it might be valuable to add the shortest of epilogues about what elapsed in the years that followed.

After the strike, a hundred returning prison officers elected to move to posts in other prisons. Those who had served in and around Colin Allen's management team, the 'Muswell Hill Group', also came to leave Holloway: Jeffrey Bayes, the chairman of the Board of Visitors, in 1988; Ann Hair, the Deputy Governor, in June 1989; Dorothy Speed, the Principal Medical Officer, in September 1990; and Norman Hindson, the Senior Medical Officer, in 1992. With the widespread scattering of people who had been critical to this history, with the more general and continuing turnover of prison inmates and staff,[12] in the absence, moreover, of any formal or informal record of what had happened,[13] those who work and live in the prison have, in effect, lost their corporate memory and tradition.[14] They now know few details of the events between 1968 and 1988, and they have little apparent curiosity about them. They are aware that the prison has had a crisis-laden past, but the precise course, nature and bearing of that past have grown quite remote and obscure.

What they *have* inherited is a building that stays confused, dingy and ill-lit: Holloway's dog-leg corridors and small spaces are still difficult to supervise by the application of conventional methods. Still filling that building is a transient, reluctant and variegated population (38 per cent of its average daily population were remand prisoners in 1992). What they have also inherited is a structure of control and management that stays riddled with difficulties. And, finally, Holloway itself remains a complex social world with abundant possibilities of change and reform. There has been a continuing train of new initiatives: for instance, inmates' children were admitted for extended visits in early 1991[15] and renewed efforts were made to deal with drug use in 1992. Rates of mutilation, assault and suicide remain comparatively low. Yet security is still an abiding preoccupation (the second ever, and much publicized, escape from the prison occurred in May 1994[16]) and it seems as difficult as before to organize the administration of the medical units. Complaints have issued periodically about the maltreatment of 'disturbed' women. In 1993, for instance, the Board of Visitors criticised poor medical recording procedures, the over-prescription of medicine and the abuse of drugs. Their criticisms led to an external enquiry into standards of health care that came in its turn to condemn the medical units not only for their overcrowding, seclusion and inadequate monitoring of cases but

---

[12] See *HM Prison Holloway: Report by HM Chief Inspector of Prisons*, (London: Home Office, 1992), 91.

[13] I explained, for example, how, in 1993, the Board of Visitors had minutes of almost no meetings that had taken place during the twenty years covered by this book.

[14] There is a propensity, for instance, to credit governors *after* Colin Allen with changes deemed crucial to the prison's reformation. No doubt those later governors were also reformers: Michael O'Sullivan was certainly such a one (see the report in The *Guardian*, 3 Jan. 1990), but Colin Allen has been quite eclipsed in the collective amnesia of the place.

[15] See *Children Visiting Holloway Prison*, (London: Save the Children, 1992).

[16] See *Evening Standard*, 16 May 1994.

also for the poverty of relations prevailing between members of the medical, nursing and discipline staff. It is evident that there has been no resolution of the many engrained dilemmas of control and treatment that this book has outlined. Judge Tumim's problems of 'balance. . . between security, humanity and help' remain. Perhaps they will always remain. No doubt the extraordinarily harmonious conditions of the prison during the weeks of the 1988 strike could be sustained only during an extraordinary time of crisis.

Yet it is my conviction that the cathartic conflict of 1988 did mark a transformation. Staff, inmates and outsiders may continue to claim that the prison is a dreadful place on occasion, but their memories are short and the contrasts they trace cannot but be less extreme: however oppressive the regime may be from time to time, however uncertain its legitimacy, Holloway has not yet reverted to the conditions of the late 1970s and early 1980s.

INDEX